I0885433

Cases on Lean Thinking Applications in Unconventional Systems

Eduardo Guilherme Satolo
São Paulo State University, Brazil

Robisom Damasceno Calado
Fluminense Federal University, Brazil

A volume in the Advances in Healthcare Information Systems and Administration (AHISA) Book Series

IGI Global
PUBLISHER of TIMELY KNOWLEDGE

Published in the United States of America by
IGI Global
Engineering Science Reference (an imprint of IGI Global)
701 E. Chocolate Avenue
Hershey PA, USA 17033
Tel: 717-533-8845
Fax: 717-533-8661
E-mail: cust@igi-global.com
Web site: http://www.igi-global.com

Library of Congress Cataloging-in-Publication Data

Names: Satolo, Eduardo, 1984- editor. | Calado, Robisom, 1964- editor.
Title: Cases on lean thinking applications in unconventional systems / Eduardo Satolo and Robisom Calado, editors.
Description: Hershey, PA : Engineering Science Reference, an imprint of IGI Global, 2022. | Includes bibliographical references and index. | Summary: "This book offers unconventional application related to lean thinking, a management philosophy described as an approach with which organizations develop skills to gradually eliminate waste and create value"-- Provided by publisher.
Identifiers: LCCN 2022023468 (print) | LCCN 2022023469 (ebook) | ISBN 9781668451854 (h/c) | ISBN 9781668451861 (s/c) | ISBN 9781668451878 (ebook)
Subjects: LCSH: Health facilities--Waste minimization--Case studies. | Health facilities--Management--Case studies. | Industrial efficiency--Case studies.
Classification: LCC RA969.45 .C37 2022 (print) | LCC RA969.45 (ebook) | DDC 362.1068--dc23/eng/20220715
LC record available at https://lccn.loc.gov/2022023468
LC ebook record available at https://lccn.loc.gov/2022023469

This book is published in the IGI Global book series Advances in Healthcare Information Systems and Administration (AHISA) (ISSN: 2328-1243; eISSN: 2328-126X)

British Cataloguing in Publication Data
A Cataloguing in Publication record for this book is available from the British Library.

For electronic access to this publication, please contact: eresources@igi-global.com.

Advances in Healthcare Information Systems and Administration (AHISA) Book Series

Anastasius Moumtzoglou
Hellenic Society for Quality & Safety in Healthcare and P. & A. Kyriakou Children's Hospital, Greece

ISSN:2328-1243
EISSN:2328-126X

Mission

The **Advances in Healthcare Information Systems and Administration (AHISA) Book Series** aims to provide a channel for international researchers to progress the field of study on technology and its implications on healthcare and health information systems. With the growing focus on healthcare and the importance of enhancing this industry to tend to the expanding population, the book series seeks to accelerate the awareness of technological advancements of health information systems and expand awareness and implementation.

Driven by advancing technologies and their clinical applications, the emerging field of health information systems and informatics is still searching for coherent directing frameworks to advance health care and clinical practices and research. Conducting research in these areas is both promising and challenging due to a host of factors, including rapidly evolving technologies and their application complexity. At the same time, organizational issues, including technology adoption, diffusion and acceptance as well as cost benefits and cost effectiveness of advancing health information systems and informatics applications as innovative forms of investment in healthcare are gaining attention as well. **AHISA** addresses these concepts and critical issues.

Coverage

- E-Health and M-Health
- Management of Emerging Health Care Technologies
- Role of informatics specialists
- Rehabilitative Technologies
- Telemedicine
- Clinical Decision Support Design, Development and Implementation
- Pharmaceutical and Home Healthcare Informatics
- IT Applications in Physical Therapeutic Treatments
- Nursing Expert Systems
- Medical Informatics

IGI Global is currently accepting manuscripts for publication within this series. To submit a proposal for a volume in this series, please contact our Acquisition Editors at Acquisitions@igi-global.com or visit: http://www.igi-global.com/publish/.

The Advances in Healthcare Information Systems and Administration (AHISA) Book Series (ISSN 2328-1243) is published by IGI Global, 701 E. Chocolate Avenue, Hershey, PA 17033-1240, USA, www.igi-global.com. This series is composed of titles available for purchase individually; each title is edited to be contextually exclusive from any other title within the series. For pricing and ordering information please visit http://www.igi-global.com/book-series/advances-healthcare-information-systems-administration/37156. Postmaster: Send all address changes to above address.

Titles in this Series

For a list of additional titles in this series, please visit: www.igi-global.com/book-series

Handbook of Research on Mathematical Modeling for Smart Healthcare Systems
Debabrata Samanta (CHRIST University (Deemed), India) and Debabrata Singh (Siksha 'O' Anusandhan (Deemed), India)
Medical Information Science Reference • © 2022 • 503pp • H/C (ISBN: 9781668445808) • US $470.00

Handbook of Research on Healthcare Standards, Policies, and Reform
Ubaldo Comite (University "Giustino Fortunato" Benevento, Italy)
Medical Information Science Reference • © 2022 • 408pp • H/C (ISBN: 9781799888680) • US $480.00

Building Resilient Healthcare Systems With ICTs
Patrick Ndayizigamiye (University of Johannesburg, South Africa) and Macire Kante (University of Johannesburg, South Africa)
Medical Information Science Reference • © 2022 • 298pp • H/C (ISBN: 9781799889151) • US $325.00

Approaches and Applications of Deep Learning in Virtual Medical Care
Noor Zaman (Taylor's University, Malaysia) Loveleen Gaur (Amity University, Noida, India) and Mamoona Humayun (Jouf University, Saudi Arabia)
Medical Information Science Reference • © 2022 • 293pp • H/C (ISBN: 9781799889298) • US $325.00

Prospects of Blockchain Technology for Accelerating Scientific Advancement in Healthcare
Malaya Dutta Borah (National Institute of Technology (NIT), India) Peng Zhang (Belmont University, USA) and Ganesh Chandra Deka (Ministry of Skill Development and Entrepreneurship, Government of India, India)
Medical Information Science Reference • © 2022 • 289pp • H/C (ISBN: 9781799896067) • US $315.00

Quality of Healthcare in the Aftermath of the COVID-19 Pandemic
Anastasius Moumtzoglou (P&A Kyriakou Children's Hospital, Greece)
Medical Information Science Reference • © 2022 • 403pp • H/C (ISBN: 9781799891987) • US $360.00

Handbook of Research on Applied Intelligence for Health and Clinical Informatics
Anuradha Dheeraj Thakare (Pimpri Chinchwad College of Engineering, Savitribai Phule Pune University, India) Sanjeev J. Wagh (Shivaji University, India) Manisha Sunil Bhende (Dr. D.Y. Patil Institute of Engineering, Management, and Research Akurdi, India & Savitribai Phule Pune University, India) Ahmed M. Anter (Beni-Suef University, Egypt) and Xiao-Zhi Gao (University of Eastern Finland, Finland)
Medical Information Science Reference • © 2022 • 470pp • H/C (ISBN: 9781799877097) • US $470.00

IGI Global
PUBLISHER of TIMELY KNOWLEDGE

701 East Chocolate Avenue, Hershey, PA 17033, USA
Tel: 717-533-8845 x100 • Fax: 717-533-8661
E-Mail: cust@igi-global.com • www.igi-global.com

Editorial Advisory Board

Table of Contents

Detailed Table of Contents

Lean production is recognized as an administrative approach associated with a minimization or constant waste system that reduces production and the lean production system. Implementation through tools help various areas of the organization. Although conceptually disseminated and applied in various sectors of the economy, publications in the agribusiness sector are scarce. This chapter presents the results of the application of és lean, action research carried out with a small-scale dairy producer. Through the use of lean tools, such as a flowchart, Ishikawa diagrams, value stream mapping, and the PDCA cycle, it was possible to guide a set of improvements in the property under study, adding profitability gains.

The use of the lean philosophy in healthcare environments has been reported in different countries, both in the private and the public sectors. However, there is not much information on how to apply the Kaizen concept to healthcare services, notably in hospitals and emergency services, which are increasingly challenging environments given the aging of the world population and the degradation of human conditions in several countries. Existing publications on the topic expose different forms of Kaizen use in healthcare services, which may cause misunderstanding and confusion. This chapter describes and brings light to the Kaizen approach in lean implementations and discusses its challenges, barriers, and success factors using a case study of a non-governmental organization (NGO) that started its lean journey with Kaizen implementation in late 2019. It also describes strategies to use it according to up-to-date publications and presents the benefits, the challenges, and the framework to successfully implement Kaizen.

Overcrowding in emergency hospital units represents a serious problem in the health system and is a phenomenon faced worldwide. And when investigating the origin of this disorder, it is observed that the great demand for care of cases considered low risk directly influences the quality of the service provided. Thus, it is necessary to apply tools and methods to improve the service offered. The Lean Six Sigma methodology allows the construction of problem-solving proposals based on statistical data and effective mechanisms. And with the use of the DMAIC method, which is also the methodological framework of Lean Six Sigma, it is possible to clearly direct the resolution of problems through process improvement and restructuring in an organization. The present study aims to present a successful experience in the application of DMAIC to improve patient care and assistance in UPA Cumbica, located in the city of Guarulhos, SP.

This study aims to demonstrate the importance of waste analysis and similarity of results. For that, the HFMEA-FUZZY was used as a tool. The study used waste results from 20 emergency care units (ECUs) from different regions of Brazilthrough the HFMEA criteria and complemented with the concepts of logic Fuzzy with the COPPE COSENZA methodology. The use of HFMEA-FUZZY aims to contribute to research in the health area where Lean healthcare will be or is already implemented. For that, it served as a basis for reports prepared after visits carried out in the emergency care units (ECUs).

The objective of this work is to carry out a literature review on indicators for emergency and urgent healthcare units aimed to identify the main measures within the context of healthcare services. A search was conducted on the Scopus and PubMed databases using two strategies aimed to conduct research on studies about indicators for emergency and urgent healthcare units. This work allowed identifying the main indicators used in the context of emergency and urgent medical services, which are length of stay, left without being seen, national emergency department overcrowding scale, among others. In addition, it was found that such indicators provide suitable and viable means to assess, review, and display the quality of health systems. It was found in some studies that the use of indicators is used only as a measure whose value is monitored by systems, but it does not lead managers to an action plan.

Lean healthcare presents as a potential means to overcome barriers in the health sector by eliminating unnecessary movements, waiting, transport, and stockpiles. However, time spent in set-up activities does not add value to the process because the patient is not receiving service. One of the Lean tools that can help mitigate waste in those activities is the single-minute exchange of die (SMED); therefore, this study aims to evaluate the implications of using SMED in the health context. The authors conducted an exploratory search in scientific documents to achieve this goal. The content analysis was based on Bardin. From the findings, it is possible to identify the implications of the use of SMED in the health context, sort activities between internal and external setup, and reduce time spent on wasteful tasks, while increasing time available for value-adding activities.

The objective of this chapter is to expand the discussions regarding the application of the Fast Track method and the standardized work in emergency services with the Lean healthcare approach. In this chapter, the authors present some fundamental concepts to broaden the understanding of the theoretical/methodological implications necessary for the application of the Fast Track method and standardized work in the healthcare area, with the Lean healthcare approach. They present the case study resulting from the execution of the Lean project in the 24-hour UPA, which was carried out in 50 selected emergency care units, as a result of the agreement with the Ministry of Health through the Department of Hospitals and Urgencies (DAHU/MS) and with the Rector of the Fluminense Federal University.

This study analyzes the contributions and applications of queuing theory (QT) in the field of health service management problems. This review presents a classification system of healthcare examined with the aid of queuing models. The purpose of this is to analyze the contributions and applications of QT in the field of problem management in health services and to give indications of when and how to use QT in order to enhance daily management decisions. A literature review was carried out to investigate the health areas supported by queuing models, searching articles that described problem models and their topics or keywords related to QT and population health or health problems. The present study analyzed 314 articles that address the applications of QT in healthcare management between 2014 and 2020. This review demonstrates that QT can contribute to the improvement of health services and provide resource managers to achieve this improvement. A discussion of why, when, and requirements to apply QT is presented.

This chapter analyzes Lean interventions in emergency care units (ECUs) with a focus on learning theory and knowledge management. The use of data served to understand the effectiveness of Lean methodology in transforming knowledge in ECUs. The method was a systematic and descriptive ex-post survey in the Lean project database, quantitative, and qualitative analysis aiming to establish relationships between the foci. The virtual platform is an effective tool for dissemination and generates reliable answers for analysis and decision making. The benefits of interventions through the use of Lean tools are unquestionable, visible, and useful for the daily life of the units. However, the internalization of the Lean culture for permanence and improvements is a point of attention as well as the content, form, and conduction of the actions. Committed people, management by processes, Lean flows, shared information, and agile communication are guarantees for the transformation and consolidation of the improvements.

This chapter is the result of a project signed between the Universidade Federal Fluminense and the Ministry of Health in 2019 and executed in 2020. Its objective was to identify intersections of ideas between the national humanization policy (PNH) and the Lean methodology. The path used was to seek ideas in the Lean methodology similar to the ideas present in the principles of the PNH. These intersections are understood as opportunities for actions that consider both the reduction of waste and the strengthening of aspects of the humanization of health. The authors identified seven common ideas: focus on the customer, the importance of the collective as a space for transforming work, the importance given to the workplace, shared management of processes, user inclusion, transversality of both, acting in the way of thinking about work. The conclusion is that such coincidences exist and are opportunities to deepen the dissemination of the principles and guidelines of the PNH through the actions of the Lean methodology and vice versa.

The world is suffering from a new coronavirus-type pathogen, namely COVID-19. Health professionals are obliged to protect themselves with personal protective equipment (PPE); however, we encountered some problems: most of this equipment is not self-cleaning. How do you protect professionals from contaminated personal protective equipment? How do you dispose of used personal protective equipment? For the construction of this equipment, the authors used the methodology of define, measure, analyze, improve, and control (DMAIC). The developed prototype was applied in a primary care sector clinic, where the pre-test (swab sampling procedure) was performed to identify cross-contamination of the environment. The cost of the prototype developed was low in relation to existing market options. The tests carried out allowed the authors to observe its effectiveness in the sterilization of equipment. However, new, more complex tests are still needed to better validate the prototype and to study its economic viability as a product.

Foreword

Cases on Lean Thinking Applications in Unconventional Systems, edited by Eduardo Guilherme Satolo and Robisom Damasceno Calado, has as main objective to approach the philosophy of Lean Production in different segments of the one that was initially conceived. In this case, the precursor company was Toyota Motor Company, which developed in Japan in the post-World War II period, what was called the Toyota Production System, under the coordination of Taiichi Ono and his collaborators, which aimed to eliminate the different types of waste in organizations.

In accordance with this proposal, the book develops relevant concepts and techniques of Lean Production in important areas, including the agribusiness and health services segments.

Regarding the agribusiness segment, discussed in Chapter 1 of the book, it proposes to use the approach of minimizing waste in a sector of significant importance in several countries, among which Brazil stands out as an important international player. Publications on the use of the Lean Production approach in this agribusiness segment are scarce, so the reader has the opportunity to deepen their knowledge in the application of tools used in Lean Production (Flowchart, Ishikawa diagrams, Value Stream Mapping and others), with the main focus on PDCA cycle approach as an improvement mechanism carried out with a small-scale dairy producer.

The remaining chapters of this book address the application of Lean Health Care concepts related to Health Care Services (Chapters 2, 10, 12, and 13) and Emergencies Care Units (Chapters 3, 4, 5, 6, 7, 8, 9, and 11).

Regarding the approach related to Health Care Services, the reader can deepen knowledge in health areas on topics related to how to apply the Kaizen concept to healthcare services (chapter 2); applications of Queuing Theory in the field of health service management problems (chapter 10); utilization of DMAIC for construction of equipment for sterilizing personal protective equipment focusing on the safety procedures for COVID-19 (Chapter 13) and intersections of ideas between the National Humanization Policy (PNH) and the Lean Methodology (Chapter 12).

With regard to Emergencies Care Units, the scope is broader, and the process of implementing traditional Lean Production methods and tools can be verified, such as: DMAIC (Chapter 3), HFMEA-FUZZY (Chapter 4), Performance Indicators (Chapters 5 and 9), SMED (Chapter 6), Standardized Work (Chapter 7), Lean practices and assistive technology (Chapter 8) and Learning Theory (Chapter 11).

Also the reader will be able to contemplate the use of different research methods throughout the book, highlighting: action research (Chapters 1, 9, 12, and 13); case studies (Chapters 2, 3, 4, 7, and 8); literature review (Chapters 5, 6, and 10) and qualitative/quantitative analysis (Chapter 11).

Another important point in the book refers to the diversity of knowledge and skills of authors and related institutions, involving Professors, Researches, Health Care Professionals, Professionals linked to public agencies of the Federal Government, acting in Universities, Hospitals and Minister of Health in Brazil, which provides to the reader a knowledge considering different cultural approaches.

In this sense, this book constitutes a source of special value and reference for university students, researchers, professors, and professionals working in the area of knowledge related to the implementation of Lean Production concepts in the fields of Agribusiness and Health Care.

Felipe Araújo Calarge
Technical School, Campinas State University (UNICAMP), Brazil

Preface

This book contains information obtained from authentic and highly regarded sources, in which the authors present *Cases on Lean Thinking Applications in Unconventional Systems* as a way of improving strategy in manufacturing organizations and service providers to the population, such as the health service area.

There is a better way to lead organizations. A way that makes more sense than the traditional methods taught in business schools. The Lean way of designing work involves all levels of the organization, from the leaders who create a culture of continuous improvement to the person who gets the work done.

This book addresses current and relevant topics on Lean Thinking:

- Applications of lean tools in small-scale
- Assistive Technology
- Define, Measure, Analyze, Improve, and Control (DMAIC)
- Failure Mode and Effects Analysis (HFMEA) and FUZZY logic
- Humanization Policy
- Indicators for Medical Services
- Kaizen Implementation
- Knowledge Management
- Lean Healthcare and Fast Track
- Monitoring Patient Flow in the Emergency Care
- Queuing Theory in Health Service
- Single-Minute Exchange of Die (SMED)

By using the Lean Thinking Applications in Unconventional Systems approach presented in this book, you can produce the same amount of value using far fewer resources, which will benefit all your stakeholders and the environment. Or you can do much more with the resources you have now. This improved productivity and culture change can, in turn, be used to expand productive capacity, conquer new markets, and increase the profitability of your public or private company.

We are pleased to organize this literature because we wish all readers a learning experience and an excellence in Lean journey, be prepared to be surprised at the amount of improvements you will be able to make with the application of the knowledge presented here.

Chapter 1 covers how lean production is recognized as an administrative approach associated with a minimization or constant waste system that reduces production and the lean production system. Implementation through tools that help various areas of the organization. Although conceptually disseminated and applied in various sectors of the economy, publications in the agribusiness sector are scarce. This chapter presents the results of the application of és lean, action research carried out with a small-scale dairy producer. Through the use of lean tools, such as a flowchart, Ishikawa diagrams, Value Stream Mapping and the PDCA cycle, it was possible to guide a set of improvements in the property under study, adding profitability gains.

The use of the Lean philosophy in healthcare environments has been reported in different countries, both in the private and the public sectors. However, there is not much information on how to apply the Kaizen concept to healthcare services; notably in hospitals and emergency services, which are increasingly challenging environments given the aging of the world population and the degradation of human conditions in several countries. Chapter 2 is built around that notion. Existing publications on the topic expose different forms of Kaizen use in healthcare services, which may cause misunderstanding and confusion. This chapter describes and brings light to the Kaizen approach in Lean implementations and discusses its challenges, barriers and success factors using a case study of a Non-Governmental Organization (NGO) which started its Lean journey with Kaizen implementation in late 2019. It also describes strategies to use it according to up-to-date publications, and presents the benefits, the challenges and the framework to successfully implement Kaizen.

Overcrowding in emergency hospital units represents a serious problem in the health system and is a phenomenon faced worldwide. And when investigating the origin of this disorder, it is observed that the great demand for care of cases considered low risk directly influences the quality of the service provided. Thus, in Chapter 3 we learn it is necessary to apply tools and methods to improve the service offered. The Lean Six Sigma methodology allows the construction of problem-solving proposals based on statistical data and effective mechanisms. And with the use of the DMAIC method, which is also the methodological framework of Lean Six Sigma, it is possible to clearly direct the resolution of problems through process improvement and restructuring in an organization. The present study aims to present a successful experience in the application of DMAIC to improve patient care and assistance in UPA Cumbica, located in the city of Guarulhos - SP.

The study in Chapter 4 aims to demonstrate the importance of waste analysis and their similarity of results. For that, the HFMEA-FUZZY was used as a tool. The study used waste results from 20 Emergency Care Units (ECUs), from different regions of Brazil, through the HFMEA criteria and complemented with the concepts of logic Fuzzy with the COPPE COSENZA methodology. The use of HFMEA-FUZZY aims to contribute to research in the health area where Lean healthcare will be or is already implemented. For that, it served as a basis for reports prepared after visits carried out in the Emergency Care Units (ECUs).

The objective of Chapter 5 is to carry out a literature review on indicators for emergency and urgent healthcare units aimed to identify the main measures within the context of healthcare services. A search was conducted on the Scopus and PubMed databases using two strategies aimed to conduct research on studies about indicators for emergency and urgent healthcare units. This work allowed identifying the main indicators used in the context of emergency and urgent medical services, which are: Length of Stay, Left Without Being Seen, National Emergency Department Overcrowding Scale, among others. In addition, it was found that such indicators provide suitable and viable means to assess, review and display the quality of health systems. It was found in some studies that the use of indicators is used only as a measure whose value is monitored by systems, but it does not lead managers to an action plan.

Lean Healthcare presents as a potential means to overcome barriers in the health sector by eliminating unnecessary movements, waiting, transport, and stockpiles. However, time spent in set-up activities does not add value to the process because the patient is not receiving service. One of the Lean tools that can help mitigate waste in those activities is the Single-Minute Exchange of Die (SMED); therefore, the study in Chapter 6 aims to evaluate the implications of using SMED in the health context. The authors conducted an exploratory search in scientific documents to achieve this goal. The content analysis was based on Bardin (2011). From the findings, it is possible to identify the implications of the use of SMED in the health context, sort activities between internal and external setup, and reduce time spent on wasteful tasks, while increasing time available for value-adding activities.

The objective of Chapter 7 is to expand the discussions regarding the application of the Fast Track method and the Standardized Work in Emergency services with the Lean Healthcare approach. In this chapter we will present some fundamental concepts to broaden our understanding of the theoretical/methodological implications necessary for the application of the Fast Track method and Standardized Work in the healthcare area, with the Lean Healthcare approach. We present the case study resulting from the execution of the Lean Project in the 24-hour UPA, which was carried out in 50 selected emergency care units, as a result of the agreement with the Ministry of Health through the Department of Hospitals and Urgencies (DAHU/MS) and with the Rector of the Fluminense Federal University.

Chapter 8 deals with the application of lean and inclusive practices in order to mitigate the problems of the healthcare system in Emergency Care Units (UPAS), especially when dealing with people with disabilities. The lack of qualified professionals, endless waiting queues causing overcrowding, waste, lack of supplies and equipment are, among others, common "pathogenic" examples in the UPAS. The combination of practices and methods to combat waste and add value derived from Lean Healthcare with the Assistive Technologies are fundamental for the adequacy of accessibility and improvement of care for people with disabilities. These practices provide mobility and autonomy to these patients, allowing their inclusion, improving their self-esteem and quality of life. The objective of this study was to investigate what is known about facilities and difficulties in the use of auxiliary devices, lean and inclusive methods and practices to improve the care of people with disabilities in UPAS.

Chapter 9 covers how performance indicators are an important tool for managers to identify how their organization is performing over time. Thus, a concept of the patient's timeline within the health unit was defined, which consists of monitoring from entry to exit, considering all the steps that patients went through during their stay in the Emergency Care Units (UPA). This concept was applied to allow the monitoring of the performance of two UPA's being classified as (1) and (2) in the city of Guarulhos - SP. Data treatment was realized by Excel and were collected from 383 patients (UPA 1 only odd days) and 1123 patients (UPA 2 all days), between 02/01/2021 and 02/28/2021. Then proceeded to the organization of data to analyze the processes flow involved. Patients were grouped according to risk classification – red, orange, yellow, green and blue – and specialty – medical clinic, orthopedics, pediatrics, dental attendance. To both UPA evaluated the major attendance were classified with green and blue and in terms of treatment the clinic medical was priority when compared with others offered in these UPA.

The study in Chapter 10 analyzes the contributions and applications of Queuing Theory (QT) in the field of health service management problems. This review presents a classification system of health care examined with the aid of queuing models. The purpose of this to analyze the contributions and applications of QT in the field of problem management in health services and to give indications of when and how to use QT in order to enhance daily management decisions. Methodology: A literature review was carried out to investigate the health areas supported by queuing models, searching articles that described problem models and their topics or keywords related to QT and population health or health problems. Results: The present study analyzed 314 articles that address the applications of QT in health care management between 2014 and 2020. Conclusion: This review demonstrates that QT can contribute to the improvement of health services and provide resource managers to achieve this improvement. And, a discussion of why, when and requirements to apply QT is presented.

Chapter 11 analyzes Lean interventions in Emergency Care Units (ECUs) with a focus on learning theory and knowledge management. The use of data served to understand the effectiveness of Lean methodology in transforming knowledge in ECUs. The method was a systematic and descriptive ex-post survey in the Lean Project database, quantitative and qualitative analysis aiming to establish relationships between the foci. The Virtual Platform is an effective tool for dissemination and generates reliable answers for analysis and decision making. The benefits of interventions through the use of Lean tools are unquestionable, visible and useful for the daily life of the Units. However, the internalization of the Lean culture for permanence and improvements is a point of attention as well as the content, form and conduction of the actions. Committed people, management by processes, Lean flows, shared information and agile communication are guarantees for the transformation and consolidation of the improvements.

Chapter 12 is the result of a project signed between the Universidade Federal Fluminense and the Ministry of Health, in 2019 and executed in 2020. Its objective was to identify intersections of ideas between the National Humanization Policy (PNH) and the Lean Methodology. The path used was to seek ideas in the Lean methodology similar to the ideas present in the principles of the PNH. These intersections are understood as opportunities for actions that consider both the reduction of waste and the strengthening of aspects of the humanization of health. We identified eight common ideas: focus on the customer, the importance of the collective as a space for transforming work, the importance given to the workplace, shared management of processes, user inclusion, transversality of both, acting in the way of thinking about work. Our conclusion is that such coincidences exist and are opportunities to deepen the dissemination of the principles and guidelines of the PNH, through the actions of the Lean methodology, and vice versa.

In Chapter 13, we look at how nowadays, the world is suffering from a new coronavirus-type pathogen, namely, COVID-19. Health professionals are obliged to protect themselves with the greatest number of Personal Protective Equipment (PPE), however, we encountered some problems: most of this equipment is not self-cleaning. How do protect professionals from contaminated personal protective equipment? How to dispose of used personal protective equipment? For the construction of this equipment, we used the methodology of Define, Measure, Analyze, Improve, and Control (DMAIC). The developed prototype was applied in a primary care sector clinic, where it was performed the pre-test (swab sampling procedure) to identify cross-contamination of the environment. The cost of the prototype developed was low in relation to existing market options. The tests carried out allowed us to observe its effectiveness in the sterilization of equipment. However, new, more complex tests are still needed to better validate the prototype and to study its economic viability as a product.

Eduardo Guilherme Satolo
Sao Paulo State University, Brazil

Robisom Damasceno Calado
Fluminense Federal University, Brazil

Acknowledgment

The construction of a literary work is never carried out without partners who believe in its proposal. In this way, the editor's express gratitude to the publisher IGI Global, Ana Carolina Sanches Zeferino for supporting the authors, the chapter authors and other partners involved in the cases reported in this book.

Chapter 1
Applications of Lean Tools in a Small-Scale Dairy Farm

Guilherme Andrade Ussuna
São Paulo State University, Brazil

Eduardo Guilherme Satolo
https://orcid.org/0000-0002-8176-2423
São Paulo State University, Brazil

Priscilla A. B. Mac-Lean
São Paulo State University, Brazil

EXECUTIVE SUMMARY

Lean production is recognized as an administrative approach associated with a minimization or constant waste system that reduces production and the lean production system. Implementation through tools help various areas of the organization. Although conceptually disseminated and applied in various sectors of the economy, publications in the agribusiness sector are scarce. This chapter presents the results of the application of és lean, action research carried out with a small-scale dairy producer. Through the use of lean tools, such as a flowchart, Ishikawa diagrams, value stream mapping, and the PDCA cycle, it was possible to guide a set of improvements in the property under study, adding profitability gains.

INTRODUCTION

Organizational Background

There are many processes of high importance that generate notoriety in the field, among them, the process of managing rural properties. This process is seen as an opportunity for the rural producer to develop his knowledge in a holistic way on his property, recording and controlling activities, analyzing the results and planning the necessary actions to maximize or minimize the actions related to production costs,

DOI: 10.4018/978-1-6684-5185-4.ch001

analyze the profitability of the activity, reduce expenses and generate indicators that help their progress in rural activity (Paris et al., 2012).

The advance is conditioned to the process of globalization and international competition. Such market behavior triggered changes in relation to the legal requirements of production, health and the environment, resulting in the need to incorporate efficiency in processes within the agribusiness scope. In this way, it is necessary to manage these processes, through professionalization and it is exactly at this point that the management process becomes valid. The growing insertion of agribusiness in the globalized economy has led the sector to play a significant role in national economic development. This role therefore requires improvement in management mechanisms for the survival of these rural enterprises (Cyrne et al., 2017).

In this scenario, family farming stands out in national agribusiness, which, according to the Brazilian Institute of Geography and Statistics (IBGE), constitutes the economic base of 90% of Brazilian municipalities with up to 20 thousand inhabitants, and corresponds to 35% of the gross domestic product (GDP) absorbing 40% of the country's economically active population. The sector employs 74% of people working in the countryside, and of every ten jobs in rural areas, seven come from family farming, in addition to being highlighted in various agricultural productions (Brasil, 2017).

In turn, Lourenzani et al. (2008) demonstrated that the main managerial problem of the family farmer is not found in the agricultural techniques that, within the reality of each producer, are fully available. It resided, in the understanding of the functioning of the markets, new forms of negotiation and practices of management of the productive process. Furthermore, a significant part of rural family producers ignored the evolution of the market and changes in consumption habits, observing only their activity as if it were disconnected from other productive segments, or from the consumers' own habits.

Given the scope of the study, contextualizing the dairy activity and its importance for the world agribusiness, it obtained a growth of more than 58% in the volume of production in the last three decades (1987-2017) reaching a total of more than 828 million tons in mid-2017. Such production was generated by approximately 150 million producers worldwide, characterized by production, mostly in developing countries and by small farmers, who carry out it for its ability to provide rapid returns to producers of low scale (FAO, 2019).

In Brazil, the aforementioned scenario is similar. The dairy activity was extremely valuable for family farming, with a production of around 30 billion liters in 2017. Family farming participated in this activity because it is part of a productive scenario of almost 58% of the national diversified agricultural production seen from the perspective from the 2017 agricultural census (IBGE, 2017).

It is noteworthy that the dairy activity is seen as a stabilizer for family farming as it increases income and is an ally in the food security of producing families (Carvalho, Tourand, Poccard-Chapuis, 2012). That said, the management process in the milk agribusiness stands out, as it proposes ways to leverage the productivity and profitability of the sector.

Borges, Guedes, and Castro (2015) described that as the family model advances in the production of culture, the need for management emerges as a process of learning and incorporation of technology that must be incorporated into its organizational model. As such actions advance, rural companies and individuals increase their profitability, competitiveness in relation to the market and adapt to the demands arising from livestock farming.

It is in this event that the role of the family producer stands out when looking for cooperatives or opting for the individual sale of milk to processing industries. In the milk market, the constant fluctuation of prices is a factor of destabilization of the relations between the agents, and therefore the companies form coalitions that guarantee stable conditions of access to the raw material. This relationship is analyzed in the light of the economic incentives that companies offer to producers, which is the type of incentive that traditional companies and cooperatives normally use (Magalhães, 2007).

Magalhães (2007) argued that milk quality regulation led to restructuring in production systems and in the relationship between processing agro-industries (dairies) and producers, especially after the validity of the Normative Instruction Ordinance IN 56, of March 30, 2006, of the Ministry of Agriculture, which sets new technical, hygienic and sanitary standards for milk production.

Other regulations stood out in the milk regulation process, such as Normative Instruction IN 51 of 2002 (MAPA, 2002), which started the process of regulating dairy activities, establishing minimum criteria for milk production, identity and quality. In 2011, with the publication of Normative Instruction nº 62, annexes I and VI, the minimum requirements for the quality of milk and the process of collecting refrigerated raw milk, as well as its transport, were regulated. At this time, it was established that the collection of the product in trucks with tanks on the rural property must occur through the transmission system of the truck itself, directly from the cooling tank, allowing the collective use of bulk cooling tanks ("community tanks") by milk producers (MAPA, 2011). Finally, replacing the regulations presented above, Normative Instructions No. 76 and No. 77, of November 2018, which came into force in May 2019, set new maximum temperature limits, as well as sensory characteristics to be monitored upon receipt, in the conservation and dispatch of milk as well as its conservation in milk processors (MAPA, 2018).

Such standardizations, if not adequate, cause economic losses and difficulty in negotiating the product on the part of producers soon, thus it is up to producers to quickly adapt to the established requirements. Thinking about the cut and delimitation of this study, linked to the arranged relationships of dairy management issues, it was decided to work with the lean production tool, envisioning lean thinking to help the management process of dairy properties, aiming at the process of milking of the properties studied.

The origins of lean production theory (also known as lean manufacturing, lean production and lean manufacturing) date back to the Toyota production system from the 1950s. This was a system created to identify and eliminate waste, with the objective of minimizing costs and increasing the quality and delivery of products to customers (Jones and Womack, 2003).

The Toyota production system, as it represents a way of producing avoiding waste, was called lean production by James Womack and Daniel Jones, in their book The machine that changed the world, published in 1990, serving as a reference for production management in various types of organization in various parts of the world (Chay et al., 2015).

Gonçalves, Santos and Gohr (2013), in this sense, ensured that one of the main objectives of lean production is to reduce the waste of human effort, eliminate losses and activities that do not add value to the product, producing quality products efficiently and economic.

Therefore, lean production is a system created to provide tools for people to continually improve their work. It is, therefore, a culture, going beyond a set of techniques for efficiency and improvement (Deimiling and Zanin, 2011).

Lean production is applied in traditional industries and has been in existence since 1950. Despite this; in Brazil, companies are recognizing its importance only in recent decades and, in agribusiness, more precisely in recent years, the latter being the focus of very few studies (FORNO; FORCELLINI; CRESTANI, 2010).

As lean production aims to improve the competitiveness of companies, this study focuses on working the lean tool in the particularities of agribusiness, precisely in the practice of milking family dairy production located in the municipality of Tupã, in the Midwest of the state of São Paulo, Brazil.

The city of Tupã, located in the Midwest of the state of São Paulo (Brazil), was chosen as the headquarters of the study due to the economic and social representation that the dairy activity has for the municipality.

According to data from IBGE (2017) and Instituto de Economia Agrícola (2018), the municipality has a total of 58,436 bovine animals, of which approximately 67% are dairy cows.

Scalco (2006), based on information from the Regional Development Office (EDR) of Tupã, highlighted the significant participation of the dairy activity in the formation of gross income from municipal products, with milk being responsible for being the main activity and, for many, as only source of income and survival. Despite the importance of dairy production for the local rural producer, there are many obstacles that compromise the development of the activity in favor of competitiveness. Among so many factors, the absence of management techniques linked to the activity is mentioned.

Therefore, this chapter has as a research problem: how can lean production system tools help a small-scale dairy farmer to improve the milking management process? Thus, the objective of this chapter is to apply tools associated with the lean production system to improve the milking management process of a small-scale dairy farm.

SETTING THE STAGE

The conduct of this chapter is methodologically based on action research, given that the chapter seeks to identify the problems involved in the milking process of a small-scale dairy producer, and, by intervening by proposing practical and joint solutions to solve such problems and carry out a mapping of the pre- and post-intervention situation.

Action research is a qualitative method of approaching problems commonly used to solve collective problems with the cooperative and/or participatory participation of those involved (Mello et al., 2012). It is a generic term, covering forms of action-oriented research and indicating a diversity in theory and practice among researchers using this method, providing a wide range of options for potential researchers for what may be appropriate for their research questions (Coughlan and Coughlan, 2002).

Therefore, action research is a research strategy that aims to produce knowledge and solve a practical problem. The relationship between these two concerns is variable, but to achieve a desirable balance, two objectives are worked on, namely (Mello et al., 2012):

- Technical objective that involves the survey of solutions and proposals for corresponding actions;
- Scientific objective to obtain information that would be difficult to access through other procedures, thus increasing the knowledge base.

The action-research characteristic of this research is highlighted, as it seeks to understand the problems with the target audience, the transformation of the target audience's gaze in the face of the problems of the milking process, in addition to having a Socratic role in proposing reflection and encouragement in the face of to the identified problems, acting in a cooperative way, respecting the relationship between the researcher and the target audience.

Action Research Steps

Given the information from the dialogue between the theory of Coughlan and Coughlan (2002) with the proposal by Mello et al. (2012), and due to the specific characteristics of action research, the theoretical detailing of the phases, stages and activities was necessary.

These steps were performed and their details between theoretical and practical are described in the next subsections.

Define Context and Purpose

Exploratory phase that was driven by questions related to rationality for action and research. At this point, the reality of the subject studied was understood, identifying and characterizing the small milk producer and the need for improvement in the management process and specifically in the milking process.

This theme has gained notoriety of study for seeking to understand economic, political, social and technical factors that permeate the milking stage of the dairy activity.

Subsequently, the profile of the small-scale producer was surveyed, respecting the following pre-established criteria: opinion-forming producer who have milk as their main productive crop, with a minimum of 15 dairy heads (in the process of lactation or not) and history of participation in training with rural dairy programs linked to the municipality and competent bodies.

At this stage, the research problem that guided the construction of this work was defined, namely: how can the tools of the lean Production system help a small-scale dairy producer to improve the milking management process?

Finally, the criteria for evaluating the results of lean tooling that are guided in this chapter were applied.

Define Conceptual-theoretical Framework

The literature review stage was constructed by proposing a critical view, based on three conceptual sections (i) lean production, (ii) characterization of milk production and (iii) dairy farm management. Such sections served as the basis for a critical view of reality in the form of published works.

Select Unit of Analysis and Data Collection Techniques

As the theory points out, the criteria for selecting the small-scale producer were defined based on the reality of the local producer, as well as the availability of participation. The producer/selected property is portrayed in this work as anonymous in order to maintain the confidentiality of his identity. Data collection took place through the techniques of direct observation of the participant researcher on the property, followed by unstructured interviews and application of lean tools.

Collect Data

Data collection has the characteristic of primary data. Collected through direct observation and generation of reports for later consultation, unstructured interviews in order to collect pertinent information not available in the environment and that have value for the construction of the work and with the application of lean tools: flowchart, Ishikawa diagram and map of value stream that allowed to visualize problems arranged in the milking process of such properties. Data collection took place through active involvement in the day to day of the property, in loco. All data are available throughout the work, thus allowing an informational feedback process whenever necessary.

Analyze Data and Plan Actions

The tabulation of the data took place after the data collection stage and remains arranged throughout the work. Data analysis was performed by the researchers, in view of the results found by the application of tools: flowchart, Ishikawa diagram and value stream map. As for the planning of corrective actions, it took place in partnership with the producer, based on the theorization of action research that assumes that the small-scale dairy producer knows better his property and business niche and, as such, needs to be heard in the decision-making process.

Implement the Actions

At this stage, the small-scale dairy farmer participating in the study, with the input of the researchers, applied the proposed corrective action plan. The action plan was built based on the identifications found by the lean tooling, and after a meeting to define the problems that should be solved, a PDCA cycle was elaborated to follow the steps involved in the solution. Among the problems, the highlight was the elaboration of a control of the volume of milk per animal via a control sheet, a control of production costs via a cost calculation sheet, the acquisition of a mechanized milking via financial investment, the construction of containment bars and allocation of a cooling tank via project creation, a herd vaccination control via a control sheet and finally, the renovation of a milking shed via financial investment.

Evaluate Results

At this stage, a comparison was made between the pre- and post-intervention scenario within the property through the application of a questionnaire with the producer focus of the study, resulting in theoretical and practical implications, in addition to the construction of final considerations relevant to the study.

CASE DESCRIPTION

The case presented is a small-scale dairy farmer, who owns a rural property with an extension of seven and a half hectares of land and leases three hectares, totaling 10.5 hectares for dairy production, of which five hectares are irrigated. It has a total of 70 bovines, 56 females of these 30 cows in the lactation process, with a total daily production of 400 liters and a productive disposal of only two heads of cattle/year.

Among the specifications of the sample, compliance with the delimitation proposed throughout the methodology was found.

Regarding the zootechnical indices of the properties, shown in Table 1, they were calculated based on the data at the end of the research, calculating the indices having as animal unit (AU) an animal of 450 kg of live weight (1AU = 450kg).

Differences in relation to the initial data of the producer profile and the zootechnical indexes are highlighted. Such distancing occurred due to the time span of collection, the first being carried out in the initial six months of this study and the second in the final six months. Since, for the calculation of the zootechnical indexes, only the relation of hectares was considered from the initial collection.

As for the number of animals (lactating cows, dry cows, heifers, and calves) and their live weight, the data collected in the second period mentioned above were taken into account.

To calculate the AU of the property, the total weight of all animals on the property was divided by 450. To calculate the animal unit per hectare, the value found in the AU of the property was divided by the number of hectares available on the property (AU /there is). As for the percentage of lactating cows, the calculation was based on the number of lactating cows x 100 divided by the total number of cows, resulting in the percentage per property. To find the production per hectare, the total milk production in the year 2018 was used and the area of the property was divided into hectares (Production/ha).

Such calculations, presented in Table 1, allow an understanding of the current scenario of dairy activity on the property that is the focus of the study.

Table 1. Zootechnical indices of the small-scale dairy farm participating in the study.

Zootechnical Indices	Property
Hectares (ha) milk production	10.50
Total weight of animals* (Kg)	37,080
AU of the property	82.40
AU/ha	7.84
Total number of cows* (un)	56
Total number of lactating cows (un)	30
% of lactating cows	53.57
Total milk production year (Kg/year)	154,758
Total milk production year/ha (Kg/ha.year)	14,738

*All animals involved in milk culture (Kg)
**Total number of cows between Jul/19 and Nov/19
Source: Prepared by the authors

Among the various collection techniques, this chapter was supported by direct observation and the unstructured interview. In the initial visits, information was collected regarding the dimensions of the properties, specificities of each producer. For this initial unstructured interview, a conversation was carried out between the researcher and the subjects, combining observation perceptions regarding the information provided there.

In subsequent meetings, after obtaining authorization from the producer, mechanisms such as photographs were used together with the process of direct observation and interviews in the application of lean tools, to facilitate the collection of information.

There were 7 visits to the property between September 2018 and November 2019.

In the first quadrant of visits, we tried to understand the profile of the producer and the peculiarities that permeate his production. On the second visit, with the support of lean tooling, the flowchart was applied to understand the milking process and its possible failures. On the third visit, it was decided to apply the Ishikawa diagram to identify potential causes visually. Finally, on the fourth visit, data collection was carried out to establish the mapping of the value stream to complete this preliminary stage of problem identification.

CURRENT CHALLENGES FACING THE ORGANIZATION

To identify the current challenges for the property under study, the first tool worked with the producer was the flowchart (Table 2). The application took place in November 2018 at the first milking of the day, around 5:30 am. In this application, we worked with the total batch during the observation of the ordering process, but the sampling of the tooling was based on the batch of the first 10 cows of a total of 20 milked in the day.

Analyzing the results obtained with this tool, it was found that the milking management process has flaws during its execution.

In the milking process, important steps such as number six, which refers to the process of washing the milker's hands, are not carried out, thus compromising the sanitary management necessary for the execution of the activity. Other recommended points, such as animal accommodation in the waiting room and milking line, are not considered by those who perform the process, and there is no standard in the process.

Another point of alert occurred with the disposal of the pre-dipping solution, which did not take place in garbage bags, but was dispensed in a bucket and was exposed throughout the milking process.

The hygiene of mechanical milking, despite not following the standard proposed by the manual of good practices by Rosa et al. (2009) strictly followed a cleaning in running water and chlorine for each milked cow.

As for the transport of milk, it follows a standardization, being transported in buckets of 40 liters and after the bucket is filled.

Finally, it was possible to verify with the application of the flowchart that the producer does not have an exactitude regarding the volume of milk withdrawn per animal. There is no mechanistic control and so little electronic control, leaving a margin of error impossible to be verified. Such an estimate is visually projected and validated only when placing the total milk volume in the tank that has collective measurement.

Subsequently, in February 2019, the morning milking was monitored again, with the aim of applying the Ishikawa diagram tooling, through the observation method and understanding the points that affect the management of the activity in what concerns the 6M'S.

As for the workforce, in this aspect factors related to people were considered, in relation to the material, materials used in the process, being automated or not. As for the method, there was a lack of standardization of work processes/methodologies; machinery was considered, maintenance status, presence, or absence of automated machinery or not. Quality measuring instruments were considered. The results are shown in Figure 1.

In view of the application of the Ishikawa diagram, it was perceived for the producer that there are points to be worked on so that the property can leverage its production. Some solutions are practical and simple, others are more complex and require investment of time and money to adapt.

Table 2. Flowchart of the milking process for the small-scale producer participating in the study

Step	Activity/Animal	Realize	Observations
1	Driving the cows to the milking place calmly, without running, screaming or hitting.	Yes	
2	Accommodation in the corrals or waiting room for the cows to rest for a few minutes.	No	
3	Conducting the milking line, following the order: 1st. first-calf cows, 2nd. cows that never had mastitis; 3rd. who have had mastitis but are cured; 4th. cows with mastitis.	No	Does not have standard.
4	Driving the cows to the milking parlor and placing them on the kennel or chains.	Yes	
5	Attachment of straps (ropes on the hind legs) *Optional, use only when necessary.	Yes	
6	Handwashing	No	
7	Place your hand on the leg or udder before the teats to avoid scaring the animal.	Yes	
8	Cleaning the ceilings with running water (Be careful not to soil the udder).	Yes	
9	Withdrawal of the first three jets of milk from the breasts in the mug with a black background.	Yes	
10	Analysis of the presence of "lumps" in the milk in the mug.	Yes	
11	Pre-dipping application (used to disinfect teats) using a non-return applicator cup.	Yes	
12	Wait 30 seconds.	Yes	
13	Cleaning of the teats with disposable paper.	Yes	
14	Dispose of the pre-dipping solution in a garbage bag.	No	Maintains pattern throughout the batch.
15	Placing the teat cups on the cow.	Yes	
16	Removal of teat cups only after exhaustion of milk from the udder/cutting the vacuum from mechanical milking.	Yes	
17	Application of post-dipping on the teats.	Yes	
18	Keeping the animal upright after milking to close the sphincter.	Yes	
19	Sanitized mechanical milking.	16	Occurs after step 16.
20	Transport of milk to the tank can occur in step 21 or post 16.	17	Occurs after step 17.
21	Cleaning of the milking place	Yes	
	Approximate average milked volume (L)	**12**	

Legend: Y - Yes; N - No.
Source: Prepared by the authors.

Figure 1. Ishikawa diagram of producer
Source: Prepared by the authors.

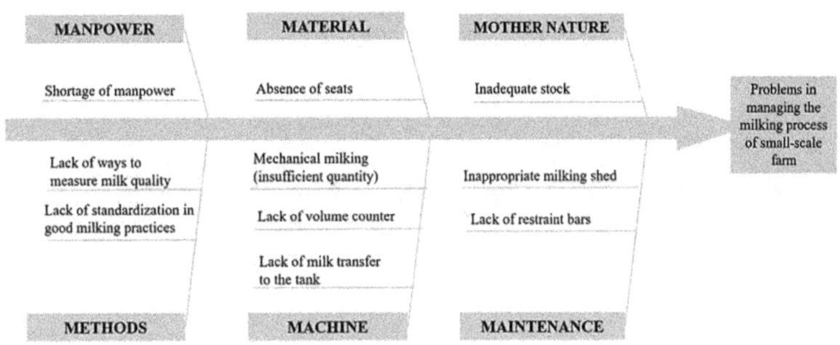

- **Manpower:** the family structure has only three people for the milking work, the (recurrent) absence of a professional greatly impairs the speed with which the activities are performed. As for the material, the greatest absence is that of benches so that workers can sit and work in the proper position without causing wear and tear.
- **Method:** the main flaw is that they do not follow best practice techniques exactly. Regarding the need for machinery, it was possible to identify that a milk volume meter is necessary, as well as a milk transfer from the milking place to the cooling tank and the purchase of a new milking to improve the uptime of milk collection, not creating idleness for a worker.
- **Measure:** it was found as an aggravating factor at this point, the producer only has information regarding the quality of his production when he is informed by the buyer dairy, he has no other means of verification. Another aggravating factor is the lack of knowledge regarding its production cost and profitability.
- **Mother nature:** it was found that logistical factors impact this scenario, the distance between the handling shed and the cooling tank is approximately 30 meters. Another important point in this scenario is the absence of containment bars for the animals in the handling shed.

The third and last tool applied to identify the problems involved in the milking process of the property/producer was the mapping of the value stream. This application took place in March 2019, during the morning milking process, on this day 22 cows were milked (Figure 2).

In view of the elaboration of the VSM with the producer, it was possible to visualize which steps are involved in the milking activities (and that can interfere with it) and what is the impact of the milk flow visualized in a macro way.

With the application of this tool, it appears that most of the actions performed during the process are mechanistic, which is a reality of the culture subject to change with technological advancement.

A point identified with alert is the high stock of inputs. There is an inadequacy in the storage process, which is in a reduced place and susceptible to possible losses due to the actions of time.

The application of the VSM detected that there is a cyclical behavior in the activity, with a weekly forecast of the dairy industry for the property, it produces according to a daily forecast, the product being stored in cooling tanks and collected three times a week by the dairy industry.

Figure 2. VSM for the property under study
Legend: (') minute and (") seconds
Source: Prepared by the authors.

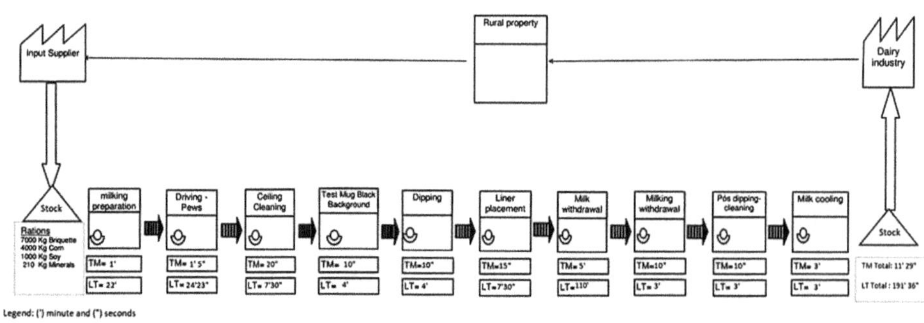

Another important point visualized was the supplier of inputs that, being an important link in this chain, has an influence on the production process. Its interaction with the property link occurs once a month via the delivery of inputs for animal supplementation.

With the VSM, it was possible to verify that the 10 production stages illustrated are part of the current value stream and add value to the customer, since if not performed correctly, they impair the quality of the milk and make it difficult to sell by the other links in the chain.

It is worth mentioning that the alert points for this VSM were related to the Mean Time (TM) of the activities, the TM that was portrayed as the time calculated in relation to the average for performing the step in an animal and the Lead Time (LT) that was portrayed as the interval time between start and end of milking activity.

In this regard, the removal of milk becomes the onerous process, since, with only two mechanized milkings, the process cannot be streamlined. Such a step consumes a TM of five minutes per worker and a LT of 110'. The activity also takes considerable time, with a total TM of 11'29" per animal and a total LT of 191'36". On the property, this activity routine is performed twice a day, and considering that there are other productive activities and other treatments in relation to the culture itself, such as pasture adequacy, treatment of male cattle, calves, medicinal interventions in other animals, among others, the LT of the activity is high and must be rethought so as not to harm too many tasks.

SOLUTIONS AND RECOMMENDATIONS

The property under study showed as the main problems involved in the milking management process (Table 3): the need to invest in another mechanized milking, a milk volume counter, a milk transfer from the milking to the tank, containment bars for the animals, new ways of measuring the quality of the milk and the relation of the storage of the stock that is in an inappropriate place.

The improvement proposals were exposed to the producers through the PDCA cycle, as suggested by the methodology, and together with them, it was defined which problems to act on and which solutions. A priori, 8 problems were identified, of which only 6 became viable for solution, since problems linked to investment, time and the producer's option were considered. Thus, problems 1 to 6 were worked on and are displayed in Table 4.

Table 3. Problems identified in the small-scale dairy farm

#	Problem	Root Cause
1	Failure to fully guide the milking process through the steps of good practice	Method
2	Lack of knowledge of the volume of milk produced	Machine
3	Lack of production cost control	Measure
4	Two milkings a day, with a high volume of production conducted manually	Machine
5	Absence of animal restraint bars	Mother Nature
6	Absence of milk transfer to the tank	Machine
7	Lack of ways to measure milk quality	Measure
8	Inadequate stock storage location	Mother Nature

Source: Prepared by the authors.

Table 4. PDCA of property issues

Problems	Plan	Do	Check	Act
11	Lack of knowledge of good milking management practices	Training conduction	Check fortnightly the performance of good milking management practices	Conduct additional training if necessary
2	Control volume of milk per animal	Control sheet	Producer/Researcher	Daily control
3	Control production costs	Cost calculation worksheet	Financial reality impact	Periodic control
4	Mechanical milking	Equipment acquisition	Improved milking environment	Environment suitability
5 e 6	Containment bars / Cooling tank	Project creation/ construction	Improved milking environment	Environment suitability

Source: Prepared by the authors.

After defining which issues should be tackled with the producers and building the PDCA, the project was put into action. This stage was centered between the months of August and November 2019 with biweekly visits, totaling 8 visits to the property. For ease of understanding of this study, the improvements are exposed by problems following the logic of action of the whole work.

Improvement Actions - Problem 1

The milking process is a fundamental step in obtaining high-quality dairy products, and factors related to animal hygiene, milking equipment and milkers lead to milk contamination (Simões and Bauer, 2017). Therefore, it was decided to initiate the improvements through training in connection with this process. For this purpose, we used the manual of good milking management practices developed by Rosa et al. (2014).

Improvement Actions - Problem 2

To solve this problem and with the support of the Brazilian Integral Technical Assistance Coordinator (CATI), a control worksheet was created. This worksheet (Table 5) aims to help the producer to measure the number of liters of milk withdrawn per animal in a temporal space and validate if the production is in accordance with food issues related to pastures, feed and other minerals and even with in relation to productivity that are deposited in the cooling tank.

Faced with the difficulties of daily control by the producer, a control was agreed every 15 days, so that during this period the productive reactions (constant or with positive and/or negative oscillations) within the milking can be compared.

The control requires filling in the current month, production data collection date, information relevant to the earring and/or name of the animal, volume of milk withdrawn in the first and second milking of the day and the sum of the total volume, in addition to possible observations. relevant to this process. Another requested point and agreement are in relation to the number of dry cows, the presence in the volume spreadsheet is important, as the producer can periodically monitor the entry and exit of cows in this cycle.

Table 5. Control table of the property milk volume

Month:_______________					
DAIRY CONTROL – DATE ____/____/____					
No.	Cow name	Producion (liters)			Comments
		1st Milking	2nd Milking	Total	

Source: Prepared by the authors.

The spreadsheet was printed, exposed to the producer and introduced into their daily lives as a way to control and understand the milking management process.

Improvement Actions – Problem 3

The lack of control over the cost of production and the profit margin against the crop has become a loose end and a recurring problem for producers, as the IFCN study (2018) points out, the lack of knowledge of such variables causes problems in relation to the competitiveness of Brazilian milk market.

With the support of the technical circular: spreadsheet for calculating the cost of milk production in Embrapa's family farming, prepared by Tupy et. al (2002) and the collection of information from the producers made it possible to measure the cost of milk production and the profitability of all properties (Table 6).

The initial calculation was performed following the guidelines proposed by the literature. It should also be noted that the amounts worked are annual. The result presented by the property is shown in Table 6.

With the realization of the relevant calculations to the cost of production of the producer, it was possible to verify that despite the high costs with feeding the herd, about BRL 118,994.70 per year the property operates in a positive situation, since the sale of milk generates a annual income of BRL 226,891.92, totaling a net income of BRL 41,240.16 more precisely a monthly income of BRL 3,438.68. Another relevant finding is the price received per liter, which follows a line of R$ 1.48 per liter during the year, award for quality, since it is above the state average of BRL 1.41 according to data from the Center for Advanced Studies. in Applied Economics – CEPEA from the Luiz de Queiroz Higher School of Agriculture – ESALQ/USP in November 2019 (CEPEA, 2019).

Finally, the profitability per liter of milk produced is verified, since the property has a positivity of BRL 0.26 per liter of milk.

However, it is noted here the need to minimize costs linked to bovine feed so that the producer's profit margin can be greater, which is, therefore, a possibility of advancement for this study. Such data were never accessed by the producer and, with the conclusion of this stage, corrective measures to improve this stage must be put into practice.

Table 6. Producer's worksheet for production cost control

Milk Production Cost Worksheet		
Producer name: Producer X		
Property name: Property X		
County: Tupã, Brazil		
Month:	Year: 2019	
#	**Items**	**BRL (Brazilian Reais)**
1	Labor expenses	11,700.00
2	Food expenses	118,994,70
3	Other expenses	20,623.44
4	Capital costs [(1) + (2) + (3)] x 0.20	30,263.62
5	Financial expenses	7,000.00
6	TOTAL COST (1) + (2) + (3) + (4) + (5)	188,581.76
7	TOTAL REVENUE	229,891.92
8	Milk sale	226,891.92
9	Other sales	0,00
10	NET PROFIT	41,240.16
11	Total milk product (liters)	154,758.00
12	Milk sold (liters)	152,958.00
13	Cost/liter of milk produced	1.21
14	Value received per liter of milk	1.48
15	Profit/liter of milk produced	0.26
16	Number of cows in the herd (unit)	56
17	Milk production per cow in the herd (liters	2,763

Source: Prepared by the authors adapted from Tupy et al. (2002).

Improvement Actions - Problem 4

The property under study presented problems with the speed of milk removal, high number of animals and idle professionals in the milk withdrawal stage. After such identification, it is concluded the need to acquire a new mechanized milking system to assist in the adequacy and improvement of the milking environment. The mechanized milking was budgeted in accordance with the needs of the property and the producer and the acquisition in the amount of BRL 2,839.00 was carried out.

As a result of the acquisition, an improvement in the milking environment was identified since the process became more agile and required greater participation of the three workers in the activity.

Improvement Actions - Problems 5 and 6

The fourth problem identified was the inadequacy of the property's milking shed, it was noted the need to build containment bars for the animals. Such construction will positively impact the safety of milkers, animals as well as the agility of the processes linked to the activity. In conjunction with this problem, the need to relocate the cooling tank was identified, since it is located at more than 30 meters from the milking shed and causes health and logistical damage to the property.

After on-site measurements and construction of the floor plan in an AutoCad® system, visualizations of the changes became possible, as seen in Figure 3.

The improvements focused on the construction of containment bars to organize the milking of the animals as well as the construction of an annex (see figure 19 lower left corner) to bring the cooling tank closer to the milking place and thus facilitate the transport links to the tank as well as the plumbing that assists in sanitary relationships.

This preposition respected the real metrics and was presented to the producer along with a model, he agreed with the improvement steps and started the adaptation process by building a new annex to adapt the cooling tank, as shown in Figure 4.

Figure 3. Floor plan of milking shed before and proposals of improvements
Source: Prepared by the authors.

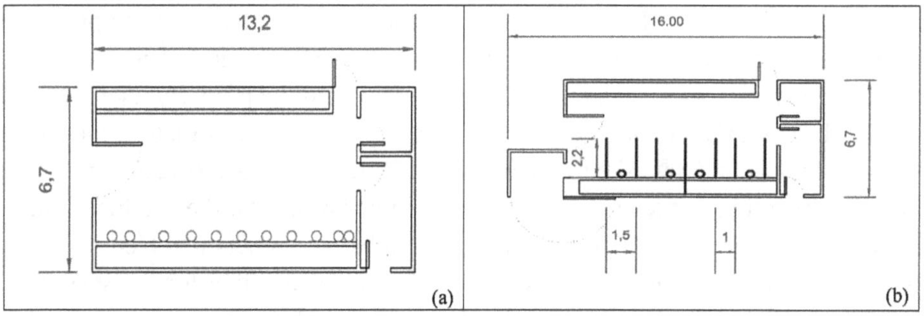

Figure 4. Attachment to allocate cooling tank under construction
Source: Authors' personal file

POST-INTERVENTION SCENARIO

Within this stage, a questionnaire with 10 questions was applied in order to identify the impact of the intervention on the efficiency in milking management in the properties studied, for which the questions were analyzed.

In the first question, it was asked whether the problems identified throughout this work are in line with reality. For the producer participating in the research "Yes, they are in compliance, among many problems identified, especially the structural ones, they match reality".

Subsequently, the question raised was related to the support of the researcher during the survey of the problems, if it occurred in an adequate way. At this point, the producer said that he is in full compliance and understands that the high number of visits, observations, questions and support from the researcher positively corroborated the identification of the problems.

The third question sought to understand whether, in the producer's perception, all the suggested improvements can be carried out in a long-term space of time. Once again, the response was positive, with emphasis on the statement that: "The biggest challenge must be the implementation of a milk volume meter, due to the high cost". The fourth question sought to understand if the producer can verify improvement in the milking process after the execution of this project, indicating that "Yes, in relation to the milking time and in relation to the transport process within the property itself".

Subsequently, the possibility of having noticed an improvement in relation to some indicator of milk quality due to the interventions was asked, and the producer indicated that he did not know how to answer.

Regarding possible problems for the introduction of improvements, the producer understands that they did not exist, since there was support from the researcher and others involved in the research.

As for the continuity of improvements, the producer understands that for the survival of the dairy activity on the properties, the continuity of improvements is necessary.

When asked if the research brought satisfactory results, it was indicated in a positive way.

The ninth question was in relation to the support given by the researcher for the implementation of corrective actions, if the same occurred properly. As in question number two, the emphasis was on the researcher's concern to solve the problems and the introduction of a working committee, always respecting and considering the opinion of the owners and employees.

Therefore, in the tenth question, it was asked how this research could have gone better. For the producer "the construction of a meter would help a lot".

With such an answer, it was possible to verify the opening for the advancement of this study, since the possibility of developing an electronic equipment to solve this common problem among producers arises.

It is also noteworthy that, given the timeframe for carrying out this study, it was not possible to develop such an experiment, which is a possible idea for advancing the study in the near future.

CONCLUSION OF THE EXPERIMENT

Finally, it is possible to conclude through this project that the lean tools were extremely valuable for identifying problems, preposing improvements, and implementing improvements in relation to the management of milking management in the dairy farms worked on in this study.

The implementation of improvements linked to the return of the producer demonstrate that it is possible to link different areas of knowledge to solve problems, leaving a legacy in relation to new control mechanisms for solutions to problems that affect agribusiness, family producers, especially of milk.

To solve such problems, it is important, above all, the contribution of public policies and universities. There is still a need to develop, through an educational process, training so that family producers can have access to information, new consumer markets and understand the new market dynamics so that culture becomes increasingly profitable and survives over generations.

ACKNOWLEDGMENT

Project funded by the Brazilian agency Conselho Nacional de Desenvolvimento Científico e Tecnológico (CNPq - grant number 424722/2018-6) and to Coordenação de Aperfeiçoamento de Pessoal de Nível Superior (CAPES – grant number CAPES/DS nº 88881.593696/2020-01).

REFERENCES

Borges, M. S., Guedes, C. A. M., & Castro, M. C. D. (2015). A gestão do empreendimento rural: Um estudo a partir de um programa de transferência de tecnologia a pequenos produtores [The management of the rural enterprise: a study from a technology transfer program to small producers]. *Revista de Ciências da Administração, 17*(43), 141–156. doi:10.5007/2175-8077.2015v17n43p141

BRASIL. Secretária Especial de Agricultura Familiar e do Desenvolvimento Agrário. (2017). *Brasil: 70% dos alimentos que vão à mesa dos brasileiros são da agricultura familiar* [Brazil: 70% of the food on the table of Brazilians comes from family farming]. http://www.mda.gov.br/sitemda/noticias/brasil-70-dos-alimentos-que-vao-a-mesa-dos-brasileiros-sao-da-agricultura-familiar

Carvalho, S. A., Tourrand, J. F., & Poccard-Chapuis, R. (2012). Atividade leiteira: Um desafio para a consolidação da agricultura familiar na região da transamazônica, no Pará [Dairy activity: a challenge for the consolidation of family farming in the trans-Amazonian region, in Pará]. *Cadernos de Ciência & Tecnologia, 29*(1), 269–290.

CEPEA - Centro de Estudos Avançados em Economia Aplicada. *Série de preços* [Price series]. https://www.cepea.esalq.usp.br/br/indicador/leite.aspx

Chay, T., Xu, Y., Tiwari, A., & Chay, F. (2015). Towards lean transformation: The analysis of lean implementation frameworks. *Journal of Manufacturing Technology Management, 26*(7), 1031–1052. doi:10.1108/JMTM-10-2013-0143

Coughlan, P., & Coghlan, D. (2002). Action research for operations management. *International Journal of Operations & Production Management, 22*(2), 220–240. doi:10.1108/01443570210417515

Cyrne, C. C. S., Rempel, C., Haetinger, C., & Bortoli, J. (2015). O (não) uso de indicadores de gestão em propriedades leiteiras na Galícia – Espanha [The (non) use of management indicators in dairy farms in Galicia – Spain]. *Holos, 5*(31), 308–321. doi:10.15628/holos.2015.3249

Deimiling, S. F., & Zanin, A. (2011). Produção enxuta no agronegócio: análise em uma agroindústria do Oeste de Santa Catarina [Lean production in agribusiness: analysis in an agroindustry in the west of Santa Catarina]. Proceedings of Simpósio Engenharia de Produção, 1-15.

FAO - Food and Agriculture Organization of the United Nations. (2019). *Gateway to dairy production and products 2019*. https://www.fao.org/dairy-production-products/production/en/

Forno, A. J., Forcellini, F. A., & Crestani, P. A. (2010). A abordagem enxuta aplicada ao agronegócio: estudo de caso em viveiro de mudas florestais [The lean approach applied to agribusiness: a case study in a forest seedling nursery]. Proceedings of Encontro Nacional de Engenharia de Produção, 2-12.

Gonçalves, J. M. S., Santos, L. C., & Gohr, C. F. (2013). Uma análise das publicações sobre produção enxuta nos principais periódicos nacionais de Engenharia de Produção [An analysis of publications on lean production in the main national journals of Production Engineering]. *Produção em Foco*, *3*(2), 252–277. doi:10.14521/P2237-5163.2013.0004.0003

IEA - Instituto de Economia Agricola. (2018). *Valor de produção: Estatística de produção dos principais produtos da agropecuária Paulista 2018* [Production value: Production statistics of the main agricultural products from São Paulo 2018]. http://ciagri.iea.sp.gov.br/nia1/subjetiva.aspx?cod_sis=1&idioma=1

IFCN - International Farm Comparison Group. (2018). *The IFCN Dairy Report 2018: For a better understanding of dairy world*. https://ifcndairy.org/wp-content/uploads/2018/10/Dairy-Report-Article-2018.pdf

Lourenzani, W. L., Pinto, L. B., Carvalho, E. C. A., & Carmo, S. M. (2008). A qualificação em gestão da agricultura familiar: A experiência da alta paulista [Qualification in family farming management: the experience of high São Paulo]. *Revista de Ciências em Extensão*, *4*, 62.

Magalhães, R. S. (2007). Habilidades sociais no mercado de leite. *Revista de Administração de Empresas*, *47*, 1–11.

MAPA - Ministério da Agricultura. Pecuária e Abastecimento. (2002). Instrução Normativa N° 51, de 19 de Setembro de 2002 [Normative Instruction No. 51, of September 19, 2002]. Brasília: Mapa.

MAPA - Ministério da Agricultura. Pecuária e Abastecimento. (2018). Instrução Normativa N° 76, de 26 de Novembro de 2018 [Normative Instruction No. 76, of November 26, 2018]. Brasília: Mapa.

Mello, C. H. P., Turrioni, J. B., Xavier, A. F., & Campos, D. F. (2012). Pesquisa-ação na engenharia de produção: Proposta de estruturação para sua condução [Action research in production engineering: a structure proposal for its conduction]. *Production*, *22*(1), 1–13. doi:10.1590/S0103-65132011005000056

Rosa, M. S, Costa, M. J. R. P., Sant´Anna, A. C., & Madureira, A. P. (2009). *Manual de Boas Práticas de Manejo-Ordenha* [Manual of Good Milking Management Practices]. Jaboticabal: Funep.

Scalco, A. R., & Souza, R. D. C. (2006). Qualidade na cadeia de produção de leite: Diagnóstico e proposição de melhorias [Quality in the milk production chain: diagnosis and improvement propositio]. *Organizações Rurais & Agroindustriais*, *8*(3), 368–377.

Simões, J., & Bauer, A. (2017). Reproductive and milk production profiles in Serrana Goats. In *Sustainable Goat Production in Adverse Environments* (Vol. 2, pp. 233–243). Springer. doi:10.1007/978-3-319-71294-9_17

Tupy, O., Manzano, A., Esteves, S. N., Novaes, N. J., Camargo, A. C., Freitas, A. R., & Machado, R. (2002). Planilha para Cálculo do Custo de Produção de Leite na Agricultura Familiar [Spreadsheet for Calculating the Cost of Milk Production in Family Farming]. *Circular Técnica Embrapa*, *32*, 1–11.

Womack, J. P., & Jones, D. T. (2003). *Lean Thinking: Banish Waste and Create Wealth in Your Corporation*. Free Press.

KEY TERMS AND DEFINITIONS

Action Research: Type of research method, commonly applied in the social sciences and research that seeks to link change through the simultaneous process of action and research, which are aligned by critical reflection between researchers and researchers.

Family Farm: A farm that is owned and operated by a family, especially one that has been handed down from one generation to another.

Ishikawa Diagram: Is a diagram that shows the causes of an event and is often used in manufacturing and product development to outline the different steps in a process.

Lean Tools: Lean tools provide frameworks to solve problems, measure performance, analyze and optimize work processes while helping to manage people and change.

PDCA Cycle: The Plan-Do-Check-Act (PDCA) Cycle is a four-step problem-solving iterative technique used to improve business processes.

Value Stream Mapping: VSM is defined as a lean tool that employs a flowchart documenting every step in the process.

Chapter 2
Kaizen Implementation: A Lean Strategy to Improve Healthcare Performance

Ana Carolina Sanches Zeferino
https://orcid.org/0000-0003-1213-0964
Fluminense Federal University, Brazil

José Ricardo de Souza Ramos
Fluminense Federal University, Brazil

Alexandre Beraldi Santos
Fluminense Federal University, Brazil

Eduardo Guilherme Satolo
https://orcid.org/0000-0002-8176-2423
Sao Paulo State University, Brazil

Olavo Braga Neto
Fluminense Federal University, Brazil

Saulo Cabral Bourguignon
Fluminense Federal University, Brazil

EXECUTIVE SUMMARY

The use of the lean philosophy in healthcare environments has been reported in different countries, both in the private and the public sectors. However, there is not much information on how to apply the Kaizen concept to healthcare services, notably in hospitals and emergency services, which are increasingly challenging environments given the aging of the world population and the degradation of human conditions in several countries. Existing publications on the topic expose different forms of Kaizen use in healthcare services, which may cause misunderstanding and confusion. This chapter describes and brings light to the Kaizen approach in lean implementations and discusses its challenges, barriers, and success factors using a case study of a non-governmental organization (NGO) that started its lean journey with Kaizen implementation in late 2019. It also describes strategies to use it according to up-to-date publications and presents the benefits, the challenges, and the framework to successfully implement Kaizen.

DOI: 10.4018/978-1-6684-5185-4.ch002

INTRODUCTION

Organizational Background

Health systems around the world face similar difficulties, such as an aging population; the increase in demand for health services; new technologies and expensive services; all while experiencing increasing financial constraints. In this context, providing high quality services that meet patient expectations with minimal resources is a major challenge, and has led some healthcare organizations to explore Lean methodology – which focuses primarily on improving processes, reducing and eliminating waste (Kelendar et al., 2020).

The authors present the case of Kaizen practice as part of a Lean implementation strategy for a Non-Governmental Organization (NGO) – specifically, a Social Health Organization –, with contracts in the countryside of Rio de Janeiro, Brazil. Non-Governmental Social Health Organizations are nonprofit institutions of the third sector, responsible for managing Brazilian public Health System (SUS) institutions throughout the country, in partnership with municipal and state health departments. Despite being characterized as a private company, it is subjected to the same public compliance regulations, which in turn have implications on company directions and strategy when compared to purely private companies. They are guided by the needs of the population and not by capital.

The company in question operates at all levels of public health, managing primary care, secondary care, and tertiary care units. Primary care is guided by the Family Health Strategy and was designed to be a space for health promotion and prevention, operating mostly with scheduled appointments and not answering to emergencies. Secondary care, which is sometimes referred to as "hospital and community care", can either be planned (elective) care such as medical treatment with specialties like physical therapy, or urgent and emergency care such as the treatment fractures (the facilities are called UPAs). Tertiary care refers to highly specialized treatment, for which hospitals are allocated.

Non-Governmental Social Health Organizations are funded by public resources according to Brazilian regulation. Human capital is based on the contract established with the municipalities, which in turn is supposed to be based on technical guidelines provided by the Ministry of Health. It is also important to note that this kind of contract is based on compliance requirements, and each contract lasts between 1 and 4 years.

The company operates in four different municipalities. For this case they will be referred to as A, B, C and D. Table 1 presents information about each of these municipalities.

SETTING THE STAGE

Lean Practices in Healthcare

The adoption of Lean practices has been studied and reported as success stories of strategic changes in healthcare organizations (Lordelo et al., 2021). Many authors report success cases like the ones of Bolton Improving Care System – BICS –, Virginia Mason Medical Center (Womack & Jones (2003), Kelendar et al. (2020); ThedaCare (Barnas, 2014), Baptist Hospital in Pensacola, IU Health Goshen Hospital, Franciscan St. Francis Health, Newton Medical Center (Kansas), Riverside Medical Center (Kankakee, Illinois), Seattle Children's Hospital (Seattle, Washington), Delnor Hospital (Geneva, Illinois), Denver

Table 1. Detailing of each municipality where the company has operations in place

	Municipality A	Municipality B	Municipality C	Municipality D
Public units managed	1 hospital 3 primary care units and its 16 subunits	1 hospital 1 secondary care unit	1 hospital 4 secondary care units (3 emergency care and 1 specialty unity) 18 primary care units	2 secondary care units (2 emergency care)
Start of Lean implementation	October, 2018	May, 2021	February, 2020	Contract 01: June, 2021 Contract 02: December, 2021
Population (number of inhabitants)	10,392	54,273	91,938	999,728
Population density (inhabitants per km^2)	12.67	56.273	209.96	4,035.90
Human Development Index (HDI)	0.668	0.700	0.709	0.739

Source: IBGE.

Health, Flinders Medical Centre (Australia), and the Royal Bolton Hospital NHS Foundation Trust (England) (Graban & Swartz, 2012); IOV – Valley Oncology Institute (Brazil) (Pinto, 2014).

All the stories told by the institutions that decided to take the Lean journey reported significant results in patient care and business indicators (Bowerman & Fillingham (2007), Kollberg et al. (2006); Lodge & Bamford (2008) and Manos et al. (2006)). A common element to these implementations is the development of the Kaizen mentality across the institutions. These results come from the Lean thinking approach, which can be explained by the promotion and leveraging by Leadership guidance, example, and coaching; structured processes with proper methods and tools; and people development in continuous improvement mentality and commitment to the business purpose.

The authors compare the continuous improvement implementation process to the development of a plant. At the beginning there is a choice in what tree to plant, based on customer needs. Once the plant has been chosen, there is a need to water it, fertilize the ground and promote an environment for its growth. At the beginning, the plant's structures are fragile. When the structures are robust but flexible, no storm can take it down. The choice in which plant to cultivate relates to the purpose of the business. The gardeners are the company's leadership and employees, taking good care and cultivating the plant so that it can survive and grow. The plant's structures are the processes, the ways through which food reaches its leaves. And the flowers are business results.

In this growing process, there is the formulation of a strategy, with the definition of methods and tools to support the strategy, along with a capability development and communicating plan. The definition of a strategy must take into consideration the context in which the company is inserted, its existing culture and the expected objectives with the implementation of the Lean mentality. The choice of methods and tools follows the strategy and must consider a proper method for solving each issue. It is important to internalize that there is not a one-size-fits-all solution. Another mandatory aspect of the continuous improvement implementation process is to plan an investment in the development of people – leaders, caregivers, service providers –'s capabilities. The capabilities to develop are associated with the employees' roles. Every member of the institution, employee or outsourced, is supposed to have training in continuous improvement principles, methods and tools. A Leader will lead the initiative and must develop people management skills. And, finally, as every implementation is a call for change and since people do not deal well with change, a good communication plan must be put in place.

One approach to build continuous improvement capabilities in people is to establish a Kaizen strategy.

Kaizen Fundamentals

One of the practices of Lean thinking is Kaizen. The concept of Kaizen was initially explained by Imai (1986) as "*continuous improvement involving all employees*", "*an umbrella concept that covers most of the typical Japanese practices that have gained fame around the world*". By typical Japanese practices, Imai refers to the concept of TQC (Total Quality Control), quality circles, suggestion systems, TPM (Total Productive Maintenance), Kanban, JIT (Just In Time), etc. After Imai, many authors studied and published on the same concept. For Ferreira & Saurin (2019), Kaizen, or continuous improvement, is a fundamental principle of Lean production, which implies that work systems must continually evolve towards better performance, addressing the weaknesses of previous projects. Kaizen initiatives are characterized by small improvements made as part of daily work, preferably by those who work on the front lines and constitute the lowest hierarchical echelons. However, what counts as "small" is not precisely defined, and the scope of Kaizen varies substantially, from individual operations to entire value streams – a broader initiative referred to as a 'Kaizen project', which usually takes place over weeks or months, aimed at improving performance using Lean production principles (Spear & Bowen, 1999; Suárez-Barraza & Ramis-Pujol, 2010).

In his book, Imai delineates 3 different approaches for using Kaizen, according to the nature of the employee's role in the company structure. He postulates that, the closer an employee's role is to top management functions, the more it relates to improving the business and innovating. In contrast, the closer to operational functions, the more a professional's role relates to keeping and improving standards. This definition implies that Kaizen has different scopes and, in consequence, requires different approaches and tools when executed by teams in each role. As a result, Imai proposed a structure of three types of Kaizen.

- **Type I Kaizen**: Type I Kaizen is the approach used by anyone, at any time, to contribute with improvements, in the form of an idea, a proposition to improve any activity. Usually related to changing standards. Mostly performed in specific activities and based on common sense. To fulfill the requirement of data driven decision, one should use tools like the seven statistical tools. Considered to boost engagement of employees on continuous improvement culture. Results are captured locally. Does not take long to be concluded and happens at any time. Usually requires only employees' work hours and materials present in the company, with no investment needed.
- **Type II Kaizen**: Type II Kaizen is the approach used by groups of people, to solve issues in a group-oriented fashion. The group is multidisciplinary and involves operational functions with management as sponsors. The initiative becomes a medium-term project, four to five months long. Results impact processes and are captured locally and in the system. Considered to solve problems, improve morale, and develop employees through practical experience in the use of continuous improvement tools. Usually requires only employees' work hours and materials present in the company to be concluded, with no investment needed.

- **Type III Kaizen**: Type III Kaizen is the approach used by groups of people, to solve issues in management-oriented fashion. The group is multidisciplinary and involves managers in its execution. The initiative is a medium-to-long-term project that focuses on systems and procedures. Results impact systems – might be a new system – and procedures. Considered to boost company performance. Sometimes requires small investments.

Kaizen in Healthcare Services

Healthcare systems are complex institutions. Contrary to a manufacturing company that has one line of products that bear a certain similarity, aggregating pieces along the way or process industries in which from one line many products are delivered per stage, in a healthcare environment there is a great number of different products (each patient in treatment is a different product) that can be generated. The interconnection and crossing of flows create in caregivers a wrong impression, a preconception that industry originated methods should not work in health services. Evidence, however, has shown the opposite. Literature shows different experiences, as summarized in Table 2, in selected published Kaizen cases in the healthcare section that follows.

In formal literature, it is very important to cite Graban & Swartz (2012) insight on Kaizen. They use the translation from Japanese to English of Kaizen, change for the better – a small change for the betterment of the overall system – as its broader definition. They construe that Kaizen are small improvement ideas, connected to measurable results, made by those who do the work, challenging and empowering them in the process of their daily work improvement. It can include team projects, called "Kaizen Events" or "Rapid Improvement Events" (RIE), depending on the scope and time of the improvement. They also explore that Kaizen is a way for organizational learning and personal pride and satisfaction, and for boosting engagement. Graban & Swartz (2012) describe the same three types of Kaizen as Imai does, all based on the Plan-Do-Study-Act (PDSA) cycle. They affirm that the healthcare institutions usually work on many small issues, few medium issues and very few large issues. For each approach, different tools should be applied.

- **Small issues**: is related to Imai's Type I Kaizen, the individual-oriented approach. Uses methods such as Daily Kaizen, A3 problem solving and Quick and Easy Kaizen. Daily Kaizen refers to the establishment of daily continuous improvement, implementing ideas. A3 problem solving refers to the use of PDSA or DMAIC approaches to problem solving, when dealing with themes that require deeper discussion and study compared to Quick and Easy Kaizen. And Quick and Easy Kaizen refers to a five-step method: (1) find opportunities or problems to solve, (2) discuss the idea with the team, (3) implement the improvement idea, (4) document the Kaizen and (5) share the Kaizen – before and after Kaizen report.
- **Medium issues**: is related to Imai's Type II Kaizen, the group-oriented approach. Uses methods such as Rapid Improvement Event (aka Workshop), Six sigma projects and A3 problem solving. Rapid Improvement Event refers to a usually weeklong effort, by a multidisciplinary team, focused on solving an issue following the PDSA cycle. Six sigma projects refer to projects using the DMAIC methodology. And A3 problem solving was the same approach used in type I Kaizen.
- **Large issues**: is related to Imai's Type III Kaizen, the management-oriented approach. Uses methods for Large Projects, Major strategic initiatives, and Lean transformation projects – a company-wide initiative.

These authors tell us the stories of companies that have developed and refined the Lean structure – sometimes called the Lean system – of the company, of which Kaizen is a part. But what about recent implementations? What changed in the 10 to 15 years before these publications, considering the evolution of technology and society?

Over the last two decades, many other private and public healthcare companies around the world started their Lean implementations.

Kaizen Published Selected Cases in Healthcare

In this section the authors present some of the published Kaizen approaches healthcare companies are using, explaining their method and results.

Mazzocato et al. (2016) presents the use of Kaizen in a Swiss hospital based on a program of suggestions for improvement. The authors explain that the hospital uses "Kaizen Blitz", which they describe as long-term initiatives for which those involved regularly meet.

Beattie et al. (2018) present the use of Kaizen at Osprey House – an English institution for the recovery of drug and alcohol addicts – in the RPIW (rapid process improvement workshop) format, described as an event divided into three phases: planning (12 weeks before the workshop), a one-week workshop, and the monitoring of results at 30, 60, 90 and 180 days.

Knechtges & Decker (2014) present results from the application of Kaizen in a radiology department using 5-day events, although they do not restrict the use of Kaizen to just this format.

Elsheikh et al. (2017) present the case of a project to revitalize the documentation of a hospital in Saudi Arabia with Lean practices and cite Kaizen as the improvements identified for the points discussed, using a model of suggestions for improvements and support of employee initiatives.

Blouin-Delisle et al. (2020) present the case of two geriatric units in which Kaizen was used to improve the patient's journey, in the Kaizen project format, following the DMAIC methodology (acronym in English for the Define, Measure, Analyze, Improve and Control phases), in which planning is done 45 days before a 3-day event is held, which, in turn, is followed by a 12-week implementation and control period.

Lamm et al. (2015) present the use of Lean principles, including Kaizen, in a chemotherapy clinic. In this article, the improvement model used starts with data preparation and collection, followed by a 5-day Kaizen event, using the Lean Six sigma method and A3 thinking.

Carney et al. (2020) presents the application of Kaizen at Children's Hospital Colorado, in Colorado, USA. The authors describe an initiative which lasted for more than 1 year, with the purpose of improving emergency department indicators, namely, door-to-office time, abandonment rate, percentage of visits in less than 30 minutes, and patient satisfaction. It is, therefore, a systemic approach. The use of Kaizen presented begins with the interest of the top leadership, who hired an external expert (consultant) to assist in the implementation. In the first year, a committee was formed, and employees were trained. Only after this initial approach were the mapping of opportunities done by applying the Value Stream Map (VSM). After surveying opportunities, Kaizen was carried out in a 5-day event format with pilot implementation and sustainability monitoring for a period of 2 months. The article deals with this event and does not discuss the application of Kaizen at other times.

Hitti et al. (2017) presents the application of Kaizen in the radiology division within the emergency department of the American University of Beirut Medical Center (AUBMC), Lebanon. The authors describe the use of Kaizen by an existing multidisciplinary team in the hospital's emergency department. This team was motivated by patient complaint records and aimed to reduce the radiology department's response time. This initiative took place over a period of more than 1 year, with 6 months of preparation, 1 month of interventions in which the VSM and chrono analyses were carried out (the Kaizen event) and results were monitored for the following 6 months. This article also does not delve into the application of Kaizen at other times and how the institution forms and maintains the Kaizen spirit

Medina-León et al. (2014) presents the application of Kaizen in the gynecology and obstetrics division of the emergency department of a Public Hospital in Mexico City, Mexico. The authors present a framework for defining when Kaizen should be used. In the structure presented, the study of the process to identify bottlenecks is carried out and, if the opportunity to address the bottleneck refers to the implementation of 5S, use of the SMED technique, implementation of Kanban, process standardization, use of visual management, or elimination of unnecessary processes, then a Kaizen approach shall be used.

Phillips et al. (2016) presents the application of Kaizen in the emergency department of the Virginia Mason Institute hospital in Seattle, USA. The article deals with the maturation of the previous Kaizen process in the Virginia Mason Institute. It is about the concept of daily Kaizen (called everyday Lean idea). In this article, the authors note that Kaizen is done with the support of its leaders who use huddles, rounds, and visual management boards to train and recognize teams when proposing and executing improvements. This article is therefore not about a project focused on business results, but about the leader's standard work as a developer of a culture of continuous improvement.

Kovacevic et al. (2016) presents the application of Kaizen in the emergency department laboratory of Vidant Health Centers, in Greenville, North Carolina, USA. The article presents Kaizen as part of a Six sigma project, after defining the project team to ensure understanding of the topic.

Phillips et al. (2016) presents Kaizen in the form of an unfolding of the program that deals with the standard work of leadership based on the execution of established routines (daily huddles, leader round, gemba walks, daily Kaizen – everyday Lean idea).

Even though each institution uses the approach considered most suitable to solve its internal issues, it is possible to identify Imai's Kaizen individual-oriented, group-oriented and management-oriented structures in every initiative. Regardless of the company type (public or private) or country of origin (in the articles selected they are the USA, Mexico and Lebanon).

One common approach used by all those institutions is to conduct Kaizen in 3 major steps: preparation, execution and sustaining phases. A summary of the strategy followed and results for the articles selected is in Table 2.

It is possible to see there are great differences in the way institutions choose to follow their path to Lean strategy using Kaizen of a means for it.

The company presented in this cases also choose Kaizen as a means for their Lean initiative.

CASE DESCRIPTION

Kaizen Strategy

The implementation of Lean in municipality A started in October 2018, when the company president invited a consultant to train his team and help him propose a process to initiate his Lean implementation process. At that moment, the scope was only in municipality A, considering the hospital and 3 Primary Care units.

Table 2. Kaizen strategy and results of healthcare companies

Author	Location	Work Model
Carney et al. (2020)	Pediatric emergency department at Children's Hospital Colorado, Colorado, USA	Preparation phase: • Hiring a specialist to support the initiative with the support of the executive leadership (June/2015). • Formation of a multidisciplinary committee (June/2015). • Training of a larger team of employees (June/2016). • Application of quality improvement tools and Lean methods (VSM). Execution phase: • Conducting 5-day Kaizen (November/2016): o Days 1 to 3 – elimination of Non-Value Adding activities (NVA). o Day 4 – Pilot test of the proposed new work system. o Day 5 – Pilot adjustments. Sustainability phase: • After the 5 days of Kaizen, a new 18-hour test was carried out, testing in the next period of greatest demand, at the first opportunity (9 days after the end of the Kaizen event). • Work carried out concurrently with a multidisciplinary team (information technology, compliance, and facilities) on the hospital information record system (SRIH) and changes in the physical arrangement. • Change support team working 24 hours a day in the 2 weeks following the deployment of the final implementation of the improvements. • 2 months of monitoring and reporting of results by project leaders. Results: • Number of calls: increase of 4.7%. • Door-to-office time (IIQ): reduction of 49%. • Abandonment rate (leaving without being attended): reduction of 56%. • Percentage of attendance in less than 30 minutes: increase of 77%. • Average length of stay: 8% reduction. • Percentage of "excellent" evaluation in the satisfaction survey: increase of 4.9%. • Return percentage in 72 hours: 0.5% reduction.
Hitti et al. (2017)	Emergency department radiology at American University of Beirut Medical Center (AUBMC), Lebanon	Preparation phase: • 6 months of preparation (October/2012 to April/2013). • The emergency department of the hospital studied has a multidisciplinary process improvement committee that makes up the Kaizen team. • Kaizen based on trend analysis of patient comments and complaints. Execution phase: • 1 month of interventions. • VSM and time and motion study. • Inclusion of the radiology department in the Kaizen team. Sustainability phase: • 6 months of post evaluation (May/2013 to November/2013). Results: • Radiology response time: 57% reduction in mean and 32% in standard deviation.
Medina-León et al. (2014)	Emergency department obstetrics/gynecology at Public Hospital in Mexico City, Mexico	Preparation phase: • An initial analysis is carried out which determines the time of the bottleneck process, the causes of waiting, the opportunities for improvement, the possible improvement actions. • The problem is classified so that, for non-complex problems that require the direct participation of employees, a Kaizen event is prepared. • For the use of Kaizen, preparation is made: an area is chosen, the problem is defined, the baseline and goal of the event are defined, and the event's agenda is established. • The author considers holding Kaizen events for the following types of approaches: implementation of 5S, use of the SMED technique, implementation of kamban, process standardization, use of visual management frameworks, elimination of unnecessary processes. Execution phase: • According to the presented framework, Kaizen is not performed in the case study. Sustainability phase: • According to the presented framework, Kaizen is not performed in the case study). Results: • According to the presented framework, Kaizen is not performed in the case study.

continues on following page

Table 2. Continued

Author	Location	Work Model
Phillips et al. (2016)	Hospital emergency department at Virginia Mason Institute, Seattle, USA	Preparation phase: • Implementation of standard leadership work, which includes Daily Huddles, Leader Round, Gemba Walks, Daily Kaizen (everyday Lean idea). Execution phase: • Employees execute ideas with support from their leaders. • - Leaders used huddles, rounds, and visual management boards to train and recognize teams. Sustainability phase: • It is not discussed how the follow-up is carried out if the ideas generate actions that need to be monitored. Results: • Increase in the number of contributions (everyday ideas – Kaizen).
Suarez-Barraza & Miguel-Davila (2020)	Admission to the emergency department of a large public hospital at Mexico	Preparation phase: • Method developed by the author Suárez-Barraza: o (1) Diagnosis of the current situation. o (2) Practical seminars on the method (20 hours of training and coaching) for key people o (3) Training and formation of Kaizen teams. Execution phase: • 3 (three) months of measurement of the current state. • Prioritization of problems (Pareto chart). • Survey of root causes (Ishikawa diagram). • Construction of the improvement action plan. • Implementation of the proposed actions (3 to 5 months depending on available resources). Sustainability phase: Not described in the article. Results: It does not present practical results from indicators.
Kovacevic et al. (2016)	Emergency Department Laboratory at Vidant Health Centers, Greenville, North Carolina, USA	Preparation phase: Kaizen is used as part of a six-sigma project, after defining the project team to ensure understanding of the topic; Execution phase: Does not describe the steps during the event. Sustainability phase: Continues with the six-sigma approach, delivering the Measure, Analyze, Improve and Control phases. Results: Reported results are from the six-sigma project. The Kaizen event used was not intended to deliver results in indicators, but to engage the team.

Source: The authors.

The first step was to train the company corporate lead team along with the local (municipality A) lead team. The following people participated in the training: the medical director, the head nurse, the administrative director, and the chief nutritionist of the hospital; the head nurses of the primary care units; the contract manager of the municipality, the financial director, the technical consultants (doctors of different specialties) and the president of the company. The training workload was 16 hours, covering basic Lean principles, fundamentals, methods, and tools.

The second step proposed was to start a Kaizen to map the opportunities for patient flow improvement. A Kaizen event was opened to survey opportunities. At this event, the medical director, the head nurse, and the administrative director of the hospital participated. At the end of the event, a list of 22 actions was generated. From then on, some of the actions were fully implemented (45%), some were canceled (36%), and others have not been completed (18%).

The third step proposed was to standardize processes while developing people's capabilities on Lean thinking. Process standardization started with Kaizen events for 5S implementation. And people capabilities were developed by 5S Kaizen events and the ideas implementation program (they have been named Valuable Ideas by the internal team).

The same approach used for municipality A was adopted in municipalities B, C and D.

Examples of Team Kaizen Efforts

Rescheduling a Medical Appointment

Municipality A is a very small city, for which doctors of some specialties in clinical practice are not provided daily. The hospital has a roster of specialists who attend it on a weekly or fortnightly basis. Patients underwent consultation and the doctor verbally indicated the return. Armed with this information, the patient went to the reception desk and asked to reschedule the appointment. Often, as reported by the hospital receptionists, patients requested a return date before the date requested by the doctor, occupying a vacancy that should be available for another patient. It impacts patient waiting time for an appointment with a specialist. The solution presented by the team is presented in Figure 01. The idea, works as follows:

- the patient goes to the medical appointment with the specialist;
- the specialist requests their return and delivers a colored paper to the patient;
- the patient goes to the reception desk and requests the return, delivering the colored paper to the receptionist;
- the new appointment is scheduled properly.

Each color has a meaning. Red paper means the patient has to return in 7 days. Yellow paper means the patient has to return in 14 days. Green paper means the patient has to return in 20 days. And blue paper means the patient has to return in 30 days. Figure 1 that follows has the original picture and an explanatory image on its right side with proper translations.

Standard Medication List

The company must follow the public rules when dealing with supplying medicines. SUS has a standard medicine list, and it is not allowed to buy, nor, consequently, prescribe medications that are not in the standard list. Doctors' work schedule is part-time, and they often also work in other public or private institutions. In private institutions, even though there might be a standard list, it may not be the same. After visiting the wards, the doctor updates the treatment plan of the patients and prescribes the necessary medications for each patient. Doctors used to prescribe medications outside of the list and nurses had to go after them to ask for changes. Sometimes, the doctor was not at the hospital anymore. Another problem encountered was having medication be out of stock. Similarly, after the nurse read the prescription, they sometimes found that there was no stock left in the nurses' station. At that moment, the nurse walked to the pharmacy to order the medication and found it was out of stock. Again, the nurse had to go after the doctor. To reduce waste such as with errors in prescriptions, unnecessary displacement of the nursing team and delay in patient treatment, the team proposed to make the list visible in front of the computer on the side of the ward entrance signaling the level of the stock. Green means high stock level, yellow means intermediate stock level, red means out of stock and blue means that the medicine has been substituted. If the doctor sees a yellow or red stock level, they should try to prescribe another medicine with the same characteristics. The idea impacts patient treatment and clinical staff satisfaction. Figure 1 presents the instrument created by the team. The table has 5 columns: first column is the medicine name, second column is the green level of stock (out of risk), third column is yellow level of stock (low stock level, please substitute if possible), fourth column is red level of stock (out of stock) and fifth column is the signalization, in blue, for the information of a medicine substitution. Figure 2 that follows has the original picture and an explanatory image on its right side with proper translations.

Figure 1. Medical appointment schedule requisition form standard.
Source: Prepared by the authors

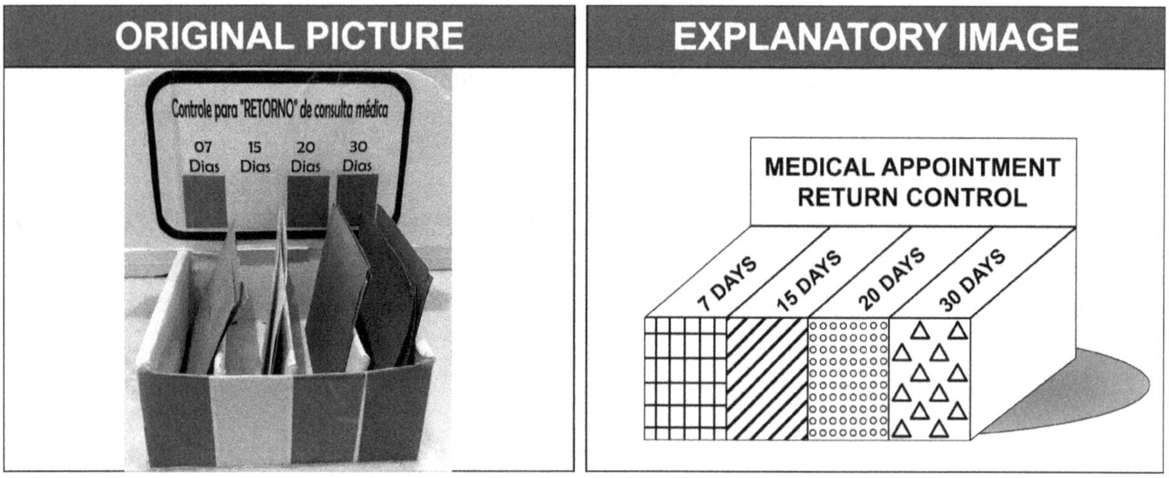

Figure 2. Standard medication list.
Source: Prepared by the authors

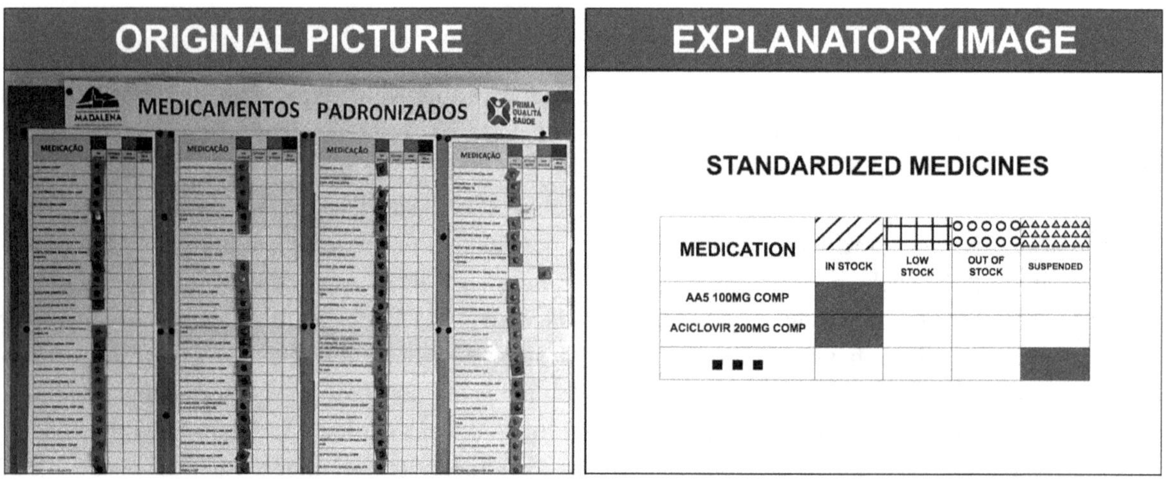

Oxygen Supply Control Board

During the SARS-CoV-2 pandemic, Brazil went through a serious crisis in supply of medicinal oxygen, caused by the exacerbated growth in consumption by patients who needed respiratory support. The hospital in municipality A is in a remote access region and needs to apprise the purchasing department of its needs quickly. Although the consumption was followed by the purchasing department and hospital administration, with consumption and routine verification, the hospital team decided to identify, outside the gas house, the state of the oxygen cylinders stock level, thus allowing gas fitters to alert about an uncommon increase in consumption, preventing a lack of oxygen. It is known that controls fail sometimes, and that is the reason inventories are required. Figure 2 shows the oxygen control board implemented. On the left side, there are the oxygen supply branches to the hospital. On the right, there are two cylinders; the one at the top is the trauma room consumption point where there is also a cylinder, and at the bottom is the SARS-CoV-2 clinic consumption point where there is also a cylinder. The darker gray in the image refers to a green status, and means the cylinder is full. The lighter gray refers to a red status, and means the cylinder is empty. Figure 3 that follows has the original picture and an explanatory image on its right side with proper translations.

Figure 3. Oxygen supply control board.
Source: the authors.
Source: Prepared by the authors

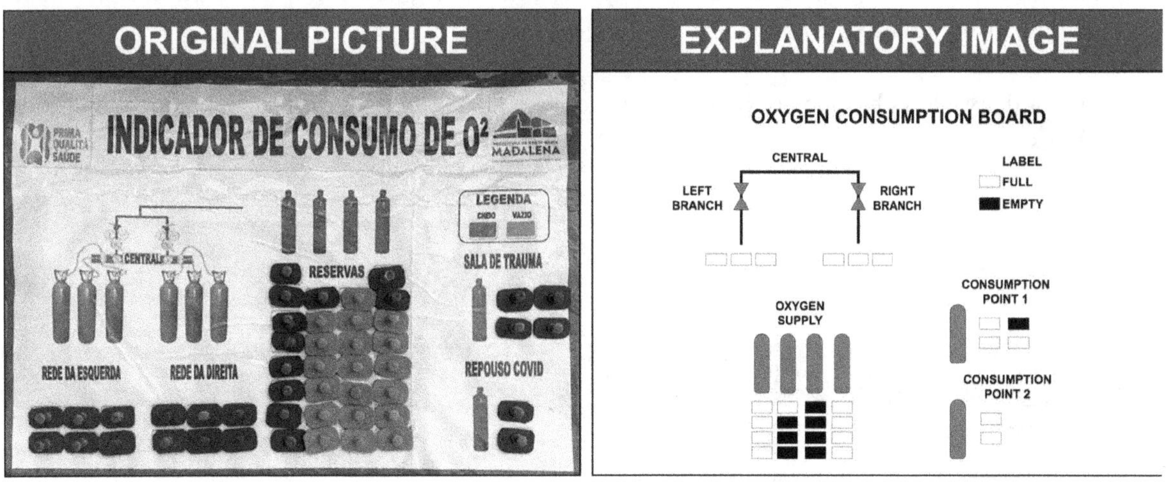

Office Occupancy Chart

In municipality C, there is a polyclinic of medical specialties. The demand for its services was reassessed by the technical team along with the municipal team, from which it was established that a series of new doctors would be hired to meet the demand. The space available to carry out the services, therefore, had to be reevaluated, since there was a great chance of needing to expand the infrastructure. Since there were plans to relocate the rehabilitation team to another location and any need for expansion would take many months from the submission of a technical project to the completion of the infrastructure expansion, the team decided to discuss the topic using the Lean approach. The approach followed the PDSA method. A team consisting of the unit administrative manager, the head of nursing, the reception supervisor, the administrative analyst and a quality analyst was formed. The demand was raised and the number of rooms needed were defined. After understanding the demand, the team organized the internal information on a board. The board gathered information about all available rooms and their current allocation. Once the board was organized and the team could see the whole, it was clear that there were many vacancies and no need for investments. Nevertheless, there was room for adjustments to the doctors' scale. The PDSA process culminated with showing the team they had no problems with allocation, but with the doctors' scale and the discipline to follow a fixed schedule (some doctors arrived at 11 a.m. and worked until 3 p.m., when the schedule to be followed should be from 8 a.m. to 12 a.m.).

Figure 3 is a picture of the board created by the team. The columns represent the medical offices. The gray lines separate the days of the working week. Each working week has 2 lines, each one representing a block of 4 hours of work. Spaces in dark gray are vacancies in the schedule. Summarizing the PDSA steps followed:

- **Plan (P):** team understands the demand and compares it with the capacity and finds out there is no occupancy problem.
- **Do (D):** team discusses and treats doctors' scale and discipline issues.
- **Study (S):** team verifies the results and confirms they don't need additional offices but need to keep up with the upcoming hires.
- **Act (A):** team reviews the board daily to update considering new information on doctors' issues and the hiring process.

Figure 4 that follows has the original picture and an explanatory image on its right side with proper translations.

Figure 4. Polyclinic occupancy board.
Source: the authors.
Source: Prepared by the authors

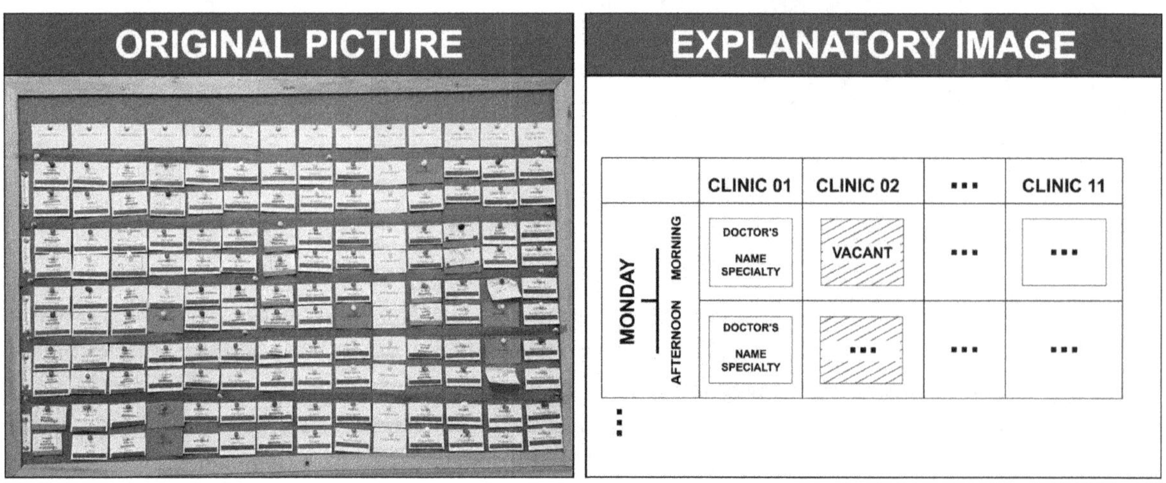

As mentioned in the cases reported in the literature and stated previously, the NGO considered Kaizen as part of the Lean implementation strategy. Also, the authors mentioned the low percentage of fully concluded actions, which was less than half. Along the journey the company choose to invest in promoting Kaizen by giving incentives to employee ideas, which led to the ones presented, and it explains the company having more initiatives related to local ideas than to solving strategic issues.

There are numerous factor affecting the evolution of a Lean mindset through Kaizen that the next section will address.

CHALLENGES TO KAIZEN IMPLEMENTATION

Kaizen is a strategic part of a company-wide Lean transformation process. If a company has already embraced such a way of transformation or is planning to do so, it will face great challenges. Although healthcare environments face unique challenges due to their complex environments, many experiences shared during the last 10 years report common barriers such as:

- lack of investment in a focused improvement team;
- lack of leadership from the hospital board in the change process;
- companies' focus on short term results without investment in creating a culture of continuous improvement;
- top-down decisions;
- distrust in the application of techniques from industry environments;
- difficulty to engage physicians;
- Kaizen used as "pockets of best practices" instead of a systematic approach and strategy to implement and sustain the initiative (Henrique & Godinho Filho, 2020);
- conflicting goals;
- poor management support;
- organizational silos;
- inadequate resources (Lima et al., 2021);
- employee perception and attitude;
- satisfaction and well-being at work;
- group professional norms and policies (Stelson et al., 2017)

If, on one side the literature reports barriers, on the other, they report success factors, such as:

- project management and selection;
- training and education;
- management commitment and leadership;
- business strategy;
- communication;
- customer focus;
- organizational culture;
- selection of staff;
- organizational infrastructure (Juliani & Oliveira, 2019).

Challenges Faced by the Institution on Kaizen Implementation

The challenges faced by the company in the case described can be sorted into:

- cultural factors;
- engagement factors; and
- resources-related factors.

Culture Impact on Kaizen

By "cultural factors", the authors mean external and internal variables that influence the institution. Once the company provides managerial services for public healthcare institutions, it is regulated by the same laws as public companies. It influences the way resources – financial and human – are allocated. There is a limit to reallocating financial resources when identified posthumously. As for human resources, there are employees who work in different hiring regimes. Employees who follow the labor law code and are hired by the institution, and employees who follow the public regiment, who were approved by means of a test and have job stability.

Another issue related to public services is that the company is restricted when it needs to create a new structure, as a Lean office to help deploy the continuous improvement strategy. It is easier to hire a consultant for a specific job than to institute, even temporarily, a Lean office.

Internal cultural factors are associated with the institution promoted and tolerated behaviors that imprint on its values. Most of the internal cultural factors challenging the Kaizen implementation are related to the way Leadership guides and helps develop employees and the existing practices for routine management and improvement.

There is also another cultural variable impacting Kaizen implementation, the orientation to short-term results. Not only but also, healthcare companies are driven by results. When a company is driven by short-term results, their strategy and actions will promote and recognize employees engaged in short-term results. The overall message will be that creating processes and developing a Kaizen culture are secondary, when they need to be enrolled in the same effort.

The institution chose to hire a consultant to help them with the strategy and deployment. The issue with that approach is that consultants have partial dedication and need a key user and the strong engagement of the leadership to deploy Kaizen.

For the leadership, the institution has very loyal and truthful leaders and is promoting, via the human resources department, a strategy leadership training. There is no leader standard work in practice, but technical people to run technical businesses (nurses and doctors).

Due to the types of contracts, the institution has only 2 to 4 years to promote Kaizen from the ground up when assuming a new contract. A specific strategy is required for such companies.

Engagement Impact on Kaizen

By engagement factors, the authors mean the strategies and approaches used to promote employee engagement. Such practices include: training, participating in Lean activities, formal and informal recognition, communicating the changes and leading the way.

A belief, by the part of the leaders, that training is all that is needed, leaves a gap to be filled in employee engagement. When the leadership believes that a single instance of training will get people ready to collaborate and construct, there is great risk of failing. The leadership expected trained employees to leave the training executing properly, ignoring that many issues require a joint, multidisciplinary work. It is about educating people, and that takes time and effort.

In health institutions, the teams are always too busy to stop and train. There is a need to create room for such an activity, organizing the agenda and employee substitution during training. The same is true for participating in Lean activities.

Assertive communication is crucial. Contradictions between formal and informal communication or between formal communication and the actions taken create an immense risk for a misunderstanding of the objectives and benefits, which generates insecurity and resistance on the part of employees.

The communication about Lean initiatives in the institution is being held by the president himself, who emphasizes the importance of Lean and his interest in it in every speech. However, there is still a gap between the president's speech and the intermediate leaders' practice.

To promote engagement, training and Kaizen events are promoted with the assistance of quality department personnel.

Resources Impact on Kaizen

By "resources factor", although mentioned above, the authors mean the absence of human and material resources to execute both the institution's routine and the improvements identified. Material resources are related to the provision of the minimum infrastructure and materials required to execute the job. Human resources are related to the availability of competent employees in the region.

The location of the units managed influenced the availability of suppliers of any nature as well as educational institutions to qualify personnel. As presented in Table 1, some municipalities have less than 60,000 citizens, which is considered very small. This places a responsibility on the institution to bring in proper professionals from outside, when necessary, while training local professionals in collaboration with government agencies.

Due to their location, size and small proceeds, the demand of some locations is not interesting to suppliers, leading to a lack of local suppliers for services and a lack of interest in some suppliers to get enrolled in a bid for materials.

In literature Mintzberg (2017) discusses how the way resources are understood and divided influences health care services. He proposes that health institutions should stop believing they are supposed to be managed as a company that has to maximize business results and must turn the mindset for a maximization of value for patients. The same way, he proposes that leadership role has goes from the businessman managing from reports to a leader that managers in the contact with the operations and caregivers, providing then the necessary resources so then can do their best work. Both are critical to business strategy and kaizen implementation because they relate to a stated culture thar is present in public and private companies, the same way of the myth that private is always better than public.

Although separated in 3 categories, resources, engagement, and culture relate to each other, sometimes being the cause and the effect to one another.

All the aspects discussed have a great impact on Kaizen implementation. Without people there is no Kaizen, without purpose (related to leadership and culture), there are no engaged people. And the lack or inappropriate resources may be a fragile link between people's engagement and results.

KAIZEN IMPLEMENTATION PLAN

After going through the theory related to kaizen, the stories reported by other companies and the case of the NGO who started its Kaizen implementation as part of its Lean strategy, it becomes clear each institution chooses it own way of conducing kaizen.

Although the different articles brought different approaches to the application of the Kaizen concept. All presented an approach that adhered to the concept presented by Imai (1986). Despite the different formats and frameworks, there is a greater pattern among all the approaches presented in the articles, which encompasses 3 phases: 1) preparation, 2) execution and 3) sustainability. In order to describe a complete model for Kaizen implementation, the authors described the general method in sequence:

Kaizen can be implemented following three phases: the preparation comprehends the definition of the initiative's goal, and of the standard work for the leadership, so that it can promote a culture of improvement. This phase can entail team engagement, training, opportunity mapping, and team definition.

The execution phase refers to the unfolding of the main objective. It happens in the form of focused improvement events of different scopes in which the team(s) analyze, discuss, and propose and test solutions to resolve the identified situations.

The sustainability phase refers to the phase in which the results are monitored in order to identify the necessary adjustments to guarantee the sustainability of the results as routines.

To structure a Kaizen implementation plan, the authors propose a strategy composed of 3 dimensions.

- Dimension 1: Institution Alignment
- Dimension 2: People Development and Engagement
- Dimension 3: Processes

Dimension 1 – Institution Alignment

The begging of a Kaizen strategy is to understand the institution vision, mission, values and the context in which it is inserted. A plan considering the urge of results, the culture of the company and the availability of resources have to be developed.

Dimension 2 – People Development and Engagement

There is no Kaizen without people. There is no good Kaizen without engaged people. Training and engaging must be part of the strategy.

Kaizen fundamentals related to reducing wastes must be taught, such as methods to improve performance – by reducing wastes – like 5S, Visual Management, Kanban, SMED and others. The training can combine in class explanation with didactic practical exercises at the gemba. Practice of Kaizen will be refined when employees, individually or in teams, participate in Kaizen.

If, on one side, training is needed, on other side, stimulate people is also needed.

Mainly at the beginning of the implementation of a Kaizen culture, people will need to be encouraged to enroll in Kaizen, because Kaizen means change. Peter Senge once said, "People don't resist change. They resist being changed.". Engagement activities involve a communication plan along with structured processes for promoting oriented Kaizen and formal and informal recognition.

Dimension 3 – Processes

The third dimension will help initiate and sustain the Kaizen strategy. Processes with rules and roles defining why and when to do a Kaizen, which method to use considering the characteristic of each issue, who has the capabilities to conduct each type of Kaizen and how to connect the results of the new practices with the business structure must be put into practice and conducted in a disciplined manner. Also, it is important to have a process to give scope and unfold the theme worked in Kaizen initiatives throughout the company.

Once the model does not fix specific tools, it can be considered a method, proposing steps that can be pursued in different situations, for different needs (proposal of ideas, problem solving). But the method alone does not completely address the strategy and the institution have to consider developing a process and invest in engaging and communication.

KAIZEN POINTS FOR FUTURE DISCUSSION

This chapter covers the definition of Kaizen, presented and discussed how healthcare companies adapted the Kaizen into their environments, considering it as a strategy for Lean implementation or just using it as a base for project development; presented and discussed challenges, critical success factors and barriers for Kaizen implementation.

However, there are still important questions to future chapters:

- Integration of Kaizen strategy with 4.0 industry and/or artificial intelligence in healthcare institutions.
- Involvement of the supply chain in Kaizen strategy in healthcare companies, as the industry model where customers and suppliers work together to provide proper products and services.
- Impact of company context (external and internal factors) culture in the definition of the strategy for short-, medium- and long-term Kaizen strategies.

LESSONS LEARNED

In this chapter you learned:

- The definition of Kaizen;
- The types of Kaizens (management-oriented, group-oriented and individual-oriented);
- How healthcare companies adopted and adapted Kaizen into their environments;
- Critical success factor to foster Kaizen;
- Kaizen implementation framework;
- Kaizen is a people drive process;
- Public and private companies can benefit from Kaizen implementation.

CHAPTER SUMMARY

Kaizen is not only a Lean tool, but a business strategy necessary to achieve a Lean-thinking company. The Kaizen framework links the three types of Kaizen (management-oriented, group-oriented and individual-oriented) with the Lean implementation strategy for the business. Each type of Kaizen requires different expertise on the part of the team, which leads us to need a strategy for developing people's capabilities. People will not think Kaizen unless there is a system to support it as a culture, containing clear business guidelines, leadership engagement at all levels, processes to foster continuous improvement culture and an environment that provides space for continuous improvement to flourish.

ACKNOWLEDGMENT

The authors would like to thank the Brazilian Ministry of Health, the UFF – Fluminense Federal University, and the Euclides da Cunha Foundation. This Research is part of the "Lean Project in UPA 24h" that has been funded by the Brazilian Ministry of Health (TED 15/2021, number: 25000.103452/2021-14).

REFERENCES

Beattie, M., Hookway, G., Perera, M., Calder, S., Hunter-Rowe, C., & van Woerden, H. (2018). Improving wait time from referral to opiate replacement therapy in a drug recovery service. *BMJ Open Quality*, *7*(3), 1–7. doi:10.1136/bmjoq-2017-000295 PMID:30019015

Blouin-Delisle, C. H., Drolet, R., Hains, M., Tailleur, L., Allaire, N., Coulombe, M., & Vézo, A. (2020). Improving interprofessional approach using a collaborative lean methodology in two geriatric care units for a better patient flow. *Journal of Interprofessional Education & Practice*, *19*(March), 100332. Advance online publication. doi:10.1016/j.xjep.2020.100332

Bowerman, J., & Fillingham, D. (2007). Can lean save lives? *Leadership in Health Services*, *20*(4), 231–241. doi:10.1108/17511870710829346 PMID:20698096

Carney, K. P., Crespin, A., Woerly, G., Brethouwer, N., Baucum, J., & DiStefano, M. C. (2020). A Front-end Redesign With Implementation of a Novel "Intake" System to Improve Patient Flow in a Pediatric Emergency Department. *Pediatric Quality & Safety*, *5*(2), e263. doi:10.1097/pq9.0000000000000263 PMID:32426629

Elsheikh, A. M., Emam, M. S., & AlShareef, S. A. (2017). Bridging the gap between documents and practice in medication management "Documents Vitalization.". *Business Process Management Journal*, *23*(4), 830–841. doi:10.1108/BPMJ-02-2017-0030

Graban, M., & Swartz, J. E. (2012). *Healthcare kaizen: Engaging front-line staff in sustainable continuous improvements*. Academic Press.

Henrique, D. B., & Godinho Filho, M. (2020). A systematic literature review of empirical research in Lean and Six Sigma in healthcare. *Total Quality Management & Business Excellence*, *31*(3–4), 429–449. doi:10.1080/14783363.2018.1429259

Hitti, E. A., El-Eid, G. R., Tamim, H., Saleh, R., Saliba, M., & Naffaa, L. (2017). Improving Emergency Department radiology transportation time: A successful implementation of lean methodology. *BMC Health Services Research, 17*(1), 625. Advance online publication. doi:10.118612913-017-2488-5 PMID:28870249

IBGE. (2010). https://cidades.ibge.gov.br/

Imai, M. (1986). *Kaizen (Ky'zen), the key to Japan's competitive success.* Academic Press.

Juliani, F., & de Oliveira, O. J. (2019). Synergies between critical success factors of Lean Six Sigma and public values. *Total Quality Management & Business Excellence, 30*(15–16), 1563–1577. doi:10.1080/14783363.2017.1383153

Kelendar, H., Faisal, M., McIntosh, B., & Mohammed, M. A. (2020). The use of lean methodology in healthcare settings in developing countries: A narrative review. *British Journal of Health Care Management, 26*(6), 1–13. Advance online publication. doi:10.12968/bjhc.2019.0095

Knechtges, P., & Decker, M. C. (2014). Application of kaizen methodology to foster departmental engagement in quality improvement. *Journal of the American College of Radiology, 11*(12), 1126–1130. doi:10.1016/j.jacr.2014.08.027 PMID:25444067

Kollberg, B., Dahlgaard, J. J., & Brehmer, P. O. (2006). Measuring lean initiatives in health care services: Issues and findings. *International Journal of Productivity and Performance Management, 56*(1), 7–24. doi:10.1108/17410400710717064

Kovacevic, M., Jovicic, M., Djapan, M., & Zivanovic-Macuzic, I. (2016). Lean thinking in healthcare: review of implementation results. *International Journal of Qualitative Research, 10*(1), 219–230.

Lamm, M. H., Eckel, S., Daniels, R., & Amerine, L. B. (2015). Using lean principles to improve outpatient adult infusion clinic chemotherapy preparation turnaround times. *American Journal of Health-System Pharmacy, 72*(13), 1138–1146. doi:10.2146/ajhp140453 PMID:26092964

Lima, A., Barbosa, C., Sobrinho, A., Calado, R., & Sobra, A. P. (2021). Capacity Management as a Tool for Improving Infrastructure in the Lean Healthcare. *Systematic Reviews*, 298–304.

Lodge, A., & Bamford, D. (2008). New development: Using lean techniques to reduce radiology waiting times. *Public Money & Management, 28*(1), 49–52. doi:10.1111/j.1467-9302.2008.00618.x

Lordelo, S. A. V., Nogueira, S. M. S., Filho, J. R. de F., Costa, H. G., Barbosa, C. L., & Calado, R. D. (2021). Kaizen and Healthcare: a bibliometric analysis. In Advances in Production Management Systems. Artificial Intelligence for Sustainable and Resilient Production Systems (pp. 314–322). doi:10.1007/978-3-030-85902-2_34

Manos, A., Sattler, M., & Alukal, G. (2006). Make healthcare lean. *Quality Progress, 39*(7), 24–30.

Mazzocato, P., Stenfors-Hayes, T., Schwarz, U. von T., Hasson, H., & Nystrom, M. E. (2016). Kaizen practice in healthcare: A qualitative analysis of hospital employees' suggestions for improvement. *BMJ Open, 6*(7), e012256. Advance online publication. doi:10.1136/bmjopen-2016-012256 PMID:27473953

Medina-León, S. V., Medina-Palomera, A., González-Ángeles, A., Rogers, P., Gil-Samaniego-Ramos, M., Ceballos-Corral, J., & Nuño-Moreno, V. (2014). Framework for patient flow improvement. *Research Journal of Applied Sciences, Engineering and Technology*, *8*(3), 410–422. doi:10.19026/rjaset.8.987

Mintzberg, H. (2017). *Managing the Myths of Health Care_ Bridging the Separations Between Care, Cure, Control, and Community*. Berrett-Koehler Publishers.

Phillips, J., Hebish, L. J., Mann, S., Ching, J. M., & Blackmore, C. C. (2016). Engaging frontline leaders and staff in real-time improvement. *Joint Commission Journal on Quality and Patient Safety*, *42*(4), 170–178. doi:10.1016/S1553-7250(16)42021-0 PMID:27025577

Pinto, C. F. (2014). *Em busca do cuidado perfeito*. Lean Institute Brasil.

Spear, S., & Bowen, H. K. (1999). Decoding the DNA of the Toyota Production System. *Harvard Business Review*, *77*(5), 96–106.

Stelson, P., Hille, J., Eseonu, C., & Doolen, T. (2017). What drives continuous improvement project success in healthcare? *International Journal of Health Care Quality Assurance*, *30*(1), 43–57. doi:10.1108/IJHCQA-03-2016-0035 PMID:28105876

Suarez-Barraza, M. F., & Miguel-Davila, J. A. (2020). Kaizen-Kata, a Problem-Solving Approach to Public Service Health Care in Mexico. A Multiple-Case Study. *International Journal of Environmental Research and Public Health*, *17*(9), 3297. Advance online publication. doi:10.3390/ijerph17093297 PMID:32397363

Suárez-Barraza, M. F., & Ramis-Pujol, J. (2010). Implementation of Lean-Kaizen in the human resource service process: A case study in a Mexican public service organisation. *Journal of Manufacturing Technology Management*, *21*(3), 388–410. doi:10.1108/17410381011024359

Womack, J., & Jones, D. T. (2003). *Lean thinking: Banish waste and create wealth in your corporation*. Academic Press.

Chapter 3
DMAIC Application in an Emergency Care Unit

Milena Estanislau Diniz Mansur dos Reis
https://orcid.org/0000-0003-1080-8735
Federal University of Rio de Janeiro, Brazil

Melissa Felix Abreu
Fluminense Federal University, Brazil

Olavo de Oliveira Braga Neto
Ministry of Health, Brazil

Helder Gomes Costa
https://orcid.org/0000-0001-9945-0367
Fluminense Federal University, Brazil

Luis Enrique Valdiviezo Viera
Fluminense Federal University, Brazil

EXECUTIVE SUMMARY

Overcrowding in emergency hospital units represents a serious problem in the health system and is a phenomenon faced worldwide. And when investigating the origin of this disorder, it is observed that the great demand for care of cases considered low risk directly influences the quality of the service provided. Thus, it is necessary to apply tools and methods to improve the service offered. The Lean Six Sigma methodology allows the construction of problem-solving proposals based on statistical data and effective mechanisms. And with the use of the DMAIC method, which is also the methodological framework of Lean Six Sigma, it is possible to clearly direct the resolution of problems through process improvement and restructuring in an organization. The present study aims to present a successful experience in the application of DMAIC to improve patient care and assistance in UPA Cumbica, located in the city of Guarulhos, SP.

DOI: 10.4018/978-1-6684-5185-4.ch003

ORGANIZATION BACKGROUND

The Emergency Care Unit Cumbica started its activities in 2017 and is located at Cidade Industrial Satélite, Guarulhos - São Paulo, Brazil. The Unit is located in the Health Region IV - Pimentas/Cumbica, being a reference to the urgent and emergency care of 05 Basic Health Units, a region with approximately 160,000 inhabitants. Management is shared between the Guarulhos City Hall, through the Health Secretariat, and the Social Health Organization Fundação do ABC.

The Cumbica UPA is installed in an area of over 1,300 m^2. The Unit has a reception desk, three medical clinic offices, a pediatric office, and a dental office, an adult observation ward with 9 full mixed beds, 1 full isolation room, and 2 male and female bathrooms. In addition, it has a pediatric observation ward with four complete beds and four armchairs, two reception rooms for risk classification. It also has specific rooms for social service, radiology, central room for sterilized materials, for pharmaceutical supply, pharmacy for drug dispensation, electrocardiogram, utilities, and also for the application of intramuscular and oral medication, and serum therapy. Besides these, there is a room for serotherapy, an emergency room with four complete beds and a nursing station.

In UPA Cumbica, considering the year 2019, an average of 12400 attendances per month were performed. Table 1 shows the distribution of employees responsible for the management and operation of the UPA.

Table 1. Distribution of employees responsible for the management and operation of the UPA.

Professional/ Sector	Quantity
Medical Doctors	33
Dentists	7
Nurses	24
Nursing Assistants	90
Ordinance, Coordination, ADM	9
X-Rays	10
Hygiene	18
Drivers	2
Maintenance	2
Pantry	4

Source: Own Elaboration based on Descriptive Memorial – UPA Cumbica (2020)

SETTING THE STAGE

The UPA occupy the intermediate level of complexity, between the Primary Healthcare Centers (Primary Care) and Medium and High complexity, integrating the Pre-Hospital Stabilization Site Network (Oliveira et al., 2015) inside the structure of SUS (Unified Health System). Within the scope of their attributions, the UPA must meet demands 24 hours a day, perform the risk classification of patients, resolve cases of medium complexity, stabilize serious cases, as well as provide backup to primary care units (Silva et al. 2012). In Brazil, the Emergency Care Units, UPA 24h, are integrated into the Brazilian emergency care network, showing their strategic relevance by enabling the reduction of demand pressure in the emergency services of hospitals (Viera et al, 2021).

With the established objective of implementing a restructuring project - Humanization of Patient Care Flow in UPA 24 h urgency and emergency network, The Lean project in UPA 24h, a partnership was established between the Brazilian Ministry of Health and the Fluminense Federal University (Reis et al., 2021). The project team comprises 30 professors and students, and 20 specialists working in management, research, training and advising the 50 UPA distributed along 8 Brazilian states and the Federal District (Reis et al., 2021). The methodology benefited about 13 million users of the country's public health network. More than 28,300 hours of training were carried out for 548 employees of UPA between the months of April and November/2020 (Reis et al., 2021). The implementation was guided by an action research using the DMAIC method (Define, Measure, Analyze, Improve and Control) in order to improve communication and quality of service offered (Reis et al., 2021).

It is worth at this point to bring a brief explanation about Lean, Lean Six Sigma, and DMAIC. The elimination of waste (*muda*) and value creation are key factors in Lean. Value is defined by the customer, it represents something that meets the customer's needs. A patient, for example, sees waiting as something unproductive, that is, as something that does not generate value. A human activity that consumes resources but creates no value is a waste (Womack & Jones, 2003). Lean approach focuses on reducing non-value added activities (Cheung et al., 2016).

Antony et al. (2018) highlighted that in Healthcare Lean has been used for reasons such as following:

- provide better services to consumers;
- increase customer satisfaction;
- improve process and operational efficiency;
- transforming the organizational culture;
- improve service quality;
- standardize and optimize the process;
- reduce delays and operational time;
- reduce waste;
- eliminate non-value added tasks.

Lean, in healthcare context, makes it possible to improve patient care by eliminating non-value-added activities that comprise efficient treatment, reduce waiting times, and speed up processes (Al-Araidah et al., 2010).

Snee (2010) pointed out that processes do not improve by themselves. Every process has critical characteristics for quality (CTQs) which must remain within a tolerance zone established in order to achieve the goal (Chiarini, 2012). Goh et al. (2006) stated that when using Six Sigma for process improvement, the aim is to deliver what customers want, that embases the CTQ. In this sense, customer focus is crucial to the success of a process (Goh et al., 2006). For Taner at al. (2007), CTQ in the healthcare context are those attributes that are considered to be of great value to the patient.

The purpose of using Six Sigma lies in process improvement; whereas, in Lean, the focus is on process flow and speed, reducing or removing waste (Raval et al., 2018). When used together, the methodology is called Lean Six Sigma (LSS).

According to Snee (2010), Lean Six Sigma is needed because organizations and individuals need a methodology for improvement and problem solving. Lean Six Sigma proposes in a structured way to achieve process efficiency and customer satisfaction by reducing waste and variation (Cheung et al., 2016).

DMAIC can be considered as a continuous improvement methodology, being considered a key methodology used in Six Sigma projects, and can be used to improve, optimize and reorganize processes (Henrique and Godinho Filho, 2018). DMAIC refers to the 5 steps of the Lean Six Sigma methodology and resembles the PDCA (Plan-Do-Check-Act) cycle (Improta et al., 2017). Performing the steps of DMAIC allows for improving the quality of any processes at the project level or overall in the organization (Niñerola et al, 2020). Ahmed (2019) stated that applying DMAIC in a healthcare organization provides a guide on how to maintain a service quality system through patient satisfaction and makes it possible to reduce waste, variation, and work imbalance.

Therefore, the entire application of DMAIC in this chapter was performed based on the A3 Report updated in each kaizen workshop in UPA Cumbica. The A3 report is a practice pioneered by Toyota, where problem analysis, corrective action and action plan are written on a single sheet of paper (A3 size), usually using graphics and figures. These A3 reports have evolved to become a standard method for problem solving (Battaglia, 2007). Thus, supports a structured approach to improvement projects and is useful for streamlining project activities and communicating about intermediary findings during the project (Oversluizen; Slomp,2020).

CASE DESCRIPTION

In the first Kaizen Workshop at UPA Cumbica, Guarulhos - SP, held on 04/07/2020, by members of the Lean Project at UPAs team, constituted by the tutor and a nurse, the main objective was to perform the initial Diagnosis, through technical reports and photos of the UPA. The activities performed on this date are listed below:

- Knowledge of the physical installations of the UPA's as well as its staff and the number of employees per specialty/area of activity.
- Definition of the internal UPA team that will participate in the Improvement Project.
- Survey of indicators and risks.
- Survey of improvement opportunities based on knowledge of the project scope Initial analysis of the UPA layout.
- Survey of information about the physical layout of the various service sectors of the UPA's based on the impact on the patient.

The following professionals from the Unit participated in this diagnostic phase: the Administrative Coordinator, the Technical Nursing Coordinator, and the Continuing Education Nurse.

During this first Kaizen Workshop the main opportunities and "fears" were identified, which guided the proposal of improvements in the UPA by the Project team members together with the unit's representatives. In addition, objectives were listed, namely:

- reduce costs and inefficiency by 30% due to waste;
- identify 8 types of waste with the greatest impact on UPA performance;

- identify actions to mitigate or eliminate waste.

Based on the analysis of the situation and objective, the most relevant categories or areas of opportunities and fears were identified, and from this, the wastes presented in Table 2 were identified. The category General Service corresponded for 51.85% of the waste, People Management with 18.52%, and medical technology with 7.51%. Detailing the study, the wastes related to waiting obtained 33.33%, rework defects, 25,.93%, and handling, 18.52%.

Table 2. Quantity of waste per category

Category	Quantity of Waste	%
General Service (Not sector-specific)	14	51.85%
People management	5	18.52%
Medical Technology (Respirators, X-Ray, etc.)	2	7.41%
Medication and materials management	2	7.41%
Others	2	7.41%
Reception	1	3.70%
Physical installations: Rooms, consulting rooms; pharmacy	1	3.70%

Source: Own Elaboration based on Descriptive Memorial – UPA Cumbica (2020)

Thus, through the data obtained and presented in Table 2, a brainstorming was performed between the Project and the UPA team, and the conclusion was reached that the main actions that would allow waste reduction would be the review of the process needs and the encouragement of improvement groups.

After the Initial Diagnosis, a clear and structured path was followed through the DMAIC steps. In total, 9 Kaizen Workshops were held (Figure 1), including the Initial Diagnosis, to apply the project, where theoretical content related to each phase of the DMAIC method was taught, as well as dynamics that guided the practical activities of the project.

The factors listed in Figure 2 were fundamental for the implementation of Lean Six Sigma DMAIC in the Unit and guided its entire execution path. These are Lean Six Sigma DMAIC Training and Practice, Employee Involvement and Commitment, Management Support, Focus on the System User, Multidisciplinary Team, Consideration of human and technical aspects, development of critical thinking, and creation of a collaborative space for dialogue and openness.

DEFINE PHASE

In the Define step, the purpose is to define the clients, capture the perceptions about the service offered to the user, define the process in which the improvement should occur, and establish the objective to be reached, the limits of the improvement project, and the critical characteristics for quality (CTQ).

For this, during the hands-on training, the team defined the scope of the project. From this, it was possible to elaborate the Project Charter, presented in Figure 3.

Figure 1. Activities performed in each Kaizen Workshop
Source: Own Elaboration based on Descriptive Memorial – UPA Cumbica (2020)

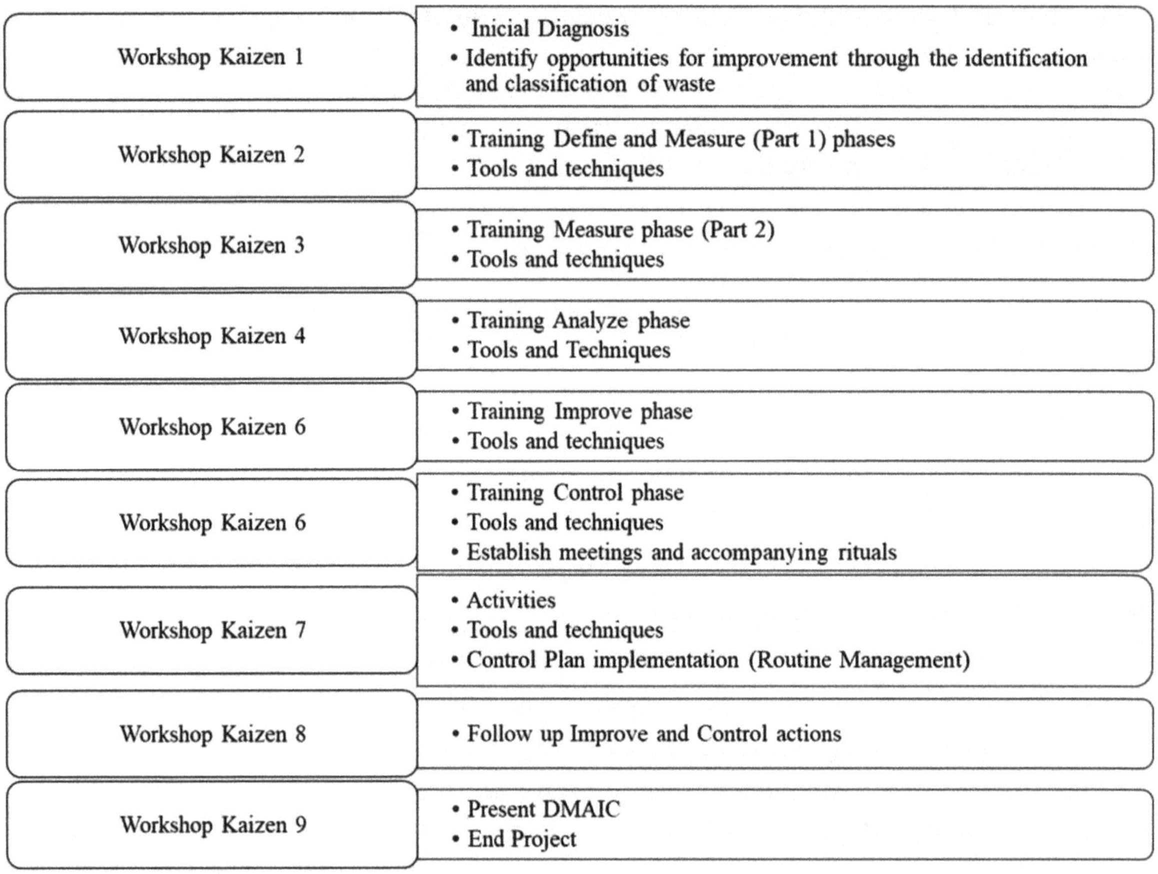

Figure 2. Key Factors
Source: Descriptive Memorial – UPA Cumbica (2020)

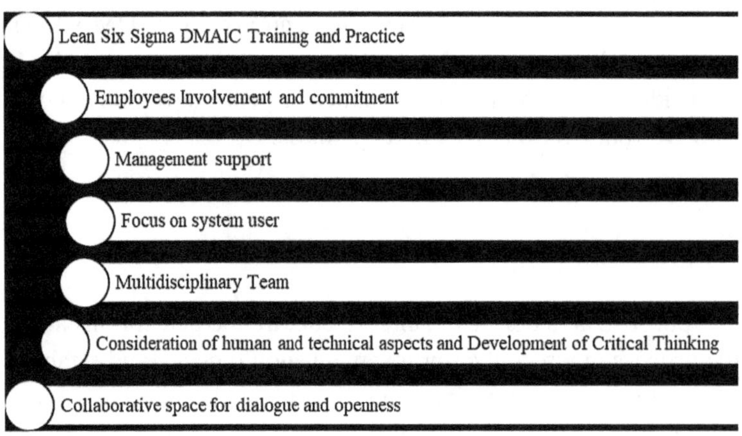

Figure 3. Project Charter
Source: Own Elaboration based on Descriptive Memorial – UPA Cumbica (2020)

Project title

Lean nas UPAs 24h - UPA Cumbica - Guarulhos - SP

Problem statement	**Objective Statement**
Inappropriate prolongation of length of Emergency care Unit for green patients	To reduce time journey of green patient.
Critical to quality	**Target**
Lenght of Emergency Care Unit stay	Realize corrective measures in order to reduce the CTQ

Team members: 1 Champion (Administative Coordinator),1 Black Belt, 1 Green Belt (Project Leader), 1 Technical Nursing Coordinator, 4 Nurses, 1 Nursing Assistant

Timeline

Define	April 2020
Measure	May 2020
Analyze	June 2020
Improve	July 2020
Control	ugust 2020

Inadequate length of stay in the Emergency Care Unit for green patients was entered into the Project Charter as the problem statement; as the goal statement, to reduce the travel time of the green patient; as Quality Critical, the length of stay in the Emergency Care Unit and to carry out corrective action as the target. In addition, it lists the team members being: one Champion, one Black Belt, one Green Belt, one technical nursing coordinator, four nurses, and one nursing assistant. Also, finalizing the chart, the project timeline was inserted.

The Voice of Customer (VOC), which aims to capture the needs of the user/patient and the service offered to the user/patient, was fundamental in this phase. This tool allowed the translation of the patient's needs into CTQ with the subsequent establishment of valid requirements and, finally, the project indicators were elaborated. In Table 3, it can be observed that the critical characteristics for patient quality are quality and service time and that the resulting indicators refer to reducing the green patient journey time by 20% and reducing the hospitalization time of 90% of the patients in up to 24h.

Table 3. Critical to quality for patients

Client	Necessity	CTQ	Valid Requirement	Indicator
Patient	Agility in service	Time	Time of care according to the recommended in the Risk Classification	Reduce the time of the green patient's journey by 20%.
Patient	Resolution of the observation process	Quality/ Time	Reduce hospital stay up to 24hours	Reduce hospital stay from 90% of patients within 24 hours

Source: Own Elaboration based on Descriptive Memorial – UPA Cumbica (2020)

In this same phase, the SIPOC tool (seeks to analyze processes in view of the connections between their suppliers, inputs, outputs and customer to give greater support to the construction of the project scope) was also applied, which allowed for a greater understanding of the Green Patient Journey Process, which is presented in Table 4.

Table 4. SIPOC to green patient journey process

S (Supplier)	I (Input)	P (Process)	O (Output)	C (Client)
Patient	Passcode Information	Reception FAA (outpatient care form) opening	Cadastre and Printed FAA	Risk Classification
Reception	Registry/Patient	Triage Risk Classification	Classified Patient Record FAA information	Doctor's Office
Risk Classification	Patient Prioritized/ Patient File	Doctor's Office Medical Evaluation	Conduct/ Prescription	Medication
Doctor's Office	Conduct/ Prescription	Medication	Medicated Patient/ FAA checked	Doctor's Office/ Discharged
Doctor's Office	Conduct/ Prescription	Exam	Patient collected/ FAA-Collection/ Exams Results	Doctor's Office
Doctor's Office	Conduct/ Prescription	Radiology exams	X-Ray Patient Performed/ FAA-Collection Information/ image available in the office	Doctor's Office
Exam/ Medication	Patient Collected/ FAA-Collection Information/ Test Results X-Ray Patient Performed/ FAA-X-Ray Information / Image Available in the Office	Medical Reassessment	Patients in need of high complexity features Test results Transfer report	Reference Hospital Unit
Exam/ Medication	Patient Collected/ FAA-Collection Information/ Test Results X-Ray Patient Performed/ FAA-X-Ray Information / Image Available in the Office	Medical Reassessment	Cured or Improved Patient Test results Orientation and Medical certificate	Patient

Source: Own Elaboration based on Descriptive Memorial – UPA Cumbica (2020)

The SIPOC tool was also applied to the Patient Observation process and can be seen in Table 5.

The In and Out Scope pointed out the limits of the project, that is, what would be included and what would be discarded from the scope of the improvement project. In Table 6 it is possible to see the Inside-Outside Scope of the Green Patient.

Similarly, the In and Out Escope for patient Observation time was prepared, which is presented in Table 7.

From the previous results of the Define phase, a survey of the history of indicators occurred and baselines were established. It was observed that the average volume of care in 2019 was 12,300 visits/ month, of which 70% were patients classified as green and stayed an average of 5 hours and 5 minutes in the unit. Concerning observation in the same period, 15% of patients remained for more than 24 h in the unit. Then, the following objectives were defined: to reduce by 20% the journey time of the green patient (low risk) and reduce the hospitalization time of 90% of the patients in 24h. As expected, qualitative gains, it was stipulated the standardization of processes, improvement in patient perception, reduction of work overload, an waste reduction.

Table 5. SIPOC to the patient observation process

S (Supplier)	I (Input)	P (Process)	O (Output)	C (Client)
Emergency Office	Medical Record (Prescription and medical evolution)/ Exams Patient	Patient Admission	Patient admitted and medicated according to prescription and conduct) Record in medical records	Nursing Observation
Nursing Observation	Medical Record (Prescription and medical evolution)/ Exams Patient	Multidisciplinary team assistance	Patient monitored and medicated according to the prescription of conduct Test results Record in medical records	Revaluation
Nursing Observation	Medical Record (Prescription and medical evolution)/ Exams Patient	Medical Revaluation	Conduct Record in Health Services Supply Regulation Center (CROSS)	Reference Hospital Unit
Nursing Observation	Medical Record (Prescription and medical evolution)/ Exams Patient	Medical Revaluation	Conduct Orientations, exams, medical certificate, and referrals	Patient/ companion

Source: Own Elaboration based on Descriptive Memorial – UPA Cumbica (2020)

Table 6. Inside-outside scope of green patient journey process

	Inside	Outside
What	Adult and pediatric observation, red, orange, yellow, green, and blue, Medical Clinic, Pediatrics, Orthopedics and Dentistry, Social Work, Nutrition and Pharmacy.	Emergency, Emergency Care, and Administrative Support.
Who	Doctors, dentists, social workers, pharma, nursing and nutritionist	-
Where	April to August	
When	Adult and pediatric observation	

Source: Own Elaboration based on Descriptive Memorial – UPA Cumbica (2020)

Table 7. In and out scope of patient observation time process

	Inside	Outside
What	Adult and pediatric observation, red, orange, yellow, green, and blue, Medical Clinic, Pediatrics, Orthopedics and Dentistry, Social Work, Nutrition, and Pharmacy	Emergency, Emergency Care, and Administrative Support
Who	Doctors, dentists, social workers, pharmacists, nursing and nutrition	-
Where	April to August	
When	Adult and pediatric observation	

Source: Own Elaboration based on Descriptive Memorial – UPA Cumbica (2020)

MEASURE PHASE

In the Measure Step (held between the 2nd and 3rd Kaizen Workshop), a Data Collection Plan was established that could contain a set of information to guide the improvement team in the search and capture of data and strategic information. The data from the Processes was collected and then filled in the spreadsheet that refers to the Data Collection Plan.

From the analysis, it could be stated that Green patients accounted for 71.25% of the total attendances in 2019. Green patients represented 66.70% of the total attendances in 2020 (in the period from 23/April to 07/May 2020). The average length of stay for Green patients in 2019 was 05:05h. The average length of stay for Green patients in 2020 was 01:16h (for the period April 23rd to May 7th, 2020). This difference is related to the 60% reduction in patient demand in this pandemic period of COVID-19. In addition to this, after surveying the data, the following data was verified:

1. 15.17% of the total number of patients were hospitalized in 2019;
2. 14.79% of total patients were hospitalized in 2020 (period from 04/23 to 05/07);
3. The average length of stay in hospitalization in 2019 was 15.33h and 15% of patients stayed over 24h;
4. The average length of stay in hospitalization 2020 (period from 04/23 to 05/07) was 14.54h and 14.79% of patients stayed over 24h.

Figure 4. Process map Green Patient Journey
Source: Own Elaboration based on Descriptive Memorial – UPA Cumbica (2020)

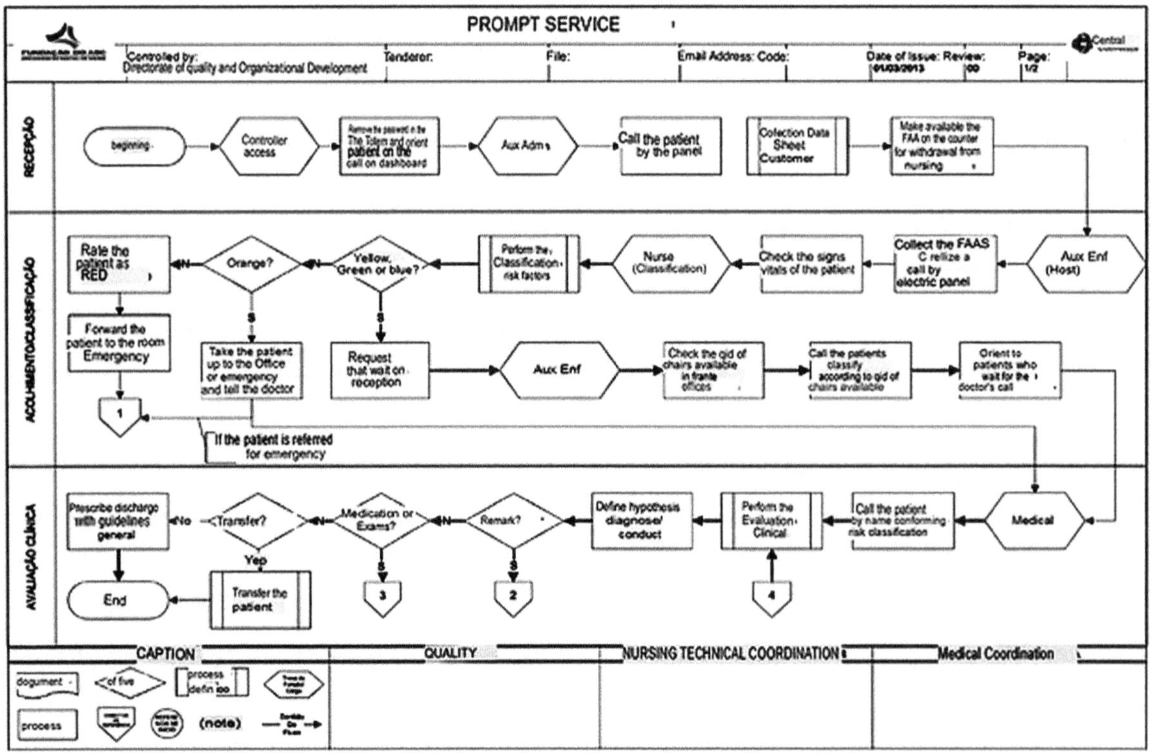

The Patient Journey and its experiences in the UPA were investigated and mapped. Maps of the processes of the green patient journey and observation (Figure 4) were prepared, taking into account the sectors of reception/classification, clinical evaluation, technical procedures, observation, and emergency to structure the key process. This understanding proved useful for the development of improvement actions in the next phases of the DMAIC.

Table 8. Matrix of prioritization of variables

Variable	CTQ1	CTQ2	Total
	Green Patient Time	**% Obs. Patient > 24h**	-
Exam failure (collection, identification, transport, result, electrocardiogram, X-ray)	9	9	180
Medication Failure	4	4	80
Exam time (collection, identification, transport, electrocardiogram - ECG, x-ray result)	4	4	80
Length of stay in the Observation (total)	0	9	90
Hospital Discharge Time (Observation)	0	9	90
CROSS Time (OBS)	0	9	90
Failure to register/update in CROSS (Observation)	0	9	50
Diagnostic Failure	1	4	50
Number of patients in Observation above 24h	0	9	50
Medication Time	4	1	50
RX Time	1	4	50
Medical Return Time	1	4	50
Social Assistance Assessment Time (Observation)	0	4	40
Error registration / updating of data	1	1	20
Color classification failed	1	1	20
Medical Evaluation Time	1	1	20
ECG Time	1	1	20
Record opening/update time	1	0	10
Classification time	1	0	10
Admission Time (Observation)	0	1	10
Pharmacy Evaluation Time (Observation)	0	1	10
Nutrition Assessment Time (Observation)	0	1	10
Hospital Discharge Failure (Observation)	0	1	10
Number of patients in the observation waiting for vacancies in CROSS	0	9	90

Source: Own Elaboration based on Descriptive Memorial – UPA Cumbica (2020)

A Matrix of Prioritization of Variables (Table 8) was developed for the variables found in the Cumbica UPA. These causes represent the "X's" of the process and will be the inputs for the implementation of Improvement Actions on the processes of medical care performed in the PAU. A weight of 10 has been set for each output.. The correlation between the X's of the process and the CTQs varies from 0 (no correlation) to 9 (strong correlation). The value of each cell was multiplied by the weight of each output and the values of each row were added together to obtain the total. As a result of the strategy outlined when assembling the Variable Prioritization Matrix, a set of variables was separated to be worked on with an Action Plan (Table 8).

From this, the see and act action plan, presented in Table 9, could be elaborated.

In this step, the final problem definition was established, and the goals were reviewed.

Table 9. Action plan see and act

Action Plan See and Act (Quick Wins)						
Process Name/ Demand: UPA Cumbica						
WHAT	**WHY**	**WHO**	**WHERE**	**WHEN**	**HOW**	**HOW MUCH**
Activity	**Objective**	**Accountable**	**Local**	**Term**	**Procedure**	**Cost**
Register the SUS Card number on the identification tag (FAA)	To save time to record (book/SADT-Therapeutic Diagnostic Support Service) exams	Nursing Assistant	Collection Room	At every medical request	Transcrever o número do CNS (national health card) na SADT	-
		Nurse				
		Supplier	Reception Module - UPA Cumbica	To check (requested on April 2020)	Include the CNS number on the identification label in the SISS System (integrated health management system)	-

Source: Own Elaboration based on Descriptive Memorial – UPA Cumbica (2020)

ANALYZE PHASE

The Analyze phase allowed the identification within the process of causes of problems and opportunities for improvement. Cause and effect diagrams were developed based on brainstorming with the team. This enabled the identification of potential causes for Observation Time and Green Patient Time. The Diagram that allows visualizing the relationship between the Effect (problem) "Time in Observation" and its causes is explained in Figure 5. Regarding the People category, the 3 causes reported were: clinical eye of the nurse; nurse's initiative, and quality of communication at shift change. In the Processes category, the 8 causes pointed out concern the record in the medical chart, absence of conduct (physician), update of CROSS (Central Regulation of Health Service Offers), delay in re-evaluation/conduct (physician), lack of communication at shift change (physician - in the figure it is written physician), physical examination, risk reclassification, and delay in hygiene.

In the Ishikawa Diagram of Figure 5, referring to the Time in Observation, the priority and non-priority causes were indicated. In addition, in the Diagram, the form of analysis of the priority causes is highlighted (2x2 Matrix or 5 Whys). The decision criteria used are shown below (Figure 6).

Figure 5. Cause and Effect Diagram concerning the "Time in Observation" Effect.
Source: Own Elaboration based on Descriptive Memorial – UPA Cumbica (2020)

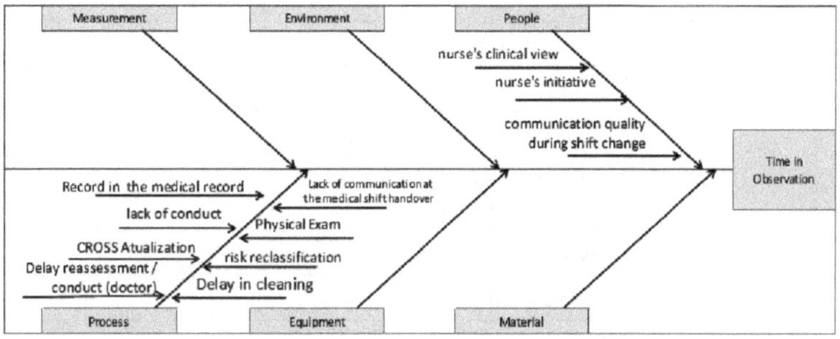

Figure 6. Decision criteria for choosing the form of analysis of priority causes
Source: Educational material – Cumbica, UFF (2020)

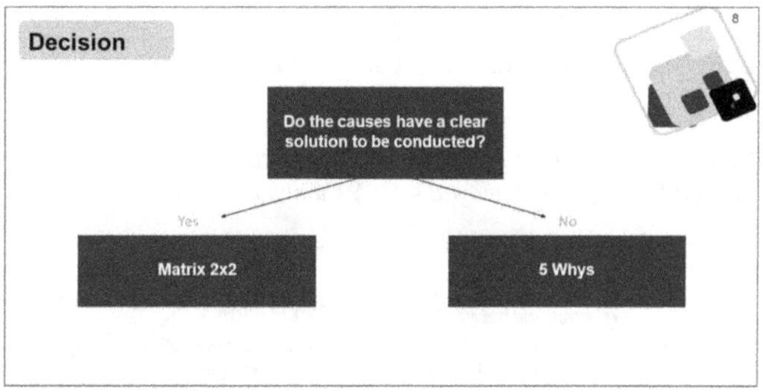

Among the 11 causes cited for the Time effect in the Observation, 7 were considered non-priority and 4 as priority. It can be seen, according to Figure 6, that only causes present in the Processes category were considered priorities. Table 10 shows, based on Figure 6, the causes considered priority and non-priority and the way these causes were analyzed. Among the priority causes, it was decided that for none of the causes the 5 Whys tool would be used. Thus, it was decided that the 2 x 2 Matrix would be used for the 4 priority causes.

The Diagram that allows visualizing the relationship between the "Green Patient Time" Effect and its causes is shown in Figure 7. Regarding the Environment category, the 3 causes reported were a change of prescription, medical certificate and lack of space (medication). In the People category, the 5 causes evidenced are listed as follows: nursing agility, patient did not notice the password, password stopped, patient arrival time (risk classification), delay to call the FAA (doctor). In the Processes category, the 25 causes pointed out concern.

In the Equipment category, the following 2 causes were evidenced: adequate equipment (risk classification) and adequate refrigerator. Finally, regarding the Material category, the only cause pointed out was the lack of medication.

In Figure 7, among the 36 causes cited for the Green Patient Time effect, 25 were considered non-priority and 11 as priority. It can be seen, according to Figure 7, that no cause from the Environment, Equipment, and Material categories was considered a priority.

Table 10. Priority and non-priority cause and form of analysis

Classification	Items
non-priority causes	nurse's clinical view
	nurse's initiative
	communication quality during shift change
	lack of communication in shift change (doctor)
	physical exam
	risk reclassification
	delay in cleaning
Priority causes	record in the medical record
	lack of conduct (doctor)
	CROSS actualization
	delay in revaluation/ conduct (doctor)

Source: Own Elaboration based on Descriptive Memorial – UPA Cumbica (2020)

Figure 7. Cause and effect diagram for the "Time in Observation" effect
Source: Own Elaboration based on Descriptive Memorial – UPA Cumbica (2020)

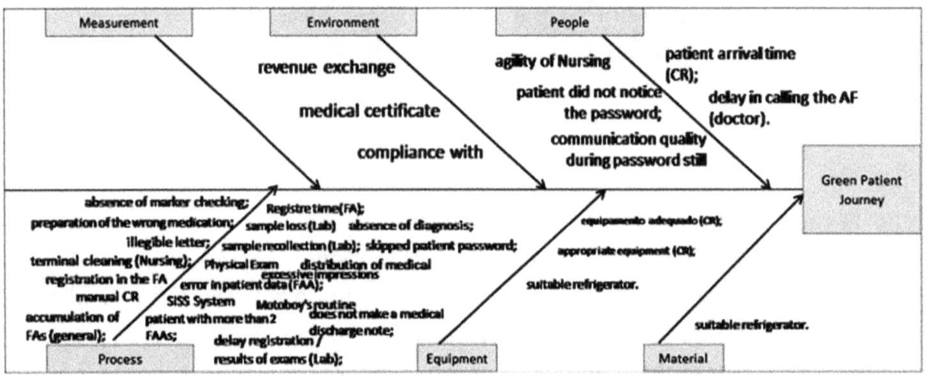

Table 11 shows, based on Figure 7, the causes considered priority and non-priority and how these cases were analyzed. Among the priority causes, it was decided that for 5 causes the 5 Whys tool would be used and for 6 causes the 2 x 2 Matrix would be used.

A 5 Whys Matrix regarding the Process/Demand entitled Green Patient Time was elaborated (Table 12). Regarding the problem "Delay to call for Doctor's Appointment, after Risk Classification" "Why" questions were elaborated in a successive manner (4 times). The answer to the final question indicates that this problem occurs because the current methodology for the distribution of medical activities is not efficient. The conclusion was reached that the solution to this problem would be to distribute the medical activities according to the profile of the physicians.

Table 11. Classification of causes of the green patient time effect according to priority and form of root cause analysis.

Classification	Items	Form of Analysis
Non-priority causes	revenue exchange	——
	medical certificate	
	lack of space (medication)	
	nursing agility	
	patient did not notice the password	
	stop password	
	absence of marker checking	
	preparation of the wrong medication	
	terminal cleaning (nursing)	
	FA record	
	manual risk classification	
	registration time (FAA)	
	sample loss (lab)	
	sample recollect (lab)	
	physical exam	
	patient with more than 2 FAAs	
	skipped patient password	
	excessive printed	
	does not make high annotation	
	lack of supply of cleaning material	
	suitable equipment (risk classification)	
	suitable refrigerator	
	lack of medicines	
Priority causes	patient arrival time (risk classification)	Matrix 2 x 2
	error in patient data (FAA)	
	SISS System	
	compliance with protocols	
	distribution of medical activities	
	the doctor refuses to see another doctor's patient.	
	delay in calling the FAA (doctor)	5 Whys
	delay registration / results of exams (Lab)	
	FAT accumulation (general)	
	motoboy's routine	
	SUS information card (FAA)	

Source: Own Elaboration based on Descriptive Memorial – UPA Cumbica (2020)

Table 12. 5 whys matrix for the process/demand green patient time

5 WHYS MATRIX						
Process Name/ Demand: Green Patient Time						
Problem	Root Cause					Solution
	Why? (1)	Why? (2)	Why? (3)	Why? (4)	Why? (5)	How?
Delay in calling the Doctor's appointment after the Risk Classification	Doctors are not always in the office	They are serving in another sector (E.g. Observation/ Emergency and Suture)	There is little support for the existing rule regarding the distribution of medical activities	The current methodology for the distribution of medical activities is not efficient, considering the profile of physicians.	-	Distribute medical activities more efficiently, considering the profile of physicians

Source: Own Elaboration based on Descriptive Memorial – UPA Cumbica (2020)

The 2 x 2 Matrix for the process/demand Observation Time is in Figure 14. Based on the choice of priority causes for Observation Time (Figure 8 and Table 11), the improvement team decided in which quadrant to allocate them. The causes inserted in quadrant A were the absence of medical conduct (2), CROSS update (3), and delay in re-evaluation/conduct (physician) (3). These have a high impact and require little effort to implement (they are easy to implement). This indicates that they are quick-wins. The cause Record in the medical record (1), placed in quadrant C, was considered to have low impact and low effort. In quadrants B and D, no causes were allocated.

Figure 8. Matriz 2 x 2 do processo/demanda "Tempo na Observação".
Source: Own Elaboration based on Descriptive Memorial – UPA Cumbica (2020)

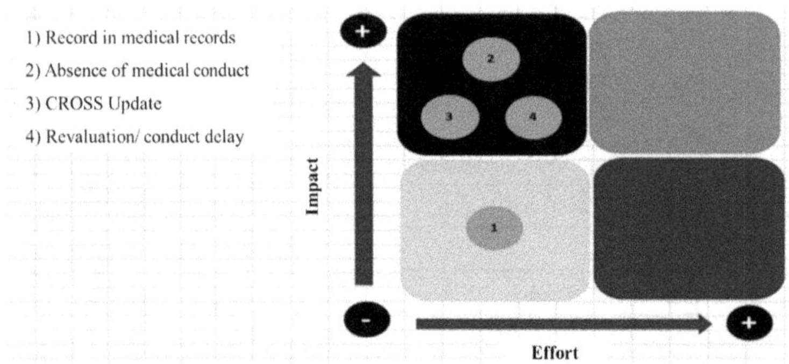

IMPROVE PHASE

In the Improve phase, to validate, finalize and replicating the project, an improvement action plan was developed and implemented using the 5W2H matrix (Table 13), where the activities to be developed, the objectives of each one, the procedure to execute them were explained, who would be responsible, location and costs. With the problems and their respective *causes* fully described, the group defined corrective actions for each issue, and then the action plan was determined. In this phase, the implementation of the 5S Program was also started, based on its importance for improving quality in the organizational environment. The team prepared reports on the Program containing information and guidance about the meaning of each S, essential criteria for each S, those responsible for implementation and maintenance, and records or observations. Good practices were implemented, in which the improvements to be made, their objectives, and also a comparison of the scenario before and after the process was scored.

Table 13. 5W2H Matrix

Activity (What?)	Objective (Why?)	Proceeding (How?)	Responsible (Who?)	Local (Where?)	Deadline (When?)	Cost (How Much?)
Distribute the medical activities more efficiently, considering the profile of the physicians	Reduce the time to call for a doctor's appointment	1) Establish a methodology / medical scale, to direct / distribute the medical activities (Ex: Observation / Emergency and Suture), according to the demand and considering medical profile.	Doctor Sérgio - technical attending physician	Medical Offices	6/17/20	Not applicable
Delay to Call for Doctor's Appointment After Risk Classification	Reduce the time to call for a doctor's appointment	1) Establish a methodology / medical scale, to direct / distribute the medical activities (Ex: Observation / Emergency and Suture), according to the demand and considering medical profile.	Doctor Sérgio - technical attending physician	Medical Offices	6/17/20	Not applicable
Accumulation of FAAs - Medication	Reduce patient time on medication	1)Revision of the flow for peak hour coverage; 2) Establish a methodology / medical scale, to direct / distribute the medical activities (Ex: Observation / Emergency and Suture), according to the demand and considering the medical profile.	1) Nurse Adriana; 2) Doctor Sérgio	1) Medication room; 2) Medical Offices	6/19/20	Not applicable
Delay in registration/test results (Lab)	Reduce examination time (external laboratory)	1) Survey sample with a time of moto boy departure x time of registration x release; 2) Survey sample with a time of moto boy departure x time of registration x release;	1) Nurse Adriana; 2) Viviane - Health Secretariat	1) Collection Room; 2 AFIP (Research Incentive Fund Association) - Health Secretariat	6/16/20	Not applicable
Motoboy's Routine	Streamline the sample transportation process (UPA-Laboratory)	1) Request addendum to the contract; 2) Establish an additional route, considering the reduction of time for all UPAs involved;	1) Viviane Hadadd - Guarulhos Emergency/ urgency Manager	1)guarulhos health secretariat; 2) AFIP	6/01/20	Not applicable
SUS FAA Card Information	SISS Supplier	1)Training/Communication of data confirmation through patient verbalization; 2) Encourage the notification of events related to registration errors;	verificar	Include the CNS number in the SISS System identification label	No access	Not applicable

continues on following page

Table 13. Continued

Activity (What?)	Objective (Why?)	Proceeding (How?)	Responsible (Who?)	Local (Where?)	Deadline (When?)	Cost (How Much?)
Patient Data Error (FAA)	Reduce registration errors and strengthen marker checking	UPA Cumbica Reception Module	1) Caio; 2) Simone	1) Reception; 2) all service areas;	6/23/20	Not applicable
SISS System	Streamline the FAA opening and screening process	Notification of SISS system failures, for the opening of Service Order; Signal the secretariat about the progress of the service orders	Caio	SISS System Health Secretariat	3/20/20	Not applicable
Resistance to evaluating another doctor's patient	Reduce the time to call for the medical realization	1) Establish a methodology / medical scale, to direct / distribute the medical activities (Ex: Observation / Emergency / Consuttory and Suture), according to the demand and considering the medical profile;	Doctor Sérgio - Medical Coordinator	Medical Offices / Observation / Emergency and Procedures	7/09/20	Not applicable

Source: Own Elaboration based on Descriptive Memorial – UPA Cumbica (2020)

CONTROL PHASE

In the control phase, we sought to sustain the improvements obtained in the processes in the long term, through the preparation of documentation, training, development of control mechanisms, monitoring of indicators, and risk assessment. In this phase, a control plan was developed (Figures 9 and 10). The control plan aims to define and establish the process parameters and product characteristics to be monitored and controlled. A Reaction plan was also prepared, which consisted of a series of actions thought out based on the Control Plan. These actions will be initiated when a non-compliant procedure or instability in the process is identified.

Visual Management was also implemented, where a board with the presentation of the whole project was assembled so that all employees could have access to the necessary information and objectives and the tools that were applied. Graphs were also prepared with the history of the data on the length of stay of the green patient and hospitalizations with time greater than 24 h. Besides, it verified the 5S applications in sectors and the user satisfaction rates.

Regarding Management at a glance, it was defined that a board (Figure 11) should be used for presentation of the A3 report, Good Practice forms, indicators, and general information. The purpose of the Management at a Glance Panel is to promote the team's engagement, update the project's actions, and show the gains obtained through the Good Practices implemented. This panel was prepared with two target audiences in mind: i) among employees for internal control of routine activities; ii) for users outside the unit for communication, guidance and Good Practices to patients.

A standardized model for holding huddle meetings was also created, and a checklist was used for the shift changeover. Standardization was also applied to the newsletters about the 5S Program.

Figure 9. Control Plan
Source: Own Elaboration based on Descriptive Memorial – UPA Cumbica (2020)

Indicator	Description (indicator name)	Where it is measured (Process/Sector)	Specification	Taxable Event	Control Media (Medication Form)	Size	Frequency (day/hours)	Analysis Method (Management)	Accountability (Who measures?)	Reaction Plan
X1	**Exam Failure (Identification, collection, transportation, result, including ECG and RX)**	Collection; ECG; X-ray	0 failures	low Failure / Protocols; Failure in adherence; Quality of materials, other	Adverse Event Notification AFIP Collection Indicators	1	At each event	Excel Spreadsheet (Charts)	Everyone (notification); Nurse - Continuing Education	Ishikawa / Five whys; Barrier (containment); Action Plan
X7	**Medication failure**	Medication	0 failures	low Failure / Protocols; Failure in adherence; Quality of materials, other	Adverse Event Notification	1	At each event	Excel Spreadsheet (Charts)	Everyone (notification); Nurse - Continuing Education	General: Ishikawa / Five Whys; Action Plan; CROSS: Trigger City Hall Pacting Group
X9	**Exam time (identification, collection, transportation, result, including ECG and RX)**	Administrative	Less or equal to 4 hours	Recollection, Confirmation; Faults Faults, Accidents Accidents; Flooding; Breakage	FAA; Attendance Time Indicator; Data Collection	01 FAA	Daily (3x per day)	Excel Spreadsheet (Charts); Sistemas Policlinicas	Administrative Assistant	Contact AFIP; X-ray: Send patient to another UPA; Collection / Correction of registration
X16	**Time to stay in THE OBSERVATION (total)**	OBSERVATION	Less or equal to 24 hours	Failure to update CROSS; Lack of reference; Conduct Conduct; Social Internment	Admission Book; Indicator - Length of Stay	1	Daily (Monthly Report)	Excel Spreadsheet (Charts)	Administrative Assistant (OBS)	Ishikawa / Five whys; Action Plan
X19	**Hospital Discharge Time (OBS)**	OBSERVATION	Less or equal to 24 hours	Failure to update CROSS; Lack of reference; Conduct Conduct; Social Internment	Book of Records: NOTE	1	At each event	Spreadsheet - Graphs(Logbook Data)	Nursing	Ishikawa / Five whys; Action Plan
X23	**CROSS time (OBS)**	OBSERVATION	Less or equal to 24 hours	Failure to update CROSS; Lack of reference; Conduct Conduct; Social Internment	CROSS Registration; Indicator - Length of Stay	1	Daily	Excel Worksheet; CROSS system	Administrative Assistant (OBS)	Ishikawa / Five whys; Action Plan
X24	**Failure to register/update CROSS (OBS)**	OBSERVATION	0 failures	Flow Failure / Protocols; Failure to enter	FAA; CROSS Registration	1	Daily	Excel Worksheet; CROSS system	Administrative Assistant (OBS)	Ishikawa / Five whys; Action Plan
X25	**Number of patients in observation over 24 hours**	OBSERVATION	0 patients	Failure to update CROSS; Lack of reference; Conduct Conduct; Social Internment	Admission Book; Indicator - Length of Stay	1	Daily	Excel Spreadsheet (Charts)	Administrative Assistant (OBS)	Ishikawa / Five whys; Action Plan

In addition, it is important to point out that the Unit has proposed to reward the two first place winners after the completion of the 5S audit. This reward system is a way to reward the employee's commitment as well as a stimulus to perpetuate the improvements.

Thus, Pareto Graphs were generated based on the Data Collection Plan regarding Collections, Examination Failures, Medication Failure, Hospital Discharge Failure (Observation), Failure to Register/Update at CROSS (Observation), Encourage Standardized Work, Establish Standard of Rituals and Meetings, Establish Meeting Schedule and Maintain the 5S Plan.

After the implementation of the control plan (routine management), the implemented actions were followed up and the team was coached, which provided a greater dissemination of Lean Culture in the organization. To this end, daily huddle meetings were held and the verification of improvements in the UPA with the placement of a notice board with the Satisfaction Survey via QR Code (without physical contact) and the organization and protection (COVID-19) of acrylic at the reception. As for the Team Coaching that was carried out with the Belts of the Project, the Project's tutor (Black belt) in the UPA to reinforce learning taught 11 professionals from the UPA concepts about Meeting Rituals, Indicators, Management by sight and 5S Plan.

Figure 10. Control Plan (part 2)
Source: Own Elaboration based on Descriptive Memorial – UPA Cumbica (2020)

X6	**Medication time**	Administrative	Less or equal to 1 hour	Complexity; Stability / Patient access; High demand	FAA; Attendance Time Indicator; Data Collection	01 FAA	Daily (3x per day)	Excel Spreadsheet (Charts); Policlinicas System	Administrative Assistant	Ishikawa / Five whys; Action Plan
X11	**RX Time**	x-ray	10 minutes	Many patients; Complexity; Absteism (Physicians)	FAA - Systems; Data Collection Sheet	01 FAA	each FAA	Data Collection Worksheet	Administrative Assistant (Reception)	Too Many Patients / Complexity: Opening a Third Practice Absenteeism: Seeking Coverage (São Francisco)
X15	**Medical Return Time**	Administrative	5 minutes	Many patients; Complexity; Absteism (Physicians)	FAA - Systems; Data Collection Sheet	1 FAA	Daily	Excel Spreadsheet (Charts); Policlinicas System	Administrative Assistant	Too Many Patients / Complexity: Opening a Third Practice Absenteeism: Seeking Coverage (São Francisco)
X6	**Doctor's Evaluation time**	Administrative	10 minutes	Many patients; Complexity; Absteism (Physicians)	FAA; Attendance Time Indicator; Data Collection	1 FAA	At each event	Excel Spreadsheet (Charts); Policlinicas System	Administrative Assistant	Too Many Patients / Complexity: Opening a Third Practice Absenteeism: Seeking Coverage (São Francisco)
X10	**ECG time**	ECG	10 minutes	Many patients; Complexity; Absteism (Physicians)	FAA System; Book of Records	1 FAA	Daily (3x per day)	Excel Spreadsheet (Charts)	Nursing	Too Many Patients / Complexity: Opening a Third Practice Absenteeism: Seeking Coverage (São Francisco)
X4	**Record opening/update time**	Administrative	2 - 4 minutes	Many patients; Absteism (Adm)	FAA - Systems; Data Collection Sheet	01 FAA	Daily (3x per day)	Excel Worksheet; CROSS system	Administrative Assistant	Too Many Patients / Complexity: Team Reassignment Absenteeism: Seeking Coverage (São Francisco)
X3	**Rating time**	Administrative	3 - 5 minutes	Many patients; Complexity; Absteism (Nursing)	FAA - Systems; Data Collection Sheet	01 FAA	Daily (3x per day)	Excel Spreadsheet (Charts); Policlinicas System	Administrative Assistant	Too Many Patients / Complexity: Team Reassignment Absenteeism: Seeking Coverage (São Francisco)
X26	**Number of patients under observation waiting for vacancies at CROSS**	OBSERVATION	0 patients/ over 24 hours	Failure to update CROSS; Lack of reference; Conduct Conduct; Social Internment	Patient Medical Record	1	Daily	Excel Worksheet; CROSS system	Administrative Assistant (OBS)	Ishikawa / Five whys; Action Plan

In addition, the 5S Audit was performed through the use of a board explaining the 5S and a 5S checklist to be used by the UPA team and have the evaluation of the sector. The evaluation grade of this list goes from 1 (bad) to 4 (great) and evidence was collected that members of the UPA team are using this tool. Also as part of the Follow up of the actions to improve and control, and specifically of Management by sight, the Cumbica UPA team has developed and implemented a series of Good Practices, as can be cited below: Lab Label; X-Ray and Electro SISS Exam Registration Screen; Removal of Observation Armchairs; Installation of intercom in the patient observation room; Placement of Organization and Social Distancing Plaques, these providences were taken due to the pandemic caused by COVID-19; designation of a nursing professional to pre-classify patients; Respiratory Symptomatic Label for patients with suspicion of COVID-19; Installation of acrylic for public attendance; Printing of the Results - AFIP; Implementation of the SUS Card with number in the patients' label; New flow of Motoboy for the removal of samples; Standardization of non-reigniting masks COVID-19; Standardization of the acrylic intubation box COVID-19.

Figure 11. Board and management information at a glance
Source: Own Elaboration based on Descriptive Memorial – UPA Cumbica (2020)

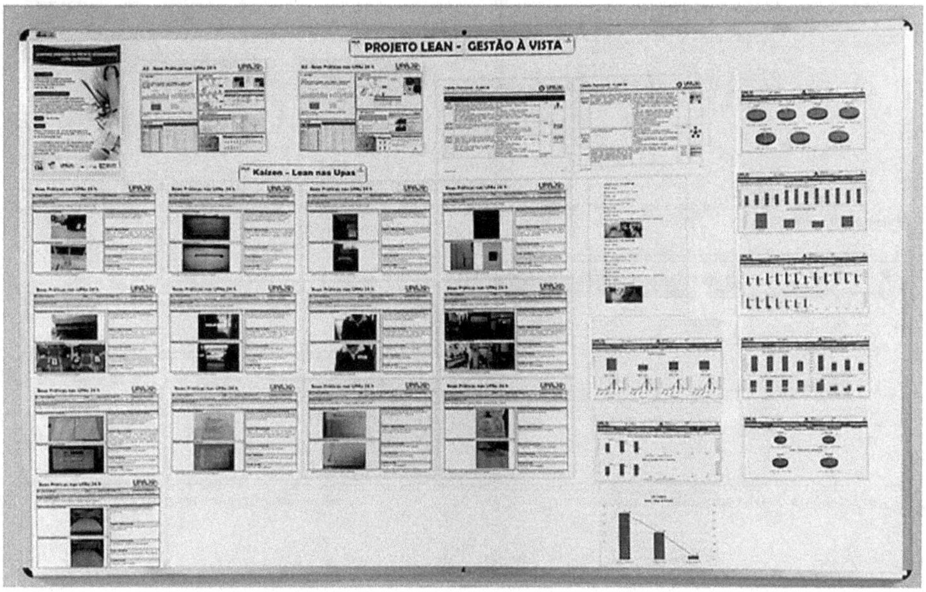

With the data complete, the Lean Project in UPA 24h team can finalize the A3 report, which was built during all phases and can be seen in figure 12. In it, the general tools used in each phase can be seen in a broad way. For the Define phase, there is the definition of the project title, the objective and the historical data. For the measure phase, there is the cause and effect matrix and the data collection plan. In the Analyze phase topic is the Ishkawa diagram, effort and impact matrix, and 5-why matrix. For the Improve phase is the see and act action plan. And finally, in the Control phase, the management chart and the control charts presenting the reduction in patient journey time.

After the control stage, the next steps of the Project were:

- maintenance of the monitoring of the Project scopes (Analysis and Improvement Actions) with the establishment of the culture of analysis of indicators x established objectives (Control / Reaction Plan);
- expansion of the methodology to the orange classification patients and
- use of the methodology for the management of Sepsis and Chest Pain protocols.

In general, as positive points of the project, we could highlight the involvement of the 24h UPA team, regarding the commitment to search and solve problems. The improvement team showed initiative and developed the activities within the planned and established schedule. No relevant negative points were found.

Figure 12. Final A3 Report
Source: Own Elaboration based on Descriptive Memorial – UPA Cumbica (2020)

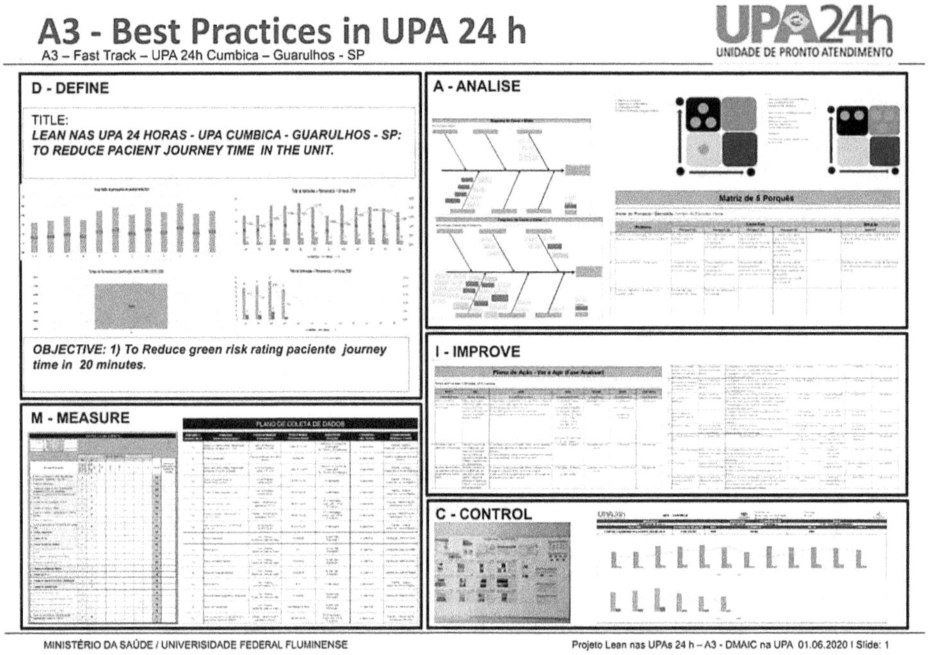

As lessons learned, the following factors are highlighted:

- Methodology for Process mapping and management.
- Analysis for waste reduction.
- Strengthening of teamwork.
- Quality tools.

DISCUSSION AND CONCLUSION

In summary, with the realization of the Restructuring Project Implementation of Humanization in the Flow of Patient Care in UPA 24h. (Lean in UPA 24h), in Guarulhos - SP, the objectives of reducing the green patient journey and hospitalization were achieved. With this, the average length of stay of low-risk cases reached a reduction of 46.9%, in the comparison between September 2019 and March 2020. It is important to report that the expected qualitative gains were achieved, such as process standardization, improved patient perception, patient safety, reduced workload, and reduced waste. An improvement was obtained in the activities implemented by the national humanization program, ensuring greater humanization in patient care from reception to discharge; the work environment became more organized and safe, thus generating greater agility and quality in patient care.

It is important to emphasize that the entire application of DMAIC was performed based on the A3 Report updated in each kaizen workshop in UPA Cumbica, which allowed the visualization of the synthesis of the implementation process of the Lean Project in UPA 24h with the presentation of DMAIC in all its stages. With respect to DMAIC applied as a Lean Healthcare tool for measuring and monitoring the performance and progress of the activities of this project, it was found that in each step of the application of this DMAIC tool, throughout the implementation of this project in this UPA 24H, the achievement of the proposed objectives was demonstrated in the kaizen workshop reports.

The importance of the application of the 5W2H tool was verified, which enabled the participation of everyone making observations in the daily work, mobilizing the team to See and Act. As the team was appropriating the concepts and principles of Lean Healthcare, the answers began to emerge simply and effectively. For this is the very purpose of management based on Lean Healthcare.

It is important to emphasize that the Lean Project in UPA 24h occurred during the pandemic caused by COVID-19, which made everything much more difficult in terms of mobility of teams and patient care in this serious moment we are going through. However, the continuous improvement team was able to participate in the meetings and brought great ideas for solutions to several identified problems, which were slowly consolidated into actions through the production of the Good Practice Report in A3 format (Reis et al, 2021).

Patient and staff safety measures were taken, with the installation of an intercom and electric lock, for an environment named Covidarium, where patients with suspected COVID-19 are safely attended to. The patients receive a protective face mask and are duly welcomed by the team, which performs the risk classification and takes the necessary steps for their humanized care.

The identification of the flow of suspected COVID-19 patients represents the creation of Fast Track to give fluidity to the service, reducing overcrowding and adding value to the patients, who stay less time in the unit. The evaluation of the effectiveness of the implementation of fast-track strategies, when operational criteria are used, is based on quantitative models and techniques. In Brazil, the efficient management of Emergency Care Units, UPAs 24h, is essential because the UPAs are a fundamental part of the Brazilian Health System. (Vieira et al, 2021)

The reduction in the length of stay of patients represents one of the main objectives in the implementation of the Lean Project in UPA 24h units with humanized reception, by the current National Humanization Policy.

Besides the reorganization of care with improvements for patients and promoting the safety of both the team and the other patients about social isolation. A system of Records was created in the Observation room that facilitates access and care to patients, with a 5S practice, which is a valuable tool used by the team, thanks to the implementation of the Lean Project in the UPAs 24h.

After the completion of the project, there was 6-month monitoring. There was a consensus that the monitoring of the improvement project would be a strategy to consolidate the implementation of Lean Project in UPA 24h.

ACKNOWLEDGMENT

The authors would like to thank the Brazilian Ministry of Health, UFF - Universidade Federal Fluminense, and Euclides da Cunha Foundation. This Research is part of the" Lean Project in UPAs 24h" that has been funded by the Brazilian Ministry of Health (TED 15/2021, number: 25000.103452/2021-14)

REFERENCES

Ahmed, S. (2019). Integrating DMAIC approach of Lean Six Sigma and theory of constraints toward quality improvement in healthcare. *Reviews on Environmental Health*, *0*(0), 427–434. Advance online publication. doi:10.1515/reveh-2019-0003 PMID:31314742

Al-Araidah, O., Momani, A., Khasawneh, M., & Momani, M. (2010). Lead-time reduction utilizing lean tools applied to healthcare: The inpatient pharmacy at a local hospital. *Journal for Healthcare Quality : Official Publication of the National Association for Healthcare Quality*, *32*(1), 59–66. doi:10.1111/j.1945-1474.2009.00065.x PMID:20151593

Antony, J., Palsuk, P., Gupta, S., Mishra, D., & Barach, P. (2018). Six Sigma in healthcare: A systematic review of the literature. *International Journal of Quality & Reliability Management*, *35*(5), 1075–1092. doi:10.1108/IJQRM-02-2017-0027

Battaglia, F. (2007). Léxico Lean. In *Illustrated glossary for practitioners of Lean Thinking*. www.Lean.org.br

Cheung, Y. Y., Goodman, E. M., & Osunkoya, T. O. (2016). No more waits and delays: Streamlining workflow to decrease patient time of stay for image-guided musculoskeletal procedures. *Radiographics*, *36*(3), 856–871. doi:10.1148/rg.2016150174 PMID:27163595

Chiarini, A. (2012). *From Total Quality Control to Lean Six Sigma: Evolution of the Most Important Management Systems for the Excellence*. Springer. doi:10.1007/978-88-470-2658-2

Goh, T. N., & Xie, M. (2003). Statistical Control of a Six Sigma Process. *Quality Engineering*, *15*(4), 587–592. doi:10.1081/QEN-120018391

Henrique, D. B., & Godinho Filho, M. (2018). A systematic literature review of empirical research in Lean and Six Sigma in healthcare. *Total Quality Management & Business Excellence*, 1–21. doi:10.1080/14783363.2018.1429259

Improta, G., Balato, G., Romano, M., Ponsiglione, A. M., Raiola, E., Russo, M. A., Cuccaro, P., Santillo, L. C., & Cesarelli, M. (2017). Improving performances of the knee replacement surgery process by applying DMAIC principles. *Journal of Evaluation in Clinical Practice*, *23*(6), 1401–1407. doi:10.1111/jep.12810 PMID:28948662

Niñerola, A., Sánchez-Rebull, M.-V., & Hernández-Lara, A.-B. (2020). Quality improvement in healthcare: Six Sigma systematic review. *Health Policy (Amsterdam)*, *124*(4), 438–445. Advance online publication. doi:10.1016/j.healthpol.2020.01.002 PMID:32156468

Oliveira, S. N. de, Ramos, B. J., Piazza, M., Prado, M. L. do, Reibnitz, K. S., & Souza, A. C. (2015). Emergency Care Units (UPA) 24h: the nurses' perception. *Text Context Nursing*, *24*(1), 238-44.

Oversluizen, G., & Slomp, J. (2020). Use of A3-method by engineering students in industry projects. *Production Planning and Control*. Advance online publication. doi:10.1080/09537287.2020.1742372

Raval, S. J., Kant, R., & Shankar, R. (2018). Revealing research trends and themes in Lean Six Sigma: from 2000 to 2016. *International Journal of Lean Six Sigma*, *9*(3), 399–443. doi:10.1108/IJLSS-03-2017-0021

Reis, M., Viera, L., Amaral, L., Farias Filho, J., Teixeira, A., & Calado, R. (2021). *Motivators to Application of DMAIC in Patient Care Processes. In Advances in Production Management Systems. Artificial Intelligence for Sustainable and Resilient Production Systems APMS 2021.* Springer.

Silva, G. S. D., Samico, I., Dubeux, L. S., & Felisberto, E. (2012). Emergency care networks: Pre-evaluation of Emergency Care Units (UPAs) in a metropolitan region of Brazil [Redes de atenção às urgências e emergências: pré-avaliação das Unidades de Pronto Atendimento (UPAs) em uma região metropolitana do Brasil]. *Revista Brasileira de Saúde Materno Infantil, 12*, 445–458. doi:10.1590/S1519-38292012000400011

Snee, R. D. (2010). Lean Six Sigma – getting better all the time. *International Journal of Lean Six Sigma, 1*(1), 9–29. doi:10.1108/20401461011033130

Taner, M. T., Kagan, G., Çelik, S., Erbas, E., & Kagan, M. K. (2013). Formation of Six Sigma infrastructure for the coronary stenting process. *International Review of Management and Marketing, 3*(4), 232–242.

Viera, L. V., Reis, M., Chaves, S., Calado, R., Bourguignon, S., & Lordelo, S. (2021). Evaluation of Fast-Track Implementation on Emergency Department: A Literature Review. In A. Dolgui, A. Bernard, D. Lemoine, G. von Cieminski, & D. Romero (Eds.), *Advances in Production Management Systems. Artificial Intelligence for Sustainable and Resilient Production Systems. APMS 2021. IFIP Advances in Information and Communication Technology* (Vol. 631). Springer., doi:10.1007/978-3-030-85902-2_30

Womack, J. P., & Jones, D. T. (2003). *Lean Thinking: Banish Waste and Create Wealth in Your Corporation*. Simon & Schuster.

Chapter 4
HFMEA-FUZZY Application: Similarity of the Eight Lean Wastes in 20 Emergency Care Units

Harvey Ribeiro Cosenza
Fluminense Federal University, Brazil

Nilra do Amaral Mendes Silva
Fluminense Federal University, Brazil

Robisom Damasceno Calado
https://orcid.org/0000-0003-3349-0344
Fluminense Federal University, Brazil

Ana Paula Barbosa Sobral
Fluminense Federal University, Brazil

Thaís Lessa Queiroz
Fluminense Federal University, Brazil

EXECUTIVE SUMMARY

This study aims to demonstrate the importance of waste analysis and similarity of results. For that, the HFMEA-FUZZY was used as a tool. The study used waste results from 20 emergency care units (ECUs) from different regions of Brazilthrough the HFMEA criteria and complemented with the concepts of logic Fuzzy with the COPPE COSENZA methodology. The use of HFMEA-FUZZY aims to contribute to research in the health area where Lean healthcare will be or is already implemented. For that, it served as a basis for reports prepared after visits carried out in the emergency care units (ECUs).

DOI: 10.4018/978-1-6684-5185-4.ch004

INTRODUCTION

Healthcare organizations have the challenge of seeking consistent and integrated techniques, methods and projects that can minimize failures in their systems, maximize results and avoid waste of own or governmental resources, often scarce. Besides also being providers of well-being, both to their employees and to patients and users, through a high technical competence, seriousness in procedures and humanization in the relationship (Pucci & Cesar, 2014). After all, institutions that promote health are directly associated with the image of preserving life. The health sector in Brazil faces some obstacles that impair health care in the country, such as the lack of beds, the overload of professionals, the lack of humanized care, the delay in care due to lack of professionals and insufficient resources (Santos, 2015; Alves, 2013). Given this context, the 24-hour Emergency Care Units (ECU) were created with the goal of offering fast patient care services to reduce the queues in hospital emergency rooms. The 24-hour Emergency Care Units are health care facilities installed in several cities in Brazil and are responsible for concentrating medium complexity services to the population's health. They offer a simplified structure with X-ray, electrocardiography, pediatrics, laboratory tests and observation beds. However, just like public hospitals, ECU have also become part of the grievances of public policy planning, suffering the same system failures as large institutions.

According to the Portal Medicina S/A (2021) 53% of healthcare costs in Brazilian hospitals are consumed by waste caused by failures in the delivery of value throughout its production chain, however, the result of this research shows that there are alternatives to increase the quality of health care to the entire population without the need to invest in resources. One of the alternatives is to collect data and analyze the performance of functionality in the desired area and make more assertive decisions from data that is qualitative. In short, it is possible to do even more and better with the available resources.

The present study aims to analyze the similarity of the 8 Lean wastes arising from system failures in 20 Emergency Care Units (EDUs) distributed throughout the regions of Brazil. To do so, the HFMEA-FUZZY was used as a tool. The study used the result of the mapping of the 8 Lean wastes through the HFMEA criteria complemented with the COPPE COSENZA methodology, of Fuzzy logic, which performs a method of crossing supply and demand matrices (Cosenza, 1981). The use of HFMEA-FUZZY aims to contribute to research in the healthcare area where Lean healthcare will be or is already implemented. Thus, internal reports from each hospital were used to analyze the data. Thus, the following objectives of the research are presented:

- Similarity of the 8 wastes in the Emergency Care Units
- Similarity among the Emergency Care Units

THEORETICAL BACKGROUND

Lean Healthcare

The Lean Healthcare approach was originally derived from the Toyota System: a continuous process improvement system comprising structured techniques for inventory management, waste reduction, and quality improvement (Santos, 2017). Lean Healthcare uses a continuous learning cycle, that is, continuous improvement in the activities that make up healthcare processes directly impacting patients, the professionals involved, and consequently the system (AlQedrah et al., 2022). Lean Healthcare philosophy involves structured methods and techniques with the purpose of solving problems that cause waste in a system (Amaral et al., 2021) Helping healthcare promoting institutions to create maximum value to their patients and workers, reducing waste, care waiting time and, where possible, standardize work practices.

For Lean Healthcare to be successful in its implementation, communication management must be frequent in the transmission of information, and must facilitate the understanding and commitment of employees, thus creating clear and measurable objectives; results that are contemplated, demonstrated, and transmitted to the right people (Barbosa et al., 2021). The implementation of Lean Healthcare philosophy results in reduced medical errors, and increased patient safety (Cosenza et al., 2021). However, the application of Lean for improving patient safety is still a relatively unexplored field (AlQedrah et al., 2022).

The Eight Lean Wastes in Healthcare

The mapping of waste in the Lean Healthcare philosophy is able to identify operational bottlenecks and contribute to the elimination of unnecessary activities that do not add value in all types of processes in the provision of health services (Lean Institute Brasil, 2014). The initial concept of the Toyota Production System (STP) was based on the complete elimination of waste (Ohno, 1997). As such, the 8 types of Lean waste adapted to healthcare from Taiichi Ohno's (1997) proposal are:

1. **Overproduction:** Producing more than necessary. For example, excessive monitoring of low urgency patients, high number of patient visits, etc.
2. **Defects:** Finished products or components (equipment, medications, etc.) that do not meet minimum quality requirements. For example, wrong medication handling, inadequate test performance, wrong patient release, errors with medications and/or surgeries, rework, etc.
3. **Waiting:** Excessive levels of materials, products and/or people between processes. For example, delays in incoming and outgoing patients, unavailability of resources, delays in accessing systems, as well as delays in the collection and results of exams.
4. **Transportation:** Energy spent with transportation of materials and information beyond what is necessary. Examples: taking and bringing medications, reports, exams, equipment in haste due to poor dispensing of those on the workbench.
5. **Processing:** Carrying out an unnecessary or incorrect process, which does not add value. For example, checking several times the same process, asking the same questions several times.
6. **Inventory:** Having more than is necessary to run a controlled system. For example, supplies and medications more than necessary, etc.
7. **Movement:** People or products moved unnecessarily, producing unnecessary movement when performing a task. For example, handling equipment, long distances to be traveled with patients, documents, equipment, employees and/or medical staff.
8. **Creativity:** Misuse of the abilities of professionals. For example, not listening to employees who are closely involved with the work, lack of staff training, limiting access to knowledge of information that is relevant for a process to progress, etc.

Reducing and/or eliminating waste increases the ability of healthcare organizations to "see" the specific faults that generate the waste.

HFMEA

Healthcare Failure Mode and Effect Analysis (HFMEA) or FMEA in healthcare is a prospective tool for risk analysis in healthcare management (Cosenza et al., 2021). Healthcare Failure Mode Effect Analysis (HFMEA) which refers to Failure Mode and Effect Analysis in Healthcare, emanates from the FMEA method, in whose translation is Failure Modes and Effects Analysis. In the 1950s the FMEA method was developed by the Grumman Aircraft Corporation to minimize failures of military systems. Since then, it has been widely used in engineering in general. In 2000, the Joint Commission Accredited of Health Organization (JCAHO) recommended that health care organizations, like industry, undertake proactive risk management activities to predict system weaknesses and make changes to minimize harm to patients (DeRosier et al., 2002; Neily et al., 2003; Adachi et al., 2005).

As a result, these efforts resulted in the effective introduction of FMEA in the healthcare industry, giving rise to the term Healthcare Failure Mode Effect Analysis (HFMEA).

The HFMEA method is a prospective risk tool divided into 5 steps: **(1)** Definition of risk area to understand the main root causes of failures, visualizing their mode and effect; **(2)** Definition of multidisciplinary team to conduct the meetings and mapping of failures; **(3)** Description of the analyzed risk area in terms of flowchart or process design for better understanding of the studied process; **(4)** Risk analysis through the criteria of occurrence, severity and detection inherent to the process analyzed; **(5)** Definition of the action plan and thus the prioritization of the worst failures, to propose suggestions for actions to reduce and/or eliminate possible errors, contributing to the strengthening of the culture in health care assistance (DeRosier et al., 2002; Neily et al., 2003). Therefore, the search for minimizing risks and failures has been one of the basic principles in the search for quality in health services (Neily et al., 2003).

Fuzzy

The effective formalization of fuzzy sets theory occurred in 1965 by Lofty Zadeh (Zadeh, 1965). While the limits of the classical sets are well defined (Crisp logic), the Fuzzy sets have nebulosity, i.e., it tries to approximate the inaccuracies of the human way of reasoning. The classical logic works the extremities with values "zero" or "one", however, the Fuzzy logic captures an infinite group of values between these extremes, with the manipulation of a gradient of values able to offer its users great precision to large levels of uncertainty (Krykhtine et al., 2013). Fuzzy consists of a theory in which everything is subject to gradation, everything has elasticity. The transition between belonging or not belonging to a set is gradual and not abrupt. The differential of Fuzzy logic is configured by the treatment of set theory with the relativization between values through the degree of pertinence of an element in relation to a universe. The pertinence is portrayed by a function that takes on values indicating the degree of pertinence of an element to a given set.

Therefore, in a decision-making approach, one can highlight the use of fuzzy logic in many models, such as in scenarios for prioritization of product portfolio in an agro-industrial system (Figueiredo & da Silva, 2014); urban and regional planning (Cereda Junior, Rohm & Lollo, 2009); accidents with oil spills at sea (Krohling & Campanharo, 2009); for supplier selection (Lima Junior & Carpinetti, 2015); risk assessment in the inspection of health services waste (Silva et al., 2017); determination of speed limit on highways (Lanzaro, 2018) among others. The use of fuzzy logic in the delineation of zones through multicriteria selection, fuzzy systems has been recurring solution for its ability to deal with a very large number of variables incorporating high degree of uncertainty and, from its processing, extract extremely accurate results. The COPPE COSENZA Model is a methodology adapted from Cosenza (1981), which is a demonstration of the robustness and flexibility of applications based on fuzzy logic.

CASE DESCRIPTION

Data Treatment

The COPPE COSENZA methodology for similarity is to evaluate the similarity between the ECU in terms of waste in 3 steps in order to elaborate the demand and supply matrices.

1. The first stage consists of characterizing the importance of the attributes in linguistic terms: a) Very Important - Absence of the factor makes the process unfeasible. b) Important - Absence of the factor compromises the success of the process but does not make it unfeasible. c) Relatively Important - Absence of the factor does not compromise the success of the process but makes it less attractive. d) Not Very Important - Absence of the factor compromises/influences the success of the process. e) No Importance - Absence of the factor makes the process unfeasible. According to table 1 in the second stage the importance weights are defined, in relation to each attribute on a scale of [0.2 to 1].

Table 1. Characterization of the degrees of importance

X_I	Degree of Importance
1	Very Important
0.8	Important
0.6	Relatively Important
0.4	Slightly Important
0.2	No Important

Source: Prepared by the authors

2. The second step was to invite 5 professionals trained and experienced in the Lean philosophy to assess the degree of importance of each waste that was listed on a scale from 0.2 to 1 (Table 1), according to the factors listed in Table 2. Then, the experts assigned weight to the wastes that they thought were important from their perspective. The HFMEA-FUZZY model considers concepts from the HFMEA tool for a deep analysis of the root causes of waste.

With this, the wastes were considered the cause of the failures committed in the processes; the way the failures were propagated were the factors, and the effects of the failures are the impacts generated by the causes (wastes) perceived by the users of the system. This result generates the demand matrix.

Table 2. Causes, modes, and effects of waste

Cause of Failure	Mode of Failure (Waste)	Effect of Failure
Lean Management/Leadership	Over-processing/Creativity	Dissatisfaction with Leadership support
Adherence to communication and interaction among staff members	Defects	Failure of staff communication and interaction
Management through indicators	Waiting/Inventory	Lack of management through indicators
Physical and technological infrastructure	Overproduction	Failure in physical and technological structure
Clear and well-defined processes	Transport/Motion	Lack of Clear and well-defined processes

Source: Prepared by the authors

Elaboration of the Demand Matrix

The Demand Matrix was elaborated considering 5 factors attributed to the 8 wastes. Table 3 shows the evaluation of the Lean experts.

Table 3. Demand Matrix Factors

Demand Matrix	Degrees of Membership				
Factors	VI	I	RI	SI	NI
1. Management and Leadership in a Lean environment	0.67	1	0	0	0
2. Adherence to communication and interaction among staff members	1	1	0.50	0	0
3. Management through indicators	0.67	1	0	0	0
4. Physical and technological infrastructure	1	1	0	0.50	0
5. Clear and well-defined processes	1	0.67	0	0	0

Source: Prepared by the authors

3. After the definition given by the experts regarding the degrees of importance of each waste (factor). After this definition, the next step competes in the elaboration of the supply matrix.

Elaboration of the Supply Matrix

The Supply Matrix was developed, from the evaluation of the internal reports, for each of the 20 ECU regarding occurrence, severity and detection, following the linguistic terms of the HFMEA tool:

Occurrence - What is the chance of this type of waste happening?

1. Very High - Up to 1 unattended point
2. High - Between 1 and 3 unattended points
3. Moderate - Between 4 and 5 unattended points
4. Low - Between 6 and 7 unattended points
5. Remote - All points are not met

6. Severity - If waste occurs, how much damage can be generated?

Low - The waste will have little noticeable effect on the discriminating patients and/or professionals;

1. Moderate - Slight deterioration in performance, with mild patient and/or professional discontent;
2. High - Significant deterioration in performance of a system with patient and/or professional dissatisfaction;
3. Very High - System stops working and there is great dissatisfaction from the patient and/or professional;
4. Extreme - Same as above, but. Affects the safety of the patient and/or professional.

Detection - If waste occurs, what is the chance of it being detected?

1. Almost certainly
2. High
3. Moderate
4. Remote
5. Nearly Impossible

Table 4. Supply and Demand Matrix Model (HFMEA Criteria)

Demand X Supply (Occurrence, Severity and Detection)					
Demand	**Supply**				
	Very Low	**Low**	**Average**	**High**	**Very High**
Very Important	1	1-1/N	1-2/N	1-3/N	1-4/N
Important	1+1/N	1	1-1/N	1-2/N	1-3/N
Relatively Important	1+2/N	1+1/N	1	1-1/N	1-2/N
Slightly Important	1+3/N	1+2/N	1+1/N	1	1-1/N
No Importance	1+4/N	1+3/N	1+2/N	1+1/N	1
N = 5					

Source: Prepared by the authors

Table 5 represents the crossing of the data from the demand and supply matrices (Table 4) according to the occurrence, severity and failure detection criteria of the HFMEA. In summary, the degrees of importance presented (Very Important, Important, Relatively Important, Slightly Important, No Important) were related to Demand. However, the supply matrix varies with each type of HFMEA criteria (Occurrence, Severity and Detection). For this reason, at each table the degrees of importance that correspond to the supply matrices are different from each other.

Table 5. HFMEA of Supply and Demand Matrices

Demand x Supply - Occurrence					
Demand	Supply				
	Remote	Low	Moderate	High	Very High
Very Important	1	0.80	0.60	0.40	0.20
Important	1.20	1	0.80	0.60	0.40
Relatively Important	1.40	1.20	1	0.80	0.60
Slightly Important	1.60	1.40	1.20	1	0.80
No Important	1.80	1.60	1.40	1.20	1
N = 5					
Demand x Supply - Severity					
Demand	**Supply**				
	Low	**Moderate**	**High**	**Very High**	**Extreme**
Very Important	1	0.80	0.60	0.40	0.20
Important	1.20	1	0.80	0.60	0.40
Relatively Important	1.40	1.20	1	0.80	0.60
Slightly Important	1.60	1.40	1.20	1	0.80
No Important	1.80	1.60	1.40	1.20	1
N = 5					
Demand x Supply - Detection					
Demand	**Supply**				
	Almost Certain	**High**	**Moderate**	**Remote**	**Nearly Impossible**
Very Important	1	0.80	0.60	0.40	0.20
Important	1.20	1	0.80	0.60	0.40
Relatively Important	1.40	1.20	1	0.80	0.60
Slightly Important	1.60	1.40	1.20	1	0.80
No Important	1.80	1.60	1.40	1.20	1
N = 5					

Source: Prepared by the authors

RESULT

The process of converting the linguistic terms to fit the different criteria was evaluated on two similarities: as to the waste and the overall similarity between the ECU.

Similarity of the 8 Wastes in the Emergency Care Units

Occurrence

The 20 ECU were submitted to similarity analysis of the 8 wastes in health systems and related to the criteria of occurrence, severity, and detection. Thus, before each waste analyzed in terms of occurrence, Table 6 shows the result of the question: What is the chance of this type of waste occurring? The result shows that the 20 ECU, on average, have 80% chance of the 8 wastes occurring, but that the predominant wastes are those with greater failures in the Waiting/Inventory.

Table 6. Waste Similarity - Occurrence

Factors	**OCURRENCE**									
	F1	**F2**	**F3**	**F4**	**F5**	**F6**	**F7**	**F8**	**F9**	**F10**
Over-processing/Creativity	0.80	0.60	0.80	0.80	0.80	0.80	0.60	0.80	0.60	0.60
Defects	0.80	0.60	0.80	1.00	0.80	0.80	0.80	1.20	1.20	1
Waiting/Inventory	0.80	0.60	1.20	0.80	0.80	1	0.60	1.20	1.20	0.80
Overproduction	0.40	0.60	0.60	0.60	0.40	0.60	0.40	0.80	0.40	0.60
Transport/Motion	0.80	0.40	0.80	1,00	0.80	0.80	0.80	0.80	0.80	1
Factors	**F11**	**F12**	**F13**	**F14**	**F15**	**F16**	**F17**	**F18**	**F19**	**F20**
Over-processing/Creativity	0.60	1	1	0.60	0.80	0.80	0.60	0.60	0.80	0.80
Defects	0.80	1.20	1	0.80	1	0.60	1	0.80	0.80	1
Waiting/Inventory	0.60	1.20	1.20	0.80	1	0.80	1	0.80	1.20	1.20
Overproduction	0.60	0.40	0.60	0.60	0.60	0.60	0.60	0.40	0.80	0.40
Transport/Motion	0.80	0.80	0.60	0.80	0.80	0.60	0.80	0.40	0.80	0.80

Source: Prepared by the authors

These two types of waste, in this study, were related to the management indicators since they are intertwined with time. The waiting time, most of the time in the Emergency Care Units, is associated with failures in some activities of the teams responsible for part of the process. For example, patients waiting for consultations, document release, exam results, and others. The wastage of stock associated with the management indicators in health systems is caused by poor distribution of materials, medications, information that doesn't flow in the middle of the process, and there are also internal logistics problems, for example, between pharmacies and other sectors of the ECU generating stock of people. These situations are failures that need to be combated with Lead Time indicators (Length of Stay, Queue Time, among others), quality indicators, and other actions that make it possible to measure these failures so that they do not become waste.

Severity

In terms of severity, the question to be answered is: If waste occurs, what damage can be generated? According to Table 7, on average, 60% of the ECU have enough failures for waste to occur and obtain significant deterioration in performance in their system with considerable user (patient and/or professional) dissatisfaction.

Table 7. Waste Similarity - Severity

Factors	SEVERITY									
	F1	F2	F3	F4	F5	F6	F7	F8	F9	F10
Over-processing/Creativity	1	1	1	0.60	0.80	0.60	1	0.80	0.80	1
Defects	0.80	1	0.80	0.80	0.80	0.60	0.80	0.80	0.60	0.80
Waiting/Inventory	0.80	1	0.80	0.80	0.80	0.60	0.80	0.60	0.80	0.80
Overproduction	0.60	0.60	0.40	0.60	0.80	0.60	0.80	0.60	0.80	0.60
Transport/Motion	0.60	0.80	0.40	0.40	0.40	0.80	0.60	0.60	0.80	0.60
Factors	**F11**	**F12**	**F13**	**F14**	**F15**	**F16**	**F17**	**F18**	**F19**	**F20**
Over-processing/Creativity	1,00	0.60	0.80	0.80	0.80	0.80	0.80	0.80	0.80	0.60
Defects	0.80	0.60	0.80	0.60	0.60	0.60	0.60	0.80	0.60	0.60
Waiting/Inventory	0.80	0.80	0.80	0.80	0.80	1	0.80	1	0.80	0.80
Overproduction	0.60	0.60	0.60	0.60	0.40	0.60	0.60	0.40	0.40	0.40
Transport/Motion	0.60	0.60	0.60	0.60	0.60	0.60	0.60	0.60	0.60	0.60

Source: Prepared by the authors

ECU F2 draws attention by the level of importance 1, which one needs to have in relation to its processes that involve processing waste and creativity; defects and waiting/stockpiling. In this study the relationship of processing waste and creativity are aligned with the leadership, i.e., the managers of each Emergency Care Unit in an environment that uses or is still in the implementation phase of the Lean philosophy. The processing waste competes in presenting unnecessary and/or redundant steps in the activities of professionals and/or patients. For example, repetition of activities, users answering the same questions a few times, etc. The waste of creativity, i.e., not valuing the creativity of professionals competes in the lack of involvement of employees' perceptions in identifying and solving the problems with which they deal daily. The leadership of this ECU may be preventing its employees from expressing ideas that due to their experiences can contribute and prevent mistakes from being repeated or not happening. Faulty waste means rework, that is, the need to redo something as a result of incorrect or incomplete information. Communication management and meetings need to become efficient for team alignment and to get shift changes structured and effective. In short, these types of failures, or breakdowns in the system, trigger waste that generates other waste. Therefore, generating teams that identify and solve problems will be a major barrier to these failures causing waste.

Detection

In terms of Detection the question to be answered is: If the waste occurs, what is the chance of being detected? According to Table 8 there is a percentage ranging from 100~120% of the Emergency Care Units in having their failures and, consequently, the wastes almost certainly being visible in front of everyone, either by the employees (the organization) or by the patients.

Table 8. Waste Similarity - Detection

	DETECTION									
Factors	**F1**	**F2**	**F3**	**F4**	**F5**	**F6**	**F7**	**F8**	**F9**	**F10**
Over-processing/Creativity	1	1.20	1	1.20	1.20	1.20	1.20	1.20	1.20	1
Defects	1.20	1.20	1.20	1.20	1.20	1.20	1.20	1.20	1.20	1.20
Waiting/Inventory	1	1	0.80	1.20	1	1	1.20	1	1.20	1
Overproduction	1	0.80	0.80	0.80	1	0.80	0.80	0.80	1	0.80
Transport/Motion	0.80	0.80	1	1	0.80	1	1	0.80	0.80	0.80
Factors	**F11**	**F12**	**F13**	**F14**	**F15**	**F16**	**F17**	**F18**	**F19**	**F20**
Over-processing/Creativity	1.20	1.20	1.20	1.20	1.20	1.20	1.20	1.20	1.20	1.20
Defects	1.20	1	1.20	1.20	1.20	1.20	1.20	1.20	1.20	1.20
Waiting/Inventory	1	1	1	1	1	0.80	1	0.80	1	1
Overproduction	1	0.80	0.80	0.80	1	0.80	0.80	0.80	1	1
Transport/Motion	0.80	0.80	0.80	1	0.80	0.80	0.80	0.80	0.80	0.80

Source: Prepared by the authors

It is possible to infer that the waste of defects, i.e., rework, are the easiest to detect compared to the waste of overproduction and transportation/movement that are, on average, 80% from being perceived. This lack of perception can be understood as a camouflage. The waste of overproduction is related to the physical and technological structure of the Emergency Care Unit. The waste of overproduction, according to Ohno (1997), means losses derived from the waiting process. That is, medicines produced beyond the requested, improper storage of products, which by waiting to be used in certain steps of the production process become unusable, etc. The waste of transportation/movement in health systems shows that during the execution of the work, the team needs to have the materials available to be reached and accessed easily, without people, documents, equipment, and/or exams moving unnecessarily. The experience of failures such as these promotes waste that may not be easily noticed.

Similarity Between the Emergency Care Units

The Fuzzy indexes of the 20 ECU were used to calculate the similarity. Similarity is a Fuzzy notion that yields the most realistic results in systems when identifying ambiguities and uncertainties of items and users. This similarity measure is based on popularity and significance (Shojaei & Saneifar, 2021).

Occurrence

According to Table 9, the ECU F6 showed the greatest similarity between the 20 ECU under the occurrence criterion, however, it is also possible to see the ECU F15. That is, among all the other units, ECU F6 has more chances of the 8 wastes occurring. This vulnerability allows its system to be more susceptible to failures and consequently to waste, it is possible to see in the previous tables the most latent waste of this ECU.

Table 9. Similarity between ECU – Occurrence

ECU	F1	F2	F3	F4	F5	F6	F7	F8	F9	F10
F1	**1**	0.68	0.86	0.86	**1**	0.90	0.89	0.75	0.77	0.81
F2	0.68	**1**	0.67	0.67	0.68	0.70	0.76	0.58	0.59	0.70
F3	0.86	0.67	**1**	0.83	0.86	0.95	0.76	0.88	0.91	0.78
F4	0.86	0.67	0.83	**1**	0.86	0.86	0.76	0.80	0.75	0.95
F5	**1**	0.68	0.86	0.86	**1**	0.90	0.89	0.75	0.77	0.81
F6	0.90	0.70	0.95	0.86	0.90	**1**	0.80	0.83	0.78	0.82
F7	0.89	0.76	0.76	0.76	0.89	0.80	**1**	0.67	0.76	0.80
F8	0.75	0.58	0.88	0.80	0.75	0.83	0.67	**1**	0.88	0.76
F9	0.77	0.59	0.91	0.75	0.77	0.78	0.76	0.88	**1**	0.78
F10	0.81	0.70	0.78	0.95	0.81	0.82	0.80	0.76	0.78	**1**
F11	0.84	0.82	0.81	0.81	0.84	0.85	0.94	0,71	0.73	0.85
F12	0.78	0.62	0.83	0.76	0.78	0.79	0.70	0.88	0.91	0.72
F13	0.74	0.64	0.87	0.79	0.74	0.83	0.65	0.84	0.79	0.75
F14	0.89	0.78	0.86	0.86	0.89	0.90	0.89	0.75	0.77	0.90
F15	0.86	0.67	0.91	0.91	0.86	0.95	0.76	0.88	0.83	0.86
F16	0.84	0.82	0.81	0.81	0.84	0.85	0.74	0.71	0.65	0.76
F17	0.81	0.70	0.86	0.86	0.81	0.90	0.80	0.83	0.86	0.90
F18	0.83	0.81	0.71	0.71	0.83	0.75	0.82	0.63	0.71	0.75
F19	0.82	0.64	0.95	0.79	0.82	0.91	0.73	0.92	0.79	0.75
F20	0.86	0.59	0.91	0.83	0.86	0.86	0.76	0.88	0.91	0.78
TOTAL	16.80	14.13	17.02	16.47	16.80	**17.15**	15.88	15.91	15.96	16.25
ECU	**F11**	**F12**	**F13**	**F14**	**F15**	**F16**	**F17**	**F18**	**F19**	**F20**
F1	0.84	0.78	0.74	0.89	0.86	0.84	0.81	0.83	0.82	0.86
F2	0.82	0.62	0.64	0.78	0.67	0.82	0.70	0.81	0.64	0.59
F3	0.81	0.83	0.87	0.86	0.91	0.81	0.86	0.71	0.95	0.91
F4	0.81	0.76	0.79	0.86	0.91	0.81	0.86	0.71	0.79	0.83
F5	0.84	0.78	0.74	0.89	0.86	0.84	0.81	0.83	0.82	0.86
F6	0.85	0.79	0.83	0.90	0.95	0.85	0.90	0.75	0.91	0.86
F7	0.94	0.70	0.65	0.89	0.76	0.74	0.80	0.82	0.73	0.76

continues on following page

Table 9. Continued

F8	0.71	0.88	0.84	0.75	0.88	0.88	0.83	0.63	0.92	0.88
F9	0.73	0.91	0.79	0.77	0.83	0.83	0.86	0.71	0.79	0.91
F10	0.85	0.72	0.75	0.90	0.86	0.86	0.90	0.75	0.75	0.78
F11	1	0.67	0.77	0.94	0.81	0.79	0.85	0.78	0.64	0.73
F12	0.67	1	1	0.71	0.83	0.67	0.79	0.65	0.80	0.91
F13	0.77	1	1	0.74	0.87	0.77	0.83	0.68	0.83	0.87
F14	0.94	0.71	0.74	1	0.86	0.84	0.90	0.83	0.82	0.77
F15	0.81	0.83	0.87	0.86	1	0.81	0.95	0.71	0.91	0.91
F16	0.79	0.67	0.77	0.84	0.81	1	0.76	0.88	0.77	0.73
F17	0.85	0.79	0.83	0.90	0.95	0.76	1	0.75	0.83	0.86
F18	0.78	0.65	0.68	0.83	0.71	0.88	0.75	1	0.68	0.71
F19	0.64	0.80	0.83	0.82	0.91	0.77	0.83	0.68	1	0.87
F20	0.73	0.91	0.87	0.77	0.91	0.73	0.86	0.71	0.87	1
TOTAL	16.18	15.81	16.00	16.91	17.14	16.30	16.87	15.26	16.26	16.60

Source: Prepared by the authors

Severity

According to Table 10, the ECU F14 showed the greatest similarity among the 20 ECU under the severity criterion, however, it is also possible to see the ECU F17. That is, as the waste happens the damage generated by this waste makes this ECU the most damaging. It is possible to visualize in the previous tables the most latent wastes of this ECU and use this analysis to reduce and/or mitigate these waste-generating failures.

Table 10. Similarity between ECU – Severity – Part 1

ECU	F1	F2	F3	F4	F5	F6	F7	F8	F9	F10
F1	1	0.86	0.89	0.84	1	0.75	0.95	0.89	0.81	1
F2	0.86	1	0.77	0.73	0.74	0.73	0.83	0.77	0.78	0.86
F3	0.89	0.77	1	0.83	0.84	0.65	0.85	0.79	0.71	0.89
F4	0.84	0.73	0.83	1	0.89	0.78	0.83	0.75	0.75	0.84
F5	1	0.74	0.84	0.89	1	0.70	0.90	0.84	0.85	0.85
F6	0.75	0.73	0.65	0.78	0.70	1	0.71	0.83	0.84	0.75
F7	0.95	0.83	0.85	0.83	0.90	0.71	1	0.85	0.86	0.95
F8	0.89	0.77	0.79	0.75	0.84	0.83	0.85	1	0.80	0.89
F9	0.81	0.78	0.71	0.75	0.85	0.84	0.86	0.80	1	0.81
F10	1	0.86	0.89	0.84	0.85	0.75	0.95	0.89	0.81	1
F11	1	0.86	0.89	0.84	0.85	0.75	0.95	0.89	0.81	1
F12	0.84	0.73	0.74	0.88	0.79	0.88	0.80	0.83	0.84	0.84

continues on following page

Table 10. Continued

F13	0.84	0.82	0.84	0.89	0.89	0.79	0.90	0.94	0.85	0.95
F14	0.95	0.77	0.79	0.83	0.84	0.83	0.85	0.89	0.89	0.89
F15	0.84	0.73	0.83	0.78	0.79	0.78	0.80	0.83	0.84	0.84
F16	0.85	0.82	0.83	0.79	0.80	0.79	0.81	0.84	0.85	0.85
F17	0.89	0.77	0.79	0.83	0.84	0.83	0.85	0.89	0.89	0.89
F18	0.85	0.82	0.84	0.79	0.79	0.70	0.81	0.84	0.76	0.85
F19	0.84	0.73	0.83	0.78	0.74	0.78	0.80	0.83	0.84	0.84
F20	0.79	0.68	0.78	0.82	0.74	0.82	0.75	0.78	0.79	0.79
TOTAL	17.55	15.80	16.41	16.48	16.53	15.70	17.05	17.01	16.59	17.61
ECU	**F11**	**F12**	**F13**	**F14**	**F15**	**F16**	**F17**	**F18**	**F19**	**F20**
F1	**1**	0.84	0.84	0.95	0.84	0.85	0.89	0.85	0.84	0.79
F2	0.86	0.73	0.82	0.77	0.73	0.82	0.77	0.82	0.73	0.68
F3	0.89	0.74	0.84	0.79	0.83	0.83	0.79	0.84	0.83	0.78
F4	0.84	0.88	0.89	0.83	0.78	0.79	0.83	0.79	0.78	0.82
F5	0.85	0.79	0.89	0.84	0.79	0.80	0.84	0.79	0.74	0.74
F6	0.75	0.88	0.79	0.83	0.78	0.79	0.83	0.70	0.78	0.82
F7	0.95	0.80	0.90	0.85	0.80	0.81	0.85	0.81	0.80	0.75
F8	0.89	0.83	0.94	0.89	0.83	0.84	0.89	0.84	0.83	0.78
F9	0.81	0.84	0.85	0.89	0.84	0.85	0.89	0.76	0.84	0.79
F10	1.00	0.84	0.95	0.89	0.84	0.85	0.89	0.85	0.84	0.79
F11	**1**	0.84	0.95	0.89	0.84	0.85	0.89	0.85	0.84	0.79
F12	0.84	**1**	0.89	0.94	0.88	0.89	0.94	0.79	0.88	0.94
F13	0.95	**1**	**1**	0.94	0.89	0.89	0.94	0.89	0.89	0.83
F14	0.89	0.94	0.94	**1**	0.94	0.94	1.00	0.84	0.94	0.88
F15	0.84	0.88	0.89	0.94	**1**	0.89	0.94	0.89	1.00	0.94
F16	0.85	0.89	0.89	0.94	0.89	**1**	0.94	0.89	0.89	0.83
F17	0.89	0.94	0.94	**1**	0.94	0.94	**1**	0.84	0.94	0.88
F18	0.85	0.79	0.89	0.84	0.89	0.89	0.84	**1**	0.89	0.83
F19	0.84	0.88	0.89	0.94	**1**	0.89	0.94	0.89	**1**	0.94
F20	0.79	0.94	0.83	0.88	0.94	0.83	0.88	0.83	0.94	**1**
TOTAL	17.61	17.17	17.84	**17.88**	17.28	17.26	17.83	16.78	17.22	16.61

Source: Prepared by the authors

Detection

According to Table 11, ECU F2 showed the highest similarity among the 20 ECU under the detection criterion, however, it is also possible to see ECU F13 and F17, which also reached a very high similarity value. This similarity means that the effect of the waste is in plain sight of everyone in the unit, i.e., all the waste is exposed and strongly visible in front of all users. It is possible to visualize in the previous tables the most latent wastes of this ECU and use this analysis to reduce and/or mitigate these waste-generating failures.

Table 11. Similarity between ECU – Detection

ECU	F1	F2	F3	F4	F5	F6	F7	F8	F9	F10
F1	**1**	0.92	0.88	0.86	0.96	0.89	0.86	0.92	0.92	0.96
F2	0.92	**1**	0.88	0.93	0.96	0.96	0.93	1.00	0.96	0.96
F3	0.88	0.88	**1**	0.89	0.85	0.92	0.89	0.92	0.82	0.92
F4	0.86	0.93	0.89	**1**	0.89	0.96	1.00	0.93	0.93	0.89
F5	**1**	0.96	0.85	0.89	**1**	0.93	0.89	0.96	0.96	0.92
F6	0.89	0.96	0.92	0.96	0.93	**1**	0.96	0.96	0.89	0.92
F7	0.86	0.93	0.89	**1**	0.89	0.96	**1**	0.93	0.93	0.89
F8	0.92	**1**	0.92	0.93	0.96	0.96	0.93	**1**	0.93	0.96
F9	0.92	0.96	0.82	0.93	0.96	0.89	0.93	0.93	**1**	0.89
F10	0.96	0.96	0.92	0.89	0.92	0.92	0.89	0.96	0.89	**1**
F11	0.96	0.96	0.85	0.89	**1**	0.93	0.89	0.96	0.96	0.92
F12	0.88	0.96	0.85	0.89	0.92	0.92	0.89	0.96	0.89	0.92
F13	0.92	**1**	0.92	0.93	0.96	0.96	0.93	**1**	0.93	0.96
F14	0.89	**1**	0.92	0.96	0.93	**1**	0.96	0.96	0.89	0.92
F15	0.96	0.96	0.85	0.89	**1**	0.93	0.89	0.96	0.96	0.92
F16	0.88	0.96	0.92	0.89	0.92	0.92	0.89	0.96	0.89	0.92
F17	0.88	**1**	0.92	0.93	0.96	0.96	0.93	**1**	0.93	0.96
F18	0.88	0.96	0.92	0.89	0.92	0.92	0.89	0.96	0.89	0.92
F19	0.96	0.96	0.85	0.89	**1**	0.93	0.89	0.96	0.96	0.92
F20	0.96	0.96	0.85	0.89	**1**	0.93	0.89	0.96	0.96	0.92
TOTAL	18.38	**19.23**	17.83	18.32	18.95	18.81	18.33	19.19	18.49	18.60
ECU	**F11**	**F12**	**F13**	**F14**	**F15**	**F16**	**F17**	**F18**	**F19**	**F20**
F1	0.96	0.88	0.92	0.89	0.96	0.88	0.88	0.88	0.96	0.96
F2	0.96	0.96	1.00	1.00	0.96	0.96	1.00	0.96	0.96	0.96
F3	0.85	0.85	0.92	0.92	0.85	0.92	0.92	0.92	0.85	0.85
F4	0.89	0.89	0.93	0.96	0.89	0.89	0.93	0.89	0.89	0.89
F5	1.00	0.92	0.96	0.93	1.00	0.92	0.96	0.92	1.00	1.00
F6	0.93	0.92	0.96	1.00	0.93	0.92	0.96	0.92	0.93	0.93
F7	0.89	0.89	0.93	0.96	0.89	0.89	0.93	0.89	0.89	0.89
F8	0.96	0.96	1.00	0.96	0.96	0.96	1.00	0.96	0.96	0.96
F9	0.96	0.89	0.93	0.89	0.96	0.89	0.93	0.89	0.96	0.96
F10	0.92	0.92	0.96	0.92	0.92	0.92	0.96	0.92	0.92	0.92
F11	**1**	0.92	0.96	0.93	1.00	0.92	0.96	0.92	0.92	0.92
F12	0.92	**1**	0.96	0.92	0.92	0.92	1.00	0.92	0.92	0.92
F13	0.96	**1**	**1**	0.96	0.96	0.96	1.00	0.96	0.96	0.96
F14	0.93	0.92	0.96	**1**	0.93	0.92	0.96	0.92	0.93	0.93
F15	**1**	0.92	0.96	0.93	**1**	0.92	0.96	0.92	1.00	1.00
F16	0.92	0.92	0.96	0.92	0.92	**1**	0.96	1.00	0.92	0.92

continues on following page

Table 11. Continued

F17	0.96	1	1	0.96	0.96	0.96	1	0.96	0.96	0.96
F18	0.92	0.92	0.96	0.92	0.92	1	0.96	1	0.92	0.92
F19	0.92	0.92	0.96	0.93	1	0.92	0.96	0.92	1	1.00
F20	0.92	0.92	0.96	0.93	1	0.92	0.96	0.92	1	1
TOTAL	18.78	17.57	19.20	18.84	18.94	18.61	19.20	17.68	18.86	18.85

Source: Prepared by the authors

DISCUSSION AND RECOMMENDATION

Similarity comparisons between institutions are made in order to provide a preliminary indication of overall risk. These results can help ECU improve their health care processes by determining which failures and in which sectors need attention in order to seek ways to mitigate and/or eliminate existing waste. The current challenges of each ECU go beyond what the literature can report. Since the inappropriate use and poor dispensing of materials, equipment, and work teams convey the central idea that the Emergency Care Units need to be directed to a change in culture so that there are reflections on the quality of care to the user.

The ECU in turn has a risk classification for priority care of patients who undergo the initial triage, however, despite this internal standardization in relation to patient flow, even so, the entire management system of the unit suffers from lack of logical sequencing of activities. The standardization of activities should be outlined in routines and procedures to standardize the actions in order to ensure the reduction of risks to patients, since the work will be standardized and not performed in subjective ways (Dos Santos et al., 2021). The lack of basic medical supplies, the poor dimensioning of the physical structure, in most cases, the lack of technology, the shortage of professionals and investments, the lack of fluidity in the processes, etc., are some of the difficulties faced by ECU. Thus, the struggle of these health institutions, in general, is just to keep their doors open, even if under these conditions, but providing care to the population (Santos, 2015). However, a study by the University of São Paulo (USP, 2020) showed that despite the challenges faced, health professionals have appropriated creativity and effort to ensure the continuity of the work and highlighted the importance of training professionals involved in the provision of health services.

The imbalance between the financial resources applied to health and the increase in population pose a great challenge from the management perspective: finding new managerial measures to coordinate the scarce resources in order to optimize their efficiency (Ramos; Spiegel; Assad, 2018). Although no productive operation is indifferent to failures, in some it is crucial that products and services do not fail, culminating in losses, situations and places such as: an airplane in flight, hospitals, the brake of a car, for example (Slack, Chambers & Johnston, 2009). Therefore, it is necessary that managers of health institutions, whether public or private, know the problems to be faced, be agile and flexible, know how to plan, structure, organize, implement, and evaluate plans, programs, and projects (Martins; Waclawovsky, 2015). In addition, they also have access to information of technical-scientific and political-institutional nature so that they are able to intervene, in relation to the demands of the population to be met, according to the law (Coelho, 2007; De Lacerda & Santiago, 2007).

From this holistic view of how failures become waste and their impact on health institutions, we see the need for implementation of systemic and structured methods for the identification, analysis and implementation of mitigation plan to organizational failures for patient safety in Emergency Care Units. Therefore, it is necessary to motivate the professionals involved in the process to achieve changes in the assistance to users, firstly, in their work environment with improvements in the bonds between team members, so that there is a favoring of a more productive, satisfactory, reliable, and pleasant work environment (Breda et al., 2018). Since there are several elements that directly interfere in the quality of care, such as interpersonal relationships between work team and this is an extremely important factor. For, the team in ECU is the union of several professionals who work together to provide excellent care to users (Breda et al., 2018).

This study reinforces the demand for strengthening health care as the first step towards the implementation of continuing education strategies for health professionals, processes and projects that clarify to users the roles of each one in this network. Therefore, new research needs to be carried out in this context, aiming to increase the knowledge about this reality. This document can be of great esteem for professionals in the area or related ones to generate learning, research, and/or implementation of continuous improvement through the 8 wastes; for professionals who use Fuzzy logic; and the HFMEA method for risk management in the healthcare sector to improve patient safety.

CONCLUSION

This study intended to present the HFMEA-FUZZY model, through the COPPE COSENZA methodology, to assess the similarity of the 8 Lean wastes in each Emergency Care Unit (ECU), as well as the similarity of these among the 20 ECU distributed by regions in Brazil. The study used the result of the mapping of the 8 Lean wastes through the HFMEA criteria complemented by Fuzzy logic, through the crossing of supply and demand matrices. The similarity analysis of the 8 wastes demonstrated how the effects of the main failures generate the wastes in the ECU and how the healthcare organizations can see them. The similarity among the Emergency Care Units presented the 3 main ECU with the most latent wastes under the criteria of occurrence, severity, and detection. This mapping allowed us to describe and analyze the failures that generate waste occurring in the production chain of the ECU. In this context, the information works as instruments and/or tools to reduce the degree of uncertainty about the risks and unnecessary damages associated with healthcare, offering support to the decision-making process from the development of the HFMEA-FUZZY model. Given this, this work points to the need for the development of new studies and research focusing on risk management based on failure prevention and Team Leadership, as the main gap to be filled.

ACKNOWLEDGMENT

The authors would like to thank the Brazilian Ministry of Health, UFF - Universidade Federal Fluminense, and Euclides da Cunha Foundation. This Research is part of the" Lean Project in ECU 24h" that has been funded by the Brazilian Ministry of Health (TED 15/2021, number: 25000.103452/2021-14).

REFERENCES

Adachi, W., & Lodolce, A. E. (2005). Use of failure mode and effects analysis in improving the safety of iv drug administration. *American Journal of Health-System Pharmacy*, *62*(9), 917–920. doi:10.1093/ajhp/62.9.917 PMID:15851497

AlQedrah, M., Marbouh, D., Simsekler, M. C. E., & Ellahham, S. (2022, February). Opportunities for Patient Safety Improvement using Lean. In *2022 Advances in Science and Engineering Technology International Conferences (ASET)* (pp. 1-4). IEEE. 10.1109/ASET53988.2022.9735048

Alves, E. A. V. (2013). Patient safety: From error to risk prevention. *Cadernos Ibero-Americanos de Direito Sanitario*, *2*(2), 723–733.

Amaral, L. C. D., Calado, R. D., Vieira, L. W. H., & Chaves, S. M. D. A. (2021, September). Lean Healthcare in Reducing HAI an Integrative Literature Review. In *IFIP International Conference on Advances in Production Management Systems* (pp. 351-361). Springer. 10.1007/978-3-030-85902-2_38

Barbosa, C., Lima, A., Sobrinho, A., Calado, R., & Lordelo, S. (2021, September). Information, Communication and Knowledge for Lean Healthcare Management Guidelines, a Literature Revision. In *IFIP International Conference on Advances in Production Management Systems* (pp. 250-257). Springer. 10.1007/978-3-030-85902-2_27

Brazilian Health System wastes 53% of the cost of care. (2021, October 4). Retrieved May 03, 2022, from Medicina S/A https://medicinasa.com.br/desperdicio-custo-hospital/

Breda, M. E. C, Joaquim, P.N, Testoni, A.K, Schneider, C.F, Mello, V.A & Trindade, L.L. (2018). Teamwork in an emergency care unit. *Revista da Semana Acadêmica do Curso de Medicina da UFFS-Campus Chapecó, 1*(1).

Cereda, A., Jr., Röhm, S., & Lollo, J. A. D. (2009). Mapping using Multicriteria Analysis and Fuzzy Logic as a subsidy to Urban and Regional Planning. 12th Encuentro de geógrafos de america latina, Montevideo, 222-229.

Coelho, V. S. P. (2007). The democratization of Health Councils: The paradox of attracting non-allies. *Novos Estudos CEBRAP*, 77–92. doi:10.1590/S0101-33002007000200009

Cosenza, C. A. N. (1981). *An Industrial Location Model* [Working Paper]. Martin Centre for Architectural and Urban Sites Studies, Cambridge University.

DeRosier, J., Stalhandske, E., Bagian, J. P., & Nudell, T. (2002). Using health care failure mode and effect analysis™: The VA National Center for Patient Safety's prospective risk analysis system. *The Joint Commission Journal on Quality Improvement*, *28*(5), 248–267. doi:10.1016/S1070-3241(02)28025-6 PMID:12053459

Dos Santos, A. J., Ribeiro, M. I. L. C., da Silva Melo, C., da Silva, M. M., Silva, A. T., & Alves, A. C. (2021). Demand of patients medicated and referred for hospital admission after risk classification in an Emergency Care Unit. *Brazilian Journal of Health Review*, *4*(5), 18998–19012. doi:10.34119/bjhrv4n5-041

Figueiredo, C. J., & da Silva, M. H. L. (2014). Multicriteria approach and fuzzy logic for product portfolio prioritization in an agroindustrial system. *Operational Research for Development*, *6*(2), 226–242.

Krohling, R. A., & Campanharo, V. C. (2009). Fuzzy-TOPSIS for multicriteria decision making an application to the case of offshore oil spill accidents. In *XLI Simposio Brasileiro de Pesquisa Operacional* (pp. 1731–1742). Academic Press.

Krykhtine, F. L. P., Morim, A. C. D., do Vale, N. G. P., Fortes, L. E. N. S., & Neto, A. G. C. (2013). *Applying fuzzy logic in a multicriteria selection model for multiclients*. X Simpósio de Gestão e Excelência em Tecnologia.

Lacerda, W. A. D., & Santiago, I. M. F. L. (2007). Popular participation in local management of the Family Health Program in Campina Grande, Paraíba. *Journal Katálysis*, *10*, 197–205.

Lack of basic medical supplies hinders pandemic combat in UBS. (2020, August 19). Retrieved May 05, 2022, from University of São Paulo (USP) https://jornal.usp.br/atualidades/falta-de-insumos-medicos-basicos-dificulta-combate-a-pandemia-nas-ubs/

Lanzaro, G. A. (2018). *Using fuzzy logic for speed limit determination on highways*. Academic Press.

Lima, F. R. Jr, & Carpinetti, L. C. R. (2015). A comparison between TOPSIS and Fuzzy-TOPSIS methods in supporting multicriteria decision making for supplier selection. *Management & Production*, *22*, 17–34.

Martins, C. C., & Waclawovsky, A. J. (2015). Problems and challenges faced by public managers in the health management process. *Journal of Management in Health Systems, 4*(1), 100-109.

Neily, J., Ogrinc, G., Mills, P., Williams, R., Stalhandske, E., Bagian, J., & Weeks, W. B. (2003). Using aggregate root cause analysis to improve patient safety. *Joint Commission Journal on Quality and Safety*, *29*(8), 434–439. doi:10.1016/S1549-3741(03)29052-3 PMID:12953608

Ohno, T. (1997). The Toyota production system beyond production. *The Bookman*.

Pucci, M., & Cesar, A. M. R. V. C. (2014). The decision-making process of hospital managers. Anais do 14o Congresso USP de Controladoria e Contabilidade.

Ramos, L. C. F., Spiegel, T., & Assad, D. B. N. (2018). Hospital materials management: A process improvement proposal applied in a university hospital. *Journal of Health Administration*, *18*(70).

Santos, A. N. S. (2015). *Patient safety in non-hospital urgent and emergency care units: risk analysis* [Dissertation]. Federal University of Goiás.

Santos, V. M. (2017, July 5). *Lean Healthcare: What is it and how is it changing healthcare?* [Blog post]. Retrieved from https://www.fm2s.com.br/o-que-e-lean-healthcare/

Shojaei, M., & Saneifar, H. (2021). MFSR: A novel multi-level fuzzy similarity measure for recommender systems. *Expert Systems with Applications*, *177*, 114969. doi:10.1016/j.eswa.2021.114969

Silva, N. F. D. C. D., Vianna, C. M. D. M., Oliveira, F. S. G. D., Mosegui, G. B. G., & Rodrigues, M. P. D. S. (2017). Fuzzy Visa: A fuzzy logic model for Health Surveillance risk assessment for health services waste inspection. *Physis: Journal of Collective Health*, *27*(1), 127–146. doi:10.15900103-73312017000100007

Slack, N., Chambers, S., & Johnston, R. (2009). *Production Management* (3rd ed.). Editora Atlas.

Where is the waste in healthcare? (2014, January 23). Retrieved May 03, 2022, from Lean Institute Brasil https://www.lean.org.br/artigos/250/onde-esta-o-desperdicio-na-area-da-saude.aspx

Zadeh, L. A. (1965). Information and control. *Fuzzy Sets, 8*(3), 338-353.

Chapter 5
Indicators for Emergency and Urgent Medical Services

Ana Paula Barbosa Sobral
Fluminense Federal University, Brazil

Aline Rangel de Oliveira
Fluminense Federal University, Brazil

Adalberto da Cruz Lima
https://orcid.org/0000-0001-7666-4581
Federal University of Pará, Brazil

Guilherme dos Santos Silva
Fluminense Federal University, Brazil

Patrick Fernandes Ribeiro da Fonseca
Fluminense Federal University, Brazil

EXECUTIVE SUMMARY

The objective of this work is to carry out a literature review on indicators for emergency and urgent healthcare units aimed to identify the main measures within the context of healthcare services. A search was conducted on the Scopus and PubMed databases using two strategies aimed to conduct research on studies about indicators for emergency and urgent healthcare units. This work allowed identifying the main indicators used in the context of emergency and urgent medical services, which are length of stay, left without being seen, national emergency department overcrowding scale, among others. In addition, it was found that such indicators provide suitable and viable means to assess, review, and display the quality of health systems. It was found in some studies that the use of indicators is used only as a measure whose value is monitored by systems, but it does not lead managers to an action plan.

DOI: 10.4018/978-1-6684-5185-4.ch005

INTRODUCTION

In Brazil, the National Humanization Policy (PHN) is aimed at transversally encompassing the healthcare process through assistance and management by ensuring the role of actors and collectives, providing services and healthcare technologies, and offering safe and harmonious environments that provide users with comfort and well-being (Ministry of Health, 2013). However, overcrowded emergency units represent a serious problem to healthcare systems and a spontaneous demand of patients suffering from common diseases increases the number of services provided at these units. Given such conditions, there is an urgent need to plan work routines and implement projects and proposals aimed to ensure efficient and dignified service, therefore reducing pressure from such excessive demand. Thus, humanization is the only way to alleviate the impacts that plague the service routine in urgency and emergency medical networks.

Operating the National Humanization Policy in a way that values the quality of services provided in Emergency Care Units (UPAs) allows ordering medical care routines, improving the quality of services and reducing the possibilities of discontent and dissatisfaction of users. In addition, it is possible to prioritize patient care in conditions of greater severity and increase the productivity and efficiency of the unit's specialized staff, as well as reorganizing flows and ensuring humanized care.

From this perspective, a lean research project has been developed in emergency care units through a partnership between the Ministry of Health and the Federal Fluminense University in 2020 aimed to promote a new service culture that improves the quality and efficiency of services provided to users of the Unified Health System (SUS) served in Emergency Care Units 24 hours a day, seven days a week. The project prioritizes the following aspects in emergency and urgency networks: care for patients suffering from more serious conditions, increased productivity and efficiency of specialized staff, as well as a reorganization of patient flows and the assurance of humanized care.

Within the conception of difficulty and subjectivity in assessing the quality of health systems, there is a concept in literature which states that there should be criteria for suitable assessment measures composed of reproducible and comparable indicators. Such criteria offers data that could have been lost on account of the subjectivity of personal assessments with respect to the perception of quality of services rendered (Viola et al., 2014). For such a purpose, indicators are used as tools to measure how the results of Emergency Care Units can be classified with respect to the efficiency and quality of services provided to its users. In addition, through these indicators, it will be possible to compare values assumed before and after implementing the project, followed by taking managerial action.

Thus, the objective of the work is to conduct a systematic review of the literature on indicators used in emergency and urgent units to identify the major measures within the context of healthcare. The PRISMA method will be used to help the authors improve the reporting of this systematic review.

CONCEPTUAL FRAMEWORK

This section presents a general definition of indicators used to measure the quality of service in emergency and urgent units of a health system. Healthcare indicators are selected according to objectives defined for daily routines. Essentially, the objective is the expected resolution of a problem that managers face in their daily routine. In addition, every indicator must have a target, i.e., a value that must be reached in a given period of time. The difference between the current value of the indicator and the target is called a gap. Gap detection should lead managers to discover the cause and take corrective actions. In other words, indicators must lead managers to act towards achieving expected results.

It is also worth mentioning the issue of overcrowding of patients in emergency departments. Overcrowding is considered as a concern, since it significantly affects patients and healthcare professionals. The tension caused by patient overcrowding generates a deficit in the quality of emergency healthcare. It has been associated with reduced access to emergency medical services, delays in assisting cardiac patients, increased patient mortality, prolonged patient transport time, improper pain management, violence from irritated patients against staff, increased costs of patient care and decreased physician job satisfaction (Hoot et al., 2007).

Therefore, overcrowding assessment tools have been developed and implemented to quantify and evaluate overcrowding in emergency departments. These tools are also part of a list of indicators used in the context of emergency units.

- NEDOCS (National Emergency Department Overcrowding Scale) measures aspects such as length of stay in emergency departments, time it took the patient to be discharged, total number of emergency beds, total number of cared patients, among others. The NEDOCS scoring system was created to assess and quantify overcrowding in emergency department of major trauma centers, which is calculated statistically (Weiss et al., 2006).
- CEDOCS (Score for Emergency Department Overcrowding) has been created as an enhanced analysis based on the NEDOCS scoring system. It was developed for emergency departments of small trauma centres, given that NEDOCS was aimed at large centres. The CEDOCS score range is from 0 to 100, but it is doubled so that it can be compared to NEDOCS (0-200). CEDOCS appears to be valid in emergency departments with at least 18,000 patients per year.
- SONET (Severely Overcrowded - Overcrowded - Not Overcrowded Estimation Tool) is an accurate tool for estimating overcrowding in an emergency sector scenario involving a large number of patients (equal to or greater than 100,000 annual admissions) (Wang et al., 2017).
- LWBS (Left Without Beeing Seen): Patients who leave units unattended are understood as those who were admited and screened at a certain time, but have never been actually examined by a doctor (Weiss et al., 2005).
- EDWIN (Emergency Department Work Index) is an index based on Weiss et al. (2006) which can be calculated by the Equation 1.

$$EDWIN = \frac{\sum n_i t_i}{N_a \left(B_T - B_A\right)} \quad (1)$$

where n_i is the number of patients in the unit in the screening category i, t_i is the screening category, N_a is number of doctors on call, B_T is the available admittance capacity and B_A is number of admitted patients.

It is noteworthy that the Emergency Severity Index (ESI) was used as screening system, i.e. a five-level tool that has high interobserver agreement and is associated with the use of resources and hospitalization rates.

- READI (Real-time Emergency Analysis of Demand Indicators) is an indicator obtained by Hoot et al. (2007) which is calculated through the Equation 2.

$$DV = (BR + PR) \times AR \tag{2}$$

$$BR = \frac{\left(P_{total} + A_{pred} - D_{pred}\right)}{B_t}$$

$$AR = \frac{\sum n_i t_i}{P_{screen}}$$

$$PR = \frac{A_{hour}}{\sum PPH}$$

where DV = demand value, BR = bed ratio, AR = acuity ratio, PR = Provider ratio, P_{total}= number of patients, A_{pred}= number of expected arrivals (Estimated), D_{pred}= number of expected leaves (Estimated), B_t= number of licensed beds, n_i= number of patients in screening category i, t_i= reversed screening category i, P_{triage}= number of patients per assigned screening category, A_{hour}= number of arrivals in the latest hour and HPP = average of patients assisted per hour by each doctor and resident on duty.

It is worth mentioning that the original READI instrument used a four-level screening system, therefore the five-level Emergency Severity Index (ESI) was condensed into four categories by combining the two least severe acuities.

- Work Score: This score is a statistically derived calculation that relies on the following indicators: number of patients waiting, number of licensed beds, number of patients per screening category, number of nurses on call and number of hospitalized patients (Hoot et al., 2007).
- According to Hoot et al. (2007), the occupancy rate of units is obtained by the Equation 3.

$$Occupancy\, rate = 100 \times \frac{P_{bed}}{B_t} \tag{3}$$

where P_{bed} = number of patients in licensed beds and overflowing spots, such as beds or chairs in the corridor; B_t = number of licensed beds.

- Indicator to assess overcrowding based on the patient's perception obtained through a satisfaction survey. (Hoot et al., 2007)

The next section presents the research method in order to carry out the literature review focusing on the indicators used in emergency and urgent medical service sectors.

METHOD

This section describes the method for conducting the systematic review of published studies using indicators in emergency and urgent medical service sectors. Before performing a literature search of indicators used in emergency and urgent medical service sectors, the Virtual Health Library Descriptors (DeCs bvs) website was selected so as to identify the most appropriate keywords in the search of scientific publication databases. The words "Indicators", "Measure", "Emergency"; "Urgency", "Service" and "Healthcare" were sought on the DeCs bvs, and the following permuted indexes were found: "Health System Efficiency Indicators", "Healthcare Quality Indicators", "Emergency Care" and "Urgent Care". From them, the following keywords were obtained: "Indicators", "Healthcare", "Ambulatory Care" and "Emergency Medical Services".

To conduct research on published studies using indicators in emergency and urgent medical service sectors, a search was carried out on the Scopus and PubMed databases using two search strategies. The PRISMA method was used to help the authors improve the reporting of this systematic review. It is worth mentioning that research on scientific databases was carried out in April 2020.

In the first search strategy, the terms "Indicators", "Healthcare", "Ambulatory Care" and "Emergency Medical Services" obtained from the Virtual Health Library (DeCs bvs) website were filtered to find them in titles, abstracts, and keywords of publications. In addition, a filter regarding the year of publication was used, starting from 2010. Afterwards, their abstracts were read so as to exclude publications that focused on subjects other than those of interest or those that had no open access to the full article. In the second search strategy, the terms "Overcrowding Scale" and "Emergency Department" were used, which have been obtained after a discussion conducted by the lean project research team in Emergency Care Units as regards the used filters and all other steps of the first search strategy. In the second search strategy, the filter concerning the year of publication was not used.

RESULTS

In this section, the results obtained from the search on Scopus and PubMed databases are discussed using the two search strategies. In the first search strategy, databases of scientific publications were sought using the following filters: "Indicators" AND "Healthcare", AND "Ambulatory Care" OR "Emergency Medical Services" from 2010. They were initially found in 275 articles of which 172 were from Scopus and 103 from PubMed databases. After an initial analysis of abstracts, there were 33 remaining articles, of which 29 were excluded after reading their introduction sections, since they focus on different subjects than the use of indicators in emergency and urgent medical service sectors or on account of having no open access to the full article. Hence, four articles remained for a thorough analysis through this search strategy.

In the second search strategy, databases of academic publications were sought using the terms "Overcrowding Scale" AND "Emergency Department", but without filtering the year of publication, and 18 articles were initially found on the Scopus database, of which 13 were excluded after reading their abstracts, as they focused on different subjects than using indicators to quantify overcrowding in the emergency department or due to not allowing open access to the full article. As a result, five articles remained for a complete analysis through this search strategy.

The Figure 1 illustrates the flowchart of the PRISMA method with the systematic review strategies carried out in this work.

Figure 1. Flowchart based on the PRISMA method with the results of article selection
Source: Prepared by the authors.

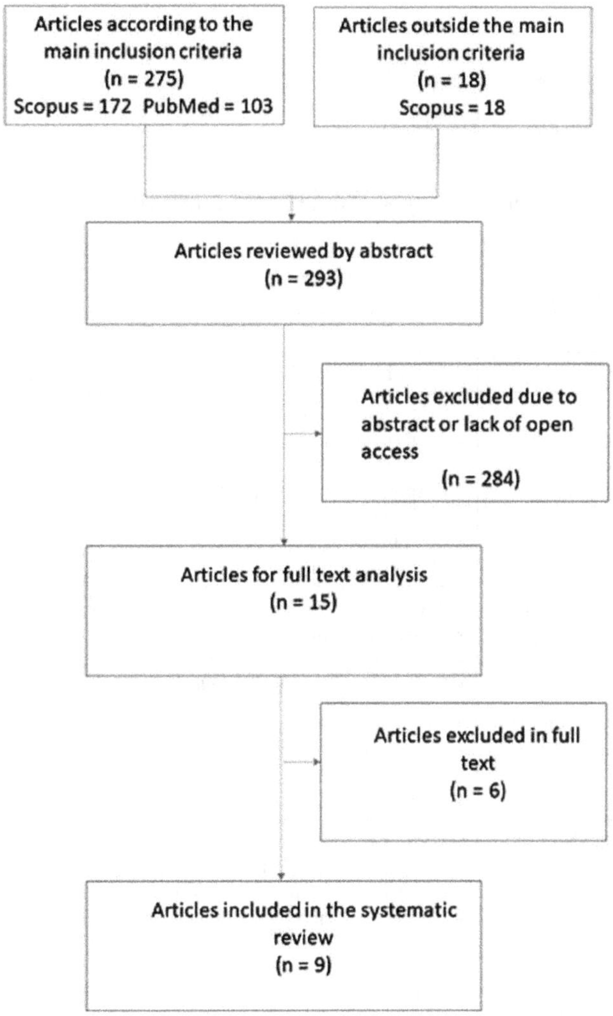

Thus, from the nine articles analysed, it was possible to identify the main indicators used to assess quality and productivity in emergency and urgency units. A co-occurrence network map regarding titles, abstracts and keywords of analysed articles is shown in Figure 2.

Figure 2 shows the presence of two clusters of words, which emphasizes the general definition of indicator in literature. There is a cluster of indicators found in articles stating that measures also required managerial action, in addition to the cluster of measures that refer to measures of patient overcrowding in emergency and urgent healthcare units, in which articles are focused on the procedure for estimating patient overcrowding without taking managerial action.

Figure 2. Co-occurrence network map of titles, abstracts, and keywords of analyzed articles
Source: Prepared by the authors.

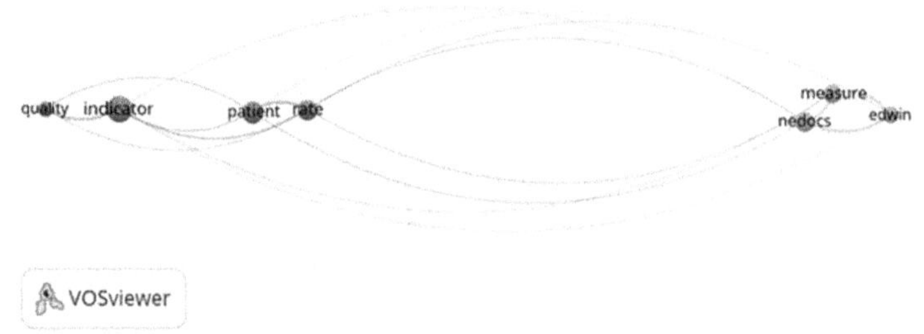

The main indicators used in emergency and urgency healthcare units were shown in Table 1.

Table 1. Indicators used by articles selected in the literature review

Articles Selected	Indicators Used in Emergency and Urgent Medical Service Sectors
Advanced units: quality measures in urgent and emergency care (Viola et al., 2014)	• Death rate in the emergency room. • Average length of stay of patients within the unit. • Unscheduled return visit fees. • Hospitalization rate of patients at level 1 screening (Emergency Severity Index). • Unfinished medical care fee. • Complaints rate. • Electrocardiogram time.
Application of Lean Healthcare methodology in a urology department of a tertiary hospital as a tool for improving efficiency (Boronat et al., 2017)	• Average length of stay of patients within the unit. • Risk-adjusted complication rate. • Risk-adjusted mortality rate. • Risk-adjusted readmission index.
Impact of Lean on patient cycle and waiting times at a rural district hospital in KwaZulu-Natal (Naidoo & Mahomed, 2016)	• Takt time. • Process time. • Waiting time. • Cycle time.
Primary Health Care in Brazil and the "Mais Médicos" (More Doctors) program: An analysis of production indicators (Lima et al., 2016)	• Total monthly medical consultations. • Number of medical referrals. • Number of educational visits by Family Health Strategy staff. • Weekly productivity rates of medical appointments.
Relationship between the National ED Overcrowding Scale and the number of patients who leave without being seen in an academic ED (Weiss et al., 2005)	• LWBS. • NEDOCS. • Number of patient admittances at the unit. • Number of times the ambulance arrived at the unit.
Comparison of the National Emergency Department Overcrowding Scale and the Emergency Department Work Index for Quantifying Emergency Department Crowding (Weiss et al., 2006)	• NEDOCS. • Number of patients (occupying beds at the unit). • Number of respirators in operation at the unit. • Longest hospital stay. • Waiting time for the latest patient taken to bed. • EDWIN. • Number of patients per screening category. • Number of attending physicians on call. • Admittance Capacity. • Number of patients admitted.

continues on following page

Table 1. Continued

Articles Selected	Indicators Used in Emergency and Urgent Medical Service Sectors
Measuring and Forecasting Emergency Department Crowding in Real Time (Hoot et al., 2007)	• EDWIN. • NEDOCS. • READI Demand Value. • Work Score (WS). • Number of patients per screening category. • Number of attending physicians on call. • Number of beds licensed for treatment at the unit. • Number of hospitalized patients. • Number of patients in licensed beds and overflowing spots, such as stretchers or chairs in the corridor. • Number of admitted patients. • Waiting time for the latest patient called to bed. • Longest time since admittance of hospitalized patients. • Number of respirators in operation. • Number of beds used for trauma treatment. • Bed occupancy rate. • Number of patients in the emergency department. • Estimated number of arrivals (Estimated). • Number of scheduled leaves (Estimated). • Number of arrivals in the latest hour. • Average number of patients assisted per hour by each physician and resident on call (Estimated). • Work Score (Work Score). • Number of patients waiting. • Number of nurses on call. • Number of hospitalized patients. • Occupation rate in the emergency department.
The role of patient perception of crowding in the determination of real-time patient satisfaction at Emergency Department (Wang et al., 2017)	• NEDOCS. • Number of patients (occupying ED beds). • Number of ventilators in operation at the ED. • Longest hospital stay. • Waiting time for the latest patient called to bed. • SONET. • Indicator of patients' perception through a satisfaction survey - questionnaire.
Effects of Lean Healthcare on Patient Flow: A Systematic Review (Tlapa et al., 2020)	• Waiting time. • Length of Stay (LoS).

Source: Prepared by the authors.

The results and advantages of selected publications are going to be presented as follows. Viola et al. (2014) evaluated, through healthcare indicators, the quality of care provided for patients requiring emergent and immediate care in an Advanced Emergency Care Unit. For such a purpose, data from management reports of 64,891 consultations carried out in Ibirapuera's Emergency Care Unit at Albert Einstein Hospital Israelite from June 1, 2012 to May 31, 2013 have been analysed. The indicators proposed for assessing healthcare were: death rate in the emergency department; average length of stay of patients within the unit; unscheduled return visit fees; hospitalization rate of patients at level 1 screening according to the Emergency Severity Index; rate of unfinished medical care; complaints rate; and electrocardiogram time. The study revealed that advanced urgent and emergency care service enables efficient and effective care for patients. Both critically ill and less complex patients can receive treatment that suits their needs.

Boronat et al. (2017) describe an application of the Lean Healthcare aimed to continuously improve the efficiency of a urology department in a hospital. It was implemented in 3 stages: training the staff and improving feedback among professionals, management by process and improving management (continuous improvement). The indicators were obtained from the hospital's information systems. The main used indicators were: average length of stay, risk-adjusted complication rate, risk-adjusted mortality rate, risk-adjusted readmission rate. A baseline was established with indicators for a comparative analysis of results after implementing the Lean Healthcare method. This study showed that it is feasible to apply the Lean Healthcare method in a hospital's urology department due to fact that it was achieved significant and continuous improvement in all its indicators, in addition to satisfaction by its professionals. Staff training, process management, continuous improvement and assignment of responsibilities are shown to be its fundamental pillars. Moreover, it is also necessary to involve health authorities as a means to increase motivation at work and prevent health deterioration.

Naidoo and Mahomed (2016) determine the impact of Lean techniques and principles on the operational efficiency of an outpatient department in a given hospital. Process and *takt time* were measured by direct observation beforehand, approximately twice a week, during and at two occasions after the Lean project implementation. A standardized data collection tool was applied by the researchers in order to find waiting time and cycle times. The application of Lean principles and techniques provides hospital managers with an evidence-based management approach to solving problems and improving quality indicators.

Lima et al. (2016) analyze the performance of medical consultations and referrals by the family health strategy staff carried out in primary care units in Brazil focusing on the "Mais Médicos" (More Doctors) Program. This is a sectional study on the conduction of work by the doctor and staff that either belong to the "Mais Médicos" (More Doctors) Program or not based on secondary data from SIAB (Primary Care Information System) and ESUS (Unified Health System electronic database) made available by the Department of Primary Care of the Ministry of Health, on which absolute indicators were found, such as total monthly medical consultations, medical referrals and educational assistance provided by ESF staff (Family Health Strategy), and relative indicators, such as productivity rates of weekly medical consultations according to the profile of Brazilian municipalities. The advantage of this work was to use secondary data to construct production indicators aimed to evaluate a health program.

Weiss et al. (2005) evaluate the correlation of results of two measures that quantify overcrowding in the emergency department: NEDOCS and LWBS. It was found that the correlation was higher for the NEDOCS score from 2 to 4 hours after patient admittance. The authors recommend that future research on overcrowding in the emergency departments should focus on evaluating other input variables in the model that generates the NEDOCS result, which are: disease severity and ambulance trip problems.

Weiss et al. (2006) evaluate the values of NEDOCS and EDWIN to estimate overcrowding in the emergency department. For such a purpose, they assume that NEDOCS and EDWIN are equally sensitive and specific to quantify overcrowding. It was found that these measures are correlated and accurate at overcrowding in the emergency department.

Hoot et al. (2007) quantified the potential to monitor and predict overcrowding in emergency departments using four measures: the Emergency Department Work Index (EDWIN), the National Emergency Department Overcrowding Scale (NEDOCS), the READI Demand Value and the Work Score. It was found that EDWIN, NEDOCS and the Work Score monitor the current overcrowding of emergency departments accurately, although none of them has exceeded the performance of occupancy rate across the range of operational points.

Wang et al. (2017) evaluated an association between real-time overall patient satisfaction and overcrowding in the emergency department, as determined by the patient's perception and the score of the overcrowding estimation tool. Although there is heterogeneity in the level of agreement between objective assessments and that perceived by the patient during emergency department overcrowding, it was observed that higher degrees of emergency department overcrowding on admission are associated with lower patient satisfaction in real time.

By means of a systematic literature review, Tlapa et al. (2020) determined that the effects of Lean Healthcare (LH) on the flow of patients reduced waiting time and length of stay (LOS) in outpatient care are mainly due to its focus on identifying and minimizing activities with no added value. However, evidence of the impact of LH on patient/staff satisfaction and reaping benefits from savings are scarce among evaluated publications.

CONCLUSION

This work allowed identifying the main indicators used in the context of emergency and urgency in relevant literature, such as: number of visits, number of beds, Length of Stay (LoS), Left Without Being Seen (LWBS), National Emergency Department Overcrowding Scale (NEDOC), among others. In addition, it was found that these indicators provide adequate and feasible means to assess, review and communicate the quality of the health system. It is noteworthy that the health indicators are selected according to the objectives defined for the daily routines. Essentially, the goal is the expected resolution of a problem that managers face in their daily lives.

Lastly, an inappropriate use of the word indicator in the context of emergency and urgent units of the health system also stands out, since every indicator must have a target, i.e., a value that must be reached in a certain period. As a consequence, the indicators should lead the manager to act towards achieving the expected result. However, in some studies, the indicator in the context of emergency and urgency units in the health system is used only as a measure whose value is monitored, but it does not lead managers to an action plan.

ACKNOWLEDGMENT

The authors would like to thank the Brazilian Ministry of Health, UFF - Universidade Federal Fluminense, and Euclides da Cunha Foundation. This Research is part of the "Lean Project in UPA 24h" that has been funded by the Brazilian Ministry of Health (TED 15/2021, number: 25000.103452/2021-14).

REFERENCES

Boronat, F., Budia, A., Broseta, E., Ruiz-Cerdá, J. L., & Vivas-Consuelo, D. (2017). Application of Lean Healthcare methodology in a urology department of a tertiary hospital as a tool for improving efficiency. *Actas Urologicas Espanolas*, *42*(1), 42–48. doi:10.1016/j.acuro.2017.03.009 PMID:28676387

Hoot, N. R., Zhou, C., Jones, I., & Aronsky, D. (2007). Measuring and Forecasting Emergency Department Crowding in Real Time. *Annals of Emergency Medicine*, *49*(6), 747–755. doi:10.1016/j.annemergmed.2007.01.017 PMID:17391809

Lima, R. T. de S., Fernandes, T. G., Balieiro, A. A. da S., Costa, F. dos S., Schramm, J. M. de A., Schweickardt, J. C., & Ferla, A. A. (2016). Primary Care in Brazil and the Mais Médicos program: An analysis of production indicators [A Atenção Básica no Brasil e o programa Mais Médicos: Uma análise de indicadores de produção]. *Ciencia & Saude Coletiva*, *21*(9), 2685–2696. doi:10.1590/1413-81232015219.15412016 PMID:27653054

Ministry of Health. (2013). *National Humanization Policy - HumanizaSUS* [Política Nacional de Humanização - HumanizaSUS]. https://www.gov.br/saude/pt-br/acesso-a-informacao/acoes-e-programas/humanizasus

Naidoo, L., & Mahomed, O. H. (2016). Impact of Lean on patient cycle and waiting times at a rural district hospital in KwaZulu-Natal. *African Journal of Primary Health Care & Family Medicine*, *8*(1), e1–e9. doi:10.4102/phcfm.v8i1.1084 PMID:27543283

Tlapa, D., Zepeda-Lugo, C. A., Tortorella, G. L., Baez-Lopez, Y. A., Limon-Romero, J., Alvarado-Iniesta, A., & Rodriguez-Borbon, M. I. (2020). Effects of Lean Healthcare on Patient Flow: A Systematic Review. *Value in Health*, *23*(2), 260–273. doi:10.1016/j.jval.2019.11.002 PMID:32113632

Viola, D. C., M., Cordioli, E., Pedrotti, C. H. S., Iervolino, M., Bastos Neto, A. da S., Almeida, L. R. N. de, Neves, H. S. de S., & Lottenberg, C. L. (2014). Advanced units: Quality measures in urgent and emergency care [Unidades avançadas: medidas de qualidade no atendimento de urgência e emergência]. *Einstein (Sao Paulo, Brazil)*, *12*(4), 492–498. doi:10.1590/S1679-45082014GS2894

Wang, H., Kline, J. A., Jackson, B. E., Robinson, R. D., Sullivan, M., Holmes, M., Watson, K. A., Cowden, C. D., Phillips, J. L., Schrader, C. D., Leuck, J., & Zenarosa, N. R. (2017). The role of patient perception of crowding in the determination of real-time patient satisfaction at Emergency Department. *International Journal for Quality in Health Care*, *29*(5), 722–727. doi:10.1093/intqhc/mzx097 PMID:28992161

Weiss, S. J., Ernst, A. A., Derlet, R., King, R., Bair, A., & Nick, T. G. (2005). Relationship between the National ED Overcrowding Scale and the number of patients who leave without being seen in an academic ED. *The American Journal of Emergency Medicine*, *23*(3), 288–294. doi:10.1016/j.ajem.2005.02.034 PMID:15915399

Weiss, S. J., Ernst, A. A., & Nick, T. G. (2006). Comparison of the National Emergency Department Overcrowding Scale and the Emergency Department Work Index for Quantifying Emergency Department Crowding. *Academic Emergency Medicine*, *13*(5), 513–518. doi:10.1197/j.aem.2005.12.009 PMID:16551777

Chapter 6
Single-Minute Exchange of Die (SMED) and Lean Healthcare:
Reducing Patient Journey in Emergency Care Units

Andrei Bonamigo
https://orcid.org/0000-0002-6670-9755
Fluminense Federal University, Brazil

Patricia Mendonça Maia Bernardes
Fluminense Federal University, Brazil

Luiz Felipe Conrado
Fluminense Federal University, Brazil

Newton Narciso Pereira
Fluminense Federal University, Brazil

EXECUTIVE SUMMARY

Lean healthcare presents as a potential means to overcome barriers in the health sector by eliminating unnecessary movements, waiting, transport, and stockpiles. However, time spent in set-up activities does not add value to the process because the patient is not receiving service. One of the Lean tools that can help mitigate waste in those activities is the single-minute exchange of die (SMED); therefore, this study aims to evaluate the implications of using SMED in the health context. The authors conducted an exploratory search in scientific documents to achieve this goal. The content analysis was based on Bardin. From the findings, it is possible to identify the implications of the use of SMED in the health context, sort activities between internal and external setup, and reduce time spent on wasteful tasks, while increasing time available for value-adding activities.

DOI: 10.4018/978-1-6684-5185-4.ch006

INTRODUCTION

The goal of the healthcare field is, for all intents and purposes, to maximize the value of services provided to clients (Singh, 2021). When thinking about hospitals, clinics, and other healthcare facilities, it's important to remember that the outcomes and items given are health and treatments for patients (Franco, 2020). One of the ways to achieve this while meeting organizational goals is through the Lean methodology adoption (Davis, 2010), which can be applied in healthcare facilities through the Lean Healthcare use. Providing reliable, safe, and quality care while constantly seeking efficiencies is one of the challenges in healthcare (Hallam, 2018). Combined with the Lean approach to cost and waste reduction, Lean Healthcare offers great opportunities to become a significant area of research.

Many systems in health care are inefficient, and they end up causing more suffering to clients (who, for this study, will particularly be referred to as patients) than benefits. Although many of these inefficiencies are culturally ingrained in the daily exchanges of the businesses, they are the main reasons for patient dissatisfaction (Leite, 2019).

One of the main factors that can greatly reduce the value of the service to the customer is the waiting time, which is usually associated with negative experiences (Barlow, 2002; Bielen and Demoulin, 2007). Given that fact, the Single-Minute Exchange of Die (SMED) technique is a Lean tool known for its focus on optimizing set-up activities, with the goal of reducing idle time. Although this is a widely known shortcoming, not many studies address the Lean implementation and SMED in healthcare, and it deals with some criticism regarding its origins in industrial manufacturing, as the cultural underpinnings and principles prevalent in manufacturing and healthcare differ in several aspects (flow, products, operations, stakeholders) (Chiarini, 2016); therefore, caution is warranted when implementing Lean and SMED in healthcare.

Most hospitals, according to the Joint Commission on Accreditation of Healthcare Organizations (2006), use "conventional management thinking", focusing on individual healthcare activities rather than processes. Local improvement (or improvement in operations) is prioritized in conventional management thought, which is still visible in manufacturing. Lean Thinking, on the other hand, transfers the focus of improvement from individual tasks to the process (or patient pathway), which is defined as "a set of activities that must be executed in the proper sequence and at the appropriate time to suit the demands of the patient" (de Souza and Pidd, 2011). Lean is most effective when applied across the entire process, from determining the need for a service to delivering that service without interruption.

Because of the large number of variables and the unpredictable nature of their interactions, healthcare systems are indeterministic, which means that future states and configurations cannot be easily anticipated by looking at and extrapolating previous data (Franco, 2020). Furthermore, the healthcare sector has faced numerous challenges around the world in the recent decade, such as limited resources (be it staff, equipment, or space), increased demand given the rise in population size and unhealthy lifestyles, and economic crisis (Franco, 2020). As a result, it's critical to find new ways to provide care more effectively while also exceeding customers' expectations (Crema and Verbano, 2021).

Delivering and financing high-quality healthcare services has been a major global goal recently, mainly because healthcare quality reflects citizens' perceptions of their quality of life. However, according to Franco (2020), this ecosystem faces important challenges such as:

- **Rising Costs:** this might be due to a variety of circumstances, such as an unanticipated increase in demand due to an aging population or lifestyle-related disorders (mainly alcohol, smoke, drugs, and obesity). The advent of new technologies and medicines, which may increase demand — but also expenses — associated with their implementation, is another factor driving up demand (Hurst, 2000).
- **Shift from Supply-Driven to Demand-Driven:** patients frequently demand the finest possible service quality at the lowest possible cost and with the fastest possible processing times. Customers have easier access to the medical information on the internet, which raises their awareness of their medical needs and desires and reduces information asymmetry. As a result, healthcare firms should place a greater emphasis on what customers desire.
- **Cybersecurity:** the health department has become an easy target for cybercrime, given the amount of sensitive information about patients collected by information systems. Not only to guarantee the confidentiality of medical records, but also to avoid injunctions for violations of security standards, healthcare organizations should strengthen their reaction to cybercriminals.

Within the Lean philosophy, various strategies can be used to optimize management and considering that waiting time is one of the biggest problems in healthcare, SMED can be a well-suited tool for this purpose because of its focus on reducing "set-up time" and "changeover time" (Ani and Shafei, 2014). Thus, this study's purpose is to identify and create guidelines based on Lean Healthcare and SMED methods to lessen wait times in emergency care units, while increasing patient satisfaction and reducing wastes.

Relating to the methodological procedures, firstly, the authors searched for articles on Lean implementation and SMED in both manufacturing and hospitals. It was created a database containing articles and books on the Lean and SMED application in different contexts, was used keywords such as "Lean Healthcare", "SMED", "Lean Manufacturing", "Patient Journey", "Flow Optimization" *et cetera*. It was then used as analysis material to specify the strategies used exclusively in manufacturing, exclusively in hospitals, and in both settings.

Then, they were compared to highlight the major difficulties in implementing Lean in both sectors and to highlight the differences between the two sectors to identify common and specific problems. A research plan was developed based on the following questions, "What are the strategies, resources, or guidelines in the current literature for implementing Lean and SMED?"; "What are the practical differences between healthcare and manufacturing?"; and "How does the SMED implementation method in healthcare differ from the manufacturing method?".

Once the analysis was completed, some guidelines were listed based on the results, also considering that each patient is different, and each healthcare facility has a different reality (Peimbert-García et al., 2021). In other words, while a strategy may be considered superior for a specific entity, it may not be as well accepted in other unrelated contexts.

Furthermore, the main goal of this study is to create guidelines for the implementation of SMED in the health care area, specifically in emergency care units.

BACKGROUND

Lean Management

The term first appeared in the Toyota Production System (Arnheiter and Maleyeff, 2005), a manufacturing doctrine introduced by Japanese engineers Taiichi Ohno and Shigeo Shingo (Inman, 1999). At that time, the traditional production strategy was characterized by high volumes, large batch sizes, and long waiting times between operations, which usually results in inferior quality because defects often remain undiscovered until subsequent operations or even until the product is completed (Arnheiter and Maleyeff, 2005). The Lean production system, on the other hand, emphasizes small batch sizes (with the goal of a single-piece batch size) and the make-to-order approach whenever possible (Arnheiter and Maleyeff, 2005).

The Lean Management philosophy is usually described as "an integrated sociotechnical system whose main objective is to eliminate waste by simultaneously reducing or minimizing variability among suppliers, customers, and within the company itself" (Rotter et al., 2019). However, as there is currently a debate in the field of operations management (OM) about what constitutes Lean Management (Rotter et al., 2019), there is currently no single definition of this term (Pettersen, 2009). It can be presented as a "systematic and focused approach to guiding the learning, training, and practice of Lean principles by employees in an organization" and includes both individual and collective organizational transformation plans for developing a Lean change management system (Charron et al., 2014).

In addition to small batch sizes and reducing inventory, the main pillars of Lean are defined as the following:

- **Waste Elimination:** Lean focuses on improving customer value rather than optimizing performance. A customer is only willing to pay for activities that add value to the end product (Hallam and Contreras, 2018). Therefore, it is necessary to highlight activities that customers do not perceive as adding value and take immediate action to eliminate them (Tlapa et al., 2020).
- **Reduction of Variability:** this includes variations in product quality characteristics (such as length, width, and thickness), variations in delivery times, and variations in working hours (especially downtime, absenteeism, and lack of employee qualifications). It can be improved through standardized work processes (in terms of variation in products and labor times) and through partnerships and other forms of collaboration between suppliers and producers (in terms of variation in supply and delivery times) (Arnheiter and Maleyeff, 2005).
- **Zero Quality Control (ZQC):** meeting quality requirements is paramount to the pillar of perfection. However, quality control can often be an inefficient, costly, and time-consuming task that, eventually, is a chore that does not contribute to the value chain of the process. Crosby (1989) defines quality as "conformance to requirements". Ideally, in a Lean enterprise, every part produced would meet quality requirements without any quality control. This can be achieved through a combination of defect assurance systems (Poka-Yoke), automated inspections and audits, statistical process control, and complete paralysis of the production system when defects occur.
- **Perfection:** represents the core of Lean Management, and is achieved through continuous improvement (kaizen). For this to be possible, processes must be standardized, stable, and transparent (Bauer et al., 2018).

Lean Healthcare

Lean Healthcare (LH) is a philosophy based on a set of principles, techniques, and tools that optimize hospital organization and management (Graban, 2009). It originated as a service strategy to reduce or eliminate waste and activities that do not add value to the healthcare process. The application of this strategy can increase the efficiency of clinical care in hospitals, reduce costs, and improve patient outcomes (Tlapa et al., 2020). LH has already been successfully implemented in some settings, including intensive care units (ICUs), cardiology, surgery, gynecologic oncology, colonoscopy, pathology, radiology, psychiatric units, ophthalmology, otolaryngology, ultrasound otolaryngology, organ transplant centers, and clinical laboratories (Tlapa et al., 2020). A national study showed that approximately 70% of hospitals in the United States include LH in their plan of care or related strategies (Shortell et al., 2018).

The tactics of LH begin with examining a healthcare process and determining what is of value to the patient (Tlapa et al., 2020), which in itself is commonly interpreted as quality divided by cost (Ken Lee et al., 2016). In addition, value in health care is "activities that improve the quality of health care and promote patient well-being to achieve better outcomes" (Tlapa et al., 2020).

According to Amaral et al. (2021), the Lean Healthcare approach and its tools have been shown to accelerate the recovery process of patients in healthcare facilities, which can improve quality of life and reduce costs. When applied properly, Lean helps measure the value of each activity in the process and identify its variation to achieve positive and repeatable results (Vats et al., 2011).

Fillingham (2007) reports that Bolton Hospitals in the United Kingdom applied Lean principles as well as tools such as kaizen, value stream mapping, standardized words, pulled systems, and continuous flows to their operations and managed to reduce hospital length of stay for hip fractures by 38%, patient turnaround time by 33%, and mortality rate by 36%.

Based on their work at Flinders Medical Center (Australia), McGrath et al. (2008) presented a set of principles to increase the success rate of Lean Healthcare projects, which are as follows:

- **Customer Specification:** compared to other sectors, the healthcare industry has difficulty identifying who its customer is — and given the complexity of the system, processes tend to focus on internal customers, namely physicians, hospitals, healthcare facilities, and the government. According to the authors, the value stream must be focused on the primary customer: the patient.
- **Leadership Efforts Made by Directors:** employees need to perceive the commitment of managers at the upper levels of the hierarchy. The Lean program should be considered a priority.
- **Multidisciplinary Teams:** problem-solving should be done in teams consisting of members directly involved in the analyzed work and supervised by process optimization specialists.
- **Implementation:** according to the authors, this is the most difficult part of the process, and the managers entrusted with this task should have change management skills.
- **Focus on Patient Flow:** patients should be sorted by similar service delivery needs to facilitate the redesign process, e.g., elderly patients with comorbidities, patients requiring emergency care, and patients who can be sent home immediately after evaluation. The value stream must be designed to meet the needs of patients and their operators.
- **Data:** solutions must be based on evidence. The redesign is about getting different points of view from the parties involved about the problem and its causes and then confronting them with the available data. This should be simple, clearly visible, and available in real-time so that errors can be analyzed and corrected.

- **Goals and Deadlines:** the desired results should be ambitious, but at the same time realistic. Achieving goals can motivate employees and inspire innovation, which together can lead to amazing results.
- **Process Management:** training and external support should be considered. The use of external consultants can be an effective tool to overcome obstacles in an employee's mindset and facilitate the team's work.
- **Project Selection:** initially, the deliberate selection of simple, quick-win projects can encourage employee engagement. High-volume patient family improvements are also a good starting point.
- **Flexibility and Persistence:** the PDSA (plan-do-study-act) method is ideal for making the implementation of improvement projects more flexible and creating space for continuous learning.
- **Sustainability:** there must be a process of revision and continuous improvement of health services to meet the needs of clients. This process should be integrated into the change process to sustain the improvements and achieve higher levels of quality and efficiency.

Finally, the authors suggest a sustainability cycle — as described below:

1. Standardization: new processes must be documented, and it must be clear who is responsible for each duty, especially when dealing with new or temporary personnel. The removal of variance from the process is a key aspect of standardized work, and employee performance should be checked to ensure that the procedures are being carried out as intended.
2. Maintenance: each stream should have its process leader. This person is in charge of regularly maintaining, measuring, and revising work using performance indicators. They should also spend some time in the location where work is done well so that they may see how the tasks are completed and identify areas for future improvement.
3. Continuous Improvement: needed to meet demand growth, technological innovation, and quality standards.

Single-Minute Exchange of Die (SMED)

Shigeo Shingo developed the SMED technique in his 1985 book, "Revolution in Manufacturing: The SMED System." Its goal is to enable a fast and efficient transition from one product to the next (Karam et al., 2018) by reducing set-up times (Ani and Shafei, 2014), with the "running product" in the healthcare context being the sick or injured patient. This method proposes that set-up time should be kept to a maximum of 10 minutes, which can be accomplished by the machine operator's work rationalization (Rosa et al., 2017).

A process, according to Shingo (1985), is "a continuous flow by which raw materials are turned into completed items," whereas an operation (or activity) is "any action is done on raw materials, intermediate, or finished products by man, machine, or equipment." SMED must go through four stages to reduce set-up time: preliminary stages, separation of internal and external set-up, conversion of internal to external set-up, and streamlining every aspect of set-up (Ani and Shafei, 2014). Furthermore, external and internal set-up is as defined as following:

- External set-up: possible to perform even while the process is still running.
- Internal set-up: possible to perform only when the process has completely stopped.

Shingo's technique had a pioneering approach to achieve the desired small-batch, flexible production systems since it involves both the theoretical background on which the methodology is based, and the practical applications that can and need to be done so to lessen set-up time to under 10 minutes (Tekin et al., 2018). Below, the steps for set-up time reduction already mentioned are described according to Shingo (2018):

1. **Preliminary stages:** internal and external set-up procedures are combined in traditional processes, and what could be done externally is classified as internal, causing machines to sit idle for longer than necessary. At this point, the person in charge must research the actual workplace conditions in great detail to have a clear picture of what is going on. A continuous production analysis using a stopwatch, work sampling research (especially in processed where there is a lot of repetition), interviewing workers, and recording the full set-up operation are some alternatives for this study.
2. **Separation of internal and external set-up:** this is the most critical stage in implementing SMED because, while most people agree that stopping a process to execute specific activities is inefficient, those same people frequently fail to realize that they themselves display this behavior when executing those tasks. Trying to treat as much of the set-up operation as possible as external could help reduce the amount of time it takes anywhere from 30 to 50%. "Mastering the distinction between internal and exterior set-up is the passport to obtaining SMED," according to Shingo. Separation can be accomplished by using a checklist or check-table of all tasks involved in an activity; however, generic lists for an entire process should be avoided. They should instead be as detailed as feasible.
3. **Conversion of internal to external set-up:** even though the decrease indicated above is excellent for process optimization, it is insufficient to meet the SMED target. This step entails two key concepts: examining activities to see whether any tasks are incorrectly considered to be internal and figuring out how to change such chores to external. Internal set-up operations can frequently be transformed into external set-up by re-evaluating their genuine purpose. Following the analysis, trial shots should be taken, and the activity should then be transitioned to the external.
4. **Streamlining every aspect of set-up:** to ensure that the set-up obtained is already the bare minimum, each part must be thoroughly examined. Even though steps 3 and 4 are separated, they don't have to be done in that order; in fact, they can be done almost simultaneously. Improvements in the storage and transportation of components and tools normally help to streamline operations for external activities, but they aren't enough on their own. Internal operations can benefit from a variety of methods, including simultaneous operations, the use of functional clamps to hold things in place with minimal effort, the elimination of adjustment demands, and the relations of combinations indicated.

While the SMED approach is known for its ability to optimize manufacturing processes, it's crucial to remember that it wasn't created with the healthcare industry in mind. Thus, it might not be completely compatible with healthcare operations. Whereas extensive literature research was undertaken on the SMED implementation process, it is important to remember that the approach should be tailored to the environment and infrastructure of the process in which it will be used.

For example, the "unfinished product" in this case is the patient who has not yet received adequate treatment; while the "final product" is that same patient after release, healthy, after being treated. Set-up processes can be traditional machine adjustments (such as setting up an X-ray machine and sterilizing rooms for surgical procedures), or they can be directly related to the patient, such as the triage process.

MAIN FOCUS OF THE CHAPTER

Issues, Controversies, Problems

Most health care practitioners are unfamiliar with the Lean mindset, and once they understand that it originated in the manufacturing industry, they dismiss it as unsuitable for a field as diverse as health care (Chiarini and Baccarani, 2016). They are also concerned about losing autonomy and flexibility in the treatment of patients, as they believe that adopting a method that includes standardized work as one of its pillars (SMED) will limit their ability to suggest nonstandard treatments (Erthal et al., 2021), and they will end up treating the patient, a human being, as a "piece of metal," compromising the humanity required to provide healthcare (Erthal et al., 2021; de Souza and Pidd, 2011).

According to Chiarini and Baccarani (2016), "physicians and nurses can perceive the project to be something forced on them if they were not involved in some way". The management area also presents barriers to Lean and SMED adoption, mostly because managers prefer to take a "fire-fighting" approach to problems, resolving them as they arise rather than preventing them from occurring in the first place (de Souza and Pidd, 2011).

Furthermore, Erthal et al. (2021) state that, while the goal for health professionals and managers is patient recovery and the ability to provide patients with the best possible treatment conditions, the financial situation of the health facilities is a factor that cannot be overlooked. Private hospitals must make a profit for their shareholders, and they may be hesitant to invest in an expensive strategy without knowing if, when, and how much profit they will receive. Public health services, on the other hand, are not available everywhere, and they are wholly reliant on the government allocating a portion of its budget to them, and if such allocations are sufficient to keep the hospital afloat.

Moreover, many public hospitals lack the necessary infrastructure to operate their procedures as efficiently as they should, which should be considered before suggesting enhancements that are incompatible with such hospitals' financial realities (Levinson and Shojania, 2011).

With that, we can say that the biggest problems are the adequacy of the nomenclature, for something close to the health area. The need to transition between models for doctors and nurses, who may see the change as a reduction in service autonomy and resource savings.

SOLUTIONS AND RECOMMENDATIONS

Based on the literature review, certain guiding points for easing the application of SMED in health context were discovered. They will now be present in the format of guidelines that should be followed in order to ease the transition from the initial state to an optimized state.

Adapting Vocabulary and Symbols

Initially, to avoid alienating team members and opening them up to the new strategy, the language and symbols employed should be adapted to the new environment (Erthal et al., 2021; Ferenhof et al., 2018). As long as the fundamental concepts are applied, complete adoption of Lean vocabulary is rarely required (de Souza and Pidd, 2011).

Terminologies like "defect" and "completed product" should be avoided, according to Chiarini and Baccarani (2016), in favor of concepts like "error" and "recovered patient." Also, it should be avoided to reference the Toyota Production System and technical jargon of Lean strategies (e.g., instead of telling workers that the hospital will now be implementing poka-yoke, it should be phrased like "a mistake-proof approach") (de Souza and Pidd, 2011).

Non-Japanese words like "takt-time," "push/pull systems," and "value-adding activities" have specific meanings in Lean and SMED that may differ from general usage. When SMED is employed in production, though, the same problem arises. Sometimes, the use of Lean terminology appears to assist employees to adjust to new work methods in some cases, as evidenced by case studies (de Souza and Pidd, 2011).

However, developing a standard vocabulary to be used across the entire organization for SMED implementation is critical. Terminological inconsistencies between departments might lead to major misunderstandings. The idea, not the label, is what matters, but some terms may have to be changed (de Souza and Pidd, 2011).

Grouping Patients in "Patient Pathways"

The idea that a Lean-based healthcare model treats patients as "pieces of metal" is a fallacy, since patients are not considered identical, but are offered similar treatments if they fall into similar categories (de Souza and Pidd, 2011).

This type of model is projected to work along with the idea of patient pathways, which can be defined as a "sequence of care operations (procedures) shared by a group of patients (cluster or 'patient-care family' that are sufficiently similar to one another" (Ben-Tovim, 2007). A health unit or hospital can be perceived as a set of parallel patient pathways that may or may not share common resources (de Souza and Pidd, 2011). This implies that patients are still treated individually by physicians and are not coerced into clusters, though they frequently do so on their own.

In other words, even though patients are not considered as being virtually equal, there are often some parallels in the activities that they must undertake to receive treatment, depending on their treatment needs. Because those activities are repeated several times for multiple patients, they could benefit from standardized work and SMED to reduce their set-up time, resulting in a significant reduction in overall process set-up time, given their repetitive nature.

It's also important to remember that enhancing a particular patient pathway may not be sufficient. In geriatric care, for example, a decrease in bed occupancy (from 100% to roughly 80%) paradoxically created a problem by retaining unoccupied beds (de Souza and Pidd, 2011). Empty beds were occupied by non-elderly patients who couldn't find a bed anyplace else in the hospital after they were available on the bed management system. It's critical to optimize parallel patient paths by carefully evaluating how they interact (de Souza and Pidd, 2011).

Enforcing Cultural Improvement and Listening to Staff Concerns

According to de Souza and Pidd (2011), "beginning a Lean program with a big-bang endeavor, no matter how well organized, can still lead to failure if it is not followed up with a cultural improvement." As a result, every level of staff should go through a lengthy (but not sluggish) training process so that they understand that the new system will help the patient journey, and truly want to be a part of it and hope for it to succeed.

Their concerns and complaints should be addressed, and their suggestions should be considered; even if they can't be used in the indicated context, they may be useful to another department. Lean Healthcare does not have to be implemented in a single big bang; instead, it can start small and yield good benefits. However, for continued and continual progress, the correct mix of quantitative and qualitative skills is required (de Souza and Pidd, 2011).

The infrastructure and funding available at the hospital in question should also be considered (Peimbert- García et al., 2021), and these instructions should be viewed as guidance to assist shape the plan of action in light of the limits and resources available, rather than a rigid set of rules to be obeyed under any circumstances.

Gathering Process Data and Knowledge of Technical Aspects

It will always be a struggle and a genuine implementation hurdle to move health care managers' focus from problem-solving and firefighting to rigorous analysis, and to convert their decision-making processes from experience-based to data/evidence-based (de Souza and Pidd, 2011). SMED demands a balance of quantitative and qualitative skills, which may imply health care practitioners learning to use quantitative tools. These may be required to improve healthcare efficiency as part of a larger effort to improve performance measurement (de Souza and Pidd, 2011).

The successful development of SMED resides in satisfactory knowledge of the technical aspects related to equipment and tools, how the work is organized, and an understanding of the method itself (Rosa et al., 2017). Nonetheless, following Shingo's (1985) original concept, the first step in applying SMED in healthcare should be to define the entire process that needs to be improved.

This operation should include not only a list of all activities performed in the process, but also a list of known bottlenecks so that KPIs can be used to determine which parts don't require immediate attention, which parts need improvement, and what the expectations and goals should be (Erthal et al., 2021; Régis et al., 2019).

Optimizing Human Resources Usage

Because doctors and nurses undertake the majority of specialized work, their labor time is seen as the most valuable, even though it is the most limited (Peimbert-García et al., 2021). As a result, each task that can be completed by someone else should be recognized and delegated to another department (internal to external activity exchange). Furthermore, the department in charge of setting up emergency services should be assisted in its activities by staff from other departments (Rosa et al., 2017) so that when a physician finish using a room, another room is already free and ready to admit the next sick person, reducing patient waiting time and avoiding unnecessary idle time for professionals (Hallam and Contreras, 2018).

Even though idle time should be avoided for every employee group, especially for physicians, it is cardinal that they have regular intervals so that it's possible for them to rest in between exhaustive treatment sessions. It is known that short active breaks at work improve work productivity, well-being, and health when controlled and well-integrated into the task (Gallis, 2013). Thus, managing fatigue at work through mandated work and rest periods would reduce the effects of fatigue and increase employee work performance (Gallis, 2013).

Communicating Expectations to Staff

The expectations should be clear and fully understood by all members involved, who should be kept motivated and engaged to truly want to meet them since it is better for the system as a whole, not only for the sake of managerial orders (Davis, 2010).

The forthcoming changes are conveyed to all employees involved in the process, including physicians, nurses, and workers from other departments, before beginning any practical work. They should also be made aware of the required conduct that they must exhibit to assist with the process implementation (Chiarini and Baccarani, 2016; Davis, 2010). This should not be done in an overbearing way. Instead, participants must be enticed to desire to enhance the process by incentives such as monetary bonuses or other benefits received as a result of ranking systems (Chiarini and Baccarani, 2016).

Creating an Integrated Lean System

Whereas SMED is a useful tool for improving health processes, it is incapable of solving every waste complication in the setting (Rosa et al., 2017); as a result, it should be used with other Lean tools and strategies, such as kanban, poka-yoke, and value stream mapping (Peimbert-García et al., 2021; Régis et al., 2019; Ferenhof et al., 2018; Lobo et al., 2018).

Finally, these standards should become a normal part of daily life, and training for them should continue indefinitely (Hallam and Contreras, 2018). Regular checks should be made to ensure that none of the processes are forgotten, and any errors should be remedied with additional training rather than punishment (Hallam and Contreras, 2018).

FUTURE RESEARCH DIRECTIONS

Based on this study's findings, we can evidence a part of the potential implications adopting SMED in healthcare has, since reducing the patient journey can lead to also lowering costs and increasing user satisfaction. SMED, which is unable to operate alone, combines people's mindsets and growth as the foundation for organizational culture modifications with the goal of continual improvement. This means that anyone who wishes to implement it must be aware that SMED does not operate like most tools, which remain relatively static once installed. SMED, on the other hand, appears to be a dynamic instrument that should be updated as needed, given the ongoing change of processes and operations.

This requires the use of incremental improvements in set-up processes. As a result, future research on the creation of a Lean organizational culture is critical for the SMED's continuation and maintenance in health care organizations. Those researches should include ideas for terminology and symbols to be used, since this has been demonstrated to be a significant factor in making it more convenient for healthcare professionals to adapt. Moreover, there are gaps in the literature for management models and frameworks to guide the SMED implementation, which can also lead to significant research opportunities.

Furthermore, there are still few studies on SMED implementation in health units that show how SMED was de facto installed, together with which other tools were used alongside it, what was the unit's infrastructure situation and possibilities before the intervention, found problems, and the specific results achieved, paired with statistical evidence. As a result, case study researches can help to expand the content of this topic, and it should be as specific as possible to allow researchers to learn exactly how it was done so that they can apply it to other undertakings.

CONCLUSION

The positive contribution of Lean Healthcare in hospital and emergency units has been widely documented in recent literature; nonetheless, there is still a gap in terms of set-up time management regarding the patient's journey. The SMED tool can be used to help determine which activities in a

process add value or not to the patient journey, and what is their impact on the set-up time. Furthermore, this tool can be used at different stages of the patient flow (e.g., scheduling, sorting, consultation, and post-consultation).

Although the SMED technique has been widely adopted in industries such as manufacturing, it is still new to the health care industry. Given the vast differences in the elements of each sector, this makes it difficult for health professionals to adjust to changes. Nonetheless, SMED implementation allows for significant contributions from the Lean Healthcare industry, and it helps pave the way for a new health approach with reduced patient wait times and stress, as well as increased production quality.

Based on the findings, it is clear that people are a critical factor in the success of SMED, as improvement actions based on Lean begin with a shift in the work routine, which necessarily involves knowledge, skills, and a holistic perspective to identify set-up waste points and address them to improve processes and shorten the patient's journey in health emergency care units.

With the presented discoveries, we hope to assist health managers, consultants, researchers, and the government in implementing activities to enhance the health management system based on SMED adoption, as well as give decision-making support from a Lean Healthcare perspective.

ACKNOWLEDGMENT

The authors would like to thank the Brazilian Ministry of Health, UFF - Universidade Federal Fluminense, and Euclides da Cunha Foundation. This Research is part of the" Lean Project in UPA 24h" that has been funded by the Brazilian Ministry of Health (TED 15/2021, number: 25000.103452/2021-14).

REFERENCES

Amaral, L. C. D., Calado, R. D., Teixeira, A. M., Silva, M. H. T. D., Bourguignon, S. C., & Costa, H. G. (2020). *Systematic review and meta-analysis of the use of lean methods and tools in healthcare services: An alternative to improve care during the pandemic*. Academic Press.

Arnheiter, E. D., & Maleyeff, J. (2005). The integration of lean management and Six Sigma. *The TQM Magazine*, *17*(1), 5–18. doi:10.1108/09544780510573020

Barlow, G. L. (2002). Auditing hospital queuing. *Managerial Auditing Journal*, *17*(1), 397–403.

Bauer, H., Brandl, F., Lock, C., & Reinhart, G. (2018). Integration of Industrie 4.0 in lean manufacturing learning factories. *Procedia Manufacturing*, *23*, 147–152.

Ben-Tovim, D. I. (2007). Seeing the picture through "lean thinking". *BMJ (Clinical Research Ed.)*, *334*(7586), 169–169.

Bertani, T. M. (2012). *Lean Healthcare: Recomendações para implantações dos conceitos de produção enxuta em ambientes hospitalares* [Doctoral dissertation]. Universidade de São Paulo.

Bielen, F., & Demoulin, N. (2007). Waiting time influence on the satisfaction-loyalty relationship in services. *Managing Service Quality*, *17*(2), 174–193. doi:10.1108/09604520710735182

Bin Che Ani, M. N., & Bin, S. M. S. S. (2014). The effectiveness of the single minute exchange of die (SMED) technique for the productivity improvement. Applied Mechanics and Material, 465, 1144-114.

Charron, R., Harrington, H. J., Voehl, F., & Wiggin, H. (2014). *The lean management systems handbook* (Vol. 4). CRC Press. doi:10.1201/b17201

Chiarini, A., & Baccarani, C. (2016). TQM and lean strategy deployment in Italian hospitals: Benefits related to patient satisfaction and encountered pitfalls. *Leadership in Health Services*, *29*(4), 377–391. doi:10.1108/LHS-07-2015-0019 PMID:27707152

Crema, M., & Verbano, C. (2021). Simulation modelling and lean management in healthcare: First evidences and research agenda. *Total Quality Management & Business Excellence*, *32*(3-4), 448–466.

Crosby, P. (1989). *Let's Talk Quality*. McGraw-Hill.

Davis, B. M. (2010). Applying Lean to the perioperative environment. *AORN Journal*, *92*(S6), S100–S104.

de Souza, L. B., & Pidd, M. (2011). Exploring the barriers to lean health care implementation. *Public Money & Management*, *31*(1), 59–66.

Erthal, A., Frangeskou, M., & Marques, L. (2021). Cultural tensions in lean healthcare implementation: A paradox theory lens. *International Journal of Production Economics*, *233*(1), 107968. doi:10.1016/j.ijpe.2020.107968

Ferenhof, H. A., Da Cunha, A. H., Bonamigo, A., & Forcellini, F. A. (2018). Toyota Kata as a KM solution to the inhibitors of implementing lean service in service companies. *VINE Journal of Information and Knowledge Management Systems*, *48*(3), 404–426. doi:10.1108/VJIKMS-11-2017-0083

Fillingham, D. (2007). Can lean save lives? *Leadership in Health Services*, *20*(4), 231–241. doi:10.1108/17511870710829346 PMID:20698096

Franco, L. (2020). *Lean healthcare application for patient flow analysis in Cardiology department* [Doctoral dissertation]. Politecnico di Torino.

Gallis, C. (2013). Increasing productivity and controlling of work fatigue in forest operations by using prescribed active pauses: A selective review. *Croatian Journal of Forest Engineering: Journal for Theory and Application of Forestry Engineering*, *34*(1), 103–112.

Graban, M. (2009). *Lean Hospitals: Improving Quality*. Patient Safety and Employee Satisfaction.

Hallam, C. R., & Contreras, C. (2018). Lean healthcare: Scale, scope and sustainability. *International Journal of Health Care Quality Assurance*, *31*(7), 684-696.

Hurst, J. (2000). Challenges for health systems in Member Countries of the Organisation for Economic Co-operation and Development. *Bulletin of the World Health Organization*, *78*, 751–760. PMID:10916912

Inman, R. R. (1999). Are you implementing a pull system by putting the cart before the horse? *Production and Inventory Management Journal*, *40*(2), 67.

Joint Commission on Accreditation of Healthcare Organizations. (2006). *Doing More with Less: Lean Thinking and Patient Safety in Health Care*. Oakbrook Terrace.

Karam, A. A., Liviu, M., Cristina, V., & Radu, H. (2018). The contribution of lean manufacturing tools to changeover time decrease in the pharmaceutical industry. A SMED project. *Procedia Manufacturing*, *22*, 886–892. doi:10.1016/j.promfg.2018.03.125

Lee, K. H., Austin, J., & Pronovost, P. J. (2016). Developing a measure of value in health care. *Value heal*, *19*(4), 323-325.

Leite, H., Bateman, N., & Radnor, Z. (2019). Beyond the ostensible: An exploration of barriers to lean implementation and sustainability in healthcare. *Production Planning and Control*, *31*(1), 1–18. doi:10.1080/09537287.2019.1623426

Levinson, W., & Shojania, K. G. (2011). Bad experiences in the hospital: The stories keep coming. *BMJ Quality & Safety*, *20*(11), 911–913. doi:10.1136/bmjqs-2011-000474 PMID:21964611

Lobo, C. V. F., Calado, R. D., & da Conceição, R. D. P. (2018). Evaluation of value stream mapping (VSM) applicability to the oil and gas chain processes. *International Journal of Lean Six Sigma*, *11*(2), 309–330. doi:10.1108/IJLSS-05-2018-0049

McGrath, K. M., Bennett, D. M., Ben-Tovim, D. I., Boyages, S. C., Lyons, N. J., & O'Connell, T. J. (2008). Implementing and sustaining transformational change in health care: Lessons learnt about clinical process redesign. *The Medical Journal of Australia*, *188*(6), S32. PMID:18341474

Peimbert-García, R. E., Gutiérrez-Mendoza, L. M., & García-Reyes, H. (2021). Applying Lean Healthcare to Improve the Discharge Process in a Mexican Academic Medical Center. *Sustainability*, *13*(19), 10911. doi:10.3390u131910911

Pettersen, J. (2009). Defining lean production: Some conceptual and practical issues. *The TQM Journal*.

Régis, T. K. O., Santos, L. C., & Gohr, C. F. (2019). A case-based methodology for lean implementation in hospital operations. *Journal of Health Organization and Management*, *33*(6), 656–676. PubMed

Rosa, C., Silva, F. J. G., Ferreira, L. P., & Campilho, R. D. S. G. (2017). SMED methodology: The reduction of setup times for Steel Wire-Rope assembly lines in the automotive industry. *Procedia Manufacturing*, *13*, 1034–1042. doi:10.1016/j.promfg.2017.09.110

Rotter, T., Plishka, C., Lawal, A., Harrison, L., Sari, N., Goodridge, D., Flynn, R., Chan, J., Fiander, M., Poksinska, B., Willoughby, K., & Kinsman, L. (2019). What is lean management in health care? Development of an operational definition for a Cochrane systematic review. *Evaluation & the Health Professions*, *42*(3), 366–390. doi:10.1177/0163278718756992 PMID:29635950

Shingo, S. (1985). *A Revolution in Manufacturing: The SMED System*. Productivity Press.

Shortell, S. M., Blodgett, J. C., Rundall, T. G., & Kralovec, P. (2018). Use of lean and related transformational performance improvement systems in hospitals in the United States: Results from a national survey. *Joint Commission Journal on Quality and Patient Safety*, *44*(10), 574–582. doi:10.1016/j.jcjq.2018.03.002 PMID:30243359

Singh, S., Verma, R., & Koul, S. (2021). A collaborative method for simultaneous operations: case of an eye clinic. *OPSEARCH*, 1-21.

Tekin, M., Arslandere, M., Etlioğlu, M., Koyuncuoğlu, Ö., & Tekin, E. (2018, August). An application of SMED and Jidoka in lean production. In *The International Symposium for Production Research* (pp. 530- 545). Springer.

Tlapa, D., Zepeda-Lugo, C. A., Tortorella, G. L., Baez-Lopez, Y. A., Limon-Romero, J., Alvarado-Iniesta, A., & Rodriguez-Borbon, M. I. (2020). Effects of lean healthcare on patient flow: A systematic review. *Value in Health*, *23*(2), 260–273. doi:10.1016/j.jval.2019.11.002 PMID:32113632

Vats, A., Goin, K. H., & Fortenberry, J. D. (2011). Lean analysis of a pediatric intensive care unit physician group rounding process to identify inefficiencies and opportunities for improvement. *Pediatric Critical Care Medicine*, *12*(4), 415–421. doi:10.1097/PCC.0b013e3181fe2e3c PMID:20975612

KEY TERMS AND DEFINITIONS

Continual Improvement Process: An ongoing effort to improve products, services, or processes over time.

Flow: The way resources or people in a process move from the first step to the last.

Lead Time: The amount of time from the start of a process or activity until its conclusion.

Lean Healthcare: Application of Lean Management strategies in the healthcare context.

Lean Management: An approach to managing an organization based on the concept of continuous improvement, focused on maximizing customer value while minimizing waste.

Set-Up Time: Time needed to adjust settings and prepare machines so that they are ready to process a job.

SMED: Abbreviation of "Single-Minute Exchange of Die"; it's a Lean Management tool used to reduce set-up time.

Toyota Production System: The manufacturing production system focused on eliminating all waste from a process to make it more efficient.

Value: In a process, is everything the customer is willing to pay for.

Waiting Time: Time an operator, machine or customer has to wait after placing a request for an action or service and before it occurs.

Chapter 7
Lean Healthcare Approach With Fast Track:
Standardized Work in Emergency Services

Sandra Maria do Amaral Chaves
Fluminense Federal University, Brazil

Luis Enrique Valdiviezo Viera
Fluminense Federal University, Brazil

Saulo Cabral Bourguignon
Institute of Biology, Brazil

Luiz Eduardo de Morais Rodrigues
Fluminense Federal University, Brazil

Ana Carolina Sanches Zeferino
https://orcid.org/0000-0003-1213-0964
Fluminense Federal University, Brazil

Alexandre Beraldi Santos
Fluminense Federal University, Brazil

EXECUTIVE SUMMARY

The objective of this chapter is to expand the discussions regarding the application of the Fast Track method and the standardized work in emergency services with the Lean healthcare approach. In this chapter, the authors present some fundamental concepts to broaden the understanding of the theoretical/methodological implications necessary for the application of the Fast Track method and standardized work in the healthcare area, with the Lean healthcare approach. They present the case study resulting from the execution of the Lean project in the 24-hour UPA, which was carried out in 50 selected emergency care units, as a result of the agreement with the Ministry of Health through the Department of Hospitals and Urgencies (DAHU/MS) and with the Rector of the Fluminense Federal University.

DOI: 10.4018/978-1-6684-5185-4.ch007

INTRODUCTION

Overcrowding in emergency departments is a serious public health problem affecting the quality of emergency care and clinical decisions about admission. (Jung et al., 2021). The increasing use of emergency departments as the first contact for health is a multifactorial issue on a global scale (Heymann et al., 2019). Emergency departments have had an increasingly growing demand for health care, and efforts to ensure quality patient care have been widely documented in specialized literature (Chaves, 2022).

Emergency departments have become increasingly crowded, which congested access to health services due to a rise in demand, the blocking of access to these types of services, and, paradoxically, an improvement in clinical capacity in emergency departments (Ahsan et al., 2019). This increase in clinical capacity of emergency departments is a result of technological advances related to care and administrative techniques. Although paradoxical, as many vacancies emergency departments have, as much they will be demanded by the population.

In Brazil, universal, equal, and orderly access to health actions and services begins with the Unified Health System (Sistema Único de Saúde – SUS) and is later fulfilled within the regionalized and hierarchical network, according to the complexity of the service.

In Brazilian health care network, that are 24-hour Emergency Care Units, called 24-hour UPA, that will be mentioned in this chapter as 24h ECU, are in charge of providing care of intermediate complexity, and – articulated with primary care units, the mobile emergency care service (SAMU 192), home care and hospital care – aim to contribute to improving the operation of the Emergency Care Network (RAU) (Brazil, 2021).

Brazilia 24h ECU are structures of intermediate complexity between the primary health units and the hospital network. They operate 24 hours a day, every day of the week, and compose an organized network of urgent and emergency care, with previously defined pacts and flows, to guarantee the reception of patients, intervening in their clinical condition, and referring them to the other points of attention of the health care networks, providing continuity of treatment with a positive impact on the individual and collective health of the population (Brasil, 2021).

The relationship between the supply of emergency departments and their demand has been studied through numerous indicators that aim to improve care in the management process. Studies on the metrics used in healthcare to assess the effectiveness of the provision of services have been studied by several authors over the last few years. The indicators most used are the length of stay (LOS) and the left without being seen (LWBS), which are of great importance for managers to assess the performance of emergency departments in regards to overcrowding (Chaves, 2022).

Reducing the LOS of low-risk patients is one of the main contributions of the Lean approach. Healthcare with the Fast-Track method reduces emergency room overcrowding due to the agility of care for patients who require the simplest resources and are performed first. It should also be considered that overcrowding in emergency departments contributes to the increased rates of patients who leave without being seen (LWBS). These patients tend to return to emergency departments in more severe conditions. Therefore, the Lean Healthcare approach and the Fast-Track method, in addition to reducing overcrowding, also reduce mortality rates (Chaves, 2022)

The idea of processes and systems must be expanded beyond the company's physical space. It is not enough to be efficient in this environment if the activities that support and add to the products produced do not follow at the same pace. "The lean and standardized model encompasses a company in its entirety, from the source of resources to the consumer and the return of a new purchase order" (Pompeu et al., 2015, p.4).

SETTING THE STAGE

Lean Healthcare

Lean was a term coined for the first time around 1990, when Womack and Jones studied and published 'The Machine that Changed the World', a book containing the results of a global benchmark research on car manufacturing practices. Lean studies evolved and were introduced in other sectors until it was identified as a valuable practice for healthcare institutions, which is now known as Lean Healthcare. Lean thinking is a management philosophy that focuses on aggregate value for customers through waste identification and elimination or reduction. Its author defined 8 types of wastes (Pyzdek, 2021; Graban, 2016; Min et al., 2019).

- **Extra-processing:** Doing work that is not valued by the customer or is guided by definitions of quality that are not in line with patient needs. Filling in or collecting the same information multiple times.
- **Excess Transportation:** Unnecessary movement of the "product" (patients, specimens, materials) in a system. Unnecessary movement of materials that should be stored in pre-established locations; the unnecessary transit of patients for surgeries or canceled exams, forcing the patient to return.
- **Overproducing:** Doing more than what is needed by the customer or doing it sooner than needed. Preparing more medications than used; filling in more forms than necessary; accumulation of completed prescriptions; or trying to predict what will happen and preparing more materials than necessary.
- **Waiting:** Waiting for the next event or next work activity to occur. It is present in the waiting lines, waiting to receive care and medication, and waiting for discharge.
- **Inventory:** Excess inventory cost through financial costs, storage and movement costs, spoilage, and wastage. Expired medicine that should not be stored; empty or open containers that should have been discarded; request for more supplies than necessary to serve the patient.
- **Excess Motion:** Unnecessary movement by employees in the system. The unnecessary movement of professionals in search of inputs they do not know where they are; lack of prior knowledge of the infrastructure and organization of the workplace; messy drawers or storeroom that make the professional move excessively.
- **Defects:** Time spent doing something incorrectly, inspecting for errors, or fixing errors. Errors in performing procedures, such as operative Non-events; incompetence or recklessness of professionals that cause harm to patients, including death; incorrect filling of information. Performing procedures, such as exams, which will not benefit the patient.
- **Human Potential:** Waste and loss due to not engaging employees, listening to their ideas, or supporting their careers. When people employed in healthcare are not utilized to the fullest, their contributions are restricted, their ideas are ignored, and their skills are underutilized (Pyzdek, 2021).

Fast-Track

Fast-Track is a term in the scientific literature that alludes to creating a quick "path" for the care of patients in emergency departments. The Fast-Track concept can be applied in emergency departments to meet the demand of low-risk patients. However, there is no precise definition of a Fast-Track. Some authors refer to Fast-Track as a flow, others as a technique or method. Chaves (2022) studied the wastes identified and treated by ECU in Brazil. By analyzing the wastes treated and improvements that were proposed and implemented, Chaves (2022) identified Fast-Track implementation as a means to reduce wastes and conceptualized Fast-Track as a method whose application occurs by ordering or sequencing actions, focused on patients of lower risk or complexity. The Fast-Track method consists of a set of actions regulated by sequencing the planning and control of resources of the "shortest operation time first" type. Shortest operation time (SOT) are the ones that require small quick tasks, targeted at lower-risk patients. Having SOT executed first helps promote continuous flow with the Lean Healthcare approach.

In Lean Healthcare, the method can be understood as a set of measures strategically carried out, aiming at the reduction of waste and, consequently, the creation of opportunities with the application of continuous improvement measures. These continuous improvements, understood as good practices, consist of actions that, when performed, impact the work process so that the set of these actions can be named by the Fast-Track method, as they lead to the development of actions in a sequencing order, obeying the rules so that the most straightforward actions are performed first, followed by the more complex ones. From this perspective, it is seen that care for low-risk patients is prioritized when applying the Fast-Track method. (Chaves, 2022)

We know that interventions in health services, aiming to minimize the effects of overcrowding in emergency departments, have a certain complexity that, depending on the type of service, the professional qualification needed and the organizational culture, demand not only a conceptual understanding about the Lean principles, its methods and tools, but a deeper and detailed discussion about the implications of Fast-Track and other pillars of Lean, as Standardized Work.

Several authors have evidenced an increase in demand for health services that exceeds the care capacity of hospital systems (Chrusciel et al., 2019; Hajjarsaraei et al., 2018; Gill et al., 2018; Fitzgerald et al., 2017). An overcrowded hospital system is an inefficient system, reflected in several performance indicators, such as:

- Increased waiting time and patient stay;
- Lower number of patient discharges;
- Lower number of calls;
- Decreased productivity of hospital resources;
- Higher number of patient dropouts.

A poor operational performance hurts financial performance and user satisfaction (Chrusciel et al., 2019; Wijnen et al., 2019). Hospital unit managers are faced with significant challenges in managing overcrowding due to investment restrictions that would allow an increase in service capacity, having to opt for implementing operational strategies that increase the supply of hospital services without increasing resource usage. The deployment of Fast-Track in hospital units is justified by the need managers face to increase capacity and mitigate the consequences of overcrowding, having proven to be effective in improving the flow of patients (Liu et al., 2019).

Deploying a Fast-Track stream consists in separating specific and organized areas intended for low risk, low complexity patient care. According to health units screening practices, these areas are created when there is an increase in demand, causing overcrowding, which, when perceived, leads managers to a decision as the demand for service increases. Patients screened for Fast-Track flow are attended by a team of health professionals designated for this type of low-complexity demand. Figure 1 briefly shows a Fast-Track flow.

Figure 1. Illustration of a Fast-Track flow: the C area, the Fast-Track, provides care to low-risk patients, these areas are created on-demand, and more areas can be made.
This is a template for the Fast-Track stream when there is high demand for care.
These areas are not permanent.
Source: Adapted from (Hajjarsaraei et al., 2018)

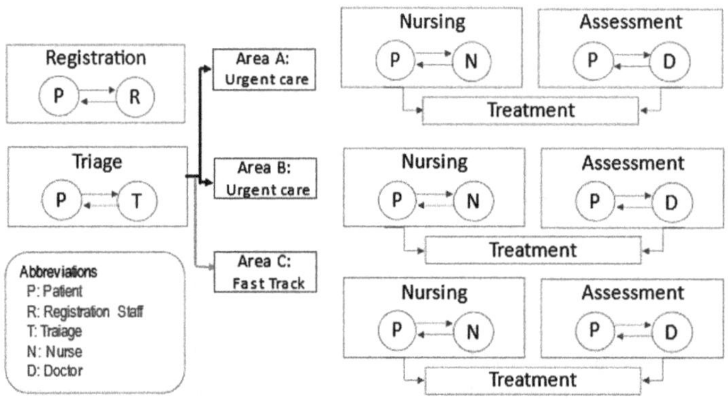

The Fast-Track as a method demands a set of actions defined according to sequencing rules, in which the least complex, or simplest, needs to be performed first. From this perspective, patients classified as blue or green by the Manchester risk classification are the low risk, low complexity ones.

Another aspect of great relevance for providing care for low-risk patients with the Lean Healthcare approach concerns the seasonality in the emergency departments. Seasonality imposes different cycles in this process, such as the day of the week, the time of day, the month, etc. The environment in which that 24h ECU is inserted, whether in far inland towns, in large cities, or in a coastal region, among other variables need to be considered when planning for service to users is carried out.

As stated before, the success of Fast-Track implementation has its foundations on standardized work.

Standardized Work

The organization of activities in a work environment is premised on the understanding and structuring of work processes. Structuring a work process means capturing customer demands by planning the provision of material and human resources. Such activities can be part of the sequence of activities inserted in the execution of the product or service, or they can be support activities such as the logistics of supplying inputs and cleaning the environments that serve the process that performs the activities inserted in the execution, directly from the health service.

At the 24h ECU, the delivery of the patient care service happens. The care process can follow a flow that comprises different sectors, from reception to the risk-classification sector, doctor's office, medication, or exam room, among other sectors, to discharge or transfer, according to user demand. For the processes to happen entirely and correctly, there must be standardization of activities.

Among the Lean approaches lies standardized work (SW). Standardized work is the management process involving all elements related to standardizing activities. Although this is not a new subject, there is still confusion between the concepts involved in work standardization. To ensure understanding, some terms need to be defined:

- **Standard:** comparative reference.
- **Standard work:** a work procedure that establishes the best and most reliable sequence for each activity and worker. Commonly called Standard Operating Procedure, or SOP.
- **Standardized work:** the practice of establishing, communicating, following, and improving standard works and standards.

The standardized work, therefore, encompasses the standard work. It consists of a people and process management strategy to guarantee customer value delivery. The development of the standardized work strategy, therefore, involves other practices such as TWI (Training Within Industry). TWI is the practice of training professionals effectively. In a simplified way, the way of training a professional recommended by the TWI is carried out in the workplace, in 3 stages:

1. The leadership explains the work according to the established standard work, including the reason for carrying out each step;
2. The professional performs the work under supervision;
3. Validation of the professional's aptitude for the function (Huntzinge, 2005, Liker & Meier, 2007, Smalley, 2005).

Standard work is the instrument of standardized work, in which standardization is formalized. Many institutions use SOP models that are more similar to documents to meet the demand of external auditors than documents to facilitate the understanding of the work and the training of teams. These SOP bring in their content, in addition to the introduction, the objectives of the procedure, the normative references that are used as bases for the construction of the document, the activities to be carried out, the definition of roles and responsibilities, and actions in case of anomalies. Such procedure format is not user-friendly, and sometimes, it is not clear even to who executes it. On the other hand, the standard work is also a document containing the sequence of activities, information on the risks of the action, demand and time for carrying out the activities, as well as the exact sequence of carrying out the activities. (Rother & Harris, 2002, Monden, 1998, Ohno, 1997).

In the Lean Healthcare approach, Standardized Work enables continuous flow, one of the Lean principles. And for the implementation of the Fast-Track method, the ordered actions obey sequencing rules that contribute to the reduction of overcrowding in emergency departments, as the service to users who were classified as low risk are provided faster, thus reducing the length of stay of patients in the emergency departments, as found in (Chaves, 2022).

As aforementioned, Fast-Track consists of prioritizing and sequencing the flow of activities in order to improve balance and allow low risk, low complexity demands to go further, making the whole process quicker. In order for Fast-Track to be in place, there are some standardization of the following activities in the process:

4. Standardization of trigger criteria to start and stop Fast-Track activities. The start of a Fast-Track process is triggered by the flow of patients and must be obeyed, since it is a protocol for the unit capacity management. It means the unit has to know the demand, its distribution over time to establish the rate of patients and/or the time to initiate it.
5. Standardization of care protocols in order to prevent variation. Once Fast-Track is a process for SOT, the risk classification process is crucial, the same way as defining care protocols for low risk, low complex lines of care that are known to be part of the demand. Those protocols have to prevent doctors from ordering resources that are not needed, like superfluous exams.
6. Standardization of professional (doctor, nurses and other care professionals) roles and attitude. During Fast-Track activities, each professional has a specific role to perform. If a professional does not follow his/her role, the flow will be interrupted, breaking the rhythm.
7. Standardization of team communication and training. The care team must act fast to assure the flow rhythm. Good and standard communication and proper training promote alignment, preventing failures and interruptions.

In order for Fast-Track to work properly, standardizing the work is mandatory.

CASE DESCRIPTION

The Lean Project in 24-hour UPA - Lean Project in 24h ECU - was conceived in partnership with the Ministry of Health, through the team of the Department of Hospital and Emergency Care and the Fluminense Federal University.

The three phases of execution of the Lean project in the 24h ECU were:

- **1st phase:** Planning, with the selection of the 24h ECU that fit the profile defined for the implementation of the project;
- **2nd phase:** Diagnosis of the current situation of each of the selected 24h ECU;
- **3rd phase:** Execution and monitoring of the progress of the planned actions.

The ECU that participated in the program had different characteristics, related to their location and size. Despite providing the same services and being a standard model, due to the availability of resources and sanitary and epidemiological realities, the ECU would have different challenges. In each of the 50 units, training was carried out to identify wastes. For the wastes identified, continuous improvement actions and projects were proposed. The 24h ECU that participated at the project, 18 (36%) were located in São Paulo state, 12 (24%) were located in Ceará state, 6 (12%) were located at the Federal State, 4 (8%) were located in Maranhão state, 3 (6%) were located in Santa Catarina state, 3 (6%) were located in Goiás state, 2 (4%) were located in Tocantins state, 1 (2%) were located in Mato Grosso state and 1 (2%) were located in Rio de Janeiro state.

In spite of each situation, the problems and wastes identified by the ECU team during the project were quite the same. The difference was their impact, more than the kind of waste identified.

The most frequent wastes identified by the teams and present in the improvements implemented were related to defects, excess movements and not using human potential. Fast-Track addresses all those wastes when standardizing processes, behaviors, communication and training (Reports Project for the Restructuring and Implementation of Humanization in the Patient Care Flow in 24h ECU).

CURRENT CHALLENGES FACING THE ORGANIZATION

Considering Fast-Track is highly dependent on standardization, there are several challenges faced by the ECU in its implementation. Some challenges are human related, others are resources related and others are processes related.

The Fast-Track method is a method that demands, first and foremost, an understanding of human interaction from a psychological viewpoint, because every change brings at least discomfort, and no matter how good the actions are, it is necessary to assess to what extent these changes will bring benefits, not for one or another person, but all (Chaves, 2022).

Based on the records of improvements implemented in the 24h ECU, Chaves (2022), clusterized the challenges using data mining conducted by IRAMUTEQ (*Interface de R pour les analyses multidimensionnelles de textes et de questionnaires*).

Data Mining Using R at IRAMUTEQ Software

Data mining was performed using the IRAMUTEQ software, which made textual statistical analysis possible. This software was developed in Python and uses features provided by the statistical software R. (LOUBÈRE, 2014; MORAES; GALIAZZI, 2006; RITTER, et.al., 2019). R is a free software for data analysis that came from a collaborative effort of people in various locations around the world (RITTER, 2019). IRAMUTEQ establishes an interface with R and prepares the multidimensional analysis of the database with the textual corpus. The preparation of the data consists of the elaboration of the scripts, later read and analyzed by the software R. The data, shown through the graphs, are the result of the junction of these two applications (FERNANDES, 2014).

Data mining with IRAMUTEQ software allowed for the clusterization of issues identified by the ECU by processing the database related to opportunities and continuous improvements. For each of these databases, six classes were clustered; these are correlated because the opportunities identified by the teams in the 50 ECU allowed these teams to intervene in the implementation of continuous improvement actions.

Clusterization Results

Cluster 1 – Work Processes

In this cluster, failures were identified as those that contribute to problems related to the lack of information in the attendance records. Records are filled manually, which causes inconvenience, both for the team and for the patients, once records will have to be filled in again, which makes patients stay longer in the unit in order to be seen by the physician.

Filling out service forms is related to the lack of complete forms, as those found in the units are old models of forms that no longer meet the needs of the teams, in addition to difficulties in filling them out manually, which further delays the patient care, especially at the reception desks (Brasil, 2013; Drei, 2020).

In the analysis of this Work Process cluster, missing information on procedures records that took place in the patient care journey was evidenced. It impacts the billing process, which compromises the purchase process, for instance (Fernandes, et al., 2020).

Related to the transport of supplies and patients, there are two important aspects to be considered: teams' report indicated that the lack of ambulances for the transport of patients diagnosed with Sars-CoV-2 has become a major problem as not all 24h ECU have a dedicated ambulance to infected patients. The lack of supplies, especially oxygen, was a serious problem faced in some 24h ECU, in addition to other material resources that were lacking, leading to a delay in service to 24h ECU users.

Waiting time for the material to perform a procedure on the patient as well as waiting for doctors to evaluate patients were evidenced. The lack of work schedules defining a moment to rest, meal and get together to share information.

The waste of the team's time affects the care of patients, who are also waiting for problems to be resolved so that they can receive care as recommended by the current National Humanization Policy (Silva, et al., 2018).

Unnecessary material was present at the materials department. The teams pointed out difficulties related to organization of rooms, drawers and cabinets. Also related to documents archived in rooms that had been planned for other purposes, avoiding the team to use the room properly and interrupting routine activities. Many things are stocked and much of it is out of use and there are even machines that are already out of order (Amaral, 2021; Ivanov, 2020).

Work process discussion passes through ergonomics, to the waste of movement, considering the time that professionals spend looking for material, which forces them to walk long distances during work hours. In addition to have to bend over to reach the material in the disorganized closets, there is also psychological exhaustion, as the patient needs to receive care as soon as possible, and the delay in finding what they need is cause for discomfort and annoyance (Oliveira, et al., 2018).

The flow of patients, if there is no signaling, becomes a problem, generating work overload, excessive movement searching for supplies, which are related to the lack of standardization of most of the tasks performed and the lack of communication between team members, which causes misinformation, does not add value to patients (Viera et al., 2021).

Cluster 2 – Patient Waiting

Visual management, without an adequate layout and sometimes located in places of difficult access, in addition to the lack of signalization to indicate the flow of patients, caused interference in the service, as care professionals were frequently interrupted to provide information to patients. It also resulted in the lack of signalization on chairs to ensure social distance, which would have been necessary for the safety of users and teams in face of the current pandemic. These problems represent the type of waste that causes service failures with increased waiting time (Drei, 2020).

The disorganization in the sectors, in cabinets, with materials unlabeled or out of place, was listed as a major problem that contributes to the delay in patient care. As well as the lack of user-login change to the system when there were changes, which generated inconvenience by delaying patient care. This problem was also signaled as relating to waste failure, as they are related (Valdiviezo, 2020).

The unnecessary use of materials to carry out procedures was identified, concerning unnecessary processes, due to the lack of standardization of procedures in the risk-classification sector. The lack of recording of vital signs on patient forms and inaccurate notes about the color of the classification assigned in the care, also lead to an increase in waiting time for patient care (Magnusson, et al., 2020).

Transport waste in terms of handling was reported as relating to the lack of material to perform the service, caused by the distributing of materials in the sectors without adequate forms for replacement requests, which in turn causes the absence that results increased patient wait times for care (Luciani-McGillivray et al., 2020).

Regarding the waste of human potential, when analyzing the reports of the teams in this cluster, we identified the lack of a visual performance board, especially about the current pandemic, as a problem that is often not perceived by most of the people.

The need for training on protocols, on safety measures related to controlled drugs, for the use of Personal Protective Equipment (PPE), and for the humanization of care for users were punctuated by the 24h ECU teams, as well as the lack of professional qualification.

The waste of human potential encompasses aspects related to qualification and recognition of people's potential in the exercise of their functions (Dorval & Jobin, 2020; Jessome, 2020; Morell-Santandreu et al., 2021).

Cluster 3 – Material in the 24h ECU

Issues related to the need to delineate social distance were analyzed in the reports of the teams of this cluster, especially to ensure the safety of teams and users regarding the risk of transmission of Sars-CoV-2, ended up evidencing the waste of excessive transport of inputs, due to the reorganization of the spaces.

Failures were evidenced by materials or equipment, highlighting the need for preventive action and maintenance by managers. In this cluster, problems related to ECU linen, in the control, distribution, and the organization of the sector. The waste "failure" in this cluster was also described as concerning risk for accidents, particularly, the contamination with Sars-CoV-2. (Brazil, 2020).

The software for traceability of the stock of medicines does not work properly, due to the absence of a printer for the forms, which impairs stock control. This problem evidenced the lack of maintenance and the demand for acquiring new materials, as well as the inappropriate use of equipment, which caused losses in patient care (Viera et al., 2021).

The stock of materials demands a distribution as needed, with control for replacement so that there is no shortage in the sectors. The worst consequence of the lack of materials is the compromise in the care that the patient needs, which can worsen their clinical condition as it increases the waiting time for care (Fernandes et al., 2020).

The disposal of sharp material in inappropriate places was a serious problem reported, with the risk of disposing of contaminated material as common waste. This is because containers of contaminated material were found where common waste is discarded.

The biological risk of contamination increases when sharps are discarded in common waste, especially amongst cleaning professionals, who, even when wearing gloves, are at risk of infection (Brasil, 2020; Medeiros, 2021).

Cluster 4 – Patient Care

The waste "failure", is related to the need to organize the queues according to the symptomatic condition, confirming the results of the analyses regarding the issues related to the waiting time for patient care.

The teams signaled the waste, focusing on the reception of patients; the problems highlighted were given the demand for care for patients with suspected or confirmed Sars-CoV-2 (Brazil, 2020; Ivanov, 2020; Morell-Santandreu et al., 2021).

Regarding patient care, humanized reception was signaled as related to waiting time as a waste that needs to be fought (Dorval & Jobin, 2020).

Cluster 5 – Teamwork

In the reports on teamwork, there were problems with the disorganization of the sectors that cause failures in patient care, the meeting room filled with boxes of old medical records and other materials, making it impossible to use the room for meetings and training.

The absence of a proper room for changing clothes was also pointed out by the 24h ECU teams in this cluster. This makes teams very fragile and exposed to contamination in the face of the current health crisis. In order to develop teamwork, meetings are essential to improving work and to providing training on the various procedures.

The waste of failure and human potential are characterized in the face of these problems, indicated by the 24h ECU teams (Amaral, 2021).

The bench was used for the preparation of medicines with little space, with a risk of error in the preparation of medicines and occupational accidents, as the bench was being used as material support.

Forms that are difficult to fill out, with unnecessary information and without fundamental information, are filled out manually. It was indicated by the teams of the 24h ECU, as a waste of unnecessary processes, which do not add value and overload the teams.

The old format of the forms, combined with the lack of computerization, in addition to not adding value, impairs patient care, as the necessary information is not obtained (Amaral, 2021; Régis et al., 2018).

Cluster 6 – Sars-CoV-2

In this cluster, the identification of problems related to the need to place acrylic barriers predominated, especially in the reception sector, according to reports on Sars-CoV-2 (Chaves, 2022).

Questions regarding the marking of social distance on the floor and chairs. Furthermore, problems with the hand-sanitizer dispenser both for teams and 24h ECU users, were reported as opportunities for improvement (Morell-Santandreu et al., 2021).

Wasteful and unnecessary processes represent a significant portion of the problems listed by the 24h ECU teams, in this cluster of work processes related to Sars-CoV-2, as they encompass issues related to activities that demonstrate inadequate performance; in particular, related to the reception sector and attendance records, which were identified as one of the biggest problems in the 24h ECU, due to the lack of personnel to fill out the service sheets correctly and organize patient passwords. Separating suspected or confirmed Sars-CoV-2 patients presented difficulties in care, as there were no protective barriers and the lack of PPE further aggravated the problem (Brasil, 2020; Esper et al., 2020).

SOLUTIONS AND RECOMMENDATIONS

The records brought light into many issues that need to be addressed related to the lack of, or inappropriateness, or even indiscipline, in executing the standards. Most of the improvements done were simple and localized actions, although, based on them, it is evident that there is room for structured actions.

But without process standardization, Fast-Track will not be possible to run properly, and risks ending up as just another initiative that did not work.

Cluster 1 – Work Process

Considering cluster 1 - work processes issues, the urge to organize processes, organize the environment and update processes for the activities is clear. And, after that, training and providing clear information.

There is also room for automation: manual activities should be considered for change. The automatization may be done using simple spreadsheets or by buying copyrighted software that has been tested and works properly for this purpose.

Some situations reported, such as the lack of ambulances, raises the question of the need for a risk assessment and contingency plan. A risk assessment would also address safety issues such as ergonomics in the workplace and professional satisfaction.

Cluster 2 – Patient Waiting

For cluster 2 – patient waiting issues, simple solutions like proper signalization would solve the majority of the situations identified in the records analyzed. Since the signalization must be effective, the teams should consider implementing 5S, which was reported.

In this section, the need for training and practicing also arose as necessary. The teams should consider not only specialized training, but to use the healthcare permanent education practices to collaboratively understand and propose better ways of training and auditing the efficacy of the training provided.

Cluster 3 – Material in the 24h ECU

In cluster 3 – material issues, solutions are related to establishing maintenance processes (preventive and corrective) or, if they are already in place, training, auditing and making it work.

In this cluster, the ECU has to consider automatizing. The number of different materials and medicines are too big to be controlled manually, and there are available and viable technologies in the market.

Another issue included in this cluster was the handling of garbage, which could be addressed by training if it is identified that the root cause is lack of conscience.

Cluster 4 – Patient Care

Regarding cluster 4 – patient care, solutions lie on proper patient risk classification and pace of the workflow. About risk classification, the ECU should consider periodic auditing and training of professionals. About pacing the workflow, all the solutions described in clusters 1 to 3 and the ones to come will work together to pace it. And here is where Fast-Track is part of the solution.

Cluster 5 – Teamwork

For the findings of cluster 5 – teamwork, not only human-related improvements help but also solutions that impact the work environment, such as organizing and providing space for the adequate execution of activities. For teamwork, communication is critical and any action that improves communication can be beneficial: visual management boards, 5S, huddles and others promoted by the teams.

Cluster 6 – Sars-CoV-2

Since early 2021, the world has been dealing with the Sars-CoV-2 pandemic by imposing practices to prevent contamination, among which is social distancing. In that direction, are the implementation of barriers between patient and care professionals (glasses on reception desks, e.g), disablement of spaces between patients (mostly chairs) and increasing the frequency for sanitization.

ANALYSIS OF IMPROVEMENTS DONE IN THE 24h ECU

The analysis of the reports of the teams of each one of the 24h ECU made it possible to understand the different actions carried out through continuous improvements. The authors conducted a cluster analysis of the solutions to identify groups of actions implemented, once, the same way as wastes are interconnected, so are the solutions.

Improvement Cluster 1 – Teamwork

Improvements in teamwork are centered on the balanced distribution of supplies for the best suitability of them in favor of patient care, aiming to ensure an improvement in the time of care. For patients diagnosed or suspected of Covid-19, improvements were made to carry out tests, according to the indications of the contingency plan to combat Sars-CoV-2 (Brazil, 2020). The improvements focused on improving the communication between teams, filling in forms, reorganization of the patient flow, aiming to reduce the length of stay of patients classified with low acuity, which characterizes the implementation of Fast-Track in the 24h ECU that participated in the project (Chaves, 2022).

These actions reflect the results obtained in reducing the length of stay of patients with low acuity, considering the set of measures, such as those that translate the implementation of the Fast-Track method, which is not limited to the creation of a fast path, but to a set of changes in the work process which encompasses various sectors of the 24h ECU (Chaves, 2021; Viera et al., 2021).

Regarding visual management, actions were taken to guide the flow of patients through adequate identification and the standardization and update of the information wall and indicators board. (Brazil, 2015; Matias, 2021)

These improvements reduced the movement of the team to search for material and reduced the waiting time of patients for care, made it possible to promote the continuous flow and reduced the average LOS, characterizing the implantation from Fast-Track (Basta et al., 2017, Chaves, 2021; Viera et al., 2021; Lira, 2018; Oliveira et al., 2018).

Training teams about the operational flow of the pharmacy and warehouse, with the implementation of standardized operational procedures for the delivery of daily billing, among others, which were established by the teams of the 24h ECU, to avoid rework (Amaral, 2021).

Improvement Cluster 2 – Qualification

In fact, professional qualification is essential for the good performance of teamwork. The continuous improvements carried out by the 24h ECU teams present in their reports the training for humanized reception, as well as measures to update on topics related to hospital infection control and actions aimed at training teams to improve patient care about filling in forms, protocols, which demand attention when filling, avoiding rework (Matias, 2021).

Professional qualification adds value to people who start to carry out their work effectively in solving problems in their daily life. The improvements contributed to the reflection on humanization concerning the reception of patients and the reception among people in the teams, with improvements aimed at the correct use of PPE (Medeiros, 2021; Santos et al., 2021).

Improvement Cluster 3 – Organization

Improvements were largely directed to the warehouse and other sectors, with a focus on tidying cabinets and rearranging physical space. These improvements have brought valuable contributions to the reduction of the length of stay of patients classified as green or with low acuity since they reduced the movement searching for supplies and continuous improvements were made to facilitate the performance of tasks (Amaral, 2021; Magnusson et al., 2020; Tavares et al., 2018).

The linen department also received continuous improvements in terms of controlling and arranging items in the right places. The improvements in cluster 3 favored structural changes that considered the safety of the team in the provision of care and the safety of patients, based on the guidelines of the contingency plans against Sars-CoV-2. There are common aspects between cluster 3 and cluster 4, which present continuous improvements aimed at risk management (Brasil, 2020).

Improvement Cluster 4 – Risk Management

The improvements prioritized the reception sector, considering the severity of the health crisis. Therefore, measures related to everyone's protection and safety became part of the routine, with the reorganization of the physical space, to separate suspected patients or patients diagnosed with Sars-CoV-2, in addition to improvements directed to the use of PPE (BRASIL, 2018b).

The changes in the flow of patients, especially those related to the organization of queues integrating the need of social distancing by signalization on the floor and chairs, were improvements that contributed to the reduction in the length of stay of patients with low acuity and with the flow of patients, which after its reordering, favored the reduction of agglomerations and problems related to the risk of contamination by Sars-CoV-2. These changes in flow allowed the introduction of Fast-Track.

Improvement Cluster 5 – Equipment

The equipment available in the 24h ECU has been the subject of many studies, which point to the need for investments that are almost always scarce concerning public health policies (Cardoso, 2020; Nino, et al., 2020).

The improvements made by the 24h ECU teams are very close to the demands presented about the organization and risk management, as demonstrated in the analysis of the teams' reports. There was coherence of the teams when proposing improvements related to the demands for acquiring supplies and their storage in the various sectors of the unit, and also the care with the equipment in handling, avoiding the occurrence of accidents. The continuous improvements made by the 24h ECU teams made a great contribution to the hospital economy, as they observed safety standards regarding preventive actions for the maintenance of equipment (Amaral, 2021; Rodrigues & Carvalho, 2001; Brasil, 2018b).

The continuous improvements made also brought contributions related to the care of the radiology sectors, whose physical structure favors overcrowding, with the training for dealing with bottlenecks in emergency departments. Continuous improvements focused on patient access and service rosters. Contributing to the improvement in the flow of patients and reducing the length of stay of patients with low acuity (Jessome, 2020; Matias, 2021; Viera et al., 2021).

There were improvements concerning the delivery of exam results, in some 24h ECU exam results were issued by phone, to help control the pandemic, maintaining social isolation when requested by the public authorities (Fisher, et al., 2016; Hitti et al., 2017).

Improvement Cluster 6 – Patient Safety

Improvements were carried out, at the reception, with the signalization of social distancing on the chairs and placement of acrylic protection on the counters (Zibrowski, et al., 2019).

Improvements in humanized reception were emphasized by units teams, corroborating the current National Humanization Policy (da Silva et al., 2021).

The reorganization of the layout, the standardization of risk classification, division of patients into low complexity, monitoring of patients during their stay in the unit, and programming visual management to guide the flow of patients, are necessary procedures to implement Fast-Track in the 24h ECU.

Furthermore, the target situation is the flow of patients and their areas of application. according to the diagnosis of bottlenecks, which can be the reception room, triage room, risk classification room, radiology room, etc.

CONCLUSION

IN order to implement Fast-Track, the changes have to occur progressively, through the execution of the improvement after improvement, reducing bottlenecks.

The three-stage process was previously presented. In the first two stages, programmatic actions were carried out in the 24h ECU, focusing on training on Lean Healthcare, approaching Lean methods and tools. About Fast-Track, each team sought to create intervention strategies that resulted in a reduction in the LOS of patients classified as having low acuity.

The application of 5S enabled the entire process of implementing continuous improvements, which gradually spread to other sectors, and the teams began largely to create simple and easy solutions that resulted in good practices (Cosenza, 2020).

In the last stage of the structured improvements, activities were carried out to obtain indicators that prove the results of the implementation of the Lea Project. With the participation of managers, the data were compiled and presented in the technical visit reports.

As discussed, the Fast-Track method was implemented in the 24h ECU.

Accounting for results was a great challenge, and not all 24h ECU were able to show positive results but compared to the total of 24h ECU that participated in the project, the result was quite encouraging, even more so when we consider that the Lean Project in UPA 24h, started in March 2020, which marked the beginning of the health crisis. Therefore, the challenge was much greater, due to the uncertainties and insecurity generated by the pandemic among the 24h ECU teams.

Regarding the waste related to Patient Waiting, it was possible to see that the improvements aimed at reducing the LOS of patients with low acuity, with the sequencing rule, thus proving the deployment of Fast-Track. The continuous improvements made contributed to a humanized reception as patients began to be treated faster, with protective measures that ensure patient safety and, as the exposure time reduced, the risk of contamination in emergency departments reduced (Chaves, 2022).

The material resources of the 24h ECU identified by the teams with the waste related to the control of equipment and handling targeted at the provision of services by technically qualified personnel committed to patient safety. These actions reflect on the agility to solve problems that delay patient care and compromise the quality of this care, putting their safety at risk (Chaves, 2022), which resulted in a reduction in the LOS of patients with low acuity, as in radiology services, for example, improvements were made that contributed to the reduction of patients who caused crowds, as well as improvements related to visual management, which directed the flow of patients, avoiding long waits (Amaral, 2021, Drei, 2020; dos Santos et al., 2020).

Waste related to patient care was identified, in which improvements favored reducing the LOS of patients with low acuity, as teamwork began to increase actions for a humanized reception, acting on the demand of what patients needed, adding value to each stage of care (Chaves, 2022).

Teamwork, through the implementation of the Lean Project in UPA 24h, leveraged discussions on repressed demands related to communication problems, work overload, lack of training, operational difficulties, among others, which made it possible to create a democratic discussion space, where the problems experienced in the daily lives of 24h ECU became part of the agenda, innovative, in which suggestions and creativity in the construction of solutions began to be increasingly heard by everyone, which provided a plan to implement improvements continually (Chaves, 2022).

The continuous improvements that were carried out started to earn a space of representation, giving voice to users, through satisfaction surveys. The 24h ECU began to criticize themselves in the search for continuous improvements for the population (Chaves, 2022).

The health crisis caused by the transmission of the Sars-CoV-2 brought the challenge of overcoming fear and courage to react, the will to help, therefore, continuous improvements, aimed at controlling patients, avoiding agglomerations, ensuring distance, and reinvigorating safety standards with the use of PPE by the teams, among other measures, which contributed to the reduction of the length of stay of patients in the 24h ECU, with the implementation of the Fast-Track method, through the care of patients with low acuity, the positive results prove the efficiency of this method.

ACKNOWLEDGMENT

The authors would like to thank the Brazilian Ministry of Health, UFF – Fluminense Federal University, and the Euclides da Cunha Foundation. This research is part of the "Lean Project in UPA 24h" that has been funded by the Brazilian Ministry of Health (TED 15/2021, number: 25000.103452/2021-14).

REFERENCES

Ahsan, K. B., Alam, M. R., Morel, D. G., & Karim, M. A. (2019). Emergency department resource optimization for improved performance: A review. *Journal of Industrial Engineering International, 15*(S1, s1), 253–266. doi:10.100740092-019-00335-x

Amaral. (2021). Lean Healthcare: Lean Thinking, Standardized Work and the 8 Wastes in Health [Lean Healthcare: Pensamento Lean, Trabalho Padronizado e os 8 Desperdícios na Saúde]. *Universidade Federal Fluminense LabDGE, 2*(1), 16.

Basta, Y. L., Tytgat, K. M. A. J., Greuter, H. H., Klinkenbijl, J. H. G., Fockens, P., & Strikwerda, J. (2017). Organizing and implementing a multidisciplinary fast track oncology clinic. *International Journal for Quality in Health Care, 29*(7), 966–971. doi:10.1093/intqhc/mzx143 PMID:29177408

BRASIL. Tribunal de Contas da União (TCU). (2018b). *Manual of Risk Management of the National Agency for Supplementary Health.* Biblioteca/CGECO/GEQIN/DIGES. http://www.ans.gov.br/images/stories/A_ANS/Transparencia_Institucional/gestao_de_riscos/manual-de-gestao-de-riscos-da-ans.pdf

Brasil, M. da S. (2020). *Instructions for PSF - CORONAVIRUS COVID-19.* Ministério da Saúde.

Brasil, S. de C. (2015). *Visual Identity Manual - 24 h UPA. version 2.0* [Manual de Identidade Visual - UPA 24 h. versão 2.0]. Academic Press.

Brasil. (2013). *Instruction manual of the Emergency Care Network in the Unified Health System (SUS).* Coordenação-Geral de Documentação e Informação/SAA/SE. https://bvsms.saude.gov.br/bvs/publicacoes/manual_instrutivo_rede_atencao_urgencias.pdf

Brasil. (2015). *Main normative milestones of the interfederative management of the SUS.* http://editora.saude.gov.br

Brasil. (2018). Architectural Program Minimum Emergency Care Unit Upa 24 H [Programa Arquitetônico Mínimo Unidade De Pronto Atendimento Upa 24 H]. *Ministério da Saúde,* (2), 10–17.

Brasil, Ministério da Saúde, C. de O. de E. em S. P.-C.-19. (2020). National Contingency Plan for Human Infection by Coronavirus COVID-19 [Plano de Contingência Nacional para Infecção Humana pelo Coronavírus COVID-19]. In *Ministério da Saúde* (Vol. 1). https://portalarquivos2.saude.gov.br/images/pdf/2020/fevereiro/13/plano-contingencia-coronavirus-COVID19.pdf

Brasil. Ministério da Saúde. FIOCRUZ. (2020). *Fiocruz Contingency Plan Facing The Pandemic Of Disease By Sars-Cov-2 (Covid-19)* [Plano De Contingência Da Fiocruz Diante Da Pandemia Da Doença Pelo Sars-Cov-2 (Covid-19)]. Author.

Brasil. Ministério da Saúde. Portaria nº 10 de 03/01/2017, 1. (2017). *Guidelines for care model and funding of 24-hour UPA of Emergency Care as a Component of the Emergency Care Network* [Diretrizes de modelo assistencial e financiamento de UPA 24h de Pronto Atendimento como Componente da Rede de Atenção às Urgências]. https://bvsms.saude.gov.br/bvs/saudelegis/gm/2017/prt0010_03_01_2017.html

Brasil. Ministério da Saúde. Secretaria de Atenção Especializada em Saúde. (2021). Ministry of Health Health Care Department specialized specialized coordination of urgency and emergency [Ministério da saúde secretaria de atenção à saúde departamento de atenção especializada coordenação geral de urgência e emergência]. In M. da Saúde (Org.), *Programa Arquitetônico Mínimo Unidade De Pronto Atendimento Upa 24 H* (pp. 1–25). Academic Press.

Cardoso, W. (2020). 1 Introduction Going back to the historical evolution of the productive systems, it is possible to see clear progress in the managerial field of the same, since everything began in an organized way with the scientific administration of Taylor. *He Broug, 9*, 360–380.

Chaves, S. (2022). Fast Track. In *The Upas 24 H - Analysis of Opportunities and Continuous Improvements* [Fast Track Nas Upas 24 H - Análise Das Oportunidades E Das Melhorias Contínuas]. Universidade Federal Fluminense.

Chaves. (2021). Fast Track in Emergency departments an Integrative Review. *IFIP Advances in Information and Communication Technology, 631*, 241–249. doi:10.1007/978-3-030-85902-2_26

Chrusciel, J., Fontaine, X., Devillard, A., Cordonnier, A., Kanagaratnam, L., Laplanche, D., & Sanchez, S. (2019). Impact of the implementation of a fast-Track on emergency department length of stay and quality of care indicators in the Champagne-Ardenne region: A before-After study. *BMJ Open*, *9*(6), 1–8. doi:10.1136/bmjopen-2018-026200 PMID:31221873

Cosenza, H. J. S. R. (2020). *5S Organization, Quality and Efficiency of the Health Environment* [5S Organização, Qualidade e Eficiência do Ambiente de Saúde]. doi:10.22409/2675-4924.1

da Silva, M. H. T., Lima, A. D. C., Teixeria, A. M., Agostinho, R., & Calado, R. D. (2021). *Lean E PNH: a metodologia lean e a política nacionalde humanização* (Vol. 1). Revista Lean Nas Upsa.

Dorval, M., & Jobin, M. H. (2020). Exploring lean generic and lean healthcare cultural clusters. *International Journal of Productivity and Performance Management, 69*(4), 723–740. doi:10.1108/IJPPM-01-2019-0057

Drei, S. M. (2020). *Lean healthcare applied in the medical clinic of a medium-sized hospital* [Lean healthcare aplicado na clínica médica de um hospital de médio porte]. Universidade Estadual de Campinas - Faculdade de Ciências Médicas. https://www.slideshare.net/maryamkazemi3/stability-of-colloids%0Ahttps://barnard.edu/sites/default/files/inline/student_user_guide_for_spss.pdf%0Ahttp://www.ibm.com/support%0Ahttp://www.spss.com/sites/dm-book/legacy/ProgDataMgmt_SPSS17.pdf%0Ahttps://www.n

Esper, G. J., Sweeney, R. L., Winchell, E., Duffell, J. M., Kier, S. C., Lukens, H. W., & Krupinski, E. A. (2020). Rapid System Wide Implementation of Outpatient Telehealth in Response to the COVID-19 Pandemic. *Journal of Healthcare Management, 65*(6), 443–452. doi:10.1097/JHM-D-20-00131

Fernandes, B. (2014). Iramuteq Manual. Academic Press.

Fernandes, H. M. de L. G., Jesus, M. V. N. de, Silva, D. da, & Guirardello, E. de B. (2020). Lean Healthcare in the institutional, professional, and patient perspective: An integrative review. *Revista Gaúcha de Enfermagem, 41*. Advance online publication. doi:10.1590/1983-1447.2020.20190340

Fisher, A. M., Ding, M. Q., Hochheiser, H., & Douglas, G. P. (2016). Measuring time utilization of pharmacists in the Birmingham Free Clinic dispensary. *BMC Health Services Research, 16*(1), 1–7. doi:10.118612913-016-1787-6 PMID:27687973

Fitzgerald, K., Pelletier, L., & Reznek, M. A. (2017). A Queue-Based Monte Carlo Analysis to Support Decision Making for Implementation of an Emergency Department Fast Track. *Journal of Healthcare Engineering, 2017*, 1–8. Advance online publication. doi:10.1155/2017/6536523 PMID:29065634

Gill, S. D., Lane, S. E., Sheridan, M., Ellis, E., Smith, D., & Stella, J. (2018). Why do 'fast track' patients stay more than four hours in the emergency department? An investigation of factors that predict length of stay. *EMA -. Emergency Medicine Australasia, 30*(5), 641–647. doi:10.1111/1742-6723.12964 PMID:29569844

Graban, M. (2016). *Lean Hospitals: Improving Quality, Patient Safety, and Employee satisfaction* (3rd ed.). Taylor & Francis Group.

Hajjarsaraei, H., Shirazi, B., & Rezaeian, J. (2018). Scenario-based analysis of fast track strategy optimization on emergency department using integrated safety simulation. *Safety Science, 107*(March), 9–21. doi:10.1016/j.ssci.2018.03.025

Heymann, E. P., Wicky, A., Carron, P.-N., & Exadaktylos, A. K. (2019). Death in the Emergency Department: A Retrospective Analysis of Mortality in a Swiss University Hospital. *Emergency Medicine International, 2019*, 1–9. doi:10.1155/2019/5263521 PMID:31565438

Hitti, E. A., El-Eid, G. R., Tamim, H., Saleh, R., Saliba, M., & Naffaa, L. (2017). Improving Emergency Department radiology transportation time: A successful implementation of lean methodology. *BMC Health Services Research, 17*(1), 1–10. doi:10.118612913-017-2488-5 PMID:28870249

Huntzinge, J. (2005). *The Roots of Lean. Lean Enterprise Institute*. Disponível em: https://www.leaninstituut.nl/publications/Roots_of_Lean_TWI.pdf

Ivanov, D. (2020). Viable supply chain model: Integrating agility, resilience and sustainability perspectives—lessons from and thinking beyond the COVID-19 pandemic. *Annals of Operations Research*. Advance online publication. doi:10.100710479-020-03640-6 PMID:32836614

Jessome, R. (2020). Improving patient flow in diagnostic imaging: A case report. *Journal of Medical Imaging and Radiation Sciences, 51*(4), 678–688. doi:10.1016/j.jmir.2020.08.014 PMID:32950432

Jung, H. M., Kim, M. J., Kim, J. H., Park, Y. S., Chung, H. S., Chung, S. P., & Lee, J. H. (2021). The effect of overcrowding in emergency departments on the admission rate according to the emergency triage level. *PLoS ONE, 16*(2), 1–9. doi:10.1371/journal.pone.0247042

Liker, J. K., & Meier, D. (2007). *The Toyota model: Application Manual* [O modelo Toyota: Manual de Aplicação]. Bookman.

Lira, E. G. (2018). *Patient flow management strategies: Multiple case study in radiotherapy clinics in Belo Horizonte* [Estratégias de gestão do fluxo de pacientes: Estudo de casos múltiplos em clínicas de radioterapia de Belo Horizonte]. Academic Press.

Liu, J., Masiello, I., Ponzer, S., & Farrokhnia, N. (2019). Interprofessional teamwork versus fast track streaming in an emergency department—An observational cohort study of two strategies for enhancing the throughput of orthopedic patients presenting limb injuries or back pain. *PLoS One*, *14*(7), 1–16. doi:10.1371/journal.pone.0220011 PMID:31318942

Loubère, L., & Ratinaud, P. (2014). *Documentation IRaMuTeQ 0.6 alpha 3 version 0.1.* Available at: http://www.iramuteq.org/news

Luciani-McGillivray, I., Cushing, J., Klug, R., Lee, H., & Cahill, J. E. (2020). Nurse-led call back program to improve patient follow-up with providers after discharge from the emergency department. *Journal of Patient Experience*, *7*(6), 1349–1356. doi:10.1177/2374373520947925 PMID:33457586

Magnusson, C., Herlitz, J., & Axelsson, C. (2020). Pre-hospital triage performance and emergency medical services nurse's field assessment in an unselected patient population attended to by the emergency medical services: A prospective observational study. *Scandinavian Journal of Trauma, Resuscitation and Emergency Medicine*, *28*(1), 1–19. doi:10.118613049-020-00766-1 PMID:32807224

Matias, D. B. (2021). *Implementation of service strategy in an emergency care unit in Belo Horizonte based on the principles of Lean Thinking and Fast Track* [Implementação de estratégia de atendimento em uma unidade de pronto atendimento de Belo Horizonte baseada nos princípios do Lean Thinking e do Fast Track]. Academic Press.

Medeiros. (2021). *Risk communication. CIEVS | CGEMSP | DSASTE | SVS | MS Number 19* [Comunicação de risco. CIEVS | CGEMSP | DSASTE | SVS | MS Número 19]. https://sbim.org.br/images/files/notas-tecnicas/212611-rede-cievs-variante-omicron.pdf

Min, L. L., Sarantopoulos, A., Spagnol, G. S., & Calado, R. D. (2014). *What's this Lean Healthcare guy?* [O que é esse tal de Lean Healthcare]. Pedro e João.

Monden, Y. (1998). *Toyota Production System: an integrated approach to just in time. 3.* Engineering and Pressure.

Moraes, R., & Galiazzi, M. D. C. (2006). Discursive textual analysis: Multi-facereconstructive process [Análise textual discursiva: processo reconstrutivo de múltiplas faces]. *Ciência & Educação (Bauru)*, *12*, 117–128. doi:10.1590/S1516-73132006000100009

Morell-Santandreu, O., Santandreu-Mascarell, C., & Garcia-Sabater, J. J. (2021). A Model for the Implementation of Lean Improvements in Healthcare Environments as Applied in a Primary Care Center. *International Journal of Environmental Research and Public Health*, *18*(6), 2876. doi:10.3390/ijerph18062876 PMID:33799752

Nino, V., Claudio, D., Valladares, L., & Harris, S. (2020). An enhanced kaizen event in a sterile processing department of a rural hospital: A case study. *International Journal of Environmental Research and Public Health*, *17*(23), 1–20. doi:10.3390/ijerph17238748 PMID:33255618

Ohno, T. (1997). *The Toyota Production System: in addition to large-scale production* [O Sistema Toyota de Produção: além da produção em larga escala]. Bookman.

Oliveira, L. D. S., Costa, D. do N., Oliveira, D. M. de L., Almeida, H. O. C., & Mendonça, I. O. (2018). Quality indicators in hospital emergency services [Indicadores de qualidade nos serviços de urgência hospitalar]. *Cadernos de Graduação:Ciências Biológicas e de Saúde Unit, 4*(3), 173–188. https://periodicos.set.edu.br/index.php/cadernobiologicas/article/view/5177

Pompeu, A. M., Antônio, J., & Pinheiro, S. (2015). Production models and standardized work: An approach from artisanal production to lean production [Os modelos de produção e o trabalho padronizado : uma abordagem da produção artesanal à produção enxuta]. *Multitemas, 47*, 89–108.

Pyzdek, T. (2021). The Lean Healthcare Handbook: A Complete Guide to Creating Healthcare Workplaces. Springer. doi:10.1007/978-3-030-69901-7

Régis, T. K. O., Gohr, C. F., & Santos, L. C. (2018). Lean Healthcare Implementation: Experiences and Lessons Learned in Brazilian Hospitals [Implementação Do Lean Healthcare: Experiências E Lições Aprendidas Em Hospitais Brasileiros]. *Revista de Administração de Empresas / FGV EAESP, 58*, 30–43. doi:10.1590/S0034-759020180103

Ritter, M. D. N., They, N. H., & Konzen, E. (2019). *Introduction to statistical software R* [Introdução ao software estatístico R]. Academic Press.

Rodrigues, R. de C. M., & Carvalho, S. V. de. (2001). A Markovian Decision Model For The Optimization of a Maintenance System With Coxian Repair Times and Unobservable Phases [Um Modelo Markoviano De Decisão Para a Otimização De Um Sistema De Manutenção Com Tempos De Reparo Coxianos E Fases Não Observáveis]. *Pesquisa Operacional, 21*(2), 159–178. doi:10.1590/S0101-74382001000200003

Rother, M., & Harris, R. (2002). *Criando Fluxo Contínuo: um guia de ação para gerentes, engenheiros e associados da produção*. Lean Institute Brasil.

Santos, A. B., Calado, R. D., Chaves, S. M. do A., Nascimento, S. D., Silva, M. B., & Bourguignon, S. C. (2021). MDE-S: A Case Study of the Health Company Diagnostic Method Applied in Three Health Units. *IFIP Advances in Information and Communication Technology, 631*, 305–313. doi:10.1007/978-3-030-85902-2_33

Santos, A. C., Reis, A. C., Souza, C. G., Santos, I. L., & Ferreira, L. A. F. (2020). The first evidence about conceptual vs analytical lean healthcare research studies. *Journal of Health Organization and Management, 34*(7), 789–806. doi:10.1108/JHOM-01-2020-0021 PMID:32945155

Silva, I. N., Pereira, V. A., & Araujo, L. C. N. (2018). Implementation of the national humanization policy (pnh): Achievements and challenges for health care [Implantação da política nacional de humanização (pnh): conquistas e desafios para a assistência em saúde]. *GEP News*, 2–7. https://www.seer.ufal.br/index.php/gepnews/article/view/4674/3281

Smalley, A. (2005). The Starting Point For Lean Manufacturing: Achieving basic stability. *Management Services, 49*(4).

Tavares, R. S. C. R., Yukita, F., Geraldini, F. L. F., Franco, B. C., & Muniz, J. Jr. (2018). Success Factors For Lean Healthcare Implementation: A Bibliometric Study [Fatores De Sucesso Para Implantação Do Lean Healthcare: Um Estudo Bibliométrico]. *Produto & Produção, 18*(2). Advance online publication. doi:10.22456/1983-8026.60442

Valdiviezo, L.E.V. (2020). *Implementation of a Fast-Track Strategy In Emergency Hospitals* [Implementação De Uma Estratégia Fast-Track Na Emergência De Hospitais]. Academic Press.

Viera, L. V., Reis, M., Chaves, S., Calado, R., Bourguignon, S., & Lordelo, S. (2021, September). Evaluation of Fast-Track Implementation on Emergency Department: A Literature Review. In *IFIP International Conference on Advances in Production Management Systems* (pp. 280-288). Springer. 10.1007/978-3-030-85902-2_30

Wijnen, B. F. M., Hemmen, B., Bouman, A. I. E., Van De Meent, H., Ambergen, T., Brink, P. R. G., Seelen, H. A. M., & Evers, S. M. A. A. (2019). Cost-effectiveness of an integrated 'fast track' rehabilitation service for multi-trauma patients: A non-randomized clinical trial in the Netherlands. *PLoS One, 14*(3), e0213980. Advance online publication. doi:10.1371/journal.pone.0213980 PMID:30901353

Zibrowski, E., Shepherd, L., Booth, R., Sedig, K., & Gibson, C. (2019). A qualitative study of the theory behind the chairs: Balancing lean-accelerated patient flow with the need for privacy and confidentiality in an emergency medicine setting. *JMIR Human Factors, 6*(1), e11714. Advance online publication. doi:10.2196/11714 PMID:30724743

Chapter 8
Lean Practices and Assistive Technology in Emergency Care Units (UPA):
Improve the Service of People With Disabilities

José Ricardo Souza Ramos
Fluminense Federal University, Brazil

Sergio Crespo da Silva Pinto
Fluminense Federal University, Brazil

Ruth M. Mariani Braz
https://orcid.org/0000-0003-2224-9643
Fluminense Federal University, Portugal

Adriana Melo Teixeira
Minister of Health, Brazil

Ana Carolina Sanches Zeferino
https://orcid.org/0000-0003-1213-0964
Fluminense Federal University, Brazil

EXECUTIVE SUMMARY

This chapter deals with the application of lean and inclusive practices in order to mitigate the problems of the healthcare system in emergency care units (UPAS), especially when dealing with people with disabilities. The lack of qualified professionals, endless waiting queues causing overcrowding, waste, lack of supplies, and equipment are, among others, common "pathogenic" examples in the UPAS. The combination of practices and methods to combat waste and add value derived from Lean healthcare with the assistive technologies are fundamental for the adequacy of accessibility and improvement of care for people with disabilities. These practices provide mobility and autonomy to these patients, allowing their inclusion, improving their self-esteem and quality of life. The objective of this study was to investigate what is known about facilities and difficulties in the use of auxiliary devices, lean and inclusive methods, and practices to improve the care of people with disabilities in UPAS.

DOI: 10.4018/978-1-6684-5185-4.ch008

INTRODUCTION

Brazilian healthcare network, SUS (Universal Health System), is based on the United Kingdom National Health System (NHS) and is composed of primary, secondary and tertiary care facilities. Primary care facilities are responsible for the promotion of health within the population through the action of family doctors, nurses and community agents. Those professionals have the responsibility to take care of the family before they get sick and, if monitor them, providing necessary assistance before the onset of any disease and worsening. Secondary care units contemplate specialized health services, like emergency care units and polyclinics. Emergency care units are institutions designed to provide the assistance for patients that are affected by some illness and need medical evaluation or treatment. Such type of medical care sometimes are low risk situations like throat inflammation and sometimes are patients in need of a hospitalization but will have the firs care in emergency care units and them be transferred to a specialized unit, a hospital. Hospitals are part of the tertiary care facilities and are designed to answer for complex and expensive care, consisting of specialized facilities with specialized professionals.

According to the Ministry of Health (MS, 2020), the Emergency Care Unit (UPA 24h) is part of the Emergency Care Network (RAE). The objective is to concentrate health care of intermediate complexity, composing a network organized together with primary care, hospital care, home care and the Mobile Emergency Care Service - SAMU 192.

The 24-hour UPA offers a simplified structure, with x-ray, electrocardiography, pediatrics, an examination laboratory and observation beds. If necessary, the patient can be referred to a hospital in the health network for a highly complex procedure. Emergency Care Units were implemented in 2007, initially in the Southeast region, and in 2016 there were 446 emergency care units considering all regions. Currently, there are 620 emergency care units in construction, indicating an expectation of expansion. Federal funding was a strong inducer of the implantation. The states planned their emergency care units, but the existence of direct negotiation between the municipalities and the Union contributed with the significant number of emergency care units built that do not work (O´Dwyer G. et al., 2017). Also, the purpose of many UPAS is diverted with inpatient services and unforeseen medical specialties. The emergency care units (24 h UPA) have been designed to UPAs are fundamentally serve urgencies and emergencies and are structured with medical services, examination rooms, x-rays, pharmacy, fracture immobilization room, electrocardiography room, observation room and material collection. The basic purpose of a UPA is to keep patients under observation, for up to 24 hours, for diagnostic elucidation or clinical stabilization, and refer those who have not had their complaints resolved with a guarantee of continuity of care for hospitalization in back-up hospital services, through the regulation of care access.

Table 1 shows the size classification of the 24 h UPA versus recommended population according to Ordinance n° 10 of the Ministry of Health for the purpose of obtaining financing and resources.

According to the same Ordinance (Art.14) the investment resource destined for 24h UPA, in the process of financing and with a published authorization decree, it is regulated according to its sizes, population and some peculiarities such as locality, seasonality, diseases, etc.

Unfortunately, Brazilian reality shows 24h UPA overcrowded and with deficits in infrastructure and professionals. To aggravate this scenario, the population, in general, has limited or none understanding of the health system structure looking for care directly in emergency rather than in basic care units, the population is aging which leads to more needs in terms of health care, costs are raising due to economic and managerial factors and obsolescence is being present faster. The management of emergency care units

Table 1. Size classification of the 24 h UPA versus recommended population

Definition of Size Applicable to UPA 24h	Population Recommended to the Area of Scope of UPA 24h	Minimum Number of Beds to Observe	Minimum Number of Beds in Emergency Room
size i	50,000 to 100,000 inhabitants	7 beds	2 beds
size ii	101,000 to 200,000 inhabitants	11 beds	3 beds
size iii	201,000 to 3000,000 inhabitants	15 beds	4 beds

is predominantly municipal, with most emergency care units located outside the capitals and classified as Size III. The main challenges identified were under-financing and the difficulty of hiring doctors.

If the scenario is bad for people in general, it is much worse for disabled people, for whom, proper care requires necessary ancillary devices such as Tactile Floor and a Sound Alert Device in the reception rooms in the 24 h UPA as well as tactile signage in elevators, bathroom doors and other facilities e. g. canes, braille maps (where there is demand), to assist visually impaired and blind people. For wheelchair users, in addition to the wheelchairs themselves, access ramps, wide doors, safety bars and handrails are required. Most of these 24h UPA do not have many of these accessibility features and, paradoxically, there are normative requirements in the construction and operation of these Units. These Standards are established by the Brazilian Association of Technical Standards (ABNT), NBR 9050:2020 for accessibility to buildings, furniture, spaces and urban equipment and ABNT NBR 16537:2018, guidelines for the preparation of projects and installation. Equally important is preparation with intensive training of health care professionals to improve the quality of care and services for people with special needs. A survey by the Brazilian Institute of Geography and Statistics (IBGE, 2019) shows that 8.4% of the Brazilian population over 2 years of age - which represents 17.3 million people have some type of disability. A great portion of this population is attended in one of these Emergency Units but, unfortunately, face care problems related to excessive waiting time, and which is further aggravated by the common issues of overcrowding in the emergency departments. In the most varied opinion polls, the public service is the worst evaluated and the issue of management is pointed out as the main problem. Recurring discussions, invariably with criticism, about the conditions of patient care in the Emergency Care Units (24 h UPA), alert the academic and scientific communities about the need to seek solutions to this serious social and public health problem. According to the Lean literature waiting is one of the most important wastes (De Amaral et al., 2021) and the application of the Lean concepts is an excellent method to eliminate or at least mitigated this problem.

SETTING THE STAGE

According to Barnas (2015, p.143),

Patients are the center of our world. They are our neighbors and family members; one day the patients will be you and me. And so it is appropriate that we begin a discussion of the future of healthcare management systems with our rapidly changing future patient population.

Many challenges arise.

The situational cut shows the growing aging of the population with an unhealthy lifestyle, in contrast, there is a control of endemic diseases, thus, chronic non-communicable diseases emerge as one of the new challenges of medicine for the coming decades (Li Min, 2019).

Lean is the recommended method to overcome management problems in healthcare.

Lean Healthcare Practices

Lean a managerial philosophy of work originated at the Toyota Motor Company that have been spread to the world with the publication of the books "The machine that changed the world" (Womack et al., 1990) and "The Toyota Production System: Beyond Large-Scale Production" (Ohno, 1988). Such managerial practices have the objective pro reach customer needs in its totality, delivering good product, when the customer wants exactly in the amount and specifications he wants. These concepts were also complemented in the book entitled "Lean thinking: banish waste and create wealth in your corporation" (Womack et al., 2003). Despite its birth in the industry, lean philosophy has been applied by different sector with success. The results achieved by non-healthcare organizations attracted the curiosity of healthcare leaders, as John Touissant from Thedacare and the Virginia Mason Institute leaders early 2000 in the United States. Another example of Measuring Lean Six Sigma and quality performance for healthcare organizations is the study that "aims to investigate applications of Lean Six Sigma approaches and quality performance in Malaysian hospitals. It identifies five dimensions of Lean Six Sigma conformance (i.e., continuous quality improvement, Lean management initiatives, Six Sigma initiatives, patient safety and teamwork) and quality performance of the hospitals based on demographics such as gender, types of hospital and working experience" (Ahmed et al., 2018).

In Brazil, the Ministry of Health embraced in implementing Lean, through a program called "Lean nas Emergências" - Lean at Hospital Emergencies (In: encurtador.com.br/lrNR2), giving continuity to it with the program "Lean nas UPA 24h" (lean at Emergency Care Units). The program already lasts for many years and provide exceptional results like the reduction in overcrowding in 43% (In: encurtador.com.br/dt389), reducing the length of stay of patients in more than 20% (In: encurtador.com.br/lyBU0), reduction in mortality rate of 57% (In: encurtador.com.br/ctuPX) and others.

Lean philosophy is based on five principles:

1. Understand customer value
2. Map the process
3. Build continuous flow
4. Push the system
5. Pursuit perfection

The first principle in healthcare can be understood as in any other segment as translating customers' needs, patient, family, employee's needs, trying to understand what aggregates and what does not aggregate value to them. The second principle is about looking for how the value is created, looking for the steps in which the customer receives its service. Looking inside allows professionals to identify wastes and compare what customers want (and aggregate value) to what is delivered. The third principle is about balancing the resources to provide on time and high-quality care. The fourth principle is about delivering what is needed only when it is necessary avoiding wastes (inventory and space, e.g.). And the fifth principle is about being aware of new ways of doing things, new methodologies, new scenarios. It's about adapting and improving.

In order to fulfill these principles, lean has methodologies and tools. Are methodologies: PDCA or PDSA cycle, kaizen, A3, 5S and others. Methodologies are steps to be followed in order to achieve a result. Tools are instruments that we can apply and get results, like visual management signals, spaghetti diagrams, Kanban cards, visual management boards and others. All these methodologies and tools can be applied to help improve the healthcare environment to be safer and more inclusive for patients in general, but for disabled patients as well.

In this perspective the "6σ" (Six Sigma) model, Quality tools and methods such as DMAIC (Define, Measure, Analyze, Improve, Control), HFMEA (Health Failure Mode and Effects Analysis) and techniques of the Lean Management model such as the VSM (Value Stream Map), "A3", KAIZEN, KANBAN, TQM (Total Quality Management), "5 S", among others came to promote an improvement in the quality of care and inclusion for users of the Unified Health System (SUS) especially in the Emergency Care Units (24h UPA).

This practice has demonstrated over the years that Lean is not just a quality program, cost reduction, deadlines, waste, set-up time and improvements in the effectiveness of machines and processes in manufacturing units, but also a transformation of an Organization's Culture.

Emergency Care Units Functioning

A 24h UPA have been described. The overall medical care process follows all or some of the steps:

- Reception
- Risk classification
- Medical appointment
- Image exam
- Laboratory exam
- Medication
- Transfer or Discharge

The reception step is the process phase in which the patient is registered for attendance. The risk classification is the step in which the patient is evaluated following the risk classification protocol. This protocol defines the urgency of the medical attendance. The medical appointment is the step in which the patient is seen by the doctor, that defines the next steps (medication, image exam, discharge or transference). The laboratory exam step in the step in which the patient pass through a sample collection and waits for the sample analysis. The medication step is the stage in which the patient who needs medication receives it. The Transfer or Discharge of the patient is the step in which the doctor defines if the patient needs more specific care and must be transferred or if it has condition to go home and must be discharged.

Patients entering the 24h UPA can arrive by him or her means, walking through the front door or by ambulance, brought by rescuers. Rescued patients usually are the ones of higher risk and that have direct attendance.

Due to its design, only real emergencies should be attended. Most of the population should be seen by family doctors at the primary care units.

Assistive Technology

Assistive Technology – "AT is a still new term, used to identify the entire arsenal of resources and services that contribute to providing or expanding functional skills of people with disabilities and consequently promote independent living and inclusion". (Bersch &Tonolli, 2006). AT is any item, piece of equipment, software program, or product system that is used to increase, maintain, or improve the functional capabilities of persons with disabilities. Assistive Technology helps people who have difficulty speaking, typing, writing, remembering, pointing, seeing, hearing, learning, walking, and many other things. Different disabilities require different assistive technologies. (In: encurtador.com.br/akqv2). Basically, assistive technologies make use of 3 types of resources:

1. **Low-Tech:** features that can be built with simple materials. They are usually inexpensive and do not require or use electronic component. E.g., thickening of a pencil or pen to facilitate its handling by people with some motor disability in the upper limbs (hands); canes; paper printing, cutting, etc.
2. **Mid-Tech:** they use electronic components, but offer simpler features, without information processing capacity. E.g., pagers, token, TV monitors, games and toys with basic electronics;
3. **Hi-Tech:** they are more expensive resources. They use electronic components and process information. E.g., computers, mobile phones, electronic wheelchairs, digital games, etc.

As for the types of disabilities addressed and their relationships with Quality of Life, dos Santos et al. (2017) notes that "for people with physical disabilities, the use of Assistive Technology is linked to independence and autonomy to carry out Activities of Daily Living; health issues related to posture and breathing; and mobility and accessibility. Assistive technology offers products, resources, methods, strategies, practices and services that promote the functionality of people with disabilities, aiming at their autonomy, independence, quality of life and social inclusion."

According to the 2010 IBGE Census, around 45 million Brazilians have some type of disability, which may vary from physical, auditory, mental, visual or multiple. Approximately a quarter of the national population faces architectural, communication and mainly attitudinal barriers on a daily basis. The fight has been fundamental to conquer rights and improve the quality of life of people with disabilities.

The Ministry of Education and Culture (MEC) stated that the access of people with disabilities to schools increased 381% between 2003 and 2014. In sports, 287 Paralympic athletes competed in the Rio 2016 Paralympics, achieving 67% more medals than in the previous edition, in London. There were 259 athletes at the Tokyo Paralympic Games in 2021, winning 72 medals with a record 22 gold for Brazil, surpassing the 21 of the London games in 2012. In addition to the athletic scholarship and so that the positive results were growing, according to Its Brasil (2018), several rights were achieved, such as the deduction of income tax for people with disabilities, the standardization of accessibility conditions, the recognition of Brazilian Sign Language (LIBRAS) for the deaf and the quota law, which reserves 2% to 5% of vacancies for people with disabilities in companies with more than 100 employees.

Unfortunately, technology utilization, advancements and management practices in the Emergency Care Units (24h-UPA) were (and in some Units, still are) far from the contemporary concepts and technologies such as Lean Philosophy applied to healthcare. Prior to the implementation of Lean Thinking, Assistive Technologies and inclusive practices were not even considered in public services. Unsurprisingly, people with disabilities have worse prospects health and because of their socioeconomic status, lower levels of education, and rates of poverty levels compared to people without disabilities. This, in part, may be related to barriers in accessing services such as architectural, attitudinal, communication, information and health.

With the "Declaration of the Rights of the Child and the Rights of Man" in the post-war period and with the precarious conditions of care for people with disabilities within segregating institutions and scientific advances, a segregation process was implemented for the society for social integration (Silva, 2009).

CASE DESCRIPTION AND TECHNOLOGY INVOLVED

The speed that technologies have been giving to the management of organizations has caused a significant change in people's lives, but it is still necessary to increase the focus on better use of new technologies in healthcare, especially in UPAS. Lean practices derived from Lean Healthcare and Assistive Technologies need to be used to improve care and ensure accessibility, autonomy and inclusion of people with disabilities.

MANAGEMENT, CHALLENGES AND ORGANIZATIONAL CONCERNS

Answering Disabled People in 24h UPA

According to the Convention on the rights of people with disabilities (Brasília, 2012): People with disabilities are those who have long-term physical, mental, intellectual, or sensory impairments, which, in interaction with various barriers, can obstruct their full and effective participation in society on equal terms with other people. According to this definition, disability is nothing more than an unfair and very unresolved situation regarding the participation of people with disabilities in all spheres of society, due to social barriers and not to a personal attribute or characteristic. Thus, disability is the result of society's inability to adapt to people with impairments and functional diversity. That is, the cause of the disability is not found in the person, nor in the impediments (blindness, paraplegia, down syndrome, etc.) that they have, but in society, which places barriers or obstacles to their full participation. As a result, disability is understood as a shared social responsibility. In this conception, the main emphasis should be given to the perspective of rights and, as a consequence, people with disabilities should not be seen as defective, imperfect or incapable people, but as people in human fullness and, therefore, as subjects with rights that need to be implemented (ITS Brasil, 2018).

Publications of this nature lead us to a reflection on carelessness with health, especially in the care and inclusion of people with disabilities. Countries invest heavily in protecting the population from terrorist attacks, but not from virus counterattacks, which can be much more deadly and cause more economic and social damage. An uncontrolled pandemic brings down economies and nations. That's why health cannot be just a problem for the Ministry of Health. Persistent and growing socioeconomic gaps result in discrepancies in the care and quality of health of the population (Bioemfoco, 2020).

There are numerous challenges in Public Health Management whose list demands a response from more than one sector, not just health. We face shared threats, and we have a joint responsibility to act. The application of Lean as a philosophy of management in the health area, combined with Assistive Technology, constitutes an important methodology for improving the safety and quality of care in public services, especially for people with disabilities. These lean practices have demonstrated over the years that Lean is not only a quality program, cost reduction, deadlines, waste, setup time and improvements in the efficiency of machines and processes in manufacturing units, but also a transformation of culture of an organization. Assistive Technology, in turn, is an area with an interdisciplinary characteristic that encompasses products, resources, methodologies, strategies, practices and services that aim to promote functionality - related to activity and participation - of people with disabilities, motor disabilities or reduced mobility, aiming for autonomy, independence, quality of life and social inclusion.

The evidence that emerged from the reviewed studies indicates that there are relevant technologies and methods available for this improvement, in addition to standardization and specific legislation on the issue of accessibility that, with some exceptions, are not respected.

Practicing Lean in 24h UPA

The implementation of the Lean Thinking requires a commitment of the sponsors for the Units and an intensive training program for the managers and professionals involved with healthcare. Usually the resistance to accept a change in the care process comes from the Unit managers which are currently associated with the lack of qualified people in health care and other resources such as auxiliary devices and equipment. Generally, the resistance in accepting a change in the current process comes from the managers of the Care Units, who usually associate it with the lack of qualified personnel in health care and other resources such as equipment and maintenance service among others.

The challenges for the consolidation and expansion of the UPA in the governmental agenda result from a confluence of historical-structural, political-institutional and conjunctural factors, as well as the contribution of resources, via federal incentives. Regions with better socioeconomic conditions and better supply of services, such as the Southeast region, are more privileged in the implementation of an UPA. According to the interviewees (O'Dwyer et al., 2017), some factors explain this scenario of varied expansion in Brazil: divergence between political interests and technical criteria; financial or operational difficulties at the municipal level, such as hiring doctors; insufficiency of resources, as federal funding; difficulty in regionalizing municipal UPAs; projects of UPA that later proved to be wrong, due to lack of planning; and lack of credibility of the UPA and state support. There was unanimity on the insufficiency of federal resources for implementation and funding, the latter theoretically shared between state and municipality".

The following functions for the UPA stand out: complementing primary care and complement the hospital emergency. Despite the impact that insufficient primary care has on the UPA, the more serious is the impact of hospital insufficiency, which has generated some distortions. Some managers they think that the UPA solves the lack of hospitals. Two serious problems are identified in the country's hospital park: a concentration of beds in small hospitals and a tendency to reduce the already undersized number of beds. Despite the mandatory hospital referral, the difficulty of admitting patients was considered the biggest challenge for the UPA (O'Dwyer et al., 2017). According to the article in the magazine Rev. Saude Publica - 2017; 51:125: currently, we are faced with an emergency care project that intends to be integrator; however, its implementation occurred in a fragmented way and with fragile articulation among its components. The strengthening of state management was indicated as a challenge for the implementation of the network, in addition to underfunding and people management. The access provided by the UPA was beneficial, even considering that its demand reflects the incipience of primary care and the hospital network. This component has merit of having technological resources and being architecturally differentiated, but to be successful and integrated into a powerful network, investment in attention is needed primary and in hospitals. Another major challenge highlighted in visits to some UPAs was the unpreparedness of the attending professionals and the lack of accessibility in the care of people with disabilities, which must be corrected urgently.

Dr. John Touissant is a leading figure in healthcare reform in the United States and R. Hamilton interviewed him in advance of his appearance at a lean management conference in Baltimore. John S. Toussaint, MD, is CEO emeritus of ThedaCare, and CEO of the ThedaCare Center for Healthcare Value. Dr. Toussaint served as president and chief executive officer of ThedaCare, Inc. from March 2000 until April 2008. The interview with Dr. Touissant illustrates well these issues and the challenges of applying the lean philosophy in the health area. The full content of the interview with Dr. Toussaint can be found on the following website: https://robinerikhamilton.com/dr-john-toussaint/). Here are some important excerpts from what Dr. Toussaint (Dr. T) think about healthcare reform in USA.

The interviewer Hamilton asked what are some of the challenges Dr. T intend to address in his speech on the Lean Healthcare: Dr. T answered:

I think that this is about leadership behavior. The tools are the tools, the tools are important, you've got to learn the tools, but you can learn the tools. The hard part is the people part. What does a lean leader look like? That's what I'll be focusing on, what it takes to be an effective lean leader. It means, pretty much, that you have to change everything that you've learned in business school, or medical school, or nursing school, and you have to pretty much retool yourself, because our existing education system is turning out autocratic control freaks who manage by the numbers, and they don't know anything about quality improvement, and they don't know how to manage a group of people to actually achieve 100% reliable results. If we don't change ourselves as leaders, we will never be able to transform our companies.

Interviewer followed with a question regarding Dr. T experience with Lean and what he thought about using it in the area of health. Dr. T replied saying the he was not sure that anyone ever becomes a true lean expert and that there´s always something new to learn. He also mentioned about uncertainty issues with the Lean implementation in health, making some comparisons with the number of defects in the manufacturing industry when applying lean methods, finalizing saying "… whatever this lean thing was that we needed to learn more about it, and head down that path". Here is the Dr. T´s full answer to the interviewer's question about what the lessons from lean could do for a hospital:

I think that the most surprising thing was that you could improve quality, lower costs, and improve staff satisfaction all at the same time. To me, that was like, why didn't anybody ever introduce this before, because when we boil it all down, that's what this whole thing is about. If you can do those three things, you're going to have a satisfied customer. It's surprising to me that in an industry so full of highly trained, intelligent people, that this methodology could have slipped by all these years without anybody latching on to it.

Hamilton asked Dr. T: "What are some of the big achievements that you've been able to make that you attribute to following some of the precepts of lean?" Dr. T replied saying that "there are some spectacular improvements. For three years in a row, having to medication reconciliation errors. That means that the patients in the collaborative care unit receive exactly the medications they are supposed to be receiving every single time, 100% reliability for three years in a row". When questioning about the key characteristic of leaders who excel at creating quality the answer was direct without hesitation: "Humbleness. I think leaders who are humble have a much higher likelihood of being successful in changing their culture than ones that aren't".

Dr. Toussaint ended his speech with a brilliant answer to an important question from Mr. Hamilton: "I guess that the rarity is that you decided to own up to whatever deficiencies, however large they were, and change your own behavior, which is perhaps one of the hardest things we all face when we find ourselves running into obstacles".

I'd be the first to admit that I didn't change it 100%. There are still a lot of bad habits in there. It's a constant struggle. If you're really serious about transforming your whole organization, you have to transform yourself first. I'm absolutely convinced that's why most organizations fail in implementing lean, because it's senior leaders, and particularly the CEOs, who are unwilling to make those changes. Until you get a change in CEO, or somebody who's actually looking at this differently... or, hopefully, over the next few years, as ThedaCare build its internal bench strength, they get a CEO who actually was a lean facilitator somewhere along the way. It's all about the leaders.

DISCUSSION, RECOMMENDATIONS AND RESULTS

The studies showed that lean practices combined with assistive technologies have direct impacts on the quality of life and accessibility of people with disabilities so that they can enjoy their fundamental rights such as health, education, services, transport and leisure.

The remarkably positive results of the application of Lean methods and Applied Technologies have also been increasingly propagated in the market and society. But health management still lacks awareness and adjustments in the implementation of lean methods and practices in a continuous and inclusive way to improve their respective processes in order to promote the social well-being of users of health services, especially in Emergency Care Units (UPA). Based on preliminary studies and practical experiences, the existence of several situations that potentially put patients at risk is verified, especially with the growing increase in demand due to the current health crisis, such as the pandemic caused by the new coronavirus (SARS-COV2). The coronavirus pandemic has profoundly affected businesses in all segments, with the healthcare sector being one of those facing even more challenging developments. In addition to the prevention and treatment of the disease itself, there is also the issue of managing medical, diagnostic and business centers: hospitals and healthcare institutions face daily high variations in terms of patient demand and administrative changes as a whole.

Overcrowding in UPA aggravates these risks, as it has been proven that the average length of stay of patients with low acuity tends to increase and this fact also contributes to the increase in the rate of patients who leave without being treated. These patients cause bottlenecks in waiting rooms and examination rooms and also compromise the care of high-risk patients, as they mobilize the teams in their care.

Other factors that require attention are related to the training and qualification of managers and professionals in the health area, the elimination of waste and the disregard for accessibility requirements for people with disabilities. The design, layout and warning system and user guidance of some UPA require a rearrangement and reorganization of their facilities, access to service rooms and consequent flow of teams and users, as well as the infrastructure related to the equipment, which they need constant repairs and a proper maintenance plan.

These aspects, among others, need to be studied in relation to safety, accessibility and the well-being of patients from an inclusive perspective and the Lean Healthcare approach.

A recent publication on the website "bioemfoco" illustrates this objective, emphasizing that it is necessary to realize that health is an investment in the future and that the population needs safe and quality care. "Countries invest heavily in protecting the population from terrorist attacks, but not from virus counterattacks, which can be much more deadly and cause more economic and social damage. An 'uncontrolled' pandemic brings down economies and nations. This is why health cannot just be a problem for the Ministry of Health. Persistent and growing socio-economic gaps result in discrepancies in the population's health care quality" (Bioemfoco, 2020).

There are numerous challenges in Public Health Management whose list demands a response from more than one sector, not just health. We face shared threats, and we have a joint responsibility to act. The application of Lean as a management philosophy in the health area and the provision of knowledge on the subject constitute an important methodology for improving the safety and quality of care, especially in public services.

Therefore, an organizational restructuring that favors a "lean" model is imperative, whose characteristics well defined by Womack, J. in his publication "The machine that changed the world" are still very current "...immense volumes of products and services variety, with ever-decreasing costs, employing teams of multi-skilled workers at all levels of the organization, plus highly flexible machines, no inventory and no defective items, and fast, quality service." (Womack, op. cit., p.3).

In this sense, awareness and commitment to ethics, safety and quality becomes imperative, and the Lean concept is an interesting strategic decision to be taken by organizations, especially in the area of Public Health.

The studies show the supply of knowledge on the subject of Lean and present the advantages and benefits of the proposed model, emphasizing that issues of quality, safety and productivity continue to be vital and indispensable for the survival of Organizations. However, the application of Lean Philosophy or Lean Healthcare and its practical implementation in Health Organizations still needs more research and a better understanding on the part of some managers, especially in Emergency Care Units (24h - UPA) of the different regions of our country.

In the most varied opinion polls, the public service is the worst evaluated and the issue of management is pointed out as the main problem. Among the problems of service to users in these UPA usually discussed in our social environment, we highlight the failures related to poor service and safety, usually caused by failures of equipment and protocol procedures, excessive waiting time causing agglomerations, malpractice, lack of professionals suitable, among others. Not to mention the neglect with the poor service of people with special needs regarding to accessibility, orientation, guidance and healthcare itself.

The risks of worsening the health conditions of patients inherent to these failures, most of the time, go unnoticed by the user community and by the responsible professionals involved in the care. The relevance of the topic should be highlighted, since the aggravation of these risks compromises patient safety, with possible harmful consequences to their own lives. Evidently, this brings us to serious considerations about the trilogy Patient/UPA/Monitoring and the need for a new Management approach - a Lean transformation.

Difficult times are opportunities to find new solutions and Lean, originating from the "TPS" (Toyota Production System) is the best example of this. When resources are scarce, it is necessary to avoid waste as much as possible and to know how to work intelligently. The Lean methodology applied to the care process in the UPA, must be understood as an important area of knowledge, with a direct influence on the quality and safety of patients, as well as on their inclusion... a powerful instrument in the transformation of culture, technology and models now used in the health area. The implementation of the Lean Healthcare model promotes quality and safe care, socially fair, economically viable and environmentally sustainable.

SOLUTIONS AND FINAL CONSIDERATIONS

Difficult times are opportunities to find new solutions and Lean, originating from the Toyota Production System is the best example of this. When resources are scarce, it is necessary to avoid waste as much as possible and know how to work smart.

In a context where the demands of the new millennium challenge Brazilian society to build a new development model to enable the relationship between science, technology, innovation and social inclusion, the application of lean practices derived from the Lean method combined with Assistive Technologies make absolutely necessary in public health care systems, especially in the Emergency Care Units (24h - UPA).

Projects of ITS Brasil are examples to be followed in the renewal of the struggle for inclusion, full participation, citizenship and protagonism for people with disabilities. Actions for the insertion of people with disabilities into the labor market and independent access to health care are provably responsible for breaking down the barriers created by traditional models, which conceived of people with disabilities as sick, incapable, dependent and unsuitable for the job market.

Recurring discussions, invariably with criticism, about the conditions of care for patients in the Emergency Care Units, alert the academic and scientific communities about the need to seek solutions to this serious social and public health problem. Therefore, an organizational restructuring is required in the UPA that considers the need for accessibility with the use of Assistive Technologies and that favors a lean model, whose characteristics are well defined by Womack, J. in his publication "the machine that changed the world" (origin of Lean), are still quite current. Digital healthcare and accessibility technologies such as Artificial Intelligence, Lean Healthcare and Assistive Technology are strategic and can solve many problems, but they also raise new issues and challenges for monitoring and regulation.

Without a deeper understanding of the ethical and social implications, these new technologies – which include the ability to create new bodies, qualification of healthcare professionals, etc. – can harm the people they intend to help. The studies show the offer of knowledge on the subject and present the advantages and benefits of the proposed model (Lean & Assistive Technology), emphasizing that the issues of ethics, safety, quality, productivity and inclusion continue to be vital and indispensable to the survival of organizations in the health and well-being of users. However, the implementation of the Lean concept still lacks a better awareness, affection, love and care for people, especially those with special needs.

ACKNOWLEDGMENT

The authors would like to thank the Brazilian Ministry of Health, the UFF – Fluminense Federal University, and the Euclides da Cunha Foundation. This Research is part of the "Lean Project in UPA 24h" that has been funded by the Brazilian Ministry of Health (TED 15/2021, number: 25000.103452/2021-14).

REFERENCES

Ahmed, S., Manaf, N. H. A., & Islam, R. (2018). Measuring Lean Six Sigma and quality performance for healthcare organizations. *Journal International Islamic University*. https://bityli.com/JOXlDzLg

Barnas, K. (2018). *Beyond Heroes – a Lean Management System for the Healthcare Area* [Além dos Heróis – um Sistema de Gestão Lean para a Área da Saúde]. Editora Lean Institute Brasil.

Bersch, R. (2017). *Introduction to Assistive Technology* [Introdução à Tecnologia Assistida]. https://www.assistiva.com.br/Introducao_Tecnologia_Assistiva.pdf

Bioemfoco. (2020). *13 Urgent health challenges for the next decade* [13 Desafios urgentes da saúde para a próxima década]. https://bioemfoco.com.br/noticia/saude-desafios-decada/

Brasil, I. T. S. (2021). *Assistive Technology* [Tecnologias Assistivas]. http://itsbrasil.org.br/tag/tecnologia-assistiva/

Brazil, Ministry of Health. (2015). *Main normative landmarks of the interfederative management of the SUS* [Principais marcos normativos da gestão interfederativa do SUS]. Editora Saúde. http://editora.saude.gov.br

Brazil. Ministry of Health. (2017). *Ordinance nº 10 of 01/03/2017. Assistance model guidelines and funding for 24-hour Emergency Care Units as a Component of the Emergency Care Network* [Portaria nº 10 de 03/01/2017, 1. Diretrizes de modelo Assistencial e financiamento de UPA 24h de Pronto Atendimento como Componente da Rede de Atenção às Urgências]. https://bityli.com/qhQQfLV

Brazil. Ministry of Health. (2020). *Emergency Care Unit* [Unidade de Pronto Atendimento (UPA 24 h). https://bityli.com/LtiZjhXC

Brazilian Association of Technical Standards (ABNT). NBR 9050. (2020). Accessibility to buildings, equipment and the urban environment [Acessibilidade a edificações, mobiliário, espaços e equipamentos urbanos]. Author.

Brazilian Association of Technical Standards (ABNT) NBR 16537. (2018). *Accessibility – Tactile floor signage - Guidelines for design and installation the preparation of projects and installation* [Acessibilidade — Sinalização tátil no piso — Diretrizes para elaboração de projetos e instalação]. Author.

Brazilian Institute of Geography and Statistics. (2010). *Discover Brazil - Population: people with disability* [Conheça o Brasil – População: pessoas com deficiência]. https://educa.ibge.gov.br/jovens/conheca-o-brasil/populacao/20551-pessoas-com-deficiencia.html

Brazilian Institute of Geography and Statistics. (2019). *Country has 17.3 million people with some type of disability* [País tem 17,3 milhões de pessoas com algum tipo de deficiência]. https://bityli.com/VLZuSw

De Amaral, L. C., Nascimento, S.D., Costa, H.G., Viera, L.E.V., Teixeira, A.M., Braga Neto, O.O., & Calado, R.D. (2021). Lean Healthcare – Lean Thinking, Standardized Work and the 8 Health Wastes [Lean Healthcare – Pensamento Lean, Trabalho Padronizado e os 8 Desperdícios na Saúde]. *Universidade Federal Fluminense LabDGE, 2*(1), 16.

dos Santos, R. F., Sampaio, P. Y. S., Sampaio, R. A. C., Gutierrez, G. L., & de Almeida, M. A. B. (2017). Assistive technology and its relationship to quality of life of people with disabilities [Tecnologia assistiva e suas relações com a qualidade de vida de pessoas com deficiência]. *Revista de Terapia Ocupacional da Universidade de São Paulo, 28*(1), 54–62.

Min, L. L., Sarantopoulos, A., Spagnol, G. S., & Calado, R. D. (2014). *What is this Lean Healthcare thing?* [O que é esse tal de Lean Healthcare]. Pedro e João.

O'Dwyer, G., Konder, M. T., Reciputti, L. P., Lopes, M. G. M., Agostinho, D. F., & Alves, G. F. (2017). The process of implementing emergency care units in Brazil [O processo de implantação das unidades de pronto atendimento no Brasil]. *Revista de Saude Publica, 51*, 125. PMID:29236876

Ohno, T. (1988). *The Toyota Production System: Beyond Large-Scale Production.* Productivity Press.

Silva, J. O. (2009). *Illusory Social Inclusion Processes: a new look at diversity in the educational context* [Processos de Inclusão Social Ilusórios: um novo olhar frente à diversidade no contexto educacional] [Dissertação de Mestrado]. PUCRS, Porto Alegre, RS.

Toussaint, J. S. (2008). *Interview of doctor John S. Toussaint on Lean Health Care by R. Hamilton.* https://robinerikhamilton.com/dr-john-toussaint/

Womack, J., & Jones, D. T. (2003). *Lean thinking: Banish waste and create wealth in your corporation.* Academic Press.

Womack, J. T., Jones, D., & Roos, T. (1990). *D. The Machine That Changed the World: The Story of Lean Production.* Rawson Associates.

Chapter 9
Monitoring Patient Flow in the Emergency Care Units (UPA) in the City of Guarulhos, São Paulo, Brazil

Newton Narciso Pereira
Fluminense Federal University, Brazil

Andrei Bonamigo
Fluminense Federal University, Brazil

Patrick Fernandes Ribeiro da Fonseca
Fluminense Federal University, Brazil

Luis Enrique Valdiviezo Viera
Fluminense Federal University, Brazil

Thaís Lessa Queiroz
Fluminense Federal University, Brazil

EXECUTIVE SUMMARY

Performance indicators are an important tool for managers to identify how their organization is performing over time. Thus, a concept of the patient's timeline within the health unit was defined, which consists of monitoring from entry to exit, considering all the steps that patients went through during their stay in the emergency care units (UPA). This concept was applied to allow the monitoring of the performance of two UPA's being classified as (1) and (2) in the city of Guarulhos, SP. Data treatment was realized by Excel and were collected from 383 patients (UPA 1 only odd days) and 1123 patients (UPA 2 all days) between 02/01/2021 and 02/28/2021 then proceeded to the organization of data to analyze the processes flow involved. Patients were grouped according to risk classification—red, orange, yellow, green, and blue—and especially medical clinic, orthopedics, pediatrics, dental attendance. Both UPA evaluated the major attendance were classified with green and blue, and in terms of treatment, the medical clinic was priority when compared with others offered in these UPA.

DOI: 10.4018/978-1-6684-5185-4.ch009

INTRODUCTION

The health attendance is a problem in all cities in the world. In development countries, government are obligated to improve new alternatives to improve the service level to population. During the last century, the cites suffer with great migration processes, where a great mass of people move to cities. Naturally, with high demand to health treatment, the public service point attendance was more demanded, and some places started a system collapse. Then, in the country as Brazil, the main part of health attendance is realized by Unified Health System - Sistema Unico de Saúde (SUS). During much time was noted that Brazilian service quality presents structural problems persist in SUS, including gaps in organization and governance, low public funding, and suboptimal resource allocation (Massuda et al. 2018) and it were noted by population. Elevate time on the queue waiting to be attendant, long time to realized exam and other problems are reported in literature (Jurberg, 2008; Massuda et al. 2018; Iasbech et al. 2018). On the other hand, there have been advances, including investments in human resources, science, and technology, and a substantial decentralization process, widespread social participation, and growing public awareness of a right to health care and primary care (Paim et al. 2011). In this context, to mitigate these problems, during the time several proposals were suggested, implemented, assessed and some could present satisfactory results.

Therefore, In Brazil, in 2007, the first Emergency Care Units (UPAs) were created in the State of Rio de Janeiro to respond to the crisis in the health system (Konder and O'Dwyer, 2016). The successful experience allowed them to be included within the strategies of the National Emergency Care Policy for better organization of care, articulation of services and definition of patient care flows. This strategy appears as one of the initiatives to address the problem of overcrowding in hospital emergencies (Oliveira et al. 2015). The UPA's are distributed throughout the country with approximately three hundred units. The main purpose is to attending cases of medium and low complexity to support large hospitals in cities (Silva and Santos, 2014).

All patients that arrive at UPA will be shared by everyone will be the service triage process (Camilo et al, 2020). The User Embracement and Evaluation with Risk Classification (AACR) protocol recommends the stratification of risk in levels of priority, referred to by color, and related to waiting time for medical attendance, presenting greater credibility, validity, and reliability in the evaluation of the patient's actual status (Pícoli et al, 2016).

The risk classification system adopted presents five colors, red being for immediate attendance, orange for severe urgency, yellow for urgency, without immediate risk of death, green being for no immediate risk of death, and blue for a chronic situation without acute suffering, or social cases (situations in which referral to the Basic Health Center is possible) and which can be attended after all the patients classified as red, yellow and green have been seen (Zanon et al. 2016; Pícoli et al, 2016; Amorim et al. 2019; Silva et al. 2021).

The Brazilian Ministry of Health's recommend that the color identifies the maximum waiting time indicated for medical care, respectively: emergency – immediate care; orange – 10 minutes; yellow – 60 minutes; green – 120 minutes, and blue – 240 minutes (Chabudé et al, 2019).

UPA has the conception to attend patients during the 24-hour per day (1440 minutes) and offers a simplified structure, with X-rays, electrocardiography, pediatrics, an examination laboratory, and observation beds (Ministry of Health, 2022).

Considering these aspects, in this paper we evaluate the patients flow of two UPA in Guarulhos, São Paulo State, Brazil considering the risk classification in function of medical specialty to quantity the timeline to attendance.

METHODOLOGY

In this paper we will evaluate the two UPA localized in the city of Guarulhos São Paulo Brazil (Figure 1).

Figure 1. Location of UPA 1 and 2
Source: The authors

Data Gathering

Data were collected to determine the patient's timeline in both UPA 1 and 2. We consider as a timeline the events that occur from the patient's arrival to his departure, that is, the length of stay (cycle time). All these data were treated and evaluated following the timeline patient presented in Figure 2.

Figure 2 presents the steps of the patient into UPA, where each procedure can generate data to be collected and evaluated. After this, data collection is possible to establish the general indicator associated with treatment time. Data related to patient profiles was not collected in this investigation.

To prepare the timeline of events developed during the patient care process. To UPA 1, data were collected from 383 patients between 02/01/2021 and 02/28/2021, considering only odd days, due to availability of investigators. UPA 2 data were collected from 1,123 patients between 02/01/2021 and 02/28/2021 (all days). Then, the data were organized to analyze the flow of patients at each stage of care.

Figure 2. Timeline patient at UPA
Source: The authors

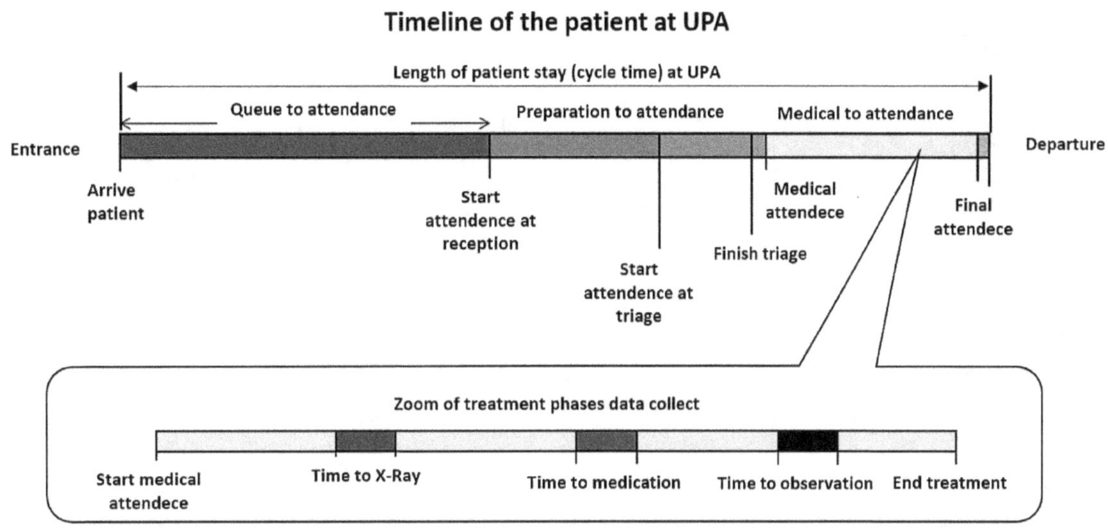

Data Treatment

Excel software was used to create a data treatment. Patients were grouped according to risk classification – red, orange, yellow, green, and blue – and specialty – internal medicine, orthopedics, pediatrics, and others. The focus was on the patient's total length of stay in the UPA, separated into times of reception, triage, first medical attendance, x-rays, medication, observation, waiting for exam result, and length of stay.

The data were analyzed and the occurrences that presented time inconsistency <0 were removed. Descriptive statistics analyze was conducted in the data base in terms of attendance time of each patient's considering the minimum, maximum, mean and standard deviation. Some problems identified in data base were evaluated individually, because inconsistences observed had to be considered in these analyses.

Our intention with this paper is to identify only the main point of the bottleneck (time of processes). The reason that can generate these bottlenecks was not identified during the data collection processes, because the focus of this research was realize a mapping of patient processes flow and their phases during each step of UPA treatment.

RESULTS AND DISCUSSION

The results were separated considering the characteristics of each UPA evaluated in same region.

UPA 1

During the month of February 2021, 383 patients were seen, considering the data made available for odd days. Figure 3 shows the daily distribution of attendances. We can observe a great deviation during these days, in terms of the number of attendances per day. The minimum and maximum varied between 8 and 36.

Figure 3. Daily distribution of attendances of UPA 1
Source: The authors

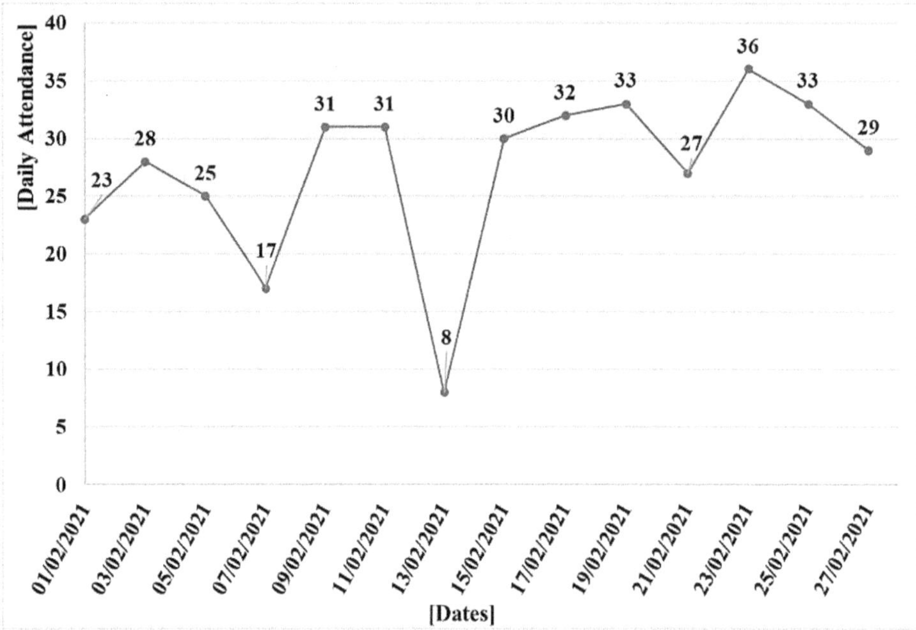

The 383 patient's timeline results are shown in Table 1, where each patient attendance step was evaluated in minutes considering the data gathered during the investigation.

Table 1. Characterization of patient's timeline for each process - time in minutes

Time Description	Min	Mean	Max	σ
Reception	1	1.48	7	0.76
Waiting for triage	1	13.42	80	14.03
Triage time	1	3.47	15	1.53
First medical attendance	2	5.31	12	1.62
X-Ray examination	2	5.87	37	4.06
Medication	2	21.66	180	25.42
Observation	30	344.81	1.135	256.92
Waiting for exam result	3	194.89	1.097	139.22
Length of stay	5	274.20	6.025	605.57

Source: Prepared by the authors

It is observed that the average time at reception did not exceed 2 min while in the next step the average waiting time for triage was 13.42 min (with a standard deviation of 14.03) indicating a bottleneck in the system service of the UPA. Another data of significant relevance is the average waiting time for the exam result with 194.89 min giving rise to a more in-depth analysis of the UPA procedures to verify the feasibility of reducing the time of this process. In this point, we can note that observation time can influence in the length of stay time of patient. It will depend on the characteristics of treatment in function of disease patient.

Global Distribution of Patients – UPA 1

The 383 patients were distributed according to the risk classification assigned in the triage stage (Figure 4). The risk classification is following the Manchester Triage System (MTS).

Figure 4. Distribution of patients in function of risk classification at UPA 1 during the February 2021
Source: Prepared by the authors

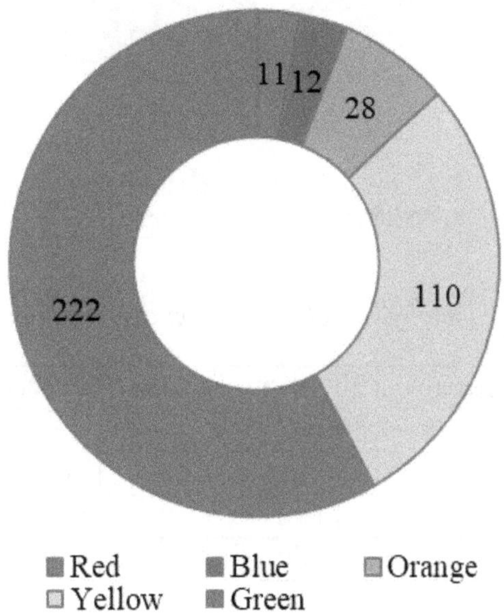

There were 234 patients in a non-urgent or less urgent situation (green and blue) equivalent to 61.1% of the total. In emergency situations – yellow, orange, and red – there were 149 patients (38.9%) and of these very urgent and emergency cases corresponded to 10.2% of the total. The Figure 5 shows the distribution of patients in relation to medical specialty.

Most patients were treated within the clinical medical specialty corresponding to 68.7% of the total. The orthopedic specialty was responsible for 21.7% of the visits while pediatrics answered for 9.4%. Finally, there was a service classified as others (0.3% of the total).

To understanding the time attendance by risk classification and medical specialty. Table 2 presents the average time for the triage medical attendance and length of stay in minutes.

Observing the most serious cases - orange and red - we can see a reduction (in relation to the average of 13.42 min) in the waiting time for triage with 11.23 min for orange classification and 9.70 min for classification red for the clinical medical specialty. A reduction of 16.3% and 27.7% respectively. For pediatrics there were two orange cases and one red case a reduction of 85.1% and 92.5%. respectively.

Figure 5. Patients' distribution by medical specialty – UPA 1
Source: Prepared by the authors

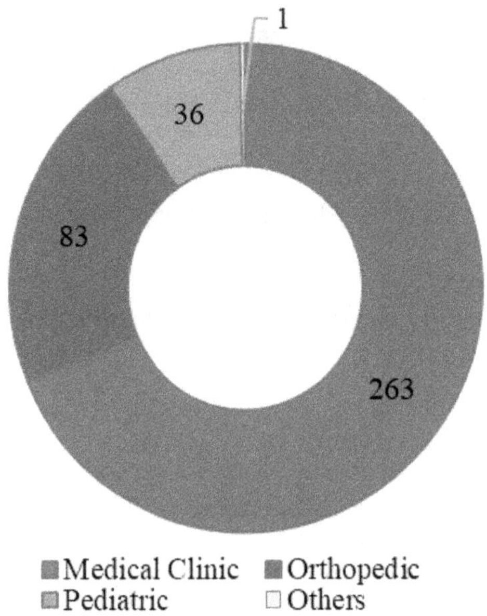

Table 2. Distribution of average time by risk classification and medical specialty – time in minutes

Risk Classification	Specialty	Waiting for Triage	Medical Attendance	Length of Stay
Yellow	Medical clinic	11.06	5.36	484.80
Yellow	Orthopedic	8.36	5.07	307.64
Yellow	Pediatric	13.38	5.88	172.75
Blue	Medical clinic	15.22	4.78	591.67
Blue	Orthopedic	22.00	5.00	14.00
Blue	Others	38.00	5.00	17.00
Blue	Pediatric	4.00	7.00	33.00
Orange	Medical clinic	11.23	4.95	442.19
Orange	Orthopedic	6.50	6.75	190.00
Orange	Pediatric	2.00	7.00	92.50
Green	Medical clinic	13.79	5.28	119.96
Green	Orthopedic	19.11	5.08	179.51
Green	Pediatric	12.42	5.74	166.26
Red	Medical clinic	9.70	5.50	1.044.22

Source: Prepared by the authors

UPA 2

During all days of February 2021, 1,123 patients were seen. Figure 6 shows the daily distribution of attendances. We can observe smooth variation during these days, in terms of the number of attendances per day. The minimum and maximum varied between 37 and 45.

Figure 6. Daily distribution of attendances of UPA 2
Source: Prepared by the authors

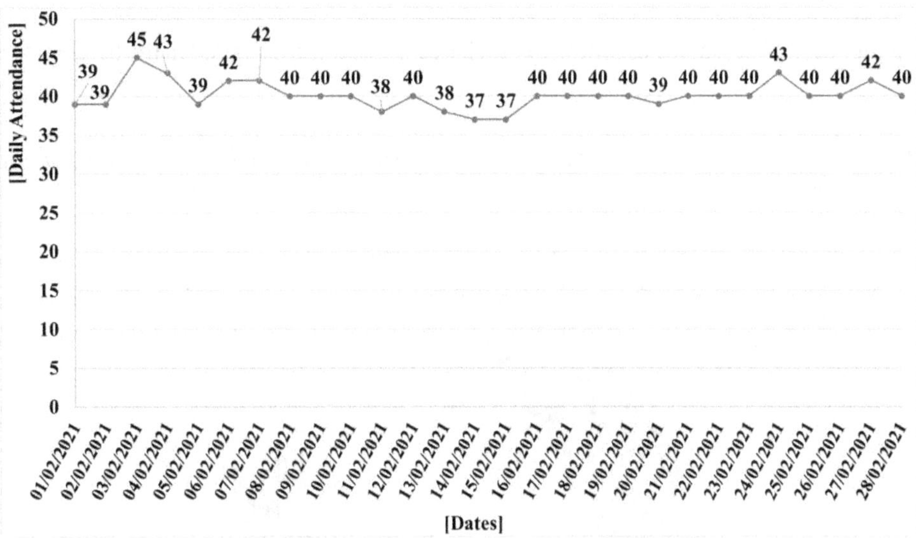

The 1,123 patient's timeline results are shown in Table 3 where each patient attendance step was evaluated in minutes.

Table 3. Characterization of patient's timeline for each process – UPA 2 - time in minutes

Time Description	Min	Mean	Max	σ
Reception	1	1	21	0.76
Waiting for triage	1	11	180	13
Triage time	1	2	12.00	1.53
First medical attendance	2	5	65	2
X-Ray examination	5	10	70	4
Medication	1	31	250	25
Observation	Not reported in the data base			
Waiting for exam result	2	41	285	49
Length of stay	1	135	1512	116

Source: Prepared by the authors

It is observed that the average time at reception is 1 min while in the next step the average waiting time for triage was 11 min (with a standard deviation of 13) indicating a bottleneck in the system service of the UPA, to start the attendance. Another data of significant relevance is the average waiting time for the exam result with 41 min giving rise to a more in-depth analysis of the UPA procedures to verify the feasibility of reducing the time of this process. When, we compare this time with UPA 1 is possible to note that UPA 2 presents a minor time in this process. An important question is that in the UPA 2 was not identified time to observation of patient in the data base.

Global Distribution of Patients – UPA 2

The 1123 patients were distributed according to the risk classification assigned in the triage stage (Figure 7).

Figure 7. Distribution of patients in function of risk classification at UPA 2 during the February 2021
Source: Prepared by the authors

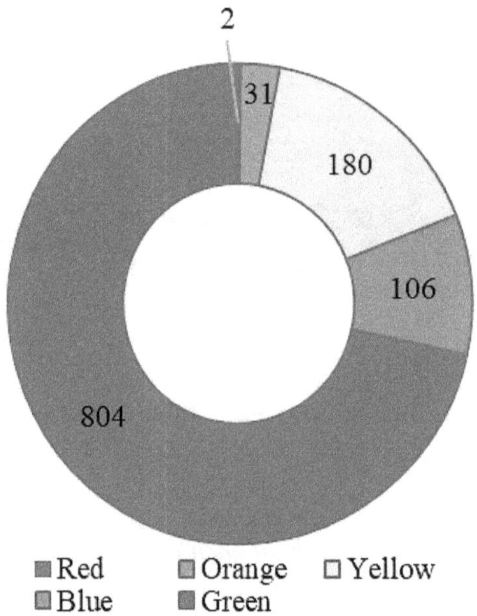

There were 910 patients in a non-urgent or less urgent situation (green and blue) equivalent to 81% of the total. In emergency situations – yellow, orange, and red – there were 213 patients (19%) and of these very urgent and emergency cases. The Figure 8 shows the distribution of patients in relation to medical specialty.

Most patients were treated within the clinical medical specialty corresponding to 83.6% of the total. The orthopedic specialty was responsible for 4.8% of the visits while pediatrics answered for 7.5% and dental attendance 4.1%. In the UPA 2 there is dental attendance differently of UPA 1 that do not offer this kind of treatment.

To understanding the time attendance by risk classification and medical specialty. Table 4 presents the average time for the triage, medical attendance, and length of stay in minutes.

Figure 8. Patients' distribution by medical specialty – UPA 2
Source: Prepared by the authors

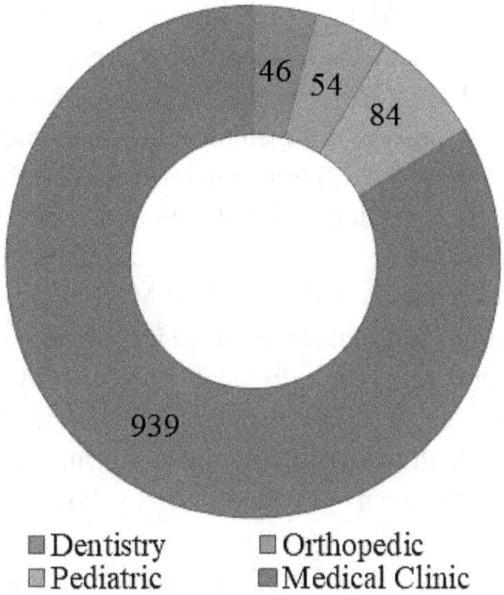

The Table 4 shows that high length of stay to patient was to medical clinic with green classification risk 149.50 minutes. It has a relation with the numbers of attendance of this classification (71.6%). Therefore, these patients can present different demands to be treated into the UPA 2.

Table 4. Distribution of average time by risk classification and medical specialty – UPA 2 - time in minutes

Risk Classification	Specialty	Waiting for Triage	Medical Attendance	Length of Stay
Yellow	Medical clinic	10.32	5.02	111.12
Yellow	Orthopedic	3.06	5	71.48
Yellow	Pediatric	9.42	5	79.21
Yellow	Dental Attendence	12.30	10	57.30
Blue	Medical clinic	10.37	5.02	139.01
Blue	Orthopedic	14.40	5	133.40
Blue	Pediatric	16.30	5	66.24
Blue	Dental Attendence	10.37	9	77.38
Orange	Medical clinic	10.14	5.02	259.38
Orange	Orthopedic	7	5	33
Green	Medical clinic	11.33	5.02	149.49
Green	Orthopedic	8.45	5	92.54
Green	Pediatric	7,16	5.01	84.16
Green	Dental Attendence	7.40	9.35	63.17
Red	Medical clinic	6	5	71

Source: Prepared by the authors

Our results present a particular characteristic of these UPA's where the main objective is offering a medical assistance for cases with low complexity. In the both cases, we can note that in total of patient's attendance were equivalent to UPA 1 - 61.1% (green and blue) and UPA 2 - 81%.

For the UPA 1 the green classification in three category represents an average length time of stay 155 minutes (cycle time). In the UPA 2 there were four green classification that represent an average length time of stay 80 minutes. In terms of red medical clinic this time is around 1.044 minutes (UPA 1) and 71 minutes (UPA 2) that show the difference in terms of severity of medical care. Both UPA's present dwindling number of treatments in red classification. It is because the UPA has a focus in the attendance of low complexity disease.

In similar system of health care unities in Brazil where MTS has been implemented similar characteristics of risk classification during the attendance can be identified in the literature. Equivalent results were identified in other studies in Brazil. Few individuals had a priority need for care according to a risk classification 53.2% of the public that seeks had their classification in blue and green colors (Guedes et al. 2014). Considering UPA with high numbers of attendances with a predominance for 'blue' classification – 34.353 (47.5%) followed by green – 31.543 (43.6%) yellow 6.312 (8.7%) and red - 151 (0.2%) (Pícoli et al. 2016).

Between 2018 and 2019, the analysis of the 390 records found that the main characteristic of the UPA demand was to attend adults aged between 25 and 59 years (54%) of both sexes (female 50,3% and male 49,7%), who sought service mainly in the afternoon shift (42,1%) which were mostly classified in green color (51,0%) and blue (30,07%) (Oliveira et al. 2019).

Other observation was realized in UPA in the city of Iguatu – Ceará regarding the risk classification, the cases classified as green and blue totaled most of the attendance, composed by 8,690 users (85.08%) while the urgent cases were composed by the minority of the attendance (De Souza Brasil et al., 2019).

In fact, the main characteristic of the UPA is the non-urgent care, this can also be evidenced in a study carried out in a large Brazilian municipality in 2017, considering 12 Basic Health Units (UBS) that were treated in a UPA. A total of 3,584 patients were analyzed, representing 7% of non-urgent risk visits. About 36.3% of users were between 41 and 65 years old, 62.3% were women, whose main symptoms were: headache; dyspnea; and abdominal, lower back, and throat pain (Schafirowitz and Souza, 2020).

In terms of utilization of UPA, some aspects need to be evaluated, considering the association between selected sociodemographic, clinical, and utilization variables and the inadequate use of an Emergency Care Service (ECS) for the population. A sample of the 791 care attendances in an ECS during the year 2012 in Ouro Preto, identified the inadequate use of the ECS using the Hospital Urgencies Appropriateness Protocol after descriptive and statistical analysis. The binary Logistic Regression was used to estimate the odds ratio that verified around 58.8% of the attendances were considered inadequate, with 78.7% of discharge after assistance. Therefore, this study presented that better structuring of the health care network and educational activities among the population for guidance on how to more effectively use the urgent/emergency system in the health region is necessary to improve the health care service (Machado et al. 2015).

On the other hand, the social implication of the UPA is to provide intermediate support to hospitals and Basic Health Units, preventing less complex cases from being referred to hospital emergencies, having as one of the effects the reduction of overcrowding in emergency rooms. In this context, the number of UPA services may vary depending on the size, location, complexity, available equipment, and areas of activity. As it was possible to verify in the cases presented for UPAs 1 and 2, the average daily attendances varied between 30 and 34 attendances on average, respectively. In other cases, we found higher numbers of daily care, such as a UPA located in the Municipality of Pelotas, which served an average of 80 patients per day, in the period 2016 and 2017. The UPA carried out 73,333 consultations, of which 68,255 patients were seen by the doctor, showing that the UPA has shown positive results, related to the reduction of visits to the local Emergency Room, in addition to providing users with specific services, as it has a simplified structure with a radius-X, electrocardiography, pediatrics, examination laboratory and observation beds, care often difficult to obtain in other hospital units (Pinto et al. 2019).

The standardized care processes in the provision of low-complexity health services give UPAs the ability to provide quality care to citizens, reducing queuing times, and waiting for low-complexity exams. However, in this study the main limitation is short period of data collection. To improve the decision-making is necessary a large period of data collection to identify a level of deviation during the health care operations. Additionally, it can allow for the development of more operational indicators and compare them for a long time. As contribution new strategies can be development associate with the performance indicators, such as implementation of fast-track patient and lean health care (Chaves et al. 2021).

CONCLUSION

In this paper we used data collected through the concept of patient's timeline applied to two UPA localized in São Paulo Brazil. Each unit care was evaluated individually in function of their characteristics. Considering both UPA the green risk classification attendance was mandatory. UPA 1 represented 57% and UPA 2 71.6%. Following this classification, the blue attendance that represent not urgent treatment represented 3% and 9.4% (UPA 1 and 2) respectively. Then, these results show that main characteristics of the unit care is focused on low complexity treatment.

Additionally, in terms of treatment the clinic medical was priority, UPA 1 (68.7%) and UPA 2 (83.6%). Other specialist was minor demanded, while orthopedics accounted for 21.7% and pediatrics for 9.4% (UPA 1) and 7.5% and 4.8% (UPA 2). Considering the each has characteristics, the UPA 2 also offer dental attendance (4.1%).

Then, we can conclude that these two UPA have been realizing their attendance with a focus on green and blue risk classification. Then, the main characteristic of UPA has been attending to provide quick service to low complexity health care, considering the reality of local where they are inserted, giving support to local Basic Health Units. Considering the times recommended by the Brazilian Ministry of Health's was possible to note that, both UPAs is committed to these parameters for the color classification of patient. Other times lost during the following patient care due to processes time and waiting time to attendance, examination laboratory and other that impact at total length stays time (cycle time) of the patient into UPA.

ACKNOWLEDGMENT

The authors would like to thank the Federal Fluminense University and the Euclides da Cunha Foundation of UFF. which made the research project funded by the Ministry of Health of Brazil viable; according to TED 15/2021 and Number: 25000.103452/2021-14.

REFERENCES

Amorim, F. F., Almeida, K. J. Q. D., Barbalho, S. C. M., Balieiro, V. D. A. T., Machado, A., Dias, G. D. F., & Dasu, S. (2020). Reducing overcrowding in an emergency department: A pilot study. *Revista da Associação Médica Brasileira*, *65*(12), 1476–1481. doi:10.1590/1806-9282.65.12.1476 PMID:31994629

Camilo, D. G. G., de Souza, R. P., Frazão, T. D. C., & da Costa, J. F. Junior. (2020). Multi-criteria analysis in the health area: Selection of the most appropriate triage system for the emergency care units in natal. *BMC Medical Informatics and Decision Making*, *20*(1), 1–16. doi:10.118612911-020-1054-y PMID:32085757

Chabudé, T.G., César, G.C., & Santana, C.J. (2019). Reception and Risk Classification in an Emergency Unit: Experience Report of the Implementation of the Manchester Triage System. *Essays and Science C Agrarian and Health Biologicals, 23*(2), 121-125.

Chaves, S. M. D. A., Calado, R. D., Coelho, S. A., Neto, O. B., Santos, A. B., & Bourguignon, S. C. (2021, September). Fast Track in Emergency Services an Integrative Review. In *IFIP International Conference on Advances in Production Management Systems* (pp. 241-249). Springer.

da Silva, M. R. B., da Silva Santos, J., de Morais, M. P. D. L., de Armada, H. C. D., de Oliveira, N. S., & Donato, A. G. (2021). Nurses' perception of risk classification in an emergency care unit in the West Zone of Rio de Janeiro [Percepção dos enfermeiros na classificação de risco em uma unidade de pronto atendimento na Zona Oeste do Rio de Janeiro]. *Global Clinical Research Journal*, *1*(1), e2–e2.

Guedes, H. M., Almeida, A. G. P., de Oliveira Ferreira, F., Júnior, G. V., & Chianca, T. C. M. (2014). Risk classification: Portrait of the population assisted in a Brazilian emergency service. *Revista de Enfermagem Referência.*, *4*(1), 37–44. doi:10.12707/RIII13108

Iasbech, P. A. B., & Lavarda, R. A. B. (2018). Strategy and practices: A qualitative study of a Brazilian public healthcare system of telemedicine. *International Journal of Public Sector Management*, *31*(3), 347–371. doi:10.1108/IJPSM-12-2016-0207

Jurberg, C. (2008). Flawed but fair: Brazil's health system reaches out to the poor. *Bulletin of the World Health Organization*, *86*(4), 248–249. doi:10.2471/BLT.08.030408 PMID:18438510

Konder, M. T., & O'Dwyer, G. (2016). The integration of the Emergency Care Units (UPA) with healthcare services in the city of Rio de Janeiro. Brazil. Interface-Communication. *Health Education*, *20*(59), 879–892.

Machado, G. V. C., Oliveira, F. L. P. D., Barbosa, H. A. L., Giatti, L., & Bonolo, P. D. F. (2015). Factors associated with the use of an emergency service, Ouro Preto, 2012 [Fatores associados à utilização de um serviço de urgência/emergência, Ouro Preto, 2012]. *Cadernos Saúde Coletiva*, *23*, 416–424. doi:10.1590/1414-462X201500040177

Massuda, A., Hone, T., Leles, F. A. G., De Castro, M. C., & Atun, R. (2018). The Brazilian health system at crossroads: Progress, crisis and resilience. *BMJ Global Health*, *3*(4), e000829. doi:10.1136/bmjgh-2018-000829 PMID:29997906

Ministry of Health. (n.d.). *Emergency Care Unit (UPA 24h)*. Available at: https://www.gov.br/saude/pt-br/assuntos/saude-de-a-a-z/u/unidade-de-pronto-atendimento-upa-24h

Oliveira, M. D. D. (2019). *Profile of the demand for services performed by the Emergency Care Unit (UPA) of Tramandaí / RS* [Perfil da demanda de atendimentos realizados pela Unidade de Pronto Atendimento (UPA) de Tramandaí/RS]. Academic Press.

Paim, J., Travassos, C., Almeida, C., Bahia, L., & Macinko, J. (2011). The Brazilian health system: History, advances, and challenges. *Lancet, 377*(9779), 1778–1797. doi:10.1016/S0140-6736(11)60054-8 PMID:21561655

Pícoli, R.P., de Oliveira Cazola, L.H., & Maurer, N. M. D. J. S. (2016). Service Users Classified as Risk Level 'Blue'in an Emergency Department. *Cogitare Enferm, 21*(1), 1-7.

Pinto, R. S., Stocker, T., & de Lima, T. M. (2019). The role of emergency care units: analysis of the performance of the first UPA in the municipality of Pelotas-RS [O papel das unidades de pronto atendimento: análise do desempenho da primeira UPA do município de Pelotas-RS]. *Revista de Gestão em Sistemas de Saúde, 8*(2).

Schafirowitz, G. D. C., & Souza, A. C. D. (2020). Adult users classified as not urgent in the Emergency Care Unit [Usuários adultos classificados como pouco urgentes em Unidade de Pronto Atendimento]. *Interface: Comunicacao, Saude, Educacao*, 24.

Silva, K. S. N., & Santos, S. L. (2014). Units of emergency care (upa) and health promotion: A look from the "system of objects" and "system of actions" [Unidades de pronto atendimento (upa) e promoção de saúde: um olhar a partir do "sistema de objetos" e "sistema de ações"]. *Rev Mov Sociais e Dinâmicas Espac, 3*(2), 224–246.

Zanon, L. R., Zanin, L., & Flório, F. M. (2016). Evaluation of the use of services provided by emergency care units in a Brazilian municipality. *RGO - Revista Gaúcha de Odontologia, 64*(4), 411–418. doi:10.1590/1981-863720160003000073043

ADDITIONAL READING

Arnous, A.H. (2014). *Experience report of risk classification of the Manchester protocol in the emergency care unit of Guarapari/ES*. Monograph presented to the Specialization Course in Nursing Care Lines – Urgency and Emergency Option of the Nursing Department of the Federal University of Santa Catarina.

de Sousa Brasil, F. M., de Sousa, M. B., & de Souza Brasil, M. (2019). Clinical and epidemiological characterization of users assisted at the Emergency Care Unit (UPA) in the city of Iguatu–Ceará [Caracterização clínica e epidemiológica dos usuários atendidos na Unidade de Prono Atendimento (UPA) na cidade de Iguatu–Ceará]. *Revista de Psicología, 13*(46), 992–1010.

Godoi, V. C. G., Ganassin, G. S., Inoue, K. C., & Gil, N. D. M. (2016). Reception with risk classification: characteristics of the demand in an emergency unit. *Cogitare enferm, 21*(3), 1-8.

Hermida, P.M.V., Nascimento, E.R.P.D., Echevarría-Guanilo, M.E., Brüggemann, O.M., & Malfussi, L.B.H.D. (2018). Reception with risk classification in an emergency care unit: an evaluative study. *Journal of the USP School of Nursing, 52*.

Pinto Júnior, D., Salgado, P. D. O., & Chianca, T. C. M. (2012). Predictive validity of the Manchester Triage System: Evaluation of outcomes of patients admitted to an emergency department. *Revista Latino-Americana de Enfermagem, 20*(6), 1041–1047. doi:10.1590/S0104-11692012000600005 PMID:23258716

Ramos, P. L., Nascimento, D. C., Fernandes, R., Guimarães, E., Santana, M., Soares, K., & Louzada, F. (2019). Medical Care in Emergency Units with Risk Classification: Time to Attendance at a Hospital based on Parametric Models. *TEMA (São Carlos), 20*(3), 571–585. doi:10.5540/tema.2019.020.03.571

Souza, C. C. D., Toledo, A. D., Tadeu, L. F. R., & Chianca, T. C. M. (2011). Risk classification in an emergency room: Agreement level between a Brazilian institutional and the Manchester Protocol. *Latin American Journal of Nursing., 19*(1), 26–33. doi:10.1590/S0104-11692011000100005 PMID:21412626

Chapter 10
Queuing Theory Contributions and Applications in Health Service:
A Study in the Field of Management Problems

Alexandre Beraldi Santos
Fluminense Federal University, Brazil

Ana Carolina Sanches Zeferino
https://orcid.org/0000-0003-1213-0964
Fluminense Federal University, Brazil

Ilma Rodrigues de Souza Fausto
https://orcid.org/0000-0003-3850-5066
Fluminense Federal University, Brazil

Sandra Maria do Amaral Chaves
Fluminense Federal University, Brazil

Saulo Cabral Bourguignon
Fluminense Federal University, Brazil

EXECUTIVE SUMMARY

This study analyzes the contributions and applications of queuing theory (QT) in the field of health service management problems. This review presents a classification system of healthcare examined with the aid of queuing models. The purpose of this is to analyze the contributions and applications of QT in the field of problem management in health services and to give indications of when and how to use QT in order to enhance daily management decisions. A literature review was carried out to investigate the health areas supported by queuing models, searching articles that described problem models and their topics or keywords related to QT and population health or health problems. The present study analyzed 314 articles that address the applications of QT in healthcare management between 2014 and 2020. This review demonstrates that QT can contribute to the improvement of health services and provide resource managers to achieve this improvement. A discussion of why, when, and requirements to apply QT is presented.

DOI: 10.4018/978-1-6684-5185-4.ch010

INTRODUCTION

The quality management processes of organizations providing health services, both in the public and private spheres, face great challenges and also great opportunities. Health is a field of social action that is constantly expanding, especially when considering the continuous increase in people's life expectancy, with increasing attention to their well-being.

Thus, in contemporary societies, improving the quality of health services has acquired increasing attention. Today, it is essential to identify the opportunities that arise, as well as the constant challenges in modern management processes.

As stated by Drucker (1997), it is considered unquestionable to observe that trying to change based on the prediction of the future is, at the very least, risky. The only things that can be said about the future is that it is uncertain and not known. However, it is also considered unquestionable, according to the same author, to be rational and to be constantly aware of the opportunities and challenges that the future may bring, as it is less risky than "continuing the trajectory with the comfortable conviction that nothing will change". (Drucker, 1994, p. 155).

Queuing theory (QT) is an immensely powerful tool because queuing models require little data and are simple and quick to use. Because of this simplicity and speed, they can be used to quickly evaluate and compare various service delivery alternatives. In addition to the more basic issue of determining how much capacity is needed to achieve a specified standard of service, queuing models can also be useful for gaining information about the appropriate degree of specialization or flexibility to use in organizing resources or the impact of several priority schemes to determine the order of work to be followed among admitted patients. With the increasing processing power of computers, there is an increasing scope of numerical methods and simulation models to be used alongside traditional queuing theory to help better understand real-life queuing systems.

This chapter aims to put some light to the QT application in healthcare, based on published work.

SETTING THE STAGE

Application of Queuing Theory in Healthcare

Many problems like these need to be addressed in health services and, Operations Research provides numerous methodologies and techniques to solve them. The operations research model offers a systematic approach to problem solving and allows characterization of activities in an existing system using mathematical modeling, which successfully addresses health system problems such as queuing.

The first analysis of QT was in the context of telephone facilities made by AK Ering in 1913. It is widely used in operations management in the industrial environment or in the retail sector, being part of the field of decision science.

The rising cost of health care can be attributed not only to an aging population and new, expensive, and modern methods of treatment, but also to inefficiencies in the delivery of health services. The use of QT to manage flow in health services is an attempt to reduce costs by minimizing system deficiencies and delays. There are many problems in the healthcare system that can be solved using this theory.

Operations research has been present as a scientific system since the 1930s, with it, it was possible to apply appropriate analytical methods for decision making. Many optimization methods, such as linear and dynamic programming models, allow for quantitative analysis. These mathematical models generally ignore the effects of uncertainty and assume that the outcome of decisions is predictive and diagnostic, which allow us to solve large and complex problems using effective mathematical methods and powerful computational models Cochrane cols. (2006).

A considerable body of research on the topic addressed in this study has demonstrated that QT can be useful in the field of health care. Preater (2001) has compiled a bibliography of queuing applications in healthcare. Also, Noseke et al. (2001), reviewed the use of queuing theory in pharmaceutical applications, with special attention to improving customer satisfaction. Customer satisfaction is improved by predicting and reducing wait times and staff compliance. Samuel Foumndame cols. (2007) researched the contributions and applications of QT in the field of health care. They summarize several QT findings in the following areas: wait time and utilization analysis, system design, and naming systems. They also considered the results of systems at different scales, including individual departments (or units), health facilities and regional health systems. (Lakshmi, 2013)

Literature Research

According to Demo (1995) methodology is an instrumental discipline for research, and a necessary condition for scientific competence. Methodology is an instrumental concern. It deals with ways of doing science. Take care of procedures, tools, paths. The purpose of science is to treat theoretical reality. To achieve this goal, there are several paths. This is what methodology deals with (Demo, 1985).

In this work, the following databases were used to survey the articles: PubMed, Scopus and Web of Science from 04/15/2020 to 04/18/2020, with an exclusive focus on articles published from 2014 to 2020. The search process strategy was divided into two stages, the first one was a query to identify works with QT that have the following word in the title, keywords or abstract: "queuing theory" (Table 1). During the second stage of the strategy, the decision to include the article was made based on the following criteria: (1) the article describes a queuing model and its applications in the management of health services; and (2) a clear association with a general phenomenon of health service management issues.

Table 1. Search criteria and selection of articles on queuing theory in health services, carried out in the Web of Science, PubMed and Scopus databases.

Registration of Bibliographic Searches			
Search Source	**Web of Science**	**PubMed**	**Scopus**
search date	04/15/2020	04/16/2020	04/18/2020
Term	("queuing theory")	("queuing theory")	("queuing theory")
Criteria (filters)	(HEALTH CARE SCIENCES SERVICES); (HEALTH POLICY SERVICES); (MEDICAL INFORMATICS); (EMERGENCY MEDICINE); (EXPERIMENTAL MEDICINE RESEARCH)	NO FILTERS	(MEDICINE)
Number of articles collected	39	105	170

Source: Author.

After collecting the initial set of articles, they were assigned according to the proposition, the decisions made in relation to the application area, professionals involved in the application areas, the desired result and how the QT was applied in the study. The reviewed articles are (directly or indirectly) related to the research of QT applications in the health area.

From the universe of 314 articles found, 14 articles were selected. To select the sample for this research, the intentional non-probabilistic sampling technique was used, based on research that discussed aspects of QT application in the field of health service management problems. Tavares et al. (2018) define non-probabilistic sampling as one that uses reasoning, depending exclusively on the criteria of the researchers to delimit and form the sample. A convenience sampling approach was chosen to control the influence of other unrelated factors and to define the scope for the selection of studies covering QT and its applications.

The PRISMA Flowchart - Main Items to Report for Systematic Reviews and Meta-analyses (Galvão, 2015) was used, which enabled the elaboration of the Researched Literature Flow Diagram with the identification, initially, of 314 records of which 14 were selected, as per Figure 1.

Figure 1. Research flow diagram used for the selection of articles involving QT and its applications in the health area.
Source: Prepared by the authors

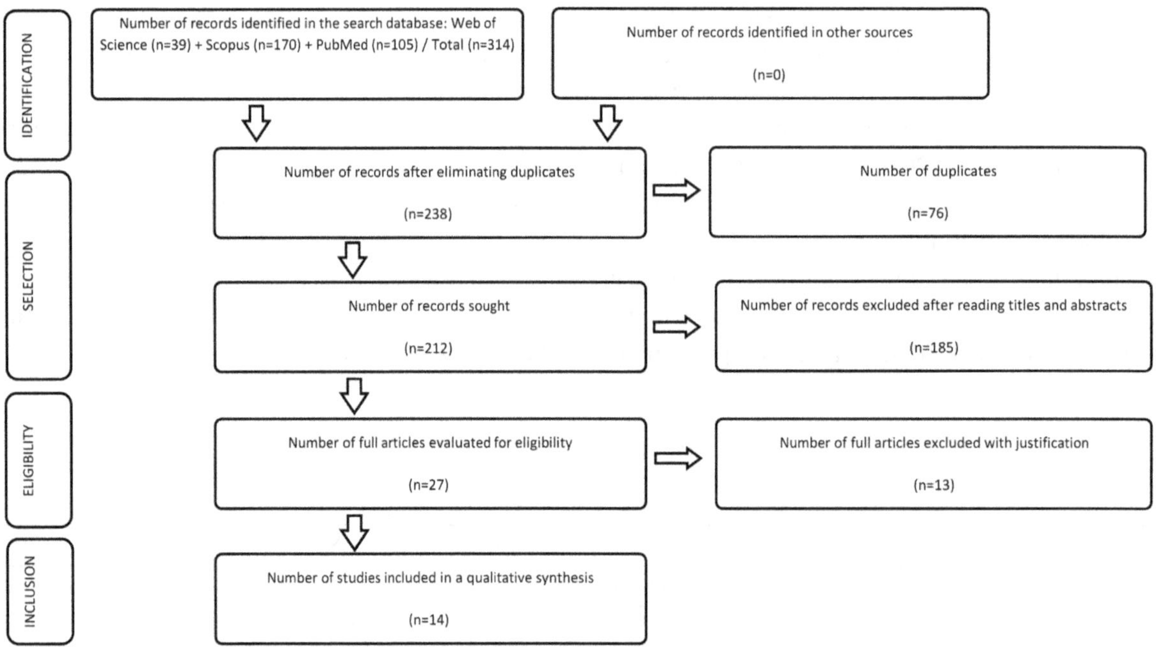

Bibliometrics

Bibliometrics is a quantitative and statistical methodology to measure indices of production and dissemination of scientific knowledge, within bibliometrics, citation analysis is one of the main areas, since it allows identifying patterns in the production of scientific knowledge (ARAÚJO, 2006). A bibliometric analysis permeates the generation of relationship networks. In the present study, the networks were generated by the Vosviewer software, the main ones being:

- **Co-citation Network:** This network shows the relationship between the references used by the articles in the base extracted from the databases. It shows the "theoretical pillars" of the articles and the topic to be analyzed.
- **Keywords Co-occurrence Network:** It presents the keywords most used by the articles in the sample and the relationship between them. it allows to identify which topics are usually addressed by the articles.
- **Co-Authoring Network:** It presents the network of authors who collaborate the most and jointly contribute to the analyzed topic.

The proposals detailed in this chapter aim to extract the terminology overlap or also known as co-occurrence, including creating a way to visualize the scientific production of the articles and the selection of title, keywords and abstracts as a unit of analysis. This part of the study was carried out using the Vosviewer Software, which searched for articles in the selected Web of Science, Pubmed and Scopus databases. The quantitative analysis with the Vosviewer software served as the basis for a subsequent qualitative analysis of the content of the selected articles, especially the categorization and co-analysis, which are important for the consolidation of the study.

Specialized studies point to three main bibliometric laws: the first, Lotka's Law of 1926 (authorship inverse square relationship), proposes to measure authors' productivity; the second, Bradford's Law of 1934 (productivity dispersion), aims to measure the dispersion of scientific knowledge in periodicals; and the third, Zipf's Law of 1949 (less effort in terminology), aims to assess the distribution of word frequencies in a text.

The Tree Map shows the hierarchical data and was built to demonstrate the sectors in the hospital units where the QT was applied. This graphic expression uses nested rectangles in its configuration, that is, smaller rectangles inside a larger rectangle. To build the map, the number of times the study was carried out in each sector of the hospital units was used. The dimensions of the rectangles are related to the quantity and color of the sectors where the theory was applied. With this, the visualization of the application of the theory in the different sectors was demonstrated (Figure 6). This map was built using Microsoft Excel software.

CASE DESCRIPTION

In Brazil, for many years, hospitals were managed by doctors, military or religious, with little specific management knowledge to manage them efficiently, which allowed for a remarkable legacy in the management models of health institutions in the country.

In hospitals, the organizational structure shows the way in which health organizations define and divide their functions and attributions, in addition to demonstrating how these attributions are grouped and coordinated (de Souza et al., 2009). According to Mintzberg (1995), an organizational structure can be segmented into: a) work specialization; b) departmentalization; c) chain of control; and d) centralization or decentralization of decision-making. According to the author, this structure defines the hierarchy of the organization, the responsibilities and the authority of individuals, in addition to demonstrating how communication and the availability of information internal to the organization occur. According to Bertani (2012), the hospital environment can be understood as that of any organization that transforms initial information (input) into a result (output). In this way, it is considered a type of production system, a real transformation unit composed of operations, having as input sick patients, infected materials, medicines, among others, which will result in healthy patients, sterilized materials and billing.

This transformation process generates what is known as a value stream. In the case of manufacturing industries, it is the set of activities necessary (adding or not adding value) to make the raw material transform into a finished product (Rother and Shook, 2003). However, in the health area, it is the set of processes that influence the transformation of the patient from a sick state to a healthy state (Graban, 2013). Figure 2 illustrates the similarity between the industrial and healthcare value streams.

Figure 2. Similarity between the industrial and health service value stream
Source: Prepared by the authors

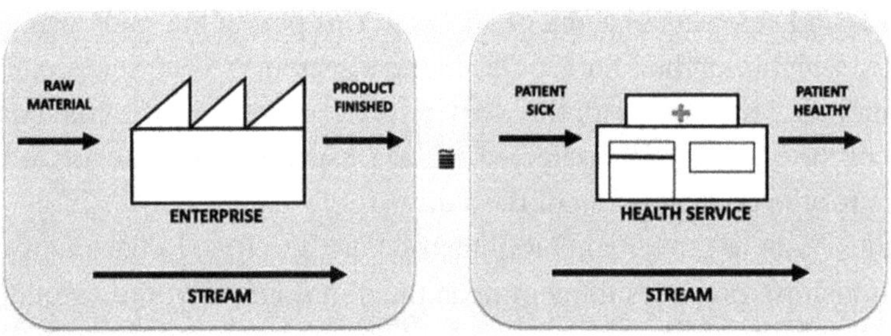

For Farias and Araujo (2017), hospital management in the 21st century is, regardless of the region, invariably complex, even though certain aspects of health services are more challenging in some countries, such as regulation, financing and available technologies. Added to the extensive list of managerial demands, the requirement for specific knowledge in the management of human and physical resources.

Effective hospital management can reduce issues that contribute to increasing complexity in hospital management, such as: a) expansion of the potential customer base; increase in the elderly population and the continuous increase in patients with chronic diseases; b) scarcity of medical resources, long waits for care; c) interpersonal differences in the organizations providing health services arising from professionals in the medical and administrative areas; and d) autonomy at work, standardization of operations and increased productivity (Farias and Araujo, 2017).

The main objective to be achieved by all organizations is to serve their public in a qualified way, optimizing costs, time and reducing waste. A management approach capable of making this possible is Lean. This approach is oriented towards enhancing results and involving teams in search of continuous improvement. Thus, the approach also proposes a business strategy focused, above all, on customer satisfaction.

Problem Situation

Health is one of the most important areas of economic and social development, presenting itself as an area of convergence between social and economic objectives, at the same time that it stimulates the full exercise of human rights and attracts a complex series of goods and services of high technology (PIMENTEL et al., 2012). Thus, health stimulates and develops technological progress and benefits society by reducing barriers to people's ability to work (Pimentel et al., 2017).

The health production chain in Brazil is made up of several relevant economic activities, which in 2015 accounted for 9.1% of the Brazilian gross domestic product (GDP) (final consumption), 6.4% of job vacancies and 9 .2% of remuneration (IBGE, 2017). Despite the great potential, there are some challenges for the future of the health sector. After the second half of the 20th century, Brazil went through the aging process of its population and, in parallel, there were changes in health demands, approaching developed countries, with the increasing prevalence of chronic-degenerative diseases.

This process also led to the emergence of new epidemics (zika, yellow fever, tuberculosis) responsible for a high incidence of deaths and disability in the country, in addition to traffic accidents and urban and rural violence. Persistent epidemiological and demographic data indicate a rapid increase in demand for health services and products, creating a tendency to increase system load (Pimentel et al., 2017).

The Brazil 2035 project (IPEA; NATIONAL ASSOCIATION OF CAREER SERVANTS OF PLANNING AND BUDGET, 2017) presents eight trends that should mark the universe of health in the horizon of 2035, which are listed below:

1. Maintenance of population aging, with the deepening of epidemiological and demographic transitions.
2. Changing the paradigm from healing to care, with an increase in people in continuous use of health services.
3. Maintenance of public underfunding in health and high private participation.
4. Maintenance of the double-entry system at health service providers.
5. Maintenance of external dependence on health technologies.
6. Maintenance of the processes of internationalization and globalization of the health system.
7. Maintenance of decentralization of federal spending on health to the neediest regions, with maintenance of inequity in health spending at the subnational level (states and municipalities).
8. Maintenance of spatial concentration and territorial inequalities of services and physical resources of high complexity in health.

Healthcare managers face the challenging task of organizing their processes more effectively and efficiently. The pressure on healthcare managers increases as demand for healthcare and expenses steadily increase. Health care is a huge field and there are many ways to look at it. How do you decide on the best locations for medical clinics and emergency vehicles to provide maximum health care coverage for a given population? How many basic medical ambulance locations are needed if the total distance between locations and hospitals must be less than a certain number? How should radiation treatment be planned to minimize the treatment time of a cancer patient? How should trauma center nurses be scheduled and reorganized to maintain an adequate level of service even in the worst-case scenario?

In these times, the preservation of information is paradoxically becoming more and more problematic for society, this is mainly due to two factors: the exponentially growing amount of information, and the almost absurd need for forces, due to their specializations, to keep the up-to-date researchers in their fields. This phenomenon was called the information explosion in the mid-1990s or, from another point of view, the ignorance explosion.

In this informational scenario, literature reviews, mainly due to their summarizing aspect, assume an important organic function, together with indexes (here in the librarianship sense), abstracts and specialized bibliographies. More time is often spent trying to identify whether a particular study has been carried out before than carrying it out (Moreira 2018).

Therefore, the objectives of this chapter are to analyze the contributions and applications of QT in the field of problem management in health services and to give indications of when and how to use QT in order to enhance daily management decisions.

CURRENT CHALLENGES FACING THE ORGANIZATION

The Challenges and Opportunities of Health Management

The quality management processes of organizations providing health services, both in the public and private spheres, face great challenges and also great opportunities. Health is a field of social action that is constantly expanding, especially when considering the continuous increase in people's life expectancy, with increasing attention to their well-being.

The current scenario of organizations permanently requires that they remain competitive throughout their existence. For Schmidt and Cohem (2014), the digital revolution that has influenced individuals, organizations, communities and national governments has led to a significant paradigm shift. It is difficult to predict the characteristics of the new society, cultural, political and commercial systems that will emerge or have their course affected by globalization in different parts of the world.

Issues such as international competitiveness, application and use of emerging technologies, sustainability and development, organizational learning and business ethical challenges make up a volatile and highly complex context for actions of innovation and permanence in the market (Bhagat, McDevitt, and Baliga, 2017; Nicolaides, 2017). On the other hand, this current context provides those who survive this competitive scenario with an environment full of opportunities for organizations. One of the challenges for success under these conditions can be seen in the existing win-win relationships between quality, innovation, competitiveness and performance (Al-Shuaibi, Zain, and Kassim, 2016).

In the healthcare environment, special challenges from a management perspective also sometimes relate to common healthcare management issues (Jorma et al., 2016). In addition to the challenges of the external scenario, many hospitals have internal problems that go through a lack of planning. Among them, there are: lack of clear processes and defined responsibilities; high degree of professional turnover; unmotivated teams; existence of fiefs within the institution; inefficiency in the billing process; lack of cost management; and cash flow problems. In addition to these, there are many others, which, experienced on a daily basis and added to external problems and changes in the market, are generating the perfect storm in health (Gordilho, 2018).

Other factors capable of accentuating the challenge of hospital management are observed in the literature, such as the absence or inefficiency of mechanisms for evaluating the management of health organizations (de Souza et al., 2009). In this regard, a study carried out by Schiesari (2014) indicated that the proper use of assessments in health organizations has the potential to make service delivery processes more efficient, helping to save resources, which they already experience, in the current context, notorious scarcity. It is noteworthy that the analysis of results and the production of recommendations are some of the main products generated by the evaluations, helping to implement improvements in hospital management.

RESULTS

Occurrence in Titles and Abstracts

Zipf's Law is a linguistic mathematical basis that analyzes the frequency and distribution of words contained in a text, whether scientific or not. By means of calculation it is possible to map and create rankings of the occurrence of words in this text (Zipf, 1949). Zipf's Law can be applied in different ways in linguistic analysis. Its application is focused on written texts, where an analysis is carried out on the occurrences of words.

Co-occurrence of terms in the titles and abstracts of the articles studied showed the presence of only 1 cluster, 33 items and 528 links. The characteristic of this configuration is the presence of 3 main terms, namely: Patient Flow, Simulation and Approach. Other 30 secondary terms appeared. What comprises the detection of words that characterize the content of the theme and the counting of the occurrences of these words in the works on the theme in focus, it is then verified that these words appear simultaneously in these works and with what frequency. From this measurement, high added value information is extracted about the proximity or distance of the main terms present in the articles, as shown in Figure 3. The presence of the words patient flow and simulation are expected, once QT in health care has a focus on improving patient flow through the simulation of scenarios to promote better managerial decisions. From the 30 words, 8 are nearer the 3 main words: combination, implementation, analysis, patient, experimental study, her, model identification and data. Also, some words were expected, like data, analysis, patient, due to the nature of the subject. About words as experimental study, model identification it shows the authors that the studies have been directed to define a model based on experimental studies, with means the studies present implementation and not just a theoretical modeling. The terms that appear less are decision making, process mining technique, Saint Petersburg, discrete event simulation, machine learning approach, diverse scenario, scipy, electronic health record, detailed simulation, realistic simulation, process, related department, Russia, multiple healthcare unit, data mining technique, programming framework, improved simulation, dos, patient length and developed solutions. These words also reinforce the connection between QT and data analysis methods for the actual situation in which records are electronic and the amount of data is huge and is growing.

Co-Occurrence of Keywords

Co-occurrence of terms was found in the keywords of the articles studied. In this specific case, the data showed the presence of 12 clusters (Figure 4) that for identification purposes are represented by each rectangle. The characteristic of this configuration is the absence of main terms demonstrating a dispersion that represents the number of low frequency elements in the set of bibliographic references studied. In this case, the keywords express concepts contained in the works, the terms found are words used in indexing to indicate an ordered collection of information and knowledge. In co-occurrence, the simultaneous occurrence indicates a close relationship between them. That is, the concepts they represent are connected among the fourteen articles studied.

Figure 3. Co-occurrence of terms found in the titles and abstracts of the 14 selected articles.
Source: Prepared by the authors

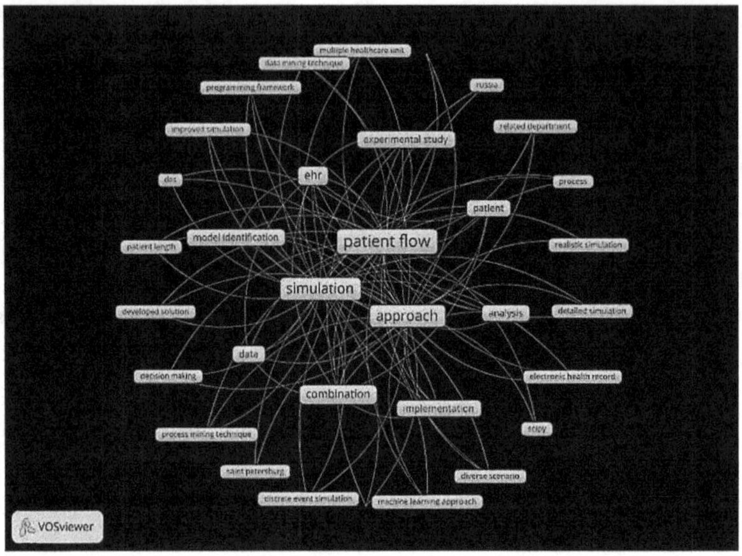

Figure 4. Co-occurrence of terms found in the keywords of the 14 selected articles, each of the terms is identified by a different color.
Source: Prepared by the authors

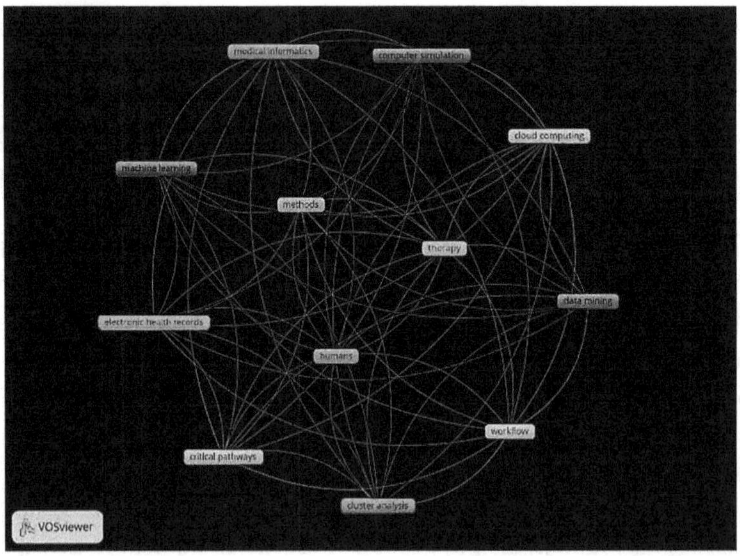

Co-Occurrence of Authorship

Lotka's Law (1926) or Inverse Square Law proposes that a limited number of researchers produce a lot in a given area of knowledge, while a large volume of researchers produces little. In this conception, the Law establishes that a field is more productive, the more articles its authors produce in the course of their careers. As a consequence of Lotka's Law, approximately 60% of authors in a field produce only one article in their entire academic life (Urbizagástegui Alvarado, 2002).

Co-authorship was found in the articles studied. In this specific case, the study showed the presence of 14 clusters, with 48 authors composing the clusters, it can be seen in Figure 5. The caption bar with the occurrence of the authors' publication distributed over the years correlated with the colors arranged, and that these clusters are not linked, the characteristic of this configuration is due to the absence of main authors in the set of publications studied and that there is no citation relationship between the authors of the works, demonstrating that this dispersion corresponds to a diversity of authors who published little in this same area of knowledge.

Figure 5. Co-occurrence of authors found and their interrelationships in the 14 selected articles.
Source: Prepared by the authors

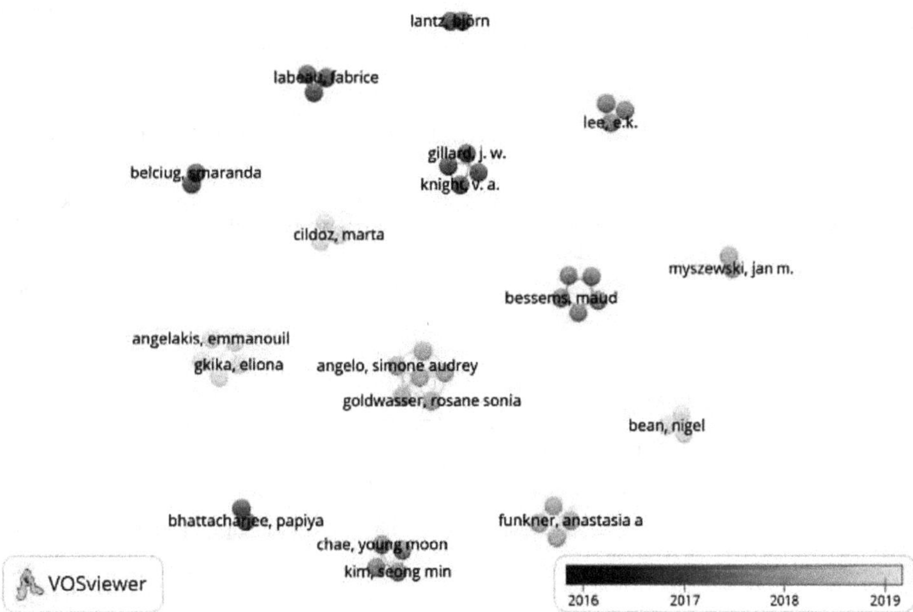

Among the articles selected in the study that address the QT, we will highlight and analyze some that focus on the central proposal of this work, which is the use of QT in the management of problems in health services.

Cildoz, Ibarra and Mallor (2019) applied the QT through a comprehensive computational analysis to show the flexibility of the queue discipline, called cumulative priority queue with finite horizon and denoted by (APQ-h) and the priority queue discipline (APQ) as well as its superiority over other pure priority disciplines in a real-world scenario and in a variety of emergency unit scenarios. Gkika, et al (2019) sought in their study to apply the QT to estimate the impact of rapid diagnosis on the average length of stay and the use of health resources.

Varney, Bean, and Mackay (2019) applied in their study on the link between patient admission and discharge behaviors, and other potential occupancy management behaviors, can create a correlation between the arrival process and length of stay distribution, QT, as a simple and robust method to test the correlations of the study and explain this correlation structure when simulating the occupancy of an ICU. Myszewski and Sinha (2018) used QT as a methodology to describe phenomena in which not all planned tasks are performed within prescribed specification limits.

For Lin, Patrick and Labeau (2014) QT was applied in the study through the development of a model with two connected queues: a queue with the patient flow to access the Emergency Department and the other queue for patients to access the Emergency Department. internment. Based on this flow model, the QT was used to estimate the mean waiting time between patients. Using specific and priority wait time targets, the required number of Emergency and Inpatient Unit resources was also estimated.

Table 2 presents the synthesis of the central proposals in the use of QT in each analyzed article.

Table 2. Authors of each analyzed article, the year of publication and the central proposal of the articles.

Author and Year of Publication	Article Proposal
Cildoz, Ibarra and Mallor, 2019	Explore the implementation of APQ-h management policies in an emergency unit and develop a simulation model that replicates a real emergency.
Gkika, Psaroulaki, Tselentis, Angelakis and Kouikoglou, 2019	Investigate the potential benefits of introducing point-of-care testing for the rapid diagnosis of infectious diseases.
Varney, Bean and Mackay, 2019	Demonstrate the problems that the correlation structure can cause e.g. link between admission and discharge behaviors, labeled in various ways, collision, demand-driven discharge, premature discharge, etc. etc.
Myszewski and Sinha, 2018	Propose a model to measure the effectiveness of quality assurance tasks in health service delivery processes.
Goldwasser, Lobo, Arruda, Angelo, Ribeiro e Silva, 2018	Determine the optimal number of adult intensive care unit beds.
Kovalchuk, Funkner, Metsker and Yakovlev, 2018	Create a hybrid simulation of patient flow with a combination of data-driven methods for automating model identification.
Cho, Kim, Chae and Song, 2017	To analyze changes in waiting times for outpatients.
Shapoval and Lee, 2017	Divide hospital clinical services into groups with the aim of efficiently allocating existing inpatient beds.
van de Vrugt and Boucherie, 2016	Investigate the various assignment policies in the medical routines of working in an emergency.
Lantz and Rosén, 2016	Develop a methodology based on queuing theory to measure effective capacity in a triage care process in a hospital.
Bhattacharjee and Ray, 2016	Conduct a case study of appointment systems to schedule patients to a hospital facility.
Green and Liu, 2015	Identify opportunities to reduce excess bed capacity in other inpatient units as well.
Belciug and Gorunescu, 2015	To analyze the allocation of resources in a hospital department, integrating in the same structure a queuing system, a compartmental model and an optimization based on evolution.
Lin, Patrick and Labeau, 2014	Develop a model to characterize the coupling effect between patient flow to access the emergency department and access to the inpatient unit.

Source: Author.

Waiting Time and Resource Usage

Some authors evaluated the waiting time in lines and the use of resources in the health area. For this analysis, we highlight the articles that focus on the queuing system used to minimize patient waiting time and consequently maximize the use of servers or resources in the health area, such as doctors, nurses, hospital beds, which are often conflicting tasks. In these studies, the objectives were divided into four categories: treatment rate (LWTR), variable arrival rate (VAR), priority queue (PQD) and minimum waiting time (MWT). Table 3 presents the main issues to be solved (application objective) using queuing theory.

Table 3. Authors and year of publication of articles with their objectives and application of queuing theory.

Author and Year of Publication	Application Objectives
Cildoz, Ibarra and Mallor, 2019	Reduce arrival time and total emergency waiting time indicators.
Gkika, Psaroulaki, Tselentis, Angelakis and Kouikoglou, 2019	Eliminate pre-diagnosis time through point-of-care testing to reduce the average length of hospital stay for infectious diseases and result in an equal reduction in bed occupancy and other resources.
Varney, Bean and Mackay, 2019	Reduce premature patient discharge through potential occupancy management behaviors.
Myszewski and Sinha, 2018	Analyze the system of factors that affect the implementation of tasks in a process.
Goldwasser, Lobo, Arruda, Angelo, Ribeiro e Silva, 2018	Reduce waiting time in the patient queue and propose policy strategies.
Kovalchuk, Funkner, Metsker and Yakovlev, 2018	Reduce patient length of stay for ACS patient flow
Cho, Kim, Chae and Song, 2017	Reduce patient wait times before and after the introduction of electronic medical record systems.
Shapoval and Lee, 2017	Solve the triple problem: 1) how many service groups to form; 2) how many beds to allocate to each group; and 3) how to partition services between groups.
van de Vrugt and Boucherie, 2016	Room allocation among residents is often unbalanced, which affects the likelihood of lockout and patient wait and stay times.
Lantz and Rosén, 2016	Measure effective capacity in the emergency department triage process.
Bhattacharjee and Ray, 2016	Reduce waiting times for all classes of patients and MRI machine utilization.
Green and Liu, 2015	Reducing the single biggest fixed cost for a hospital is the inpatient beds increase timely access to care, resulting in major savings in capital and staff costs.
Belciug and Gorunescu, 2015	Optimize bed occupancy management and resource utilization.
Lin, Patrick and Labeau, 2014	Provides decision-making support on resource allocation of Emergency / Inpatient Units in a hospital.

Source: Author.

Professionals and Sectors

Health professionals in some fields are familiar with the possibilities of mathematical decision support techniques in general and QT in particular. Population aging requires increasing care, which must be provided with limited resources. Care with rationing and its consequences has therefore become an important research topic. Decisions about which class of patients will be offered and what kind of care are inevitable. The influence of these decisions on other classes of patients, in relation to accessibility and other important issues, must be studied in detail. In addition, the dimensioning of health facilities, not only in terms of the number of beds needed, but also in terms of the care that will be offered only to certain classes of patients, will become increasingly important. Table 4 presents the sectors and professionals involved in the articles studied.

Table 4. Authors and publication date of the articles that analyzed the sectors and professionals involved in the dimensioning of health units.

Author and Year of Publication	Sector	Professional
Cildoz, Ibarra and Mallor, 2019	Emergency	Emergency response managers and professionals.
Gkika, Psaroulaki, Tselentis, Angelakis and Kouikoglou, 2019	Attendance room	health care professionals
Varney, Bean and Mackay, 2019	Intensive Care Unit (ICU)	Professionals in Intensive Care Units (ICU)
Myszewski and Sinha, 2018	All areas of medical care	Professionals from all areas of health care.
Goldwasser, Lobo, Arruda, Angelo, Ribeiro e Silva, 2018	Intensive Care Unit (ICU)	Physicians and professionals from Intensive Care Units (ICU)
Kovalchuk, Funkner, Metsker and Yakovlev, 2018	Acute coronary syndrome (ACS) patient flow care	health care professionals
Cho, Kim, Chae and Song, 2017	outpatient	health care professionals
Shapoval and Lee, 2017	Attendance room	health care professionals
van de Vrugt and Boucherie, 2016	Emergency	Resident Doctor: Surgeon and the Internist
Lantz and Rosén, 2016	Emergency	Emergency response managers and professionals.
Bhattacharjee and Ray, 2016	radiology unit	Radiology department professionals
Green and Liu, 2015	obstetrics unit	Hospital unit managers
Belciug and Gorunescu, 2015	geriatrics unit	Professionals in the geriatrics department
Lin, Patrick and Labeau, 2014	Emergency	Hospital designers and managers

Source: Author.

The QT is being applied more and more as the years go by, and this is evidence of the importance of this theory in the improvements of different sectors of health services. However, another analysis carried out through the Tree Maps (Figure 6), shows the hierarchical data of the sectors where the QT was applied in the hospital units. The result of this analysis shows that some sectors in hospital units, such as emergency, ICU and care room, QT is more applied than in other sectors. However, the sector that most stood out in the application of QT is emergency.

Figure 6. Tree map showing the number of articles published by sectors in hospital units.
Source: Author.

QT with four occurrences, followed by the two most relevant in line, the ICU sector and Care Room both with two occurrences and finally sharing the same level of relevance as the other sectors with one occurrence each.

In the set of results obtained, in this review, considering the articles included, it was possible to establish the geographical distribution by countries of publications in the period from 2014 to 2019, the occurrence of published articles reached a total of fourteen countries, with a frequency of one article pe country, named as follows: Australia, Brazil, Canada, Korea, Spain, United States, Greece, India, Netherlands, Poland, United Kingdom, Romania, Russia and Sweden.

Distribution of Publications by Periodicals

Bradford's Law focuses its description on the repetitive behavior of occurrences in a given field or scientific area, due to its characteristics of incidence of subjects and trends, Bradford observed that few journals produced many articles and many journals produced few articles (QUONIAM, 2001) .

Another relevant data found in the present review study is the distribution of publications per journal over the period from 2014 to 2019. This distribution is arranged in descending order of quantity per journal in a funnel chart Figure 7.

Figure 7. Number of articles published per journal from 2014 to 2019
Source: Author.

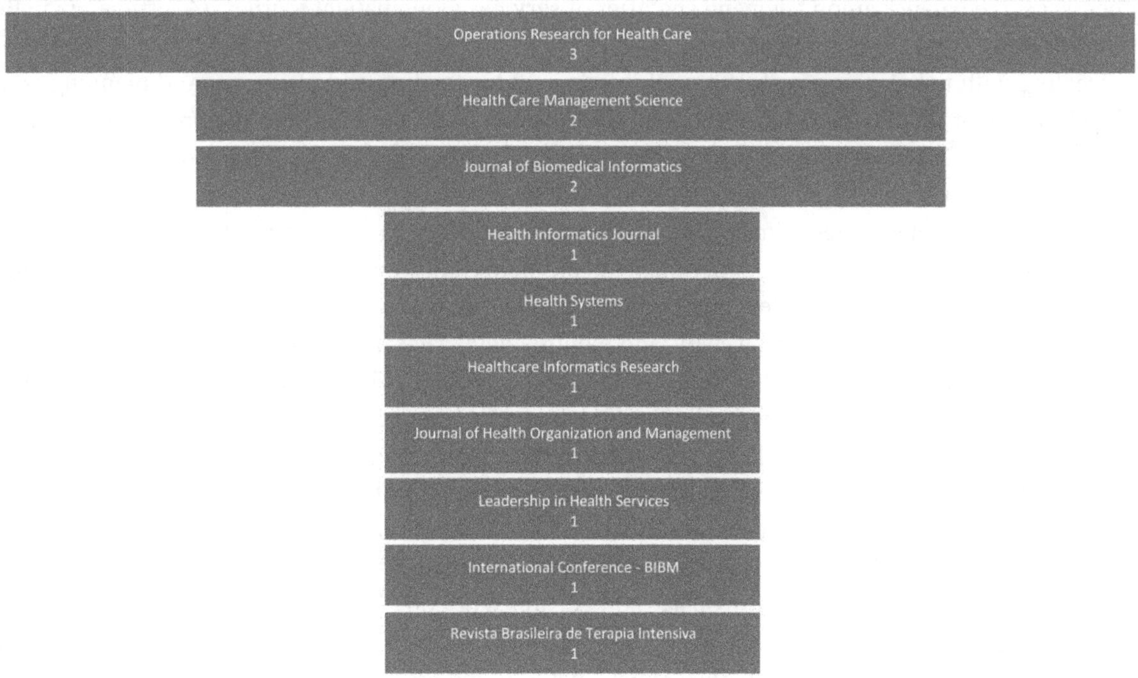

Figure 7 shows the occurrence of published articles distributed by journal, a total of ten journals are present in the set of articles studied, from which three main journals where 50% of the study publications are concentrated, as follows: Operations Research for Health Care with three articles, Health Care Management Science with two articles, Journal of Biomedical Informatics with two articles and the remaining seven journals with one publication each.

SOLUTIONS AND RECOMMENDATIONS

In this article, the applications of QT in the modeling of hospital processes were reviewed and categorized. As health services deal directly with human lives, improving system performance is a very important objective for these services and the analyzed articles clearly show that QT can contribute to this improvement. This fact can be seen in the analyzed articles, especially when it is demonstrated that the QT properly applied increases the use of resources, reduces the waiting time for patients, improves the productivity of the systems and reduces waste. It can also be concluded that QT provides an effective and powerful modeling technique, which allows managers to achieve their goals in improving the system. Another finding in this literature review carried out in the 14 selected articles is that the QT can be applied, with moderate ease, in different hospital sectors, and thus, provides good and quick estimates of the system's performance. We can observe in the selected articles that QT was applied more frequently in emergency sectors and with health care professionals.

Considering the challenges face by health care institutions described the analysis of publications on QT the authors suggest the steps in order to understand why and when to apply QT, also how to apply it.

Among the health care issues to be considered, are: (1) the lack of planning, (2) the lack of defined process, (3) the balance among demand and offer of services along patient journey, (4) efficiency in the use of resources and (team motivation.

Dealing with unbalancing passes through process understanding and planning. And planning is all related to patient journey, which, in technical terms is equal saying it is about the process flow of the patient journey. Coelho et all (2013) presents the case of medical oncology unit of Vale do Paraiba region in Brazil, in which they present the need to level the production once unevenness creates a capacity problem that promotes queues, increasing the time for a patient to access the service. They describe using VSM and waste hunting to identify the main problems and solving issues by flow design revision, integrated routine planning and leveling production. They also show how they promoted the changes and shows the importance of daily, weekly, and monthly data. That saying, there is a need to understand the company processes maturity before using QT. QT modeling is built upon data and, bad data will provide low model accuracy. To get well qualified data, it is important to have standardized processes, otherwise, the variation might be huge, also influencing the model ang promoting low accuracy in the model. Once the institution has well qualified data it should use QT to level the process. The QT model and simulations about the processes will show the real situation faster promoting real time information to manage the process. When compared to promoting studies using samples, it is more reliable and much faster. Although, the quality of the managerial decision will come from models using QT associated with team knowledge of the process.

In Augusto and Tortorella (2019), they review methods and practices in lean healthcare implementation and cite Gijo and Antony (2014) and Carvalho et al. (2013) author that discusses the levelling of production using mathematical models and an automatic sorting process to smooth and level the process. To implement such levelling an automation, QT is needed.

In Hopkins et al. (2008), the authors discuss the cost-effectiveness of reducing wait times the same way patient quality of life is increased. They discuss about the assumptions to use QT and model the process and the impact of using QT to reduce waiting times and how it reduces treatment costs. This article poses and important question related to the modeling using QT that every model has its limitations and corroborating with the need to combine modeling with people experience in the business.

To summarize, the institution seeking to increase patient flow should consider QT. The steps to decide why, when and how are:

1. Understand if queue and process unevenness is the major issue of the institution preventing patient journey from being adequate (delivering qualified care with agility, making the better use of resources);
2. Structure the processes making it possible to have reliable data;
3. Collect data and understand it, simulating in the light of the QT;
4. Use the model to define strategies and routine criteria to manage the process together with qualified personnel.

ACKNOWLEDGMENT

The authors would like to thank the Brazilian Ministry of Health, the UFF – Fluminense Federal University, and the Euclides da Cunha Foundation. This Research is part of the "Lean Project in UPA 24h" that has been funded by the Brazilian Ministry of Health (TED 15/2021, number: 25000.103452/2021-14).

REFERENCES

Al-Shuaibi, K., Zain, M., & Kassim, N. (2016). Performance indicators for quality, innovation, and competitiveness: A survey on the Saudi manufacturing sector. *International Business Research*, *9*(2), 99–113. doi:10.5539/ibr.v9n2p99

Araújo, C. A. (2006). Bibliometry: historical evolution and current issues [Bibliometria: evolução histórica e questões atuais]. *Em questão, 12*(1), 11-32.

Augusto, B. P., & Tortorella, G. L. (2019). Literature review on lean healthcare implementation: Assessment methods and practices. *International Journal of Services and Operations Management*, *32*(3), 285–306. doi:10.1504/IJSOM.2019.098351

Belciug, S., & Gorunescu, F. (2015). Improving hospital bed occupancy and resource utilization through queuing modeling and evolutionary computation. *Journal of Biomedical Informatics*, *53*, 261–269. doi:10.1016/j.jbi.2014.11.010 PMID:25433363

Bertani, T. M. (2012). *Lean Healthcare: Recomendações para implantações dos conceitos de produção enxuta em ambientes hospitalares* [Doctoral dissertation]. Universidade de São Paulo.

Bhagat, R. S., McDevitt, A. S., & Baliga, B. R. (2017). *Global organizations: Challenges, opportunities, and the future*. Academic Press.

Bhattacharjee, P., & Ray, P. K. (2016). Simulation modelling and analysis of appointment system performance for multiple classes of patients in a hospital: A case study. *Operations Research for Health Care*, *8*, 71–84. doi:10.1016/j.orhc.2015.07.005

Cho, K. W., Kim, S. M., Chae, Y. M., & Song, Y. U. (2017). Application of queueing theory to the analysis of changes in outpatients' waiting times in hospitals introducing EMR. *Healthcare Informatics Research*, *23*(1), 35–42. doi:10.4258/hir.2017.23.1.35 PMID:28261529

Cildoz, M., Ibarra, A., & Mallor, F. (2019). Accumulating priority queues versus pure priority queues for managing patients in emergency departments. *Operations Research for Health Care*, *23*, 100224. doi:10.1016/j.orhc.2019.100224

Cochran, J. K., & Bharti, A. (2006). A multi-stage stochastic methodology for whole hospital bed planning under peak loading. *International Journal of Industrial and Systems Engineering*, *1*(1-2), 8–36. doi:10.1504/IJISE.2006.009048

Coelho, S. M., Pinto, C. F., Calado, R. D., & Silva, M. B. (2013). Process improvement in a cancer outpatient chemotherapy unit using lean healthcare. *IFAC Proceedings Volumes, 46*(24), 241-246. 10.3182/20130911-3-BR-3021.00047

de Carvalho, J. C., Ramos, M., & Paixão, C. (2014). A lean case study in an oncological hospital: Implementation of a telephone triage system in the emergency service. *Risk Management and Healthcare Policy*, *7*, 1. PMID:24376365

de Souza, A., Guerra, M., Guerra, C. O., Gomide, P. L. R., Pereira, C. M., & Freitas, D. A. (2009). Management control in hospital organizations [Controle de gestão em organizações hospitalares]. *REGE Revista de Gestão*, *16*(3), 15–29.

Demo, P. (1985). *Introduction of the methodology* [Introdução da metodologia]. Atlas.

Demo, P. (1995). *Scientific methodology in social sciences* [Metodologia científica em ciências sociais]. Atlas.

Drucker, P. (1994). *Post-capitalist society* [Sociedade pós-capitalista]. Pioneira.

Drucker, P. (1997). Brave world of knowledge [Admirável mundo do conhecimento]. *HSM Management*, *1*, 63–68.

Farias, D. C., & Araujo, F. O. D. (2017). Hospital management in Brazil: Literature review aimed at improving administrative practices in hospitals [Gestão hospitalar no Brasil: revisão da literatura visando ao aprimoramento das práticas administrativas em hospitais]. *Ciencia & Saude Coletiva*, *22*, 1895–1904. doi:10.1590/1413-81232017226.26432016 PMID:28614509

Fomundam, S., & Herrmann, J. W. (2007). *A survey of queuing theory applications in healthcare*. Academic Press.

Gijo, E. V., & Antony, J. (2014). Reducing patient waiting time in outpatient department using lean six sigma methodology. *Quality and Reliability Engineering International, 30*(8), 1481–1491. doi:10.1002/qre.1552

Gkika, E., Psaroulaki, A., Tselentis, Y., Angelakis, E., & Kouikoglou, V. S. (2019). Can point-of-care testing shorten hospitalization length of stay? An exploratory investigation of infectious agents using regression modelling. *Health Informatics Journal, 25*(4), 1606–1617. doi:10.1177/1460458218796612 PMID:30179068

Goldwasser, R. S., Lobo, M. S. D. C., Arruda, E. F. D., Angelo, S. A., Ribeiro, E. C. D. O., & Silva, J. R. L. (2018). Planning and understanding the intensive care network in the State of Rio de Janeiro (RJ), Brazil: A complex societal problem. *Revista Brasileira de Terapia Intensiva, 30*(3), 347–357. doi:10.5935/0103-507X.20180053 PMID:30328988

Gordilho, R. (2018). *Strategic management in hospitals* [Gestão estratégica em hospitais]. Ledriprint.

Graban, M. (2013). *Lean Hospitals: improving quality, patient safety and employee engagement* [Hospitais Lean: melhorando a qualidade, a segurança dos pacientes e o envolvimento dos funcionários]. Bookmark.

Green, L. V., & Liu, N. (2015). A study of New York City obstetrics units demonstrates the potential for reducing hospital inpatient capacity. *Medical Care Research and Review: MCRR, 72*(2), 168–186. doi:10.1177/1077558715572388 PMID:25701578

Guedes, V. L., & Borschiver, S. (2005). Bibliometry: A statistical tool for the management of information and knowledge, in information systems, communication and scientific and technological evaluation [Bibliometria: uma ferramenta estatística para a gestão da informação e do conhecimento, em sistemas de informação, de comunicação e de avaliação científica e tecnológica]. *Encontro Nacional de Ciência da Informação, 6*(1), 18.

Henrique, D. B. (2014). *Modelo de mapeamento de fluxo de valor para implantações de lean em ambientes hospitalares: proposta e aplicação* [Doctoral dissertation]. Universidade de São Paulo.

Hopkins, R. B., Tarride, J. E., Bowen, J., Blackhouse, G., O'Reilly, D., Campbell, K., Lim, M., & Goeree, R. (2008). Cost-effectiveness of reducing wait times for cataract surgery in Ontario. *Canadian Journal of Ophthalmology, 43*(2), 213–217. doi:10.3129/i08-002 PMID:18347625

IBGE. (2019). *Macaé*. https://cidades.ibge.gov.br/brasil/rj/macae/panorama

IPEA. Associação Nacional Dos Servidores da Carreira de Planejamento e Orçamento. (2017). Brazil 2035: scenarios for development [Brasil 2035: cenários para o desenvolvimento]. IPEA.

Jorma, T., Tiirinki, H., Bloigu, R., & Turkki, L. (2016). LEAN thinking in Finnish healthcare. *Leadership in Health Services, 29*(1), 9–36. doi:10.1108/LHS-08-2015-0021 PMID:26764958

Kovalchuk, S. V., Funkner, A. A., Metsker, O. G., & Yakovlev, A. N. (2018). Simulation of patient flow in multiple healthcare units using process and data mining techniques for model identification. *Journal of Biomedical Informatics, 82*, 128–142. doi:10.1016/j.jbi.2018.05.004 PMID:29753874

Lakshmi, C., & Iyer, S. A. (2013). Application of queueing theory in health care: A literature review. *Operations Research for Health Care, 2*(1-2), 25–39. doi:10.1016/j.orhc.2013.03.002

Lantz, B., & Rosén, P. (2016). Measuring effective capacity in an emergency department. *Journal of Health Organization and Management*, *30*(1), 73–84. doi:10.1108/JHOM-05-2014-0074 PMID:26964850

Lin, D., Patrick, J., & Labeau, F. (2014). Estimating the waiting time of multi-priority emergency patients with downstream blocking. *Health Care Management Science*, *17*(1), 88–99. doi:10.100710729-013-9241-3 PMID:23690253

Mintzberg, H. (1995). Creating effective organizations [Criando organizações eficazes]. São Paulo: Atlas.

Moreira, W. (2018). *Systems of knowledge organization: theoretical, conceptual and methodological aspects* [Sistemas de organização do conhecimento: aspectos teóricos, conceituais e metodológicos]. Academic Press.

Myszewski, J. M., & Sinha, M. N. (2018). A model for measuring effectiveness of quality management practices in health care. *Leadership in Health Services*, *31*(3), 310–325. doi:10.1108/LHS-03-2018-0020 PMID:30016923

Nicolaides, A. (2017). *Promoting ethical corporate social responsibility in the events industry*. Academic Press.

Noronha, D. P., & Ferreira, S. M. (2000). Literature reviews. In *Sources of information for researchers and professionals*. UFMG.

Nosek, R. A. Jr, & Wilson, J. P. (2001). Queuing theory and customer satisfaction: A Review of terminology, trends, and applications to pharmacy practice. *Hospital Pharmacy*, *36*(3), 275–279. doi:10.1177/001857870103600307

Pimentel, V. P., Barbosa, L. M. D. L. H., Machado, L., Adão, L. F., & Reis, C. (2017). *Brazilian health system: management, institutionality and financing* [Sistema de saúde brasileiro: gestão, institucionalidade e financiamento]. Academic Press.

Pimentel, V. P., Gomes, R. D. P., Landim, A. B., Pieroni, J. P., & Palmeira Filho, P. L. (2012). *Health as a development: perspectives for bndes's performance in the health industrial complex* [Saúde como desenvolvimento: perspectivas para atuação do BNDES no complexo industrial da saúde]. Academic Press.

Preater, J. (2001). *A bibliography of queues in health and medicine*. Bibliography.

Quoniam, L., Tarapanoff, K., Araújo Júnior, R. H. D., & Alvares, L. (2001). Intelligence obtained by the application of data mining based on French theses about Brazil [Inteligência obtida pela aplicação de data mining em base de teses francesas sobre o Brasil]. *Ciência da Informação*, *30*, 20–28. doi:10.1590/S0100-19652001000200004

Rother, M., & Shook, J. (2007). *Learning to see: mapping the flow of value to add value and eliminate waste: working manual of a lean tool* [Aprendendo a enxergar: mapeando o fluxo de valor para agregar valor e eliminar o desperdício: manual de trabalho de uma ferramenta enxuta]. Lean Institute Brasil.

Schiesari, L. M. C. (2014). External evaluation of hospital organizations in Brazil: Can we do it differently? [Avaliação externa de organizações hospitalares no Brasil: podemos fazer diferente?]. *Ciencia & Saude Coletiva*, *19*, 4229–4234. doi:10.1590/1413-812320141910.21642013 PMID:25272131

Schmidt, E., & Cohen, J. (2014). *The new digital age: Transforming nations, businesses, and our lives.* Vintage.

Shapoval, A., & Lee, E. K. (2017, November). Optimizing inpatient bed capacity to improve care delivery. In *2017 IEEE International Conference on Bioinformatics and Biomedicine (BIBM)* (pp. 855-860). IEEE. 10.1109/BIBM.2017.8217767

Urbizagástegui Alvarado, R. (2002). Lotka's Law in Brazilian bibliometry [A Lei de Lotka na bibliometria brasileira]. *Ciência da Informação, 31*, 14–20.

van de Vrugt, M., & Boucherie, R. J. (2016). Assigning treatment rooms at the emergency department. *Operations Research for Health Care, 8*, 62–70. doi:10.1016/j.orhc.2015.06.004

Varney, J., Bean, N., & Mackay, M. (2019). The self-regulating nature of occupancy in ICUs: Stochastic homoeostasis. *Health Care Management Science, 22*(4), 615–634. doi:10.100710729-018-9448-4 PMID:29725895

Zipf, G. K. (1949). *Human behavior and the principle of least effort: An introduction to human ecology.* Academic Press.

Chapter 11
The Method of Applying Knowledge Management to Lean in Emergency Care Units

Christiane Lima Barbosa
Federal University of Para, Brazil

Adalberto da Cruz Lima
https://orcid.org/0000-0001-7666-4581
Federal University of Para, Brazil

Maria Helena Teixeira da Silva
https://orcid.org/0000-0001-5330-3361
Fluminense Federal University, Brazil

Milena Estanislau Diniz Mansur dos Reis
https://orcid.org/0000-0003-1080-8735
Fluminense Federal University, Brazil

Harvey José Santos Ribeiro Cosenza
Fluminense Federal University, Brazil

EXECUTIVE SUMMARY

This chapter analyzes Lean interventions in emergency care units (ECUs) with a focus on learning theory and knowledge management. The use of data served to understand the effectiveness of Lean methodology in transforming knowledge in ECUs. The method was a systematic and descriptive ex-post survey in the Lean project database, quantitative, and qualitative analysis aiming to establish relationships between the foci. The virtual platform is an effective tool for dissemination and generates reliable answers for analysis and decision making. The benefits of interventions through the use of Lean tools are unquestionable, visible, and useful for the daily life of the units. However, the internalization of the Lean culture for permanence and improvements is a point of attention as well as the content, form, and conduction of the actions. Committed people, management by processes, Lean flows, shared information, and agile communication are guarantees for the transformation and consolidation of the improvements.

DOI: 10.4018/978-1-6684-5185-4.ch011

INTRODUCTION

The connectivity by social media is favorable to the dissemination and receipt of information by various means of communication. In this market scenario, an organization uses knowledge to create social and technological environments (Xavier, Oliveira and Teixeira, 2012), generate and share individual and collective knowledge by understanding their characteristics, needs and demands (Terra, 2005).

The record of an information in each medium characterizes a document. The registration of documents in various types and forms of support are archives (Vieira, 2020). Performing knowledge management in an institution propels innovation in processes, products and services, and creates safekeeping mechanisms avoiding loss or obsolescence of knowledge.

As a consequence, there is an increase in productivity and efficiency, encouragement of innovations, better qualification of employees, and an increase in the quality of products and services, helping in the decision-making process (Fugate et al., 2012; Daud, 2012; Al-Sudairy and Vasista, 2012).

Knowledge gathers data, facts and information to be interprete by individuals in different contexts and experiences (Baskerville and Dulipovici, 2006; Tuomi, 1999), in tacit or explicit form (Silva, 2004). Tacit knowledge is subjective and comes from the individual's perception and experience. Explicit knowledge is codifiable, transferable, and organized, that is, the way and means by which knowledge is pass on, shared, and disseminated (Silva, 2004). The conversion of tacit knowledge into explicit knowledge through learning theory and organizational learning are strategies to maintain competitiveness amidst technological advances.

The question is, in what way does learning theory relate to knowledge management (KM)? Document management or knowledge management: which one does the system use in the healthcare environment? This chapter aims to relate learning theory to knowledge management in 24-hour Emergency Care Units (ECUs-24h) through their current demands by investigating the delivered products, methods, and planning at the end of the first year of the project.

It is worth highlighting that learning and knowledge will be analysed and presented from the perspectives of the researchers responsible for planning and of the teams composed of the employees of the ECUs. All participants are the protagonists in thinking, executing and achieving the results, at different stages, various forms and levels of execution. The affirmative hypothesis of the analyses is that the learning process has a beginning, a middle and an end, all based on a conceptual basis of application aiming at obtaining results. From these results is expected the transformation of knowledge and people, both coexisting in a collaborative environment. In order to identify parameters that affirm or refute the hypothesis the following documents and by-products were use for the analyses:

1. **Initial diagnosis**: applied during the project's general planning phase via a questionnaire as an instrument to collect information on the study universe, the Emergency Care Units;
2. **Road map of the Lean Project in the UPAs:** it is the detailing of the modus operandi of the improvement interventions, which was in constant improvement showing that knowledge and learning must be continuous;
3. **Lean thinking:** is the conceptual basis that underlies the execution of the Lean Project, the various stages of application and the construction of knowledge from a dynamic and practical learning of a theory in healthcare;
4. **Good practice report:** documentation that certifies the execution of improvements reported in A3 and made available in the project database;

5. **Documentation, sharing and communication strategies:** virtual meetings, technical productions, scientific articles and others.

ORGANIZATION BACKGROUND

The area of education holds a series of systematizations, procedures, and techniques for the improvement of individual or group learning whose basis is the everyday life, the environment, culture, customs, and traditions. The literature presents the humanistic thought of Carl Rogers, the behavioral thought of Skinner and Behaviorist, and the cognitive thought of Piaget and Vygotsky, all of which are base on psychology, biology, and humanities.

In the humanist view, learning requires goals, experience, and proven results from social demands. It is validated and productive when there is socialization and group work. Behavioral thinking uses positive reinforcement (successful experience) and negative reinforcement (situations with adverse responses) to stimulate actions and predict responses until they are conditioned to the individual. In cognitive theory, learning integrates the individual to the environment, stimulates critical thinking, and focuses on the process, that is, everyday experience, investigation, and discovery reinforce the acquisition of knowledge (Meirelles and Oliveir, 2013).

Once acquired, this knowledge is allie to the management function, that is, a need was created to produce, disseminate, and allow access and use of information and, on the other hand, a concern with the excess of data and excessive access to its storage banks (Alvarenga Neto, Barbosa and Pereira, 2007).

The conceptual evolution and the perception of these visions begin with the lack of innovation and association to information management, follows with the prioritization of organizational processes and activities through sophisticated techniques for obtaining and building the database and, ends in the conception of knowledge (tacit and explicit) as a driver of organizational changes and adaptations (Alvarenga Neto, Barbosa and Pereira, 2007). The management is of the context to which the knowledge is insert, not to it in itself.

A flow that promotes interaction between people, the sharing of common experiences based on actions and practices is favorable to tacit knowledge. Its consolidation via materialization, systematization, and grouping, and making it available either for use or for new production, are characteristic aspects of explicit knowledge. The interactions and conversions between the two types is know as the knowledge spiral/matrix (Nonaka, Toyama, Konno, 2000).

Other scholars argue that data and information are manageable, not knowledge because it depends on the actions, interests and dedication of the appropriating individual (Wilson, 2002; Von Krogh, Ichizo and Nonaka, 2001). The solution found by organizational managers was to institutionalize knowledge-creating environments and stimulate their use with team training, for example, without developing greater management concerns or control over the elaborated product.

Objectively, knowledge management (KM) identifies and analyzes the existing knowledge in an organization with a view to creating procedures and systems, storing, disseminating and promoting the use of knowledge for its own sake by adding value to its main asset (Owen, 1999). The key understanding of this process is the distinction between what is know by the individual and what is know as a group of people working together.

Organizational learning is complementary to knowledge management by encouraging the solution of organizational problems based on the individual and collective solving capacity of its collaborators. The good results of this conceptual junction will emerge from practical experiences that change behaviors and accumulate knowledge in the perspectives:

1. Of the worker via informal and natural learning of accumulation, control and fluidity of knowledge from the interaction individual environment (Flach and Antonello, 2010; Brito, 2008);
2. Of the environment by using habits, practices and influences of the learning culture of the individual and his nation as a basis for the success of knowledge management by stimulating the creation of a favorable environment for the assimilation and sharing of knowledge as new ideas arise (Inazawa, 2009; Pozo, 2008);
3. Of the application to each type of organization as the corporate universities responsible for the training of employees by means of the strategic needs of the organizations (Scorsolini-Comin, Inocente and Miura, 2011; Grzybovski, 2007).

Given this scenario, future challenges for knowledge management arise. The first is to incorporate the theoretical basis of KM into organizational management, and the second is to use the experiences and practices of individuals and collectives. It is known that knowledge is a continuous process intrinsic to human beings and that it can be promoted and stimulated, its management is its enhancement process and through information management.

Whether in the construction of a data or information or a document, knowledge is consolidated and is subject to processes of physical, intellectual organization, selection, disposal, and safekeeping, i.e., document management is a fundamental part of knowledge management and requires administrative procedures (Vieira, 2020).

It is in the rescue of fragmented information and structuring of informal flows that knowledge management assists the correction of actions, the identification of opportunities and anticipate activities to competitors (Valentim et al., 2003). In this way, it assumes a strategic importance as an organizational asset, of innovation and competitive advantage whose improvements are nurture back in a closed cycle of creation, acquisition, transfer and use (Vieira, 2020).

KNOWLEDGE MANAGEMENT AND PUBLIC ADMINISTRATION

The provision of service, the provision of information, the use and sharing of knowledge are daily actions in the public sector, which is not motivated by competition, but by results that can ensure the quality-of-service delivery, efficiency in the use of resources, social effectiveness and economic and social development (Cong and Pandya, 2003; Batista, 2012).

Article 37 of the Federal Constitution states that a public administration must comply with the principles of legality, impersonality, morality, publicity, and efficiency. Learn and innovation are essential to knowledge management in public administration, and only in this way will it be possible to provide improvements in the sector.

A point to be highlight is that it is not enough to identify the possibilities for improvement or the importance of knowledge management. It is essential to create measurement and intervention/implementation tools once the focus is on results. Some models (chart 1) stand out namely APQC's Road Map for Knowledge Management Results (2003), the World Bank's Organizational Knowledge Management (OKA), the Most Admired Knowledge Enterprise (MAKE), the European KM Forum's Evaluation Model, the Gespública's public management evaluation tool, an APO model focused on small and medium companies, and the one used by the Organization for Economic Cooperation and Development (OECD).

The Road Map for Knowledge Management Results is a road map for implementing KM prepared in 2003 by the American Productivity and Quality Center (APQC) and is described in five stages and each stage contains an affirmative description about the events, objectives, key employees, responsibilities, organizational structure, governance, measurement methods, budget, and finances.

Stage I or initial stage is to define the vision, justification and use of a technological resource for KM. The second stage is to develop strategies, focus on the development and implementation of pilot projects. The evaluation of these will occur in stage III from the design and implementation of the practices. Next, stage IV expands the project and applies it throughout the organization, so that, in the last stage, institutionalization occurs via alignment with the organization's management model. It is in the fifth stage that continuous evaluation will take place, with the establishment of a governance structure and the alignment of KM with institutional goals.

KM is defined by the OECD as an activity that brings together the collection, use, and sharing of knowledge in the organization. Among the activities can be highlighted the sharing of information among the various units, provide resources to acquire knowledge, encourage older employees to disseminate experiences, document the learnings either in manuals, protocols, best practices, magazines, external publications, etc. (OECD; Industry Canada, 2003).

Table 1. Knowledge management models

KM Models	Features and Objectives	Structure
Knowledge Management Results Roadmap (APQC, 2003)	• It is a model/method of CG implementation. • Evaluate the effectiveness of implementation in organizations. • Describe the steps to implement KM. Identify the stage of implementation of KM.	• Beginning: vision, mission, I.T. • Strategy development. • Design and implementation of Knowledge Management practices via pilot project. • Expansion and support. • Institutionalization.
OKA (Fonseca, 2006)	• It is an assessment tool that allows the organization to know its degree of maturity in KM. • Identifies key areas to be improve to advance and institutionalize KM. • Align KM to the objectives and goals of the organization. • Use technology to support KM. • Focus on leadership to institutionalize KM. • Build an organizational culture to encourage and stimulate the active participation of people in KM. • Associate KM with the management of support and final processes. • Use indicators to monitor the management of intellectual assets and value generation.	• People: culture, sharing, practical execution, knowledge and learning. • Processes: leadership, strategy, flows, operationalization, alignment, indicators, monitoring. • Systems: technological support, access to knowledge, content management, environment infrastructure.

continues on following page

Table 1. Continued

KM Models	Features and Objectives	Structure
Gespública	• It is an instrument for evaluating the implementation of managerial processes in Public Management. • It diagnoses the degree of maturity in KM in public organizations.	• Assesses the development, creation, and sharing of knowledge. • Evaluates how knowledge is maintained and protected. • Identifies how the organization ensures that KM is use to improve its processes, products and services.
APO (2009)	• It is an approach that acts in an integrated way to create, share, and apply knowledge to increase productivity, profitability, and organizational growth. • It is a method and a model that describes KM and guides its implementation.	• Accelerators: leadership, technology, people, and processes. • KM process: identify, create, store, share, and apply knowledge. • Results: productivity, quality, profitability and growth.
OCDE (2002) - Survey of Knowledge Management Practices for Ministries / Departments / Agencies of Central Government	• To know the performance of public organizations of OECD member governments in relation to the challenges of the knowledge economy. • KM as a top management priority; the implementation of KM practices. • The results of KM strategies.	• Organizational changes: decentralization of authority, debureaucratization of management units, information and communication technologies. • People development: mentoring and training. • Transfer of competencies: database, good work practices. • Managerial changes and knowledge sharing incentives: performance evaluation, promotion due to knowledge sharing, evolution of the role of managers.
MAKE (*The know network*, 2011)	• It is a methodology to diagnose the maturity level of organizations in KM and innovation. • It points out critical success factors and processes to be insert in the KM of a public administration.	• Organizational culture. • Leadership. • Innovation. • Intellectual capital. • Sharing. • Learning. • Customer Relationship Management (CRM). • Shareholder Return.
European Forum Evaluation Model		• Strategies. • Social and human criteria. • CG organization. • KM Processes. • Technologies. • Leadership. • Performance evaluation. • Implementation and business cases.
KM Model for Public Administration (Batista 2012)	• It is a study that describes a generic, holistic, results-focused model for KM in public administration in Brazil.	• Strategic drivers: vision, mission, objectives, strategies, and goals. • Enablers: leadership, technology, people, processes. • Processes: identify, create, store, share, and apply. • KDCA cycle: make the plan, execute, check, correct, and store. • Results: immediate (learning and innovation) and final. • Stakeholders: citizen-user and society.

Source: Adapted from Batista (2012).

In general, the literature consolidates some KM implementation models and intertwines them with organizational maturity assessment methods regardless of the area or environment to which they were developed. In a complementary way, the theory defines as constituent processes of knowledge management the identification, creation, storage, sharing, and application. The effectiveness of KM results, for the public administration, in the creation of mechanisms of response to new challenges, establishment of management practices that promote innovation and quality improvement of processes, products and services.

BRAZIL'S PUBLIC HEALTH SYSTEM

The National Humanization Policy - NHP is a transversal public policy applied to the whole health work process, from assistance to management, the subject and the collective are protagonist agents, encompassing the offer of services, care technologies, and the construction of safe, harmonious environments that ensure comfort and well-being to users.

The emergency services have a serious problem of overcrowding and a spontaneous demand of patients with simple diseases that amplifies the number of attendances in these units. Planning work routines and implementing projects and proposals aimed at ensuring efficient and dignified care that alleviates the pressure of this excessive demand is configure as a way out to change this scenario. Thus, humanization is the only way to influence the effects that plague the routine care in the urgency and emergency network.

The training in National Humanization Policy provides for simultaneous application in 50 24-hour units distributed in different states of Brazil. The goal is to add specialized implementation capacity pertinent to the area belonging to the Restructuring Project Implementation of Humanization in the Flow of Patient Care in 24-hour ECUS.

The Emergency Care Units (ECUs) occupy the intermediate level of complexity between the Basic Health Units (primary care) and the medium and high complexity, integrating the Fixed Pre-Hospital Network. Its premise "Open Doors" is direct to the way the health system proposes to guarantee a desired medical care free of access restrictions, requires broad compliance of the environment and of the multidisciplinary team, under the risk of a drop in the quality of the service provided. It operates 24 hours a day, every day of the week, and has care teams composed of qualified multi-professionals who are compatible with the care needs of a locality.

The intention is to promote a new culture of care that supports the improvement in the quality and efficiency of the services provided to the users of the Unifield Health System seen at the ECUs, giving priority to the care of patients with more serious conditions, increasing the productivity and efficiency of the Unit's specialized teams, as well as reorganizing the flows and guaranteeing care provided in a humanized way.

The Lean Project in ECUs is a project of the Ministry of Health/National Health Fund run in partnership with the Fluminense Federal University (UFF) to optimize the patient flow in 50 ECUs distributed in the national territory, from the risk classification, resulting in the structuring of a fast flow (Fast Track). It is manage by UFF with the advice of the Brazilian Institute of Public Policy (IBRAPP).

The objectives are: i) Implement the project to restructure the Humanization of the Flow of Patient Care in the urgency and emergency network ECU - 24 hours; ii) Empower the humanized training of health professionals in humanized care; iii) Institute humanized reception to users and family members and contribute with the multidisciplinary team of the Emergency Room, meeting the National Humanization Policy in urgency and emergency health services; iv) Reduce the MTT (Average Time of Stay); v) Point out potential opportunities to improve the flow and process aiming at a more efficient management of resources; vi) Train professionals in new management methodologies (Lean Healthcare, Theory of Constraints, Theory of Queues, among others).

In conducting the project, the methodology called HUMANIZA-SUS was elaborate in the scope of the National Humanization Policy. In the operational strategies, the Lean methodology based on Lean Healthcare as well as in the monitoring through Lean Healthcare consulting services for process improvement employing the DMAIC (Define, Measure, Analyze, Implement, and Control) methodology in conducting the projects in all their phases. The execution timeline and application plan stipulated three goals: Goal 1: Support the development of organizational and care skills (deadline 04/2020) - Planning: Alignment with MOH/Health Secretariats and Directors. Structuring of Support Material in the meetings and educational materials. Technical Visit and Initial Evaluation of the Services; Goal 2: Support in the use of tools and in leading teams for changes and reorganization of processes (deadline: 04/2020 to 07/2020) - Review of instruments, tools and construction of guiding diagrams. Elaboration of educational and support materials related to the intervention/change processes. Monitoring of activities (technical visits); Goal 3: Monitoring and Results Presentation (deadline: 07/2020 to 01/2021) - Project follow-up. Final presentation of results of the services.

In a joint action with the hired Consulting Company, a plan with goals was elaborate until 01/2021 for the restructuring of 50 Emergency Care Units (ECU - 24 h) - Train 250 servers in specialists in improvement and welcoming of the patient care flow. Train 50 managers in leadership and humanization of the patient care flow. Reduce the overcrowding scale of the community emergency department by one level. Implement 100 Kaizens to support the humanization and patient flow improvement projects Monitor patient, family and staff satisfaction indicators.

The Lean methodology reflects a philosophy of process improvement based on time, value, continuous flows, and elimination of waste. In healthcare it has as indicators the NEDOCS that creates a scale of overcrowding of the National Emergency Department to measure the overcrowding in emergency rooms and their risk to patients. The second indicator is the LOS (Length of Stay) that measures the length of stay of the patient in the emergency room. Therefore, the use of Lean methodology will act in the rational management of resources, spaces, and supplies.

SOLUTIONS AND RECOMMENDATIONS

The Initial Diagnosis

The initial diagnosis was the primary source of information about the universe of study, because it was necessary to understand the operation, the structure and the real needs to be prioritise by the actions of the Lean Project. Thus, it was possible to verify the understanding of the employees of the ECUs, their level of knowledge in relation to the workplace and the extent of their involvement with the management as well as the on-site verification of the determinations provided in legislation.

The 50 ECUs participating in the Lean Project were distributed in the states of Maranhão, Ceará, Distrito Federal, Goiás, Mato Grosso, Santa Catarina, São Paulo and Rio de Janeiro being distributed in type I (3), type II (20) and type III (27) as per Ordinance No. 10 of January 3, 2017, chapter V, Art. 13. It was up to the Ministry of Health to choose and invite the Units contemplated with the 24-hour ECUs Lean Project.

The data were collect through a semi-structured questionnaire with 38 questions sent to the Emergency Care Units and answered by their managers. The structure of the questionnaire can be share into four pillars: the architecture of the unit, the infrastructure, the human material, and the flow of care with its metrics.

Although the questionnaire is made of direct questions, its understanding and answers are far from the objective that is required of the respondents. This leads to a failure to interpret the data because there is no uniformity in the answers. In this sense, many of the answers were discard in the data analysis after being plott in spreadsheets. However, they were considere in the conclusions of each unit within the state under study.

After returning the questionnaire and in view of the answers, the project coordination passed it on to the researcher in charge to treat the data with an approach on Capacity Management in the Lean Healthcare environment. This is the model to be develop for implementation in the Emergency Care Units - ECUs according to the Work Plan describe in Term of Decentralized Execution of Resources No. 125/2019 whose goal is to promote a new culture of care that supports the improvement in quality and efficiency of services provided to users of the Unified Health System seen in ECUs.

The conclusion of the analysis of the Initial Diagnosis shows that within the four pillars described as study parameters - Architecture, Infrastructure, Human Resources and Flow of Care - there is no uniformity of implementation of the various Emergency Care Units studied related to the pillars established as study parameters. In the Architecture pillar, it is observes that there is no uniformity in relation to the type of EDU that should follow the standards determined in Chapter V, Article 13 (Table 2).

Table 2. Standard of architecture and infrastructure of the ECUs

Definition of Sizes Applicable to ECU 24h	Recommended Population for the ECU 24h Area	Minimum Number of Observation Beds	Minimum Number of Beds - Emergency Room
Type I	50.000 to 100.000 residents	7 beds	2 beds
Type II	100.001 to 200.000 residents	11 beds	3 beds
Type III	200.001 to 300.000 residents	15 beds	4 beds

Source: Lean Magazine in ECUs (2020)

Some ECUs type I and type II serve far above what is recommended by the architecture considering their coverage area. Type III UAPs also present a discrepancy in relation to their architecture, since the actual service is much lower than the projected demand, which demonstrates a certain idleness in relation to patient care, while others are swollen and cannot provide, minimally, a humanize and efficient service.

Another important factor in the architecture of the ECUs is the infrastructure project designed according to the type of unit. In relation to the minimum number required for observation beds, this classification by type does not meet in most cases what the Ordinance 10 determines. It was observe in the Initial Diagnosis that none of the studied ECUs meets the minimum required, regardless of their type.

In relation to the minimum number of beds in the emergency room, the Type I ECUs meet the requirement because they consider that this is the minimum number required for operation, but the Type II and Type III ECUs do not meet the architecture requirements. However, when the number of chairs in the service is evaluate, many of these ECUs present a high number of chairs characterizing that there is inefficiency in the service and that these chairs are necessary due to the low level of service affecting the flow of the patient.

Analyzing the human material, table 3 shows the standards of care according to the types of units architected and their infrastructure. In view of the answers to the questionnaire, it is observe that there is a very large variation regarding the distribution of professionals in these units. A Type I ECU may have a high number of professionals in relation to a Type II or Type III ECU and vice versa.

Table 3. Human Resource Standard for ECUs

Definition of Sizes Applicable to ECU 24h	No. of Medical Professionals/24h for the Unit's Operation	Nr. of Medical Appointments/Month	Nr. of Risk Classification Consultations Risk Classification/Month
Type I	2 (1 diurnal, 1 nightly)	2250	2250
Type II	3 (2 diurnal, 1 nightly)	3375	3375
Type III	4 (2 diurnal, 2 nightly)	4500	4500

Source: Source: Lean Magazine in ECUs (2020)

The minimum number of risk classification rooms and the high number demanded does not provide fluidity and effectiveness to the care; affect the efficiency of the flow of care and consequent increase in the waiting for the patient. This fact is contrary to the theory of Humanized Care.

It is notorious that in certain units there is an excess of medical professionals, disregarding what Ordinance 10 determines. On the other hand, the number of other professionals varies according to each unit, with no relation to the type of unit established.

It was not clear in the Initial Diagnosis how the flow of care is process in relation to the waiting time of the entire process, from the entrance to the exit of the patient. It is understood that this must be influence by the high volume of demand due to the Covid19 pandemic, where many managers had no parameters to answer this question.

However, both medical care and risk classification were impeded by a more detailed analysis of the architecture and infrastructure in each unit studied. It is important to level the staffing of the units according to the demand, thus eliminating idleness in some units and overload of work in others. It is also necessary that the back up staff be better size to meet the emergency and urgency requests in a shorter cycle time.

A no less critical factor in this Initial Diagnostic study and that goes through the Type of ECU is the number of medical offices. There is no clear evidence about the relationship between the type of the unit and the demand required; it is not clear if the architecture took into consideration the medical specialty in relation to the real need of that unit in the environment where it is installe.

Likewise, in relation to the structure of equipment and exams, it is observed that almost all have X-ray and Basic Laboratory with their own use and some outsourced. However, the waiting line for results is long, which characterizes a waste for the service flow, since the patient needs to return another day to continue the service.

It is concluds then, that the 50 ECUs studied in relation to Capacity Management (Lima et al., 2021) in the care of urgency and emergency patients need an improvement project that meets the Decentralized Execution of Resources Term No. 125/2019 with humanized care and continuous flow. It is also necessary to have more flexibility in the care process (Fast Track) and adjustments in the infrastructure of the units, so that there is no interruption in the flow of patient care with waste of waiting and unnecessary displacement.

Thus, the analysis of the results of the initial diagnosis showed that the architecture, the infrastructure, the human material and the service flow are opportunities for improvement adherent to the Lean Project in the 24-hour ECUs. The application of Lean Healthcare in the Emergency Care Units is a proposal for the improvement of fast and humanized care to patients, a new vision of management in the health area and the training of employees in the units to use modern management tools consolidated in other productive segments, thus generating a model of care in these units effectively and efficiently.

ROAD MAP FOR THE LEAN PROJECT IN ECUS

Just as in the construction of knowledge teaching-learning methodologies are used, the Lean Project sought active methodologies and facilitating instruments for this process, for example the DMAIC for the creation of a road map. This is a point in common with what was observes in the literature and before discussed in table 1.

Based on the results of the initial diagnosis, at the beginning of knowledge construction, and aiming to structure an application method in the Emergency Care Units, a road map was prepared using the DMAIC to structure the sequenced steps for Project implementation. Table 4 presents the details of the actions per phase and their main agents.

Table 4. Road map for the Lean Project in ECUs

Road Map	Ministry of Health	Fluminense Federal University
D (define)	• Consensus on the Project Scope (Fast Track and Humanization). •Define the invited ECUs.	• Ministry of Health. • Define the implementation method in the ECU aligned to the Validation Protocol. • Define the focus of the subprojects to be implemented (Fast Track and Humanization - HUMANIZA-SUS) with the Ministry of Health. • Guide the Good Practices in the ECUs. • Define the profile of the team, which cannot change during the project. •Agree with the Ministry of Health on the indicators to be use. •Define the audit methodology. •Elaborate the Project Contract, in order to guarantee the sensitization and integration of the involved entities. • Start the Project (A3 Report). • Validate the Initial Diagnosis, and may take advantage of a Value Stream Mapping of the current state to identify opportunities. • Hold an Awareness Meeting.
M (measure)	• Identify, through indicators and strategy, which PAUs will be invite. • Send the terms of commitment.	• Performing the Initial MDE-S Self-diagnosis. • Training of multipliers and cross-functional leadership in Lean Healthcare/ DMAIC. • Advisory and Implementation of DMAIC/KAIZEN; • Apply DMAIC/KAIZEN: - Design the VSM's of the current state of Fast Track and Humanization (respect for people) flows; - Perform SIPOC and VOC of the patient flow; - Draw the Spaghetti, Cause and Effect and Process Flow diagrams; - Identify the critical variables of the two processes. • Fill out A3 Report.

continues on following page

Table 4. Continued

Road Map	Ministry of Health	Fluminense Federal University
A (analyse)	• Analyze the return of the terms by the ECUs. • Analyze the Initial Diagnosis reports delivered by UFF. • Send to UFF the ECUs participating in the Project. • Analyze the proposals and schedules from UFF.	• Analyze the current measurement system; • Define list of Problems and Proposals (Action Plan). • Design the VSM's of the future state of the Fast Track and Humanization flows, contemplating possible layout adjustments and resource allocation (material, human) to meet such demands. • Fill out the A3 Report, as a basis for dissemination of the activities developed. • Analyze sectorial indicators. • Analyze the relationship of indicators (dwell time and waiting time) with the risk classification of sectors. • Evaluate and implement the 5 Senses (5S).
I (improve)	• Participate and Support the implementation of the Project. • Provide feedback during the course of the Project.	• Implement the actions of the Action Plan at GEMBA, through practical and theoretical training of employees in Lean Healthcare tools. • Implement monitoring of the waiting times and length of stay of patients in the ECU, defining the formula for calculating them. • Fill out Good Practice forms with the implemented actions and photographic records. • Implement project huddle meeting system and Visual Management. • Complete A3 Report. • Implement method (and train employees) for data collection. • Establish and disseminate the organization's guidelines and results. • Implement 10 steps of Patient Safety.
C (control)	• Participate in remote meetings for effectiveness analysis - audit (coordinated by UFF) • Analyze the performance indicators. • Determine corrections, if necessary. • Monitor number of technical visits to the ECUs. • Officialize the end of the training and advisory stage. • Analyze the monitoring of indicators.	• Perform staggered audits. • Follow up on performance indicators. • Perform new FINAL MDE-S self-diagnostic, as well as VSM's, and compare with previous ones (effectiveness analysis). • Close DMAIC/KAIZEN. • Conclude A3 Report. • Deliver the Good Practices carried out. • Hold a face-to-face meeting. • Report results to the MH (UFF). • Socialization: Live with all the ECUs through the LabDGE website. • Meeting every 45 days between the representative of the ECUs and the UFF representative. • Systematize the monitoring of the results of the HUDDLE meetings through performance indicators on the implementation of best practices, disseminating the knowledge acquired, also aiming at advising new collaborators.

In allusion to a process with beginning, middle, and end, the road map has well-defined inputs planned by the sponsoring agency, guided and mediated by the University with the execution performed by the partner companies. Each step of the DMAIC has an expect output, namely: i) Define - consensus between MS and UFF; define a project contract per hospital; ii) Measure - define KPIs, guidelines, A3 report and average length of patient stay (LOS); iii) Analyze - analyze action plans, fast track flow, humanization flow and best practices; iv) Improve - implement fast track flow and humanization; v) Control - establish continuous improvement plans, average length of patient stay (LOS).

The parallelism to the learning process presents the road map as the main reference of the Lean Project because it is in constant updating; it is based on teaching methods, application, and collection of results in a systematised and structured way. It integrates people to the processes, standardises actions and defines analysis procedures or even evaluations, which refer to the initiation of a teaching-learning process applied to the ECUs.

LEAN KNOWLEDGE MANAGEMENT IN ECUS

The development of the Lean Project in the ECUs involved three agents: the individual (collaborator), the group (improvement teams) and the organization (the ECUs and the UFF researchers). Table 5 presents the 5W1H tool and the planning of actions directed to the consolidation and dissemination of knowledge among the participating units. The knowledge transformation is present in figure 1 and built based on Nonaka and Takeuchi's (1997) model.

Table 5. Knowledge strategies applied in the Lean Project in ECUs

5W1H	Magazines	Lives
What?	Fascicles containing methods and tools of the lean healthcare approach in a simple, compact and easily understandable way.	Live broadcasts with the participation of ECU professionals, researchers, and external participants.
Why?	Disseminate the knowledge to all members of the Lean Project teams in the 24h ECUs.	Expose and share the knowledge and results obtained by the ECUs improvement teams.
Where?	Public access via LabDGE website.	LabDGE's official youtube channel and a closed Facebook group for project participants.
Who?	Authorship, editing and publication of the issues under the responsibility of the project's scientific researchers.	Aimed at ECUs professionals, UFF representatives, University researchers, and external public.
When?	Monthly posting at the end of each on line meeting.	A monthly meeting.
How?	Elaboration of the content by answering "what?", "what for?" and "how is it applied?" regarding each Lean method and tool relevant to the project.	Participation of at least one ECU representative to socialize the results obtained in the application of the Project.

Figure 1. Knowledge conversion model applied to the Lean Project in ECUs.

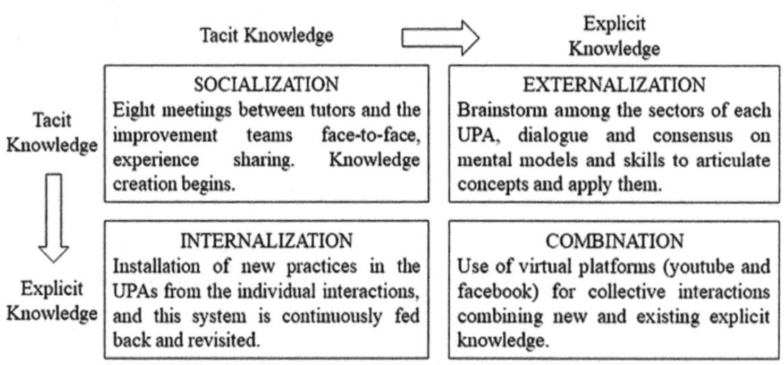

It is possible to identify the main KM processes in the experience of the Lean Project in the ECUs. One form of knowledge identification was the meeting and maintenance of a multidisciplinary team that received training and allied to their daily work practices to establish guidelines and intervention strategies in the Unit.

The permanent teaching method was the proposal implemented during the first year of the Lean Project. The starting point was the use of learning by doing, where tutors passed on the theory in the environment and in accordance with the work practice. The training themes also followed a logical order of implementation of the actions foreseen in the project schedule.

The evaluation of the Lean implementation admitted the conception of new knowledge using the new ideas, new ways to execute the work processes and introduction of new management practices. Examples are the huddle meetings, the application of 5S, the definition of indicators, the establishment of management by sight, the reorganization and standardization of internal processes and routines, and the training of the team.

The record of the knowledge created in loco has evidence: i) the development of technical reports of each of the nine visits to the Units; ii) the constitution of the best practices of Lean implementation; iii) the change or organization of the layout of internal rooms; iv) schedule modifications such as shift change, use of cafeterias, etc.; v) updating the database with the removal of incorrect or incomplete information or duplicate patients.

The development of an intervention schedule and the formation of a multidisciplinary team facilitated the sharing of information in the organization, because each member could intervene and manage their own work environment. However, it was noticed that the discipline and engagement of the team contributed to the adherence, maintenance, and sharing of improvements in the ECUs. Some internal processes were computerized and, in other cases, went through updates or were complement to meet the new scenario.

Therefore, the individual collaborator can expand his knowledge and skills, stimulate his own initiative, obtain greater insight into his work activities, and become active in the learning process. It is in the sum of individual knowledge, skills, and attitude that it is possible to improve or increase the resolutive capacity of the ECU group. The work methodology was broken into steps summarized in Figure 2 and described below.

Figure 2. Steps of learning and coaching implementation methodology.

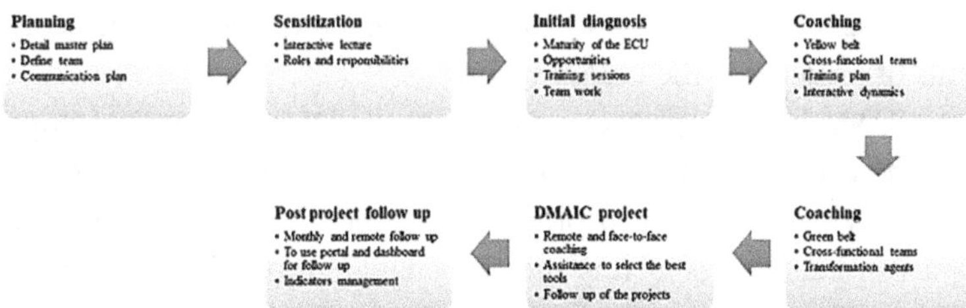

- **Step 1:** Planning/Alignment - In this phase assumptions were established for the following topics: Raising expectations; Planning activities by developing a detailed master plan; Establish the core team for the process; Develop the Stakeholder Map and the RACI (Responsibility Matrix); Create the communication plan; Customize the course material for the specific information and language; Develop the material for the awareness of the senior management of the ECUS -24hs; Develop the assessment tool for the maturity of the ECU - 24hs.

- **Step 2:** Kick Off Sensitization - Stage of sensitization of the ECUS' top executives with the objective of raising awareness by presenting the context of the program through an interactive lecture with the following programmatic content: Lean Healthcare Concepts; DMAIC Methodology; Metrics; Lean structure (Green and Yellow Belt); Criteria for choosing Belts; Roles and responsibilities; Project Selection/Survey and Evaluation of Themes of the organization. The lecture took place remotely and in person, both containing interactive dynamics, simultaneous teams - 5 workshops of 4 hs/day to attend 50 ECUS executives.
- **Step 3:** Pre Project - Operational Diagnosis - simultaneous teams in the 50 ECUs with 1.5 days in each and it is the moment for the assessment that will direct current state of maturity of the ECU. The macro-opportunities that will be work on within the training sessions and projects. The prioritization based on SMART; The definition of the team to work on ECU's projects.
- **Step 4:** Yellow Belt Training in Lean Healthcare - The Yellow Belts are members of cross-functional teams specialized in their processes, with the ability to develop Lean Healthcare projects in their work areas. A priori, they have partial dedication and participate in projects led by Green Belts. The program content is composed of: Overview of Lean Healthcare; Roles and functions within Lean Healthcare; Integration of Lean Six Sigma Tools to the DMAIC method - VOC/SIPOC; Process Map; Patient Journey; Cause and Effect Matrix; Pareto, Histogram; Brainstorming; The Herringbone Diagram or 6 M's; Action Plan; 5S; Sight Management; Standardized Work; Practical Exercises. The training was planned to be remote or face-to-face, both containing interactive dynamics planned for a 10-day load, 1 day per class (10 classes), 25 participants per class.
- **Step 5:** Green Belt Training in Lean Healthcare - Green Belts are members of cross-functional teams, with the ability to develop Lean Healthcare projects in their work areas, because they are employees specialized in their processes. They also play the role of transformation agents. A priori, they have partial dedication and participate in Lean Healthcare projects, often led by Black Belts. The training can be remote or face-to-face, both containing interactive dynamics for 10 days, 5 days per class (2 classes), 25 participants per class. Throughout this process, professionals will be trained to: Understand and apply the Lean Healthcare methodology; Understand the steps of the methodology and its supporting tools; Conduct projects focused on improving existing processes, products or services; Apply statistical methods and calculate project gains; Evaluate and report the results of projects to the organization.
- **Step 6:** Project – DMAIC: The project will follow the DMAIC methodology with its sequences of tools, with remote or face-to-face coaching. This support has the commitment of IBRAPP in the following activities: Support in project selection according to the SMART methodology; Assistance to the candidates in selecting the best analysis tools for the problems dealt with in each situation and stage of the process (DMAIC), helping them to choose the most appropriate ones and giving the direction of the next steps; Critical analysis of the tools and content used by the Belts; Critical analysis of the technical conclusions reached by the Belts; Follow-up of the projects within the Lean Healthcare methodology, pointing out the status of each project and defining deliverables until the next coaching session; Correction of project routes in terms of the need for further analysis or new directions; Orienting the Belts so that they have the capacity to interpret and align the results of the analyses with the business objectives (Savings Calculations); Recall the deliverables at each coaching session and report the deliverables through a report to the Belt/team.

Expected time of 600 days with the execution of the work by simultaneous teams in 8 visits of 1.5 days each for 50 ECUS. Each week a team will make 3 ECUS based on the locality near the ECUS with 5 Consultants. The planning of the visits totaled nine face-to-face meetings whose contents were:

- Visit 1 - Diagnose: dissemination of the Project in the ECUs, survey of opportunities, list metrics, primary analysis of the phase track, layout verification, maturity score, define team and schedule;
- Visit 2 - Define/Measure (phase 1): elaborate A3, VSM, list waste and define a data collection plan;
- Visit 3 - Measure (phase 2): data analysis, see and act;
- Visit 4 - Analyze: Ishikawa diagram, 5 whys, 2x2 matrix, queue theory, improve;
- Visit 5 - Follow up on the see and act actions, establish an action plan for the validated causes;
- Visit 6 - Follow up on the improve actions, control training, start 5S, management by sight, establish follow-up meeting rituals;
- Visit 7 - Follow up of the improve and control actions, team coaching, implementation of the control plan (routine management) and establish culture;
- Visit 8 - Follow up of the improve and control actions, team coaching;
- Visit 9 - Tollgate presentation, finalize the project.

Step 7: Post Project - Follow up: In this stage we will perform a monthly follow up through a remote portal/dashboard to follow up: PMCS - Process Managment Control System implementation; Management of the area's specific project indicators; Management of the program's driver indicators, such as CEDOCS; Follow-up of the project's pending actions; Verification and validation of the controls established by the project, feeding back the system; Issuing status reports to managers. With these actions the prospect is to ensure the sustainability and dissemination of Humanization within the system ECUS - 24hs for 30 days and simultaneous teams.

THE ROLE OF INFORMATION AND COMMUNICATION IN THE KM OF THE LEAN PROJECT IN ECUS

The objective of KM is also to reach the target audience that is the consumer of information, stakeholders, managers, leaders, employees, etc., as quickly and reliably as possible, and the means of transmission must be adapted to each reality and available resources.

Barbosa et al. (2021) proposed a generalized flow (figure 2) thinking about knowledge management to bring together people and process and feed the system at a certain periodicity. The dynamic reality of ECUs and the offer of a list of services create the need to register, document, and consolidate the knowledge management practice, considering, for example, the transfer between shifts. Before, during, and after each of these steps, it is fundamental to establish training sessions for the appropriate follow-up.

Thinking about a Lean information flow is to prioritize the diagnosis, planning and monitoring of its components, to seek continuous improvement, eliminate waste of resources and value information against the demands and other contexts. The standardization of the activities related to information and communication follows the premise of clarity, organization, trust, proper and intelligible identity.

Figure 3. Proposed generalized flow of information to the health environment
Source: Barbosa et al. (2021)

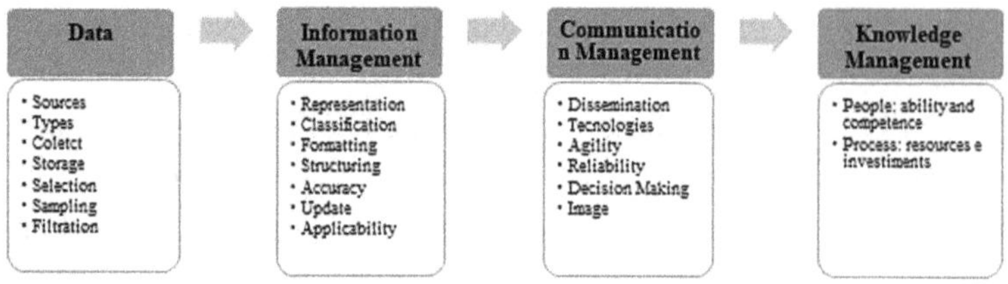

After a descriptive, documentary and explanatory research followed by consultation of the A3 reports available in the database of the Lean Project in 24h ECUs, the official website and media platforms followed by graphic analysis of the results, KM was present in the following forms:

- Literature content produced in 8 technical-scientific books and the proposal is to comprehensively present the methods and tools of the Lean methodology to all participants of the Project Restructuring Implementation of Humanization in the flow of patient care in 24-hour ECUs. All of then can be read at the project website. They are namely: Lean design and leadership in ECUs, v.1, n. 1, jul/2020; Good practices: A3 thinking, the PDCA cycle and good practices, v. 1, n. 2, sep/2022; 5S: organization, quality and efficiency of the healthcare environment, v.1, n. 3, oct/2020; Lean and NHP: the Lean methodology and the National Humanization Policy, v. 1, n. 4, dec/2020; Lean healthcare: Lean thinking, standardized work and the 8 waste in health, v. 2, n. 1, jan/2021; Pulled flow and sequencing of patient care, v. 2, n. 2, feb/2021; Fast track in 24h ECUs, v. 2, n. 3, feb/2021; The 7 quality tools, v. 2, n. 4, mar/2021; HFMEA: an alternative for risk management, v. 2, n. 5, apr/2021; VSM: value stream mapping, v. 2, n. 6, may/2021; Monitoring patient care: using power BI, v. 2, n. 7, jul/2021;
- Ten virtual meetings, one per month, with themes versed in Lean Six Sigma tools and principles;
- Dashboard to follow up on the actions and monitoring of the 677 good practices using power BI;
- A virtual media for registration and certificate;
- A virtual platform composed of digital media (LabDGE portal), social media (YouTube, Facebook) and a closed social network (Lean Project in ECUs).

Aiming to reach the public, promote communication, create a network of relationships, consolidate and disseminate knowledge among all members of the ECUs teams, the strategy of sharing experiences via virtual meetings was fruitful due to the circumstances of the pandemic scenario and an attempt to bring together the participating units. However, the insertion of participants in the first four meetings, with a relative value of 31% in the first Live, had a significant drop after the fourth.

FUTURE RESEARCH DIRECTIONS

The challenges of knowledge management involve, in particular, the simplification of it to the use of information and communication technologies. If on one hand we have the exacerbated use of media resources and the creation of content, on the other hand we have the appropriation, use, and transfer!

To think that each individual carries within him his own knowledge, his change depends on his ability to apprehend, to be receptive, and to disseminate among his peers. People are not afraid of information technology, but they are concerned about how it affects their daily work.

Organizations that use the internal environment to stimulate permanent education in their collaborators make possible the personal development to meet a labor specialty need. However, knowledge management requires a deeper transformation, that is, the human being must develop his or her skills and competencies, have the ability to transfer the new knowledge and combine it with processes, research, and investments.

The clarity of the processes, standardized procedures, work routines, and a committed team are primordial variables for knowledge management. In this analysis, two points should be made. The first corresponds to the sequencing planned and executed, and the second refers to the capacity and availability of the teams to perpetuate the improvement actions. Institutionalizing the culture through the postponement positioning or even changes of its members as well as data surveys and delays in the implementations are other challenges to be perceive in the management.

An undefined issue is the evaluation and quantification of knowledge. The literature presents measurable results from performance indicators, not from knowledge itself.

CONCLUSION

Humanization is the only way to influence the effects that plague the routine care in the urgency and emergency network. The restructuring of Emergency Care Units makes it possible to organize the routine of medical care, improving the quality of services provided to the population. In a complementary way, it reduces the possibilities of dissatisfaction and dissatisfaction of the users, prioritizing the care of patients with more serious conditions, increasing the productivity and efficiency of the specialized teams in the Unit, as well as reorganizing the flows and guaranteeing the care in a humanized way.

The Lean Project in the ECUs acted as a facilitator and, with the help of researchers, guided the creation and consolidation of knowledge management in the 50 units. A challenge was to gather data and manage information to minimize losses and increase communication, being fundamental the use of social media in the dissemination of knowledge.

The scope of the project delivered more than 28,300 hours of training to 548 employees in the period from Dec/2019 to May/2021. The ten meetings reached 3,530 participants from 8 Brazilian states and the Federal District. The "socialization" and "externalization" phases were the most significant, in numbers, for generating 450 technical visit reports. The "internalization" was materialized in the form of A3 reports of good practices created as the improvements were consolidate in the units. An incremental action in the "combination" phase was the production and dissemination of three videos to integrate the teams.

The learning theory brought varied views of thinking about learning, and when associated with the Lean philosophy it allowed a broad understanding of the convergent points of establishing sequenced and logical planning, goal setting, and the use of experience in obtaining humanistic results. Having motivated and committed teams validates socialization and group work, creates successful experiences and learning in adverse situations, stimulating the behavioral side. In this way, it expects that, internally, the cognitive of an individual acts with critical thinking focused on processes, on everyday experiences, and on continuous investigation towards the discovery and apprehension of knowledge.

AKNOWLEDGMENT

The authors would like to thank the Brazilian ministry of health, the uff – fluminense federal university, and the euclides da cunha foundation. This research is part of the "lean project in upa 24h" that has been funded by the Brazilian ministry of health (ted 15/2021, number: 25000.103452/2021-14).

REFERENCES

Al-Sudairy, M. A. T., & Vasista, T. G. K. (2012). Fostering knowledge management and citizen participation via e-governance for achieving sustainable balanced development. *IUP Journal of Knowledge Management*, *10*(1), 2012.

Alvarenga Neto, R. C. D. D., Barbosa, R. R., & Pereira, H. J. (2007). Knowledge management or management of knowledge age organizations? A theoretical-practical essay based on interventions in the Brazilian reality [Gestão do conhecimento ou gestão de organizações da era do conhecimento? Um ensaio teórico-prático a partir de intervenções na realidade brasileira]. *Perspectivas em Ciência da Informação*, *12*, 5–24. doi:10.1590/S1413-99362007000100002

APO. (2009). *Knowledge management: facilitator´s Guide*. APO.

APQC. (2002). *Measuring knowledge management*. APQC.

Barbosa, C., Lima, A., Sobrinho, A., Calado, R., & Lordelo, S. (2021, September). Information, Communication and Knowledge for Lean Healthcare Management Guidelines, a Literature Revision. In *IFIP International Conference on Advances in Production Management Systems* (pp. 250-257). Springer. 10.1007/978-3-030-85902-2_27

Baskerville, R., & Dulipovici, A. (2006). The theoretical foundations of knowledge management. *Knowledge Management Research and Practice*, *4*(2), 2006. doi:10.1057/palgrave.kmrp.8500090

Batista, F. F. (2012). Knowledge management model for the Brazilian public administration: How to implement knowledge management to produce results for the benefit of the citizen/Fábio Ferreira Batista. – Brasília. *Ipea*, *132*, 2012.

BRASIL. Constitution of the Federative Republic of Brazil: promulgada em 5 de outubro de 1988. 41. ed. atual. e ampl. São Paulo: Saraiva, 2008.

Brito, L. M. P. (2008). *Competence management, knowledge management and learning organizations: instruments of appropriation by capital of the worker's knowledge*. Imprensa Universitária.

Cong, X., & Pandya, K. V. (2003). Issues of knowledge management in the public sector. *Electronic Journal of Knowledge Management*, *1*(2), 25–33.

Daud, S. (2012). Knowledge management processes in SMES and large firms: A comparative evaluation. *African Journal of Business Management*, *6*(11), 2012.

Flach, L., & Antonello, C. S. (2010). Informal Learning theory and its implications for organizations. [A teoria sobre aprendizagem informal e suas implicações nas organizações.] *Gestao. Org*, *8*(2), 193–208.

Fonseca, A. (2006). *Organizational knowledge assessment methodology.* World Bank Institute.

Fugate, M., Prussia, G. E., & Kinicki, A. J. (2012). Managing employee withdrawal during organizational change: The role of threat appraisal. *Journal of Management, 38*(3), 890–914. doi:10.1177/0149206309352881

Grzybovski, D. (2007). *Knowledge Platform and Transgenerational Learning in Family Businesses* [Doctorate in Administration. Lavras Federal University.

Inazawa, F. K. (2009). The role of organizational culture and learning for successful knowledge management. *Perspectives in Information Science, Belo Horizonte, 14*(3), 2009.

Instrument for the evaluation of public management. (2010). CICLO.

Lean Magazine in ECUs (2020). *Initial Diagnostic Report in 50 ECUs.* Author.

Lima, A., Barbosa, C., Sobrinho, A., Calado, R., & Sobral, A. P. (2021, September). Capacity Management as a Tool for Improving Infrastructure in the Lean Healthcare: A Systematic Review. In *IFIP International Conference on Advances in Production Management Systems* (pp. 298-304). Springer. 10.1007/978-3-030-85902-2_32

Meirelles, C. S. C., & Oliveir, V. M. S. (2013). Didactics, Teaching and Tutoring in Higher Education. Aracaju. *UnitPós, 2013*, 15.

Nonaka, I., Toyama, R., & Konno, N. (2000). SECI, Ba and leadership: A unified model of dynamic knowledge creation. *Long Range Planning, 33*(1), 5–34. doi:10.1016/S0024-6301(99)00115-6

OECD. (2003). *Survey of knowledge management practices in ministries/ departments/ agencies of central government.* OECD.

Owen, J. M. (1999). Knowledge management and the information professional. Information Services & Use, 9(1), 7-16. doi:10.3233/ISU-1999-19103

Pozo, J. I. (2008). The learning society and the challenge of converting information into knowledge. *Diretor Udemo, 4*(5), 2008.

Scorsolini-Comin, F., Inocente, D.F., & Miura, I.K. (2011). Organizational learning and knowledge management: guidelines for people management. *Rev. Bras. Orientac., 12*(2).

Silva, S.L. (2004). Knowledge management: A critical review guided by the knowledge creation approach. *Ci. Inf., 33*(2).

Terra, J. C. C. (2005). *Knowledge management: The great business challenge.* Terra Forum Library.

The Know Network. (2011). *Eight worldwide criteria in the international certification of auditors in knowledge management processes – Metodologia MAKE – Most Admired Knowledge Enterprises.* The Know Network.

Tuomi, I. (1999). Data is more than knowledge: Implications of the reversed knowledge hierarchy for knowledge management and organization memory. *Journal of Management Information Systems, 16*(3), 103–117. doi:10.1080/07421222.1999.11518258

Valentim, M. L. P., Lenzi, L. A. F., Cervantes, B. M. N., Carvalho, E. L. D., Garcia, H. D., Catarino, M. E., & Tomael, M. I. (2003). The Competitive Intelligence Process in Organizations. *DataGramaZero, 24*(2).

Vieira, T. de O. (2020, January/April). The contribution of document management to knowledge management in organizations: An exploratory approach [O contributo da gestão de documentos na gestão do conhecimento nas organizações: uma abordagem exploratória]. *Questão, Porto Alegre, 26*(1), 327–350. doi:10.19132/1808-5245261.327-350

Von Krogh, G., Ichijo, K., & Nonaka, I. (2001). *Enabling Knowledge Creation: Reinventing the Enterprise with the Power of Continuous Innovation* [Facilitando a Criação de Conhecimento: reiventando a empresa com o poder da inovação contínua]. Campus.

Wilson, T. D. (2002). The nonsense of knowledge management. *Information Research, 8*(1), 8–1.

Xavier, L., Oliveira, M., & Teixeira, E. (2012). Theories used in investigations on knowledge management [Teorias utilizadas nas investigações sobre gestão do conhecimento]. *RISTI*.

Chapter 12
Dialogues Between the National Humanization Policy and Lean Methodology

Maria Helena Teixeira da Silva
https://orcid.org/0000-0001-5330-3361
Fluminense Federal University, Brazil

Gabriel Nascimento Santos
https://orcid.org/0000-0002-7178-0433
Fluminense Federal University, Brazil

Laryssa Carvalho de Amaral
Fluminense Federal University, Brazil

Stephanie D´Amato Nascimento
Fluminense Federal University, Brazil

Nilra do Amaral Mendes Silva
Fluminense Federal University, Brazil

Christiane Lima Barbosa
Federal University of Para, Brazil

EXECUTIVE SUMMARY

This chapter is the result of a project signed between the Universidade Federal Fluminense and the Ministry of Health in 2019 and executed in 2020. Its objective was to identify intersections of ideas between the national humanization policy (PNH) and the Lean methodology. The path used was to seek ideas in the Lean methodology similar to the ideas present in the principles of the PNH. These intersections are understood as opportunities for actions that consider both the reduction of waste and the strengthening of aspects of the humanization of health. The authors identified seven common ideas: focus on the customer, the importance of the collective as a space for transforming work, the importance given to the workplace, shared management of processes, user inclusion, transversality of both, acting in the way of thinking about work. The conclusion is that such coincidences exist and are opportunities to deepen the dissemination of the principles and guidelines of the PNH through the actions of the Lean methodology and vice versa.

DOI: 10.4018/978-1-6684-5185-4.ch012

INTRODUCTION

Nations have been experiencing a difficult time due to the covid-19 pandemic since the beginning of 2020. By the beginning of March 2021, it had already caused more than 2,760,000 deaths worldwide and over 304,000 in Brazil, i.e., a country with over 12,330,000 infected cases. (John Hopkins University & Medicine, 2021). There are countries that are faced with a worse situation on account of scenarios in which they do not have a public health system to face such an imposed situation. This pandemic has evidenced how important it is for nations having strong health care systems to ensure the right and access to health care services for all individuals, as forecasted by the Unified Health System, SUS, which is the Brazilian healthcare system. An effective system is based on meeting the population's demand through quality services at the right time and in the right place.

Regarding healthcare in Brazil, Souza et al. (2019) consider that over time:

[...] improved performance of actions through the National Health Surveillance System, although control problems persist for large corporations, including the areas of food, tobacco and pesticides, whose practices involve risk factors related to the epidemic of chronic diseases. (p. 3)

According to these authors, the constitutional assurance of right to health has yielded positive results, nevertheless, the assertion of right "is far from being achieved" (p.3) by the population who frequently have "[...] emergency healthcare problems, gaps and errors in services, which is unacceptable in civilized societies." (p.3)

In order to combat healthcare problems faced in the latest decades, several countries have been seeking solutions through Toyota's manufacturing philosophy, a Japanese automobile company. It is known as Lean thinking, Lean methodology, Toyota Production System (TPS) or lean manufacturing which is customer-oriented and aimed at waste reduction.

In this context, it is aimed to discuss the alignment of concepts of Lean manufacturing and the National Humanization Policy adopted by SUS, otherwise known as HumanizaSus. For such a purpose, the text begins through a presentation of the National Humanization Policy (PNH) to expose the basic aspects of the Lean methodology in the following section. Then, it is discussed the identified alignments. These are understood as opportunities for introducing the HumanizaSus policy concepts into the Lean methodology, and vice versa.

ABOUT THE NATIONAL HUMANIZATION POLICY (NHP)

Among the fundamental rights established in the Federal Constitution of 1988, in the section of Social Rights, Art.6, health is enacted as the right of the Brazilian people, in addition to education, work, housing, leisure, security, social security, protection for motherhood, childhood and assistance to destitute citizens. In Art.196, the Brazilian Constitution stipulates that health is the right of all citizens and duty of the State, and that it must be ensured by social and economic policies aimed at "reducing the risk of diseases and other health predicaments, as well as universal and equal access to healthcare, practices and services for their promotion, protection and recovery." (Constituição Federal, 1988, p.55).

According to Moura (2013), the Constitution of 1988 stipulated the basis for creating an organizational structure that would ensure healthcare for everyone, in addition to indicating how this structure should be devised, as well as a definition of its objectives, thus outlining the scope of the Unified Health System.

SUS was regulated by law 8,080 in 1990, and it states its duties and functions as a public health system. Its guiding principles are universality, equity and integrality of healthcare for the Brazilian population.

The first one, universality, is the principle that promotes the idea that all Brazilian citizens, with no distinction, are entitled to health actions and services. It is this principle that best expresses the democratic feeling that health is everybody's right and the duty of the State. Before the creation of SUS, only workers with formal employment or individuals linked to the Social Security system were entitled to use public health services. In the same line of though, a free medication distribution program was launched for certain chronic diseases, which was based on the premise that access to health is a universal right and, therefore, the duty of the State.

The second principle, equity, refers to the concepts of equality and justice. It aims to guide healthcare of SUS users by considering their needs and offering more to those who need the most care. It is hoped that the differences in life and health conditions of users will be appreciated, thus the needs of users will be met by observing social differences and the population diversity using the System. According to Escorel (2008), this principle is laid down by focusing on two main aspects: health conditions, access and use of services. The former, health conditions, refers to analyzing the ratio of risks of falling ill to dying in population groups. According to the author, most health conditions are socially determined, and they are not due to natural conditions, or personal choices for reasonably healthy lifestyles. The socially and economically underprivileged are the most vulnerable to diseases, "[...] accumulating the burden of the highest frequency of disease ratio, should these be infectious, chronic-degenerative, or originating from external causes." (EscoreL, 2008, p.207). The second aspect, access and use of services, refers to the different possibilities of utilizing health services in varying degrees of complexity by individuals with equal health needs.

The third principle, integrality, considers that SUS must be prepared to listen to users and understand them in accordance with their social context. Thus, their demands and needs are going to be met. The principle of integrality is not related to a non-fragmented view of the human being, but to an integral condition. This principle is intended to combine actions aimed at establishing health as right and as service. According to Mattos (2009), it serves as a goal to be achieved, since it indicates desirable characteristics for a health system and its practices.

To make these principles viable, a policy of mainstreaming was established for all programs, projects and management agencies of SUS, i.e., the National Humanization Policy (NHP). It was the duty of SUS to operationalize such principles. Its focus is on inclusion, and it was created in 2003.

According to Pereira and Barros (2008), in the field of health policies, humanizing means transforming the models of healthcare and management of services and systems by proposing the development of new relationships between users and workers, and among themselves as well. Appreciating subjects is pointed out to make their autonomy possible and enhance their capacities to transform reality. This process occurs through shared responsibility, the creation of solidary bonds, collective participation in health management and production processes.

The NHP is linked to the Healthcare Secretariat of the Ministry of Health and is operated by teams of regional supporters who work together with the state and municipal health departments. It is through this network that action plans are collectively designed so as to propose and disseminate innovations in healthcare performance.

Humanizing, then, translates as an inclusion of differences into management and healthcare processes. Such changes are made not by an isolated person or group, but in a collective and shared way. Inclusion is aimed to encourage the proposal of new ways of healthcare and new ways of organizing work. (Ministério da Saúde/PNH, 2013).

According to the Ministry of Health (2010), humanizing is an ethical-aesthetic-political challenge. It is ethical because it starts from the premise that the ones responsible are all those involved (managers, professionals and users). It is aesthetic as it is linked to the way of doing it, i.e., to the healthcare production process. It is political once it is linked to social and institutional organization of public healthcare and management practices within the scope of SUS.

The NHP encourages communication between managers, professionals, and users as a way to develop collective processes "to confront power, work and affection relationships that often produce dehumanizing attitudes and practices that inhibit the autonomy and co-responsibility of healthcare professionals in their work and users in taking care of themselves." (Ministério da Saúde /PNH, 2013). Communication between the three groups of actors is the mechanism of change and must be considered as one of the resources for healthcare provision. The NHP states that it is the method for including actors and effecting synergy in the public healthcare network. The tools are conversation circles, the encouragement of social networks and movements, and the management of conflicts generated by the inclusion of differences. According to the Ministry of Health (2013), the inclusion of professionals is essential in management so that, daily, they can reinvent their work processes and be actors in changes in the healthcare service. As for users, according to the Ministry of Health (2013), the importance of including them and their socio-family networks into healthcare processes is a powerful resource to expand co-responsibility for self-care.

The guiding principles of the NHP are:

- **Mainstreaming:** It must be present in all SUS policies and programs. It is intended to transform working relationships through the expansion of contact and communication between people and groups. "Mainstreaming is acknowledging that the different expertise and health practices can relate to the experience of those who are assisted. Together, such knowledge can lead to healthcare in a more co-responsible way." (Ministério da Saúde - Secretaria de Atenção à Saúde, 2013)
- **Inseparability between healthcare and management:** Recognition that management decisions directly affect healthcare. It is about emphasizing the need for workers and users to get to know how management of services and how the healthcare network functions, as well as participating in the decision-making process in organizations and in collective healthcare practices. Since the responsibility for healthcare is not limited to the team of professionals, the user and "their social and family network must also be responsible for taking care of themselves in treatments, thus assuming a leading position regarding their health and those that are dear to them." (Ministério da Saúde - Secretaria de Atenção à Saúde,, 2013)
- **Protagonism, co-responsibility and autonomy of individuals and collectives:** Recognition that there will be changes in management and health care when there is the autonomy and will of people involved in sharing responsibilities. "Users are not just patients, and workers must not only follow orders: changes occur from the recognition of each participant's role." (Ministério da Saúde - Secretaria de Atenção à Saúde,, 2013)

As for its guidelines, the NHP defines concepts developed to guide and indicate ways to achieve them:

- **Acceptation:** It is about acknowledging what others can offer as a healthcare need. This acceptation must be present in relationships between staff/services and users/populations and must be built collectively from an analysis of work processes. It has a fundamental role in the network functioning.
- **Participatory management and co-management:** Co-management concerns both the inclusion of new individuals into analysis and decision processes, as well as the assignment of further management tasks. The NHP highlights two groups of co-management devices: 1- it concerns the organization of a collective management space that allows an alignment between the needs and interests of users, workers and managers; 2- it concerns the mechanisms that ensure an active participation of users and family members in the daily routine of healthcare units.
- **Ambience:** Refers to the creation of "healthy, welcoming and comfortable spaces by respecting privacy, introducing changes in the work process and places for people to meet."
- **Expanded and shared clinic:** A tool whose purpose is to contribute to a clinical approach to illness and suffering that takes into account the individual's uniqueness and complexity of the healthcare/disease process.
- **Appreciating the workforce:** This involves making the experience of workers visible and including them in decision-making processes, trusting on their ability to analyze, define and qualify work processes.
- **Defense of users' rights:** It concerns the observance of rights established by law of users of public health services. The NHP stresses the importance of encouraging the acquisition of knowledge about these rights and ensuring that they are enforced throughout the course of healthcare, i.e. from admittance to discharge.

For all principles and concepts to be applied, the NHP emphasizes the importance of training the workforce in the public healthcare network. It points out the importance of training/intervention courses and workshops, as well as discussions of work processes where guidelines and devices are experimented and reinvented in the daily routines of services. Given the social diversity of the population, working in public healthcare requires training and creativity from the professionals involved. The NHP considers that training is an intervention, and vice-versa.

According to Raimundo and Cadete (2012), the administration of public affairs and impersonal relations in healthcare in Brazil has historically focused on the disease, not on the patient. It was from the adoption of the National Humanization Policy (PNH) by the Unified Health System (SUS) that the elementary guiding principles of healthcare practices became operational, in which users, professionals and managers must be active individuals and protagonists of their actions.

Raimundo and Cadete (2012) state that, as regards the NHP, it is found that the idea of inclusion is quite present, since it is considered as one of its guidelines. This compels commitment to patients, not to the disease, by recognizing and understanding the boundaries of knowledge, starting from the premise that patients should always be worth more than the proposed diagnosis; the assurance of the clinical encounter between two individuals: healthcare workers and users; the search for a balance between damages and benefits generated by healthcare practices; trusting on multi-tasking professionals and transdisciplinary teams; and co-responsibility between different individuals towards the defense of users' rights.

According to Pereira and Barros (2008), in public healthcare policies, the term "humanization" refers to a transformation of care models and management of healthcare services and systems by including the fashioning of new relationships between users and workers, and among themselves. The authors also state that humanization, as a public healthcare policy, has been asserting itself through the creation of spaces/times that alters the way of healthcare provision, whose principles are towards increasing the degree of communication between subjects and teams (mainstreaming) and inseparability between attention and management. "This campaign is conducted by individuals who can exercise their autonomy in a welcoming, co-responsible, resolutive manner, as well as through shared management of work processes." (p.247)

Currently, it is estimated that 80% of the Brazilian population depends on healthcare provided by SUS (Duarte, Eble, Garcia, 2018). Moreover, the Brazilian population growth, the resource restriction imposed by EC 95 created on December 12, 2016, which amended the Brazilian Constitution of 1988 and has limited the growth in Brazilian government expenditure for 20 years, and the problems that have already been experienced by SUS, which are now aggravated by the covid-19 pandemic, evidence the need to seek alternatives for enhancing the efficiency and effectiveness of public healthcare services by taking advantage of existing resources and avoiding waste.

ABOUT THE LEAN METHODOLOGY

Lean methodology or manufacturing refers to a production system (*lean production*) based on three guiding principles: focus on what the customer regards as value, focus on eliminating waste and achieving perfection through small and continuous improvements. According to Womack et al. (1992), the expression "Lean production" was coined when a member of the *International Motor Vehicle Program* in research by the *Massachusetts Institute of Technology* that has listed the differences between a conventional automobile production system and the production system adopted by the Toyota company. The Toyota production system (TPS) was then classified as lean production if compared to conventional production systems, since it required less human effort; it needed a smaller amount of investments per unit of productive capacity; it required none or less inventory; its resulting products had fewer defects; it was the cause of a lower number of cases of accidents at work. Therefore, it was a production system in which less is more.

As already mentioned, the origin of Lean thinking is Japanese which lies in the TPS, also known as Lean methodology or Ohnism, in reference to Ohno, Toyota's chief engineer who had created and implemented the so-called *Kanban* method of flow control and management production using colored cards as flags, and shaped Lean thinking. In 1978, Ohno wrote the book "Toyota Production System" in which he has organized and exposed the way of thinking of the TPS. (Coriat, 1994)

Its philosophy aimed at organizing and controlling production processes is grounded in the idea of doing better with less by using available resources in the most productive way possible. Its focus is on what the customer considers as value, and its strategy is based on a continuous and systematic elimination of waste, i.e. removing the parts that do not add value to the end result according to customers.

According to the Joint Commission (2013, p.55), when applied to healthcare, examples of waste are:

- Waiting time
- Flow barriers (once they cause delays between steps and counterproductive sequence of steps)

- Communication barriers
- Bottlenecks (they cause delays and isolate responsibility and knowledge)
- Errors
- Corrections, rework, reevaluations
- Incorrect information
- Inaccessible information
- Shortage or lack of tools or equipment
- Wrong equipment
- Inappropriate equipment
- Ineffective motion
- Unnecessary motion
- Inaccessible equipment or tools
- Inflexible processes (inability to quickly switch to another product or service)
- Inadequate focus (focus on organizational needs, rather than on the customer's needs)

Some aspects of waste are directly linked to the use of physical workspace. In the Lean methodology, the physical space, i.e. the area where the work takes place, is called *Gemba* and has a special role. It has various functions, such as provision of access to information and communication, access to equipment, medicines, and transport and reception area for customers, among others. The methodology considers that devoting attention to space has positive consequences at work in terms of providing professionals and users with productivity and well-being (Joint Comission 2013, Crane & Noon 2011)

Furthermore, another aspect of workplace is pointed out by Coriat (1994) and refers to Ohno's concern about making the factory a place that is possible to be managed by using your own eyes. He adds that:

[...] and managing using one's own eyes is a management principle that is still strictly respected in each of the Toyota Motor Company's plants, as well as in factories of its main suppliers and subcontractors. Operating patterns are highlighted at each workstation. You only have open your eyes and see the sign indicating what is known as Andon which informs you about the state of lines and problems that may occasionally arise therein. (p.35)

Coriat (1994) also mentions Ohno's concern about making the space flexible according to the needs of demands. Such an objective has been reaffirmed many times by Ohno to find ways of implementing machinery and positioning workers around them, which would allow adaptations according to qualitative and quantitative variations of demands. (Coriat, 1994)

The 5S is often one of the tools used for such a purpose by the Lean methodology. The name refers to the five Japanese words seiri, seiton, seiso seiketsu, shitsuke, which mean sorting necessary items from non-necessary ones, organizing and defining the place to which each thing belongs, cleaning and standardizing based on the results of the first S, and sustaining the operation and application of the 5S, respectively (Crane & Noon, 2011).

The philosophy of this activity renders an organized, clean and functional space, and avoids waste whether in terms of transportation, handling, quality of life at work and service provision. A signposted and organized space allows users of a service to have greater autonomy for movement and access to services and information, such as colored bands on floors of some hospitals to indicate routes to users.

According to Womack (1994), as already mentioned, Ohno used visual signs and colors at workspaces for technical communication between Toyota factory workers. In addition, according to Benjamim Coriat (1994), Ohno arranged the workplace at a Toyota plant in a U-shaped layout that would allow continuous production.

According to the Lean Institute of Brazil (2020), some organizations add a sixth "S" which stands for "safety". Toyota, on the other hand, adopts four "Ss" because it considers the last one redundant, since the company holds daily, weekly, and monthly audits to verify whether there is work standardization or not. As the Institute points out, the number of S is not as important as being aware that the effort should be systematic, not isolated.

The five guiding steps of Lean manufacturing aimed to eliminate waste and improve the provision of services or product quality are:

- Identifying what customers regard as value, what they expect from the provision of a given service. This step reveals that it is necessary to think about value from the customer's point of view, in such a way as to achieve an end result which corresponds to what has value for them, i.e. customers. According to the Joint Commission (2013), the concept of value becomes clearer whenever it is established "for a product or service that meets the needs of a patient at a specific time for a specific price" (p.11). The customer defines what has value and the producer creates such value (Joint Comission, 2013). Having clarity regarding the definition of value of a product or service is important, so that it is possible to eliminate what does not add value to the customer (patient or service user) by mapping the flow of activities, which is the following step.
- Value stream mapping. It is a necessary step to identify what adds value and what is waste. It is about identifying the value chain in its entirety. Value stream mapping serves as a process map which shows how activities and information flow, from beginning to end of processes. According to the Joint Commission (2013), the easiest way to start defining the value chain is to draw up a map of the current situation, and examine it in order to identify what is and what is not waste according to customers.
- Establishing the production flow without waste. Once the steps of the value stream mapping for a given product or service are identified, activities that do not add value are eliminated, then it is necessary to ensure that changes are effected, and the following steps produce a flow capable of proceeding without obstacles or barriers. Once waste has been eliminated, it should add value and establish the chain flow, and thus develop a service from beginning to end in a continuous flow with no delay or interruption (Joint Comission, 2013). Processes are reorganized so that the flow of products or activities stream uninterruptedly through the various stages of adding value using the set of tools and lean techniques to remove all obstacles from the stream. It is about creating a stream to reduce production time or how long it takes for provision of services, otherwise known as lead time.
- Pulling production. The implementation of the first three steps is what allows achieving pulled production. Value stream mapping and producing what customers demand on time in a continuous flow allows customers to "pull" a product according to their needs. Such "pulling" makes it possible to adapt changes according to the demands of customers. (Joint Comission, 2013)
- Continuous improvement. Improving the process through an uninterrupted and endless assessment. The adoption of Lean thinking implies that workforce starts a permanent process of identification and elimination of waste. According to the Joint Commission (2013), this step is close to

> the idea of improving a process through continuous and uninterrupted assessment. In addition, it is not a difficult task to be implemented once, as an organization takes the steps of Lean thinking, the workforce starts identifying waste more and more. According to the Joint Commission (2013), "The system inherently exposes waste, failures and barriers, and as the staff members face these impediments, they start improving the process" (p.12)

It should be observed that in the first step (Identifying what has value for customers), the statement that it is the customer (patient or service user) who defines value is embedded, in addition to the idea of what is important according to customers, what they want, and how they are willing to pay for the service or product (Womack 1994; Joint Commission 2013; Coriat 1994; Lubben 1989). Obviously, when the Lean methodology is adopted in the public service, the idea of value is rethought without this aspect.

As the 5S, *Kaizen* is also one of the activities used to carry out the steps of the Lean methodology. It is a Japanese word that means continuous improvement, and, in the context of Lean manufacturing, the term expresses the idea of continuous improvement through the elimination of waste. It is not only a method, but a philosophy which has been applied in organizations and private lives based on the premise that small and continuous improvements are means to improve the total result.

As the groundwork of this methodology, there is the idea of small and continuous improvements in which waste is eliminated and changes obtained via Kaizen may even, at first, be imperceptible, but gradually made, as small improvements are achieved, they become visible.

Normally, Lean initiatives include 5 S practices, process mapping, value stream mapping (VSM), Kaizen methods, and just-in-time (JIT). The Lean methodology applied to healthcare services is based on Kaizen. The Kaizen method defines the problem of the workflows, analysing workflows, determine the cycle times of the work processes, testing improvement alternatives, and select the best alternative to solve the problem in the quality improvement work processes. (Ahmed, Abd Manaf & Islam, 2018)

Teamwork is also the basis of the Kaizen method, in which everyone must always contribute to the improvement of the whole, as well as all parts of the process.

Those involved must be committed to Kaizen actions so that it can work. For such a purpose, it requires motivation, therefore this tool should not be a top-down imposition. (Joint Commission, 2013).

For *Kaizen* to work, it is necessary to have an environment where people think and feel satisfied with the work underdeveloped (Joint Commission, 2013). Ohno guided workers on each error that occurred by ask themselves "why?" five times. This was the formula for reaching the root cause of an error and eliminating it. Ohno argued that an error should be eliminated when it manifests for the first time, and thus preventing future occurrences. In his view, on-site observation was far superior to deduction. Thus, while workers observe the consequences of problems by asking themselves "why?", they would be able to come up with a specific solution for that specific problem, which differs from the possibility based on deduction or inference. In addition to this being an opportunity for the worker to develop reasoning skills, which is considered as one of the most important assets that a worker can add to a company that has adopted the Lean methodology (Joint Commission, 2013).

Kaizen works on the elements of a process or system in order to understand how it works and then think about how to improve it. It is based on the idea of rapid learning cycles and application.

The Plan-do-check-act (PDCA), later known as plan-do-study-act (PDSA), is a four-step problem-solving process also known as a Deming, Shewhart, or control cycle. The steps involve plan (establishing the processes needed to deliver results according to the desired outcome), do (implement the new process on a small scale), check or study (measure the new process and observe any differences between that and the desired outcome), and act (analyse the difference between observed and expected to determine the cause). (Nicolay et al., 2012). The Shewart's PDSA cycle is a scientific method applied to daily work, was being implemented (Toussaint & Berry, 2013; Walley & Gowland, 2004; Esain et al., 2012)

The PDCA is a set of actions and, according to Ohno, these actions should be divided into three types according to waste (Di Marzo, 2017):

- Actions that generate value (for example, the transformation of a steel part into a car chassis)
- Actions that do not add value, but that cannot be eliminated, given the technologies and production plants (these actions are those that involve inspections, quality tests that a product or service and other actions of such nature).
- Actions that do not add value and can be eliminated immediately. These are obvious wastes; thus they must be eliminated.

As mentioned earlier, according to the Joint Commission (2013), the Lean methodology applied in healthcare by the elimination of waste contributes to solving problems such as waiting, inappropriate care, unnecessary displacement, confusing or nonexistent information. These are some of the problems that exist in Brazilian public healthcare, and that end up compromising the quality of services. These are recurrent problems in the provision of public healthcare in countries with great social inequality, where most of the population depends on public services, as in Brazil, where such situation has been aggravated by the Covid-19 pandemic.

DIALOGUES BETWEEN THE NHP AND LEAN METHODOLOGY

Given that the NHP must be inserted into all SUS actions due to its mainstreaming feature, this section will focus on the dialogues or interfaces regarding the NHP concepts and the principles and actions of the Lean methodology. In order to analyze such issue, it was opted to identify how principles and guidelines of the National Humanization Policy (NHP) conform to Lean Methodology concepts found in literature. In this process, eight interfaces were identified between them.

The first and most evident interface is focus on the customer. Once the Lean methodology is applied to healthcare, the customer is the patient or user of the service and is the focus of any public healthcare service and, therefore, of the NHP. In general, everyone who seeks healthcare services wants well-being, whether being a citizen assisted by the private or public sector.

The second one refers to the importance of collective actions. Both in the NHP and in Lean manufacturing practices, collectivity plays a central role. In the NHP, the importance of the protagonism of main actors involved in healthcare, i.e. managers, professionals and users of public health services, is present. In the NHP, the importance of active and protagonist participation of each and everyone involved in the production of public healthcare is emphasized. In Lean manufacturing, collectivity is also understood as room for reflections and decisions. Womack et al. (1992), while discussing about lean production, quote Ohno as having adopted a technique of periodic meetings at Toyota in the late 1940s for "[...] the workforce to jointly suggest measures towards improving the process". (p.47) Further on, still on lean production, the authors emphasize the importance of everyone and of the set so that the process can flow. They report Ohno's initiative to install a rope at each workstation so that workers can immediately halt the assembly line, once there is a problem that they are unable to solve. From that point onwards, the problem was not just concerning one, but everyone. The entire assembly line workforce comes to a halt and attempts to solve the problem together. In this methodology, personnel involvement at work makes it possible to see opportunities for improvement.

The third one is associated with the principle of inseparability between management and healthcare present in the NHP. This principle is based on the concept that management decisions directly interfere with healthcare, in other words, with the end result. It is found room for Lean thinking with regard to the importance given to effective connections between macro- and micro-planning and execution of projects that take into account the whole, where systems and subsystems are part of a unit and must work as a whole. Therefore, communication must flow. In Lean thinking, communication must take place in a horizontal perspective between functional areas, workforces and individuals. This principle is mentioned by Womack et al. (1992) when the authors approach the subject using the company as metaphor for a community to portray lean production.

The fourth one relates to the guideline for participatory management and co-management present in the NHP. It is pointed out by the Ministry of Health as a way of including new individuals into the processes of analysis, decision-making and performance of further management tasks. Its interface with the Lean methodology can be exemplified in the use of the Kaizen tool, which establishes common spaces for discussion and planning collective decisions for eliminating waste.

The fifth one refers to workplace enhancement. In the NHP, this idea is found embedded within a broader scope. In the Lean methodology, in several concepts and particularly the 5S tool itself, it is worked on the improvement and use of these spaces.

The sixth one refers to the concept of acceptation found in the NHP that brings the idea of inclusion, i.e. listening to what is worth by others. In the NHP, acceptation is presented as "[...] recognizing what the other offers as a legitimate and singular health need. Acceptation must be in accordance with and sustain the relationship between staff members/services and users/populations. As a value of healthcare practices, user embracement is built collectively. In the Lean methodology, this concept appears as the importance of identifying what the customer values, given that value must be defined by the customer, and not by the company. In Lean thinking, the focus is on customers, thus they are included in the process.

As for the seventh one, it refers to the mainstreaming of both the NHP and the Lean methodology. In both, in order for their objectives to be fully achieved, they must become cultures of the institution, i.e. from top to bottom.

Therefore, as the eighth one, it is emphasized that both constitute proposals for ways of thinking that interfere in acting. These are philosophies that, when properly applied, consider and lead to growth by those involved through intervention (participation) in the work process.

FINAL CONSIDERATIONS

This article was aimed to present the basic ideas regarding the NHP and the Lean methodology, and indicate the principles and actions that coincide between them. In this process, strong links between the fundamental ideas of the NHP and the Lean methodology were identified. Such ideas are: focus on the customer, the importance of collectivity as room for transforming work, the inseparability between management and the execution of work, participatory management, the importance given to the workplace, inclusion of all those involved to the success of the process, mainstreaming and change in the way of thinking and acting. Evidently, there might be others, which also pose themselves, as well as these, as suggestions to improve public service using the Lean methodology.

These coinciding ideas can serve as means to deepen the dissemination of principles and guidelines of the NHP through actions of the Lean methodology, which means working on the philosophy of eliminating waste in the service by considering quality as a guide in which humanization of services is embedded.

As the Lean methodology implies a way of thinking and acting, there must be challenges for its implementation in an institution, whether it is public or not, especially when it comes to public healthcare services in which most of the population should be considered as customers. In Brazil, it is estimated that 80% of the population is dependent on SUS. (Duarte, Eble & Garcia, 2018). It is about learning to use the notion of customer (patient or service user) when the demand for services is high, either because the customer of public services is the majority of the Brazilian population, or since its majority is poor and, therefore, more exposed to health problems.

This is a challenge due to the number of users as well as the social and cultural diversity of the Brazilian population of SUS users.

Some points also need clarification from a different perspective. For instance, while private companies act in accordance with the need to remain in the market, the public service is guided by the provision of services to the citizen, i.e. to the person in need. Moreover, such service must be of quality. However, there is no quality without the involvement of those who participate in the management and production of such service.

Taking advantage of the Lean methodology for the population requires creativity and training of those who work in public healthcare. It is believed that the public service derive gains by experiencing what has already worked in private organizations, once the objective is to solve the same problems, such as the need to eliminate waste, which is a constant need by the public service and action strategy of the Lean methodology.

Therefore, it is found that the intersections between the Lean methodology and the NHP exist and indicate possibilities of applying the principles of the NHP using the Lean methodology to contribute to quality improvement of public healthcare services, which constitute the right for all and duty of the State in accordance with the Federal Constitution of 1988.

ACKNOWLEDGMENT

The authors would like to thank the Brazilian Ministry of Health, Fluminense Federal University and Euclides da Cunha Foundation. This Research is part of a "Lean Project in UPAs 24h" that has been funded by the Brazilian Ministry of Health (TED 125/2019, number: 25000191682201908).

REFERENCES

Ahmed, S., Abd Manaf, N. H., & Islam, R. (2018). Effect of Lean Six Sigma on Quality Performance in Malaysian Hospitals. *International Journal of Health Care Quality Assurance*, *31*(8), 973–987. doi:10.1108/IJHCQA-07-2017-0138 PMID:30415620

Brazil. Ministry of Health. (2010). *National Humanization Policy: Textbooks. Basic document for SUS managers and workers. Series B. Basic Health Texts* (4th ed.). Retrieved from: http://bibliotecadigital.puc-campinas.edu.br/services/e-books/humanizasus_documento_gestores_trabalhadores_sus.pdf

Coriat, B. (1994). Thinking Inside Out: The Japanese Model of Work and Organization [Pensar pelo Avesso: o modelo japonês de trabalho e organização]. UFRJ Editora.

Crane, J., & Noon, C. E. (2011). *The Definitive Guide to Emergency Department Operational Improvement - Employing Lean Principles with Current ED Best Practices to Create the "No Wait" Department.* CRC Press.

Di Marzo, R. (2017) *The kaizen methodology: Applications and Implementation of the Japanese Model in the West: Lantech Case* [La metodologia kaizen: Applicazioni e Implementazione del Modello Giapponese in Occidente: Caso Lantech]. Division of Scienze Economiche and Aziendali "Marco Fanno", Università Degli Studi di Padova. Retrieved from: http://tesi.cab.unipd.it/61701/

Duarte, E., Eble, L., & Garcia, L. (2018) 30 years of the Unified Health System. *Journal of Epidemiology and Health Services, 27*(1). Retrieved from: https://scielosp.org/article/ress/2018.v27n1/e00100018/

Esain, A. E., Williams, S. J., Gakhal, S., Caley, L., & Cooke, M. W. (2012). Healthcare quality improvement–policy implications and practicalities. *International Journal of Health Care Quality Assurance.*

Escorel, S. (2008). Equity in Health [Equidade em Saúde]. In *Dictionary of Professional Education in Health* (2nd ed.). Rio de Janeiro: EPSJV. Retrieved from: http://www.epsjv.fiocruz.br/publicacao/livro/dicionario-da-educacao-profissional-em-saude-segunda-edicao-revista-e-ampliada

John Hopkins University & Medicine. (n.d.). *COVID-19 – Map – Coronavirus Resource Center.* Retrieved from: https://coronavirus.jhu.edu/map.html

Joint Commission Resources. (2013). Lean thinking in healthcare: less waste and queues and more quality and patient safety [O pensamento lean na saúde: menos desperdício e filas e mais qualidade e segurança para o paciente]. *The Bookman.*

Lubben, R. (1989). *Just-In-Time: an advanced production strategy. trans* (2nd ed.). McGraw-Hill.

Mattos, R. (2009, Out 20). The Meanings of Integrality in Attention and Health Care [Os sentidos da integralidade: algumas reflexões acerca de valores que merecem ser defendidos]. In *The meanings of integrality: some reflections on values that deserve to be defended.* Cepesc/IMS/Uerj/Abrasco. Retrieved from: https://lappis.org.br/site/wp-content/uploads/2017/12/Os-Sentidos-da-Integralidade-na-Aten%C3%A7%C3%A3o-e-no-Cuidado-%C3%A0-Sa%C3%BAde.pdf

Ministry of Health. Health Care Department. (2013). *National Humanization Policy.* Retrieved from: https://bvsms.saude.gov.br/bvs/publicacoes/politica_nacional_humanizacao_pnh_folheto.pdf

Ministry of Health Department of Health Care. (2010). *National Humanization Policy.* Cadernos HumanizaSUS: Training and intervention. Retrieved from: https://bvsms.saude.gov.br/bvs/publicacoes/cadernos_humanizaSUS.pdf

Moura, E. (2013, July 1). The right to health in the Federal Constitution of 1988 [O direito à saúde na Constituição Federal de 1988]. *Revista Âmbito Jurídico, Cadernos Direitos Constitucionais*. Retrieved from: https://ambitojuridico.com.br/cadernos/direito-constitucional/o-direito-a-saude-na-constituicao-federal-de-1988/

Nicolay, C. R., Purkayastha, S., Greenhalgh, A. A. S. N., Benn, J., Chaturvedi, S., Phillips, N., & Darzi, A. (2012). Systematic review of the application of quality improvement methodologies from the manufacturing industry to surgical healthcare. *Journal of British Surgery*, *99*(3), 324–335.

Pereira, H., & Barros, R. D. (2008). Humanization [Humanização]. In *Dictionary of Professional Education in Health* (2nd ed.). EPSJV. Retrieved from: http://www.epsjv.fiocruz.br/publicacao/livro/dicionario-da-educacao-profissional-em-saude-segunda-edicao-revista-e-ampliada

Planning Ministry. Constitution of the Federative Republic of Brazil. (2007). *Constitutional text enacted on October 5, 1988, with the amendments adopted by Constitutional Revision Amendments nº 1 to 6/94*. Federal Senate Undersecretary of Technical Editions. Retrieved from: https://pac.gov.br/infraestrutura-social-e-urbana/upa-unidade-de-pronto-atendimento

Raimundo, J., & Cadete, M. (2012). Qualified listening and social management among health professionals. *ACTA Paulista Nursing Journal*, 61-17. Retrieved from: https://www.scielo.br/pdf/ape/v25nspe2/pt_10.pdf

Souza, L. E. P. F. D., Paim, J. S., Teixeira, C. F., Bahia, L., Guimarães, R., Almeida-Filho, N. D., ... Azevedo-e-Silva, G. (2019). The current challenges of the struggle for the universal right to health in Brazil [Os desafios atuais da luta pelo direito universal à saúde no Brasil]. *Ciencia & Saude Coletiva*, *24*, 2783–2792.

Toussaint, J. S., & Berry, L. L. (2013). The Promise of Lean in Health Care. *Mayo Clinic Proceedings*, *88*(1), 74–82. doi:10.1016/j.mayocp.2012.07.025

Walley, P., & Gowland, B. (2004). Completing the circle: From PD to PDSA. *International Journal of Health Care Quality Assurance*, *17*(6), 349–358.

Womack, J. P., Jones, D. T., & Roos, D. (2007). *The machine that changed the world: The story of lean production—Toyota's secret weapon in the global car wars that is now revolutionizing world industry*. Simon and Schuster.

ADDITIONAL READING

Chioro, A. (2020, mar 17). *Strengthening the SUS is the main measure to stop the spread of the corona virus* [Fortalecer o SUS é principal medida para deter avanço do coronavirus]. Retrieved from: https://www.redebrasilatual.com.br/sem-categoria/2020/03/fortalecer-sus-principal-medida-conter-coronavirus

Favretto, G. (2017). *Value metrics: Management control in companies responsive to change* [Le metriche del valore: il controllo di gestione nelle aziende reattive al cambiamento] [Thesis]. Department of Engineering and Architecture, Università Degli Studi di Triestre, Triestre, Itália. Retrieved from: https://www.slideshare.net/giorgiafavretto/le-metriche-del-valore-la-lean-accounting

Harzheim, E. (2019, dez 10). *Transfer of funds to the health area of municipalities depends on the registration of users in the SUS* [Repasse de verba para área da saúde de municípios depende de cadastro dos usuários no SUS]. Retrieved from: https://www.anahp.com.br/noticias/noticias-do-mercado/repasse-de-verba- para-area-da-saude-de-municipios-depende-de-cadastro-dos-usuarios-no- sus/

Rocha, R., & Fernandes, L. (2016). The impact of 24-hour emergency care units (UPAs) on mortality indicators: evidence for Rio de Janeiro [O impacto das unidades de pronto atendimento (upas) 24h sobre indicadores de mortalidade: evidências para o Rio de Janeiro]. *Revista Pesquisa e Planejamento Econômico, 46*(3). Retrieved from: https://ppe.ipea.gov.br/index.php/ppe/article/viewFile/1626/1234

Chapter 13
SafeClean Prototype for Sterilizing Personal Protective Equipment

Ilma Rodrigues de Souza Fausto
https://orcid.org/0000-0003-3850-5066
Fluminense Federal University, Brazil

Fabiana Rodrigues Leta
https://orcid.org/0000-0002-6210-3078
Fluminense Federal University, Brazil

Maicon Gonzaga da Silva
Federal Institute of Rondônia, Brazil

Sérgio Crespo Coelho da Silva Pinto
Fluminense Federal University, Brazil

Ruth Maria Mariani Braz
https://orcid.org/0000-0003-2224-9643
Fluminense Federal University, Brazil

EXECUTIVE SUMMARY

The world is suffering from a new coronavirus-type pathogen, namely COVID-19. Health professionals are obliged to protect themselves with personal protective equipment (PPE); however, we encountered some problems: most of this equipment is not self-cleaning. How do you protect professionals from contaminated personal protective equipment? How do you dispose of used personal protective equipment? For the construction of this equipment, the authors used the methodology of define, measure, analyze, improve, and control (DMAIC). The developed prototype was applied in a primary care sector clinic, where the pre-test (swab sampling procedure) was performed to identify cross-contamination of the environment. The cost of the prototype developed was low in relation to existing market options. The tests carried out allowed the authors to observe its effectiveness in the sterilization of equipment. However, new, more complex tests are still needed to better validate the prototype and to study its economic viability as a product.

DOI: 10.4018/978-1-6684-5185-4.ch013

INTRODUCTION

These days unfortunately the world suffers from a new pathogen of the coronavirus type, designated as COVID-19. Health professionals must protect themselves with the highest number of Personal Protective Equipment (PPE), but we found some problems, most of this equipment is not self-cleaning. According to the regulation of the European Union Equipment 2016/425 of the European Parliament and of the Council of 9 March 2016, Individual Protection is

For the purposes of this regulation, the following definitions apply: 1) Personal protective equipment (PPE) a) Equipment designed and manufactured to be worn or handled by a person to protect him against one or more risks to his health or safety; b) Interchangeable components for the equipment referred to in paragraph a) that are essential for its protective function; c) Connection systems for equipment referred to in point (a), which are not operated or worn by a person, which are designed to connect such equipment to an external device or secure attachment point, which are not designed to be attached permanently and that do not require a fastening action before being used (Official Journal of the European Union, 2016, p.7).

How do protect professionals supposedly contaminated PPE in UPA Emergency Care Units, hospitals, schools, and even nursing homes? The UPA are emergency and emerging units offering medical care services 24 hours a day, every day of the week, and are associated with the Mobile Emergency Care Service (SAMU, from the Portuguese Serviço de Atendimento Móvel de Urgência). The sterilizer is equipment to destroy all germs that are harmful to human health. The function of the sterilizer is to eliminate any microorganisms that may interfere with the experiments or influence the results, eliminate the contamination generated by the burning of Liquefied Petroleum Gas (LPG) and also protect against the risks arising from liquid fuels that are ignited inside the laboratory. The sterilizer is used to purify objects such as handles, tubes, scissors, tweezers, and tips, preventing objects from coming into direct contact with the flame. It can also be very useful equipment to be placed in unidirectional flow cameras or biological security cameras in place of the Bunsen burner. The II Congress in 1932, established the standardization of the categories of ultraviolet light in A, B, and C, provisionally defined by the following filters:

Noviol -A- Barium - flint (long-wavelength UV UV-A giving approximately 4000 to 3150 Å spectral band). Barium Flint - Pyrex (medium wavelength UV or UV-B giving approximately 3150 to 2800 Å spectral band). Pyrex (short-wavelength UV, or UV-C giving approximately rays less than 2800 Å) (Coblentz, 1932)

Ultraviolet A radiation is invisible, is present from sunrise to sunset and when a person is exposed for a long time without sun protection, it can harm human health. Ultraviolet B radiation is present on the earth's surface from 9 am to 4 pm, these rays are responsible for burning and redness in the skin when exposed to the sun, for a long time without sun protection. And ultraviolet C radiation is blocked by the ozone layer, so we don't suffer its effects because they don't reach humans.

Ultraviolet radiation, at 253.7 nm, forms a part of artificially reproduced solar radiation and provides effective disinfection without causing adventurous disinfection by-products.

The UVC rays, reproduced, have a much higher radiation intensity than sunlight and are used to sterilize water and environments. This technology used for disinfection is recognized for its ability to eliminate legionella, microbes, bacteria, viruses, and protozoa while respecting the environment.

Recent research, published by Schappo (2020), mentions that at Boston University, researchers concluded that the use of ultraviolet light (UV-B) inactivates the new coronavirus. The Signify company (formerly Philips Lighting) offers three products with ultraviolet technology, including cameras, light fixtures, and disinfection vehicles. According to a statement from Signify, the material inoculated with the virus was treated with different doses of UVC radiation from a Signify light source. Experts evaluated the sterilization ability under different conditions. The results indicated that a dose of 5mJ/cm2 (unit derived from energy) caused a 99% reduction of the virus in 6 seconds ("Extreme UV", n.d.).

The technology used by the company Bio Lambda created hygiene chambers, lighting, and a purifier that sucks the air from the environment through "a filter that performs the sterilization by a mirrored chamber with high power UVC lamps and returns clean air with a capacity for with up to five people" (Schappo, 2020). Schappo (2020) also mentioned another company: Meister Safe System, which offers customized plans for biosafety systems in offices, clinics, and hospitals; hotels and inns; bars and restaurants, as well as schools and universities for the sterilization of the environment and offers a security seal.

We studied the regulatory standard (NR) No. 32, which mentions the hospital environment, establishing the "protective measures to guarantee the health and safety of everyone who works in that place" (BRASIL, 2019), and thus we seek to understand what were the measures that we should pay attention to for the development of the prototype. The Ministry of Social Security has been warning us that "the problems faced by health professionals lead to high rates of work accidents, often leading to contamination of the environment in which they are working (Prometal, 2021).

Thus, our objective was to develop equipment that uses UV-B light to sterilize low-cost personal protective equipment - PPE. We are ensuring that light does not escape and encounter people, after all, it is necessary to guarantee the integrity of the people who operate the product.

METHODOLOGY

We use the methodology with the following steps: define, measure, analyze, improve (Improve) and control (DMAIC), the prototype. In the first phase, we defined the team, selected the problem, focused on the most relevant project, and thus established the possible solutions that could be carried out. In the second we measure the success of current processes to verify the level of performance and in the third, we analyze the data collected, costs of parts, and materials that would be used. In the fourth phase, we implement the ideas, that is, we make the prototype. actions to eliminate and reduce the root cause of the problem. And in the fifth phase, we establish control and measurement standards to keep the performance of the prototype running. Thus, the DMAIC methodology can be summarized (Figure 1).

Thus, the use of this methodology helped us to define the scope and phases that we established, which equates to computational thinking, because we decompose each stage of the prototype construction, and establish the standards, for the feasibility of product quality processes. To identify the validation phases, we use the descriptive one that has well-defined objectives, with structured and formal procedures aimed at solving problems or evaluating alternative courses of action, supported by observational, due to the difficulty of carrying out experiments to validate the prototype, seen during the process. (Campana,

1999; Castro, 2001; de Souza Minayo et al., 2011). To achieve their goals, it was necessary to create a 3D model of a sterilizer, design the electronics, carry out tests and execute possible corrections.

Figure 1. Summary of the DMAIC methodology
Source: https://bit.ly/3pWm5mj

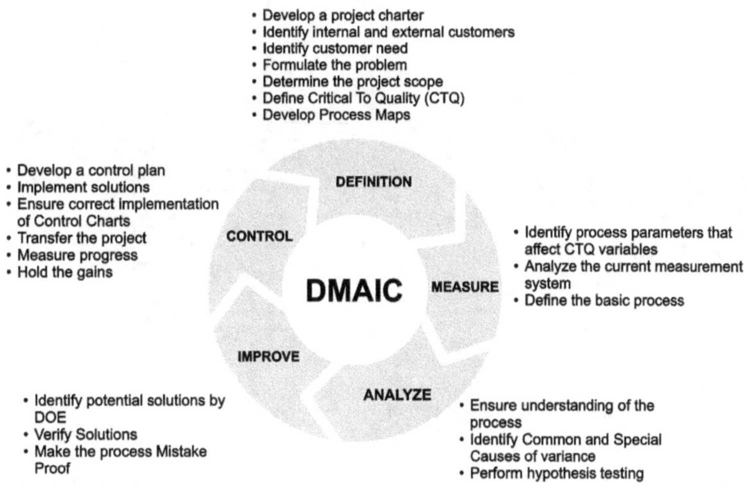

RESULTS

As a result of the first phase, the design of the pieces was carried out, initially planned to be made of acrylic, but the lack of raw material in the state forced the use of 6 mm MDF. After the production of the first parts, the necessary adjustments were made to provide a better fit and finish. Always aiming to avoid agglomerations as much as possible, the work was carried out in part in the laboratory of the student executing the project, so we were respecting international determinations about the moment we live in a pandemic. After a model of the sterilizer, the limiting dimensions that the board must have is known, then it is time to design the electronics. Our choice of materials was to reduce costs, so, in Figure 2 we can understand the project with its electronic diagram, board layout, and 3D modeling of the board. Designed by Autodesk's EAGLE program. ("What is EAGLE?", n.d.).

After cutting the board, it is necessary to apply a layer of photosensitive paint to protect against corrosion over the copper part to start the positive of the tracks. Soon after, it is necessary to place the transparency over the plate in the correct position and then place the plate in a black light oven so that the paint can polymerize where the light waves touch. After leaving the greenhouse, we can already see where the light touched. A mixture is made with a solution of water with 2% soda, this solution will remove the paint that was not reached in the previous process.

After exiting the solution, thorough verification is required to discover imperfections in the process that could render the project unusable. After the verification, the plate is ready to be corroded with ferric perchloride and after that, we will have the positive tracks as shown in Figure 3.

Figure 2. Electronic Diagram
Source: The authors

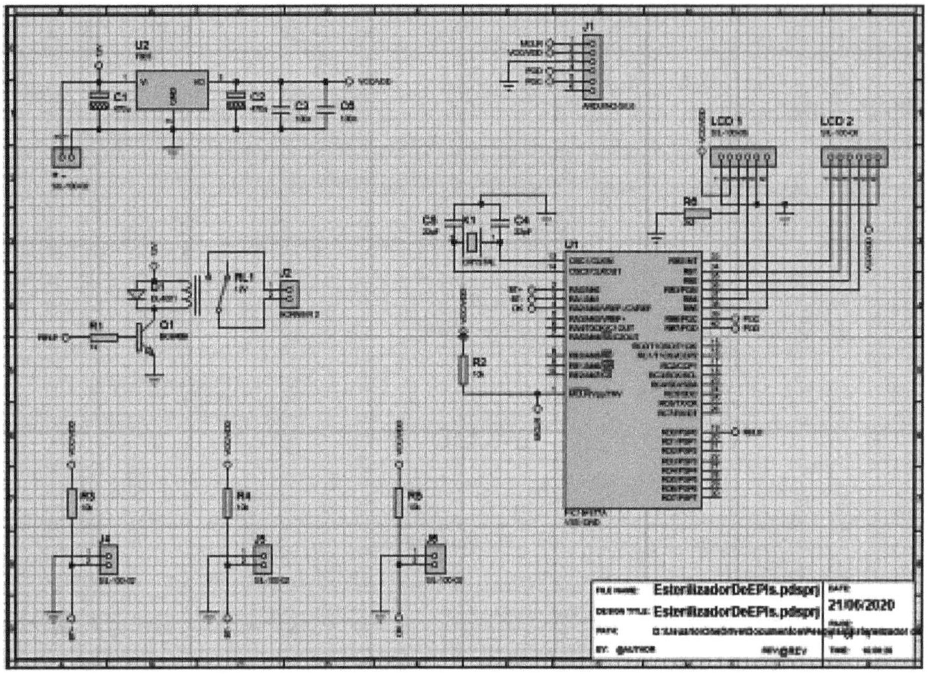

Figure 3. Board Layout
Source: The authors

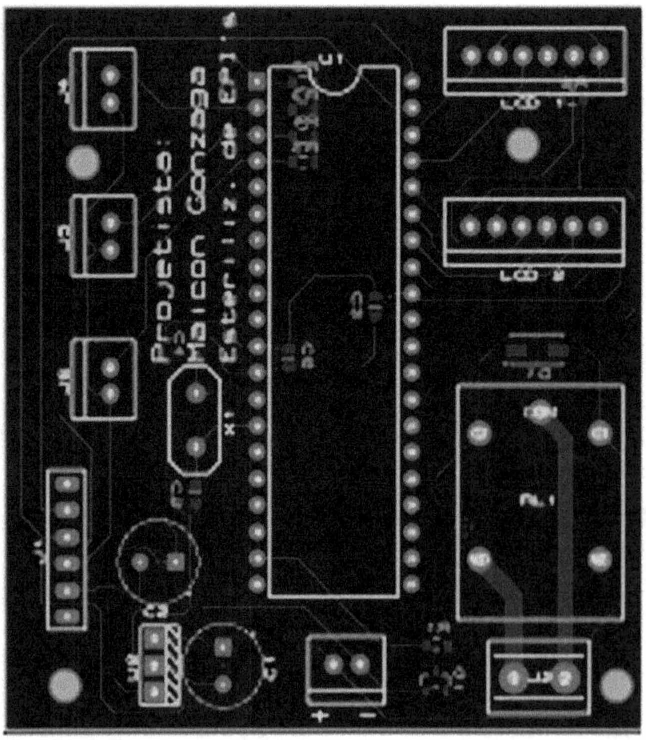

As the brain of the project, a PIC16F877A microcontroller was used, it was chosen because it is a low-cost component, for supporting up to 8192 instructions, more than enough for the project, in addition to other good configurations, as can be seen in its datasheet (manual of the electronic component). To make the PCI, it is necessary to print 3 negatives of the tracks, of protection, and component mask, generated by the EAGLE software. In Figure 4, the transparency of the tracks is observed on the photosensitive ink applied to the copper of the plate, the process is repeated for the protection of the tracks and the mask of components, respectively with their transparencies. The ink is put back on the board, but now on the other side, to write the locations of the DIP components. It is placed in the oven with the specific transparency and soon after in the 2% soda solution. Drilling is done on a CNC, where the computer drills the plate with absolute precision and after this step, the plate is ready to be assembled.

Figure 4. Plate cut under the transparency
Source: The authors

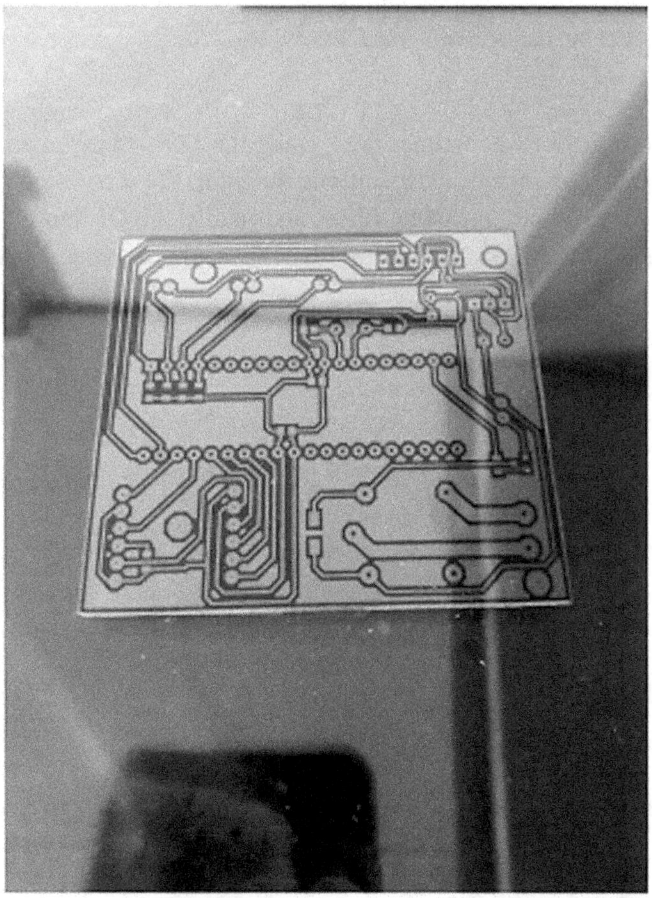

After making the PCB, using a soldering iron, tin, and anti-static gloves to maintain the integrity of the components to be handled during the soldering, the result (Figure 5).

Figure 5. Components already welded – Source: Personal archive
Source: The authors

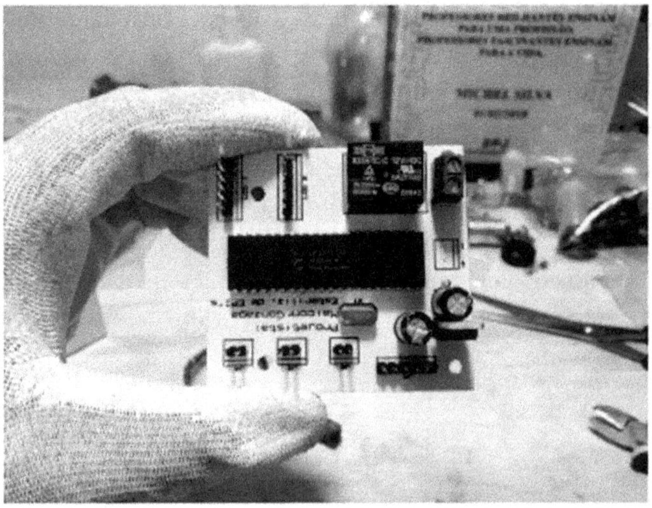

The firmware for this project was written in C, using the IDE – Integrated development Environment – PIC C Compiler and as seen in the electronic diagram, the relay is activated by PORTD0, the + button is on PORTA0, the – button is on PORTA1 and finally, the OK button is on PORTA2. As can be seen in Figure 7, the firmware is loaded using PICKIT 3. The Cabinet was mounted on laser cut 6 mm MDF, (Figure 6)

Figure 6. Loading firmware for the microcontroller.
Source: The authors

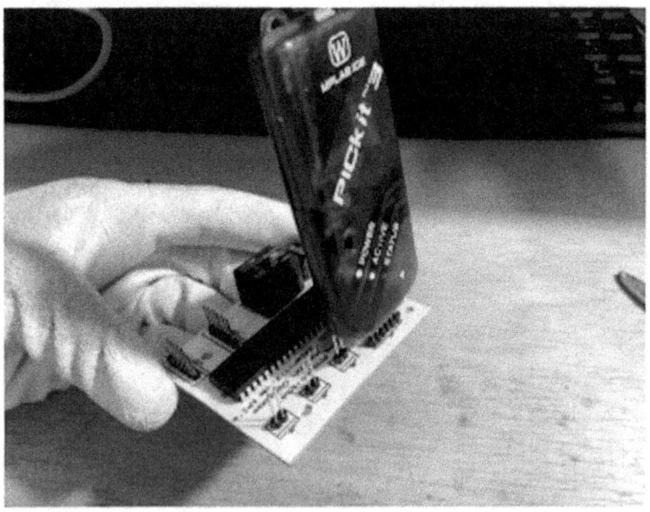

For the assembly of the project, a quick-drying superglue was used, and all parts were glued, except for the bottom cover and the cover of the display and buttons.

In the first test, it was noticed that an important part was forgotten, a piezoelectric insert, also known as a buzzer. These chips are used to convert waves into sound, among other applications, that is, the project is not emitting sounds. The equipment must warn the user of the end of the cycle, and that is why it was necessary to weld a buzzer with an internal oscillator. As the lamps are at the top, it is then necessary to turn the PPE so that the photons reach the entire surface. To be a system that saves time and energy, an internal coating was designed with a 3 mm mirrored acrylic, in this way the waves from 100 nanometers to 280 nanometers collide with the mirror and are launched on all sides, reaching the entire surface of the PPE. in a single exposure. To maintain salubrity, the surface of the equipment must be smooth and non-porous, so it was necessary to cover it with a protective film and automotive coating.

Coating and mirrored acrylic were applied to the lid in the same way. Soon after, the reactors and the 30th source were inserted, and the cover was screwed to the body of the project, (Figure 7)

Figure 7. Screwing the electronics
Source: the authors

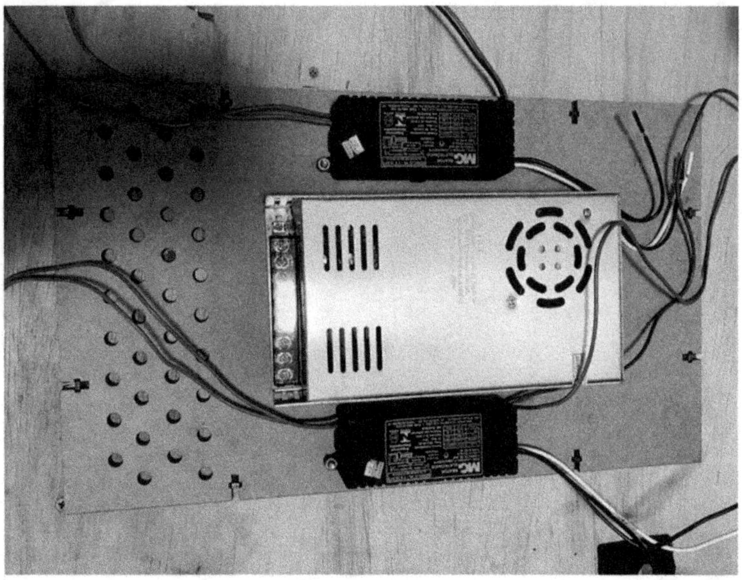

The connection of the lamps in the ballasts is given by a socket that has to be fixed on the cover and the lamps will be fitted in the socket so that it is easy to remove. (Figure 9). In the first test, it was noticed that an important part was forgotten, a piezoelectric insert, also known as a buzzer, (Figure 8).

These chips are used to convert waves into sound, among other applications, that is, the project is not emitting sounds. The equipment must warn the user of the end of the cycle, and therefore it was necessary to weld a buzzer with an internal oscillator (Figure 9).

Figure 8. Lamps in the sockets
Source: the authors

Figure 9. Project working
Source: the authors

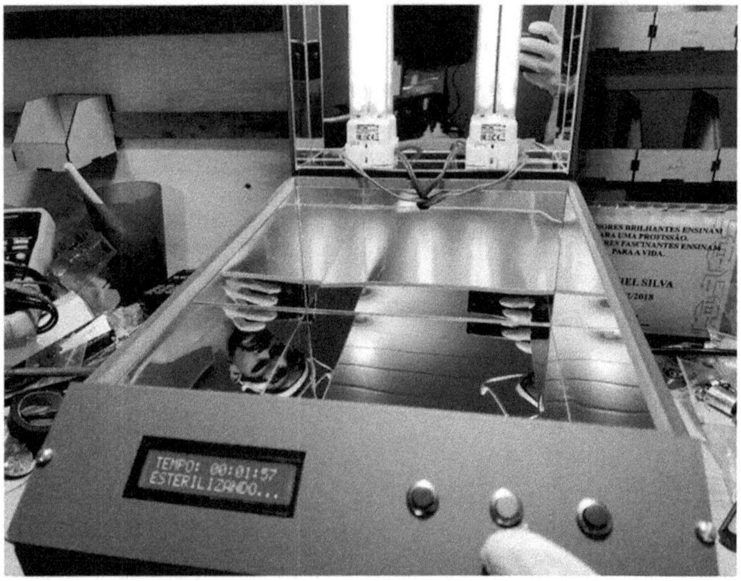

The prototype was tested in the state of Rondônia, in the city of Ji-Paraná, at the clinic center, and the disinfection mechanisms by ultraviolet radiation in personal protective equipment allowed the microorganisms to be inactivated.

As a result of photochemical damage to its nucleic acids, UV radiation is absorbed by nucleotides, the building blocks of DNA and RNA in the cell, depending on the wavelength, with the highest values near 200 and 260 nm. Absorbed UV promotes bond formation between adjacent nucleotides, creating double molecules or thiamine-thiamine dimers being the most common, cytosine-cytosine dimers, cytosine thiamine, and uracil dimerization also occur. The formation of a sufficient number of dimers within a microbe prevents it from replicating its DNA and RNA, which prevents it from reproducing. Due to the wavelength dependence of UV absorption by DNA, UV inactivation of microbes is also a function of wavelength. (Wright & Cairns, 1990, p.6).

The Fraimework used, the steps, the purposes, the activities developed for the construction of the tool were essential to achieve the value achieved.For the define phase, we mapped the phases relevant to the development of the prototype, listened to our customer's voice, defined the work team and defined the scope of the planned activities.We created a catalog with the current suppliers, identified the root and cause of the problems to determine the solutions that were necessary. We chose the most suitable statistical tools for each of the purposes under analysis. We found alternative solutions that added improvements to what was established, we evaluated the benefits and efforts of the processes so that we can redesign them. We communicate the results obtained and we are, through this article, disseminating the process developed to the scientific community.

All the phases described by the researchers were intended to promote other initiatives for the construction of more safety equipment to reduce the contamination of individual equipment used in the hospital environment.

The working prototype can be seen at (Maicon Gonzaga, 2022).

We performed the pre-test, swab sampling procedure, to identify cross-contamination of the environment. The polyester fabric used in this type of swab has a low particulate level and high collection capacity and is very effective when applied to organic sampling using Total Organic Carbon as an analytical technique. Then the swab is placed in an appropriate container, properly labeled, and sent to the laboratory for analysis. This result exceeded our expectations.

We can always improve our actions, since we evaluate the mechanisms and we will improve the current process, we control and define the actions implemented with protocols required by the laboratories, so the device developed needs to be evaluated in the use of new materials for more and more we lower costs.

All the phases described by the researchers were intended to promote other initiatives for the construction of more safety equipment to reduce the contamination of individual equipment used in the hospital environment. After surveying the costs, it amounted to R$9,993.00, a machine purchased from one of the companies that it sells today is around R$23,307.00. Thus, we can say that the DMAIC methodology used, and the phases described here can help any research group build new products.

Everyone will be affected by the environment without contamination because this brings more safety and gives reliability to patients who seek help and expect that the materials used are sterilized. We are sharing our experience so that new research groups using the DMAIC and Safeclean methodology created by us can be replicated by the industry and commercialized to save lives.

FINAL CONSIDERATIONS

In the process of building the board, we can see that it was a complex process, but there is a reason that justifies it, after all, it would be much easier to just use an Arduino where everything is already ready. However, the objective proposed from the beginning was to create low-cost equipment and design a board, and building it is cheaper than using an Arduino, not to mention that it is a professional project. The hardware program, also known as firmware, was professionally developed, but for another reason. If we had used Arduino integrated development Environment - IDE, and so the project would be open source, which is not the objective of this work, but if this happens in the future, people who read the code will understand more about electronics, because Arduino codes do not teach electronics due to much of the code comes ready-made in libraries format ("Code optimizing C compilers for Microchip PIC® and dspic® dscs. CCS, Inc. - CCS C Compilers", n.d.). Looking at the project in general, we can say that it was a success, after all, it delivers what it promises and is really low cost. In this article, we present the assembly of the prototype, with economic viability, but we need to continue experiments with other raw materials to conclude which would be the best economic results, maintaining its functionality with maximum efficiency and durability, hence the application of DMAIC to enable product quality processes.

ACKNOWLEDGMENT

The authors would like to thank the Brazilian Ministry of Health, UFF - Fluminense Federal University, and Euclides da Cunha Foundation. This Research is part of the" Lean Project in UPA 24h" that has been funded by the Brazilian Ministry of Health (TED 15/2021, number: 25000.103452/2021-14).

REFERENCES

Campana, Á. O. (1999). Methodology of scientific research applied to the biomedical area: 2. Investigations in the medical area [Metodologia da investigação científica aplicada à área biomédica: 2. Investigações na área médica]. *Jornal de Pneumologia*, *25*, 84–93. doi:10.1590/S0102-35861999000200005

Castro, A. A. (2001). Systematic review and meta-analysis [Revisão sistemática e meta-análise]. *Compacta: temas de cardiologia, 3*(1), 5-9.

Coblentz, W. W. (1932). The Copenhagen meeting of the second international congress on light. *Science, 76*(1975), 412-415. 10.1126cience.76.1975.412

Code optimizing C compilers for Microchip PIC® and dspic® dscs. (n.d.). CCS, Inc. Retrieved from http://www.ccsinfo.com/compilers.php

de Souza Minayo, M. C., Deslandes, S. F., & Gomes, R. (2011). *Social research: theory, method and creativity* [Pesquisa social: teoria, método e criatividade]. Editora Vozes Limitada.

Extreme U. V. (n.d.). *Grape Rays And UVB: Difference Between Them* [Raios Uva E UVB: Diferença Entre Eles]. Retrieved from https://www.extremeuv.com.br/raios-uva-e-uvb-diferenca-entre-eles

Maicon Gonzaga. (2022, January 4). *EPI's sterilizer* [Esterilizador de EPI's] [Video]. YouTube. https://www.youtube.com/watch?v=hUFDIk8SWIo

Official Journal of the European Union. Regulation (EU) 2016/425 of the European Parliament and of the Council of 9 March 2016, Art.3 p.7. https://bit.ly/3vgohXj

Prometal. (2021, July 20). NR 32 - Safety and health at Work in health services [NR 32 - Segurança e saúde no Trabalho em serviços de saúde]. *Prometal EPIs - Equipamentos de Proteção Individual.* Retrieved from https://www.prometalepis.com.br/blog/50-nr-32-seguranca-e-saude-no-trabalho-em-servicos-de-saude/

Schappo, M. G. (2020, June 16). How does ultraviolet light fight the coronavirus? [Como a luz ultravioleta combate o coronavírus?]. *Questo de Cienceia.* Retrieved from https://bit.ly/3t6k0WK

What is EAGLE? (n.d.). Autodesk. Retrieved from: https://autode.sk/3HztSwm

Wright, H. B., & Cairns, W. L. (1990). *UV light.* Trojan Technologies Inc. https://www.science.org/doi/10.1126/science.76.1975.412 doi:10.1126/science.76.1975.412

Compilation of References

Adachi, W., & Lodolce, A. E. (2005). Use of failure mode and effects analysis in improving the safety of iv drug administration. *American Journal of Health-System Pharmacy*, *62*(9), 917–920. doi:10.1093/ajhp/62.9.917 PMID:15851497

Ahmed, S., Manaf, N. H. A., & Islam, R. (2018). Measuring Lean Six Sigma and quality performance for healthcare organizations. *Journal International Islamic University*. https://bityli.com/JOXlDzLg

Ahmed, S., Abd Manaf, N. H., & Islam, R. (2018). Effect of Lean Six Sigma on Quality Performance in Malaysian Hospitals. *International Journal of Health Care Quality Assurance*, *31*(8), 973–987. doi:10.1108/IJHCQA-07-2017-0138 PMID:30415620

Ahsan, K. B., Alam, M. R., Morel, D. G., & Karim, M. A. (2019). Emergency department resource optimization for improved performance: A review. *Journal of Industrial Engineering International*, *15*(S1, s1), 253–266. doi:10.100740092-019-00335-x

AlQedrah, M., Marbouh, D., Simsekler, M. C. E., & Ellahham, S. (2022, February). Opportunities for Patient Safety Improvement using Lean. In *2022 Advances in Science and Engineering Technology International Conferences (ASET)* (pp. 1-4). IEEE. 10.1109/ASET53988.2022.9735048

Al-Shuaibi, K., Zain, M., & Kassim, N. (2016). Performance indicators for quality, innovation, and competitiveness: A survey on the Saudi manufacturing sector. *International Business Research*, *9*(2), 99–113. doi:10.5539/ibr.v9n2p99

Al-Sudairy, M. A. T., & Vasista, T. G. K. (2012). Fostering knowledge management and citizen participation via e-governance for achieving sustainable balanced development. *IUP Journal of Knowledge Management*, *10*(1), 2012.

Alvarenga Neto, R. C. D. D., Barbosa, R. R., & Pereira, H. J. (2007). Knowledge management or management of knowledge age organizations? A theoretical-practical essay based on interventions in the Brazilian reality [Gestão do conhecimento ou gestão de organizações da era do conhecimento? Um ensaio teórico-prático a partir de intervenções na realidade brasileira]. *Perspectivas em Ciência da Informação*, *12*, 5–24. doi:10.1590/S1413-99362007000100002

Alves, E. A. V. (2013). Patient safety: From error to risk prevention. *Cadernos Ibero-Americanos de Direito Sanitario*, *2*(2), 723–733.

Amaral, L. C. D., Calado, R. D., Teixeira, A. M., Silva, M. H. T. D., Bourguignon, S. C., & Costa, H. G. (2020). *Systematic review and meta-analysis of the use of lean methods and tools in healthcare services: An alternative to improve care during the pandemic*. Academic Press.

Amaral. (2021). Lean Healthcare: Lean Thinking, Standardized Work and the 8 Wastes in Health [Lean Healthcare: Pensamento Lean, Trabalho Padronizado e os 8 Desperdícios na Saúde]. *Universidade Federal Fluminense LabDGE, 2*(1), 16.

Amaral, L. C. D., Calado, R. D., Vieira, L. W. H., & Chaves, S. M. D. A. (2021, September). Lean Healthcare in Reducing HAI an Integrative Literature Review. In *IFIP International Conference on Advances in Production Management Systems* (pp. 351-361). Springer. 10.1007/978-3-030-85902-2_38

Amorim, F. F., Almeida, K. J. Q. D., Barbalho, S. C. M., Balieiro, V. D. A. T., Machado, A., Dias, G. D. F., & Dasu, S. (2020). Reducing overcrowding in an emergency department: A pilot study. *Revista da Associação Médica Brasileira, 65*(12), 1476–1481. doi:10.1590/1806-9282.65.12.1476 PMID:31994629

APO. (2009). *Knowledge management: facilitator´s Guide.* APO.

APQC. (2002). *Measuring knowledge management.* APQC.

Araújo, C. A. (2006). Bibliometry: historical evolution and current issues [Bibliometria: evolução histórica e questões atuais]. *Em questão, 12*(1), 11-32.

Arnheiter, E. D., & Maleyeff, J. (2005). The integration of lean management and Six Sigma. *The TQM Magazine, 17*(1), 5–18. doi:10.1108/09544780510573020

Augusto, B. P., & Tortorella, G. L. (2019). Literature review on lean healthcare implementation: Assessment methods and practices. *International Journal of Services and Operations Management, 32*(3), 285–306. doi:10.1504/IJSOM.2019.098351

Barbosa, C., Lima, A., Sobrinho, A., Calado, R., & Lordelo, S. (2021, September). Information, Communication and Knowledge for Lean Healthcare Management Guidelines, a Literature Revision. In *IFIP International Conference on Advances in Production Management Systems* (pp. 250-257). Springer. 10.1007/978-3-030-85902-2_27

Barlow, G. L. (2002). Auditing hospital queuing. *Managerial Auditing Journal, 17*(1), 397–403.

Barnas, K. (2018). *Beyond Heroes – a Lean Management System for the Healthcare Area* [Além dos Heróis – um Sistema de Gestão Lean para a Área da Saúde]. Editora Lean Institute Brasil.

Baskerville, R., & Dulipovici, A. (2006). The theoretical foundations of knowledge management. *Knowledge Management Research and Practice, 4*(2), 2006. doi:10.1057/palgrave.kmrp.8500090

Basta, Y. L., Tytgat, K. M. A. J., Greuter, H. H., Klinkenbijl, J. H. G., Fockens, P., & Strikwerda, J. (2017). Organizing and implementing a multidisciplinary fast track oncology clinic. *International Journal for Quality in Health Care, 29*(7), 966–971. doi:10.1093/intqhc/mzx143 PMID:29177408

Batista, F. F. (2012). Knowledge management model for the Brazilian public administration: How to implement knowledge management to produce results for the benefit of the citizen/Fábio Ferreira Batista. – Brasília. *Ipea, 132*, 2012.

Bauer, H., Brandl, F., Lock, C., & Reinhart, G. (2018). Integration of Industrie 4.0 in lean manufacturing learning factories. *Procedia Manufacturing, 23*, 147–152.

Belciug, S., & Gorunescu, F. (2015). Improving hospital bed occupancy and resource utilization through queuing modeling and evolutionary computation. *Journal of Biomedical Informatics, 53*, 261–269. doi:10.1016/j.jbi.2014.11.010 PMID:25433363

Ben-Tovim, D. I. (2007). Seeing the picture through "lean thinking". *BMJ (Clinical Research Ed.), 334*(7586), 169–169.

Bersch, R. (2017). *Introduction to Assistive Technology* [Introdução à Tecnologia Assistida]. https://www.assistiva.com.br/Introducao_Tecnologia_Assistiva.pdf

Bertani, T. M. (2012). *Lean Healthcare: Recomendações para implantações dos conceitos de produção enxuta em ambientes hospitalares* [Doctoral dissertation]. Universidade de São Paulo.

Bhagat, R. S., McDevitt, A. S., & Baliga, B. R. (2017). *Global organizations: Challenges, opportunities, and the future*. Academic Press.

Bhattacharjee, P., & Ray, P. K. (2016). Simulation modelling and analysis of appointment system performance for multiple classes of patients in a hospital: A case study. *Operations Research for Health Care*, *8*, 71–84. doi:10.1016/j.orhc.2015.07.005

Bielen, F., & Demoulin, N. (2007). Waiting time influence on the satisfaction-loyalty relationship in services. *Managing Service Quality*, *17*(2), 174–193. doi:10.1108/09604520710735182

Bin Che Ani, M. N., & Bin, S. M. S. S. (2014). The effectiveness of the single minute exchange of die (SMED) technique for the productivity improvement. Applied Mechanics and Material, 465, 1144-114.

Bioemfoco. (2020). *13 Urgent health challenges for the next decade* [13 Desafios urgentes da saúde para a próxima década]. https://bioemfoco.com.br/noticia/saude-desafios-decada/

Borges, M. S., Guedes, C. A. M., & Castro, M. C. D. (2015). A gestão do empreendimento rural: Um estudo a partir de um programa de transferência de tecnologia a pequenos produtores [The management of the rural enterprise: a study from a technology transfer program to small producers]. *Revista de Ciências da Administração*, *17*(43), 141–156. doi:10.5007/2175-8077.2015v17n43p141

Boronat, F., Budia, A., Broseta, E., Ruiz-Cerdá, J. L., & Vivas-Consuelo, D. (2017). Application of Lean Healthcare methodology in a urology department of a tertiary hospital as a tool for improving efficiency. *Actas Urologicas Espanolas*, *42*(1), 42–48. doi:10.1016/j.acuro.2017.03.009 PMID:28676387

Brasil, I. T. S. (2021). *Assistive Technology* [Tecnologias Assistivas]. http://itsbrasil.org.br/tag/tecnologia-assistiva/

Brasil, Ministério da Saúde, C. de O. de E. em S. P.-C.-19. (2020). National Contingency Plan for Human Infection by Coronavirus COVID-19 [Plano de Contingência Nacional para Infecção Humana pelo Coronavírus COVID-19]. In *Ministério da Saúde* (Vol. 1). https://portalarquivos2.saude.gov.br/images/pdf/2020/fevereiro/13/plano-contingencia-coronavirus-COVID19.pdf

Brasil, S. de C. (2015). *Visual Identity Manual - 24 h UPA. version 2.0* [Manual de Identidade Visual - UPA 24 h. versão 2.0]. Academic Press.

Brasil. (2013). *Instruction manual of the Emergency Care Network in the Unified Health System (SUS).* Coordenação-Geral de Documentação e Informação/SAA/SE. https://bvsms.saude.gov.br/bvs/publicacoes/manual_instrutivo_rede_atencao_urgencias.pdf

Brasil. (2015). *Main normative milestones of the interfederative management of the SUS*. http://editora.saude.gov.br

Brasil. (2018). Architectural Program Minimum Emergency Care Unit Upa 24 H [Programa Arquitetônico Mínimo Unidade De Pronto Atendimento Upa 24 H]. *Ministério da Saúde,* (2), 10–17.

BRASIL. Constitution of the Federative Republic of Brazil: promulgada em 5 de outubro de 1988. 41. ed. atual. e ampl. São Paulo: Saraiva, 2008.

Brasil. Ministério da Saúde. FIOCRUZ. (2020). *Fiocruz Contingency Plan Facing The Pandemic Of Disease By Sars-Cov-2 (Covid-19)* [Plano De Contingência Da Fiocruz Diante Da Pandemia Da Doença Pelo Sars-Cov-2 (Covid-19)]. Author.

Brasil. Ministério da Saúde. Portaria nº 10 de 03/01/2017, 1. (2017). *Guidelines for care model and funding of 24-hour UPA of Emergency Care as a Component of the Emergency Care Network* [Diretrizes de modelo assistencial e financiamento de UPA 24h de Pronto Atendimento como Componente da Rede de Atenção às Urgências]. https://bvsms.saude.gov.br/bvs/saudelegis/gm/2017/prt0010_03_01_2017.html

Brasil. Ministério da Saúde. Secretaria de Atenção Especializada em Saúde. (2021). Ministry of Health Health Care Department specialized specialized coordination of urgency and emergency [Ministério da saúde secretaria de atenção à saúde departamento de atenção especializada coordenação geral de urgência e emergência]. In M. da Saúde (Org.), *Programa Arquitetônico Mínimo Unidade De Pronto Atendimento Upa 24 H* (pp. 1–25). Academic Press.

BRASIL. Secretária Especial de Agricultura Familiar e do Desenvolvimento Agrário. (2017). *Brasil: 70% dos alimentos que vão à mesa dos brasileiros são da agricultura familiar* [Brazil: 70% of the food on the table of Brazilians comes from family farming]. http://www.mda.gov.br/sitemda/noticias/brasil-70-dos-alimentos-que-vao-a-mesa-dos-brasileiros-sao-da-agricultura-familiar

BRASIL. Tribunal de Contas da União (TCU). (2018b). *Manual of Risk Management of the National Agency for Supplementary Health*. Biblioteca/CGECO/GEQIN/DIGES. http://www.ans.gov.br/images/stories/A_ANS/Transparencia_Institucional/gestao_de_riscos/manual-de-gestao-de-riscos-da-ans.pdf

Brasil, M. da S. (2020). *Instructions for PSF - CORONAVIRUS COVID-19*. Ministério da Saúde.

Brazil, Ministry of Health. (2015). *Main normative landmarks of the interfederative management of the SUS* [Principais marcos normativos da gestão interfederativa do SUS]. Editora Saúde. http://editora.saude.gov.br

Brazil. Ministry of Health. (2010). *National Humanization Policy: Textbooks. Basic document for SUS managers and workers. Series B. Basic Health Texts* (4th ed.). Retrieved from: http://bibliotecadigital.puc-campinas.edu.br/services/e-books/humanizasus_documento_gestores_trabalhadores_sus.pdf

Brazil. Ministry of Health. (2017). *Ordinance nº 10 of 01/03/2017. Assistance model guidelines and funding for 24-hour Emergency Care Units as a Component of the Emergency Care Network* [Portaria nº 10 de 03/01/2017, 1. Diretrizes de modelo Assistencial e financiamento de UPA 24h de Pronto Atendimento como Componente da Rede de Atenção às Urgências]. https://bityli.com/qhQQfLV

Brazil. Ministry of Health. (2020). *Emergency Care Unit* [Unidade de Pronto Atendimento (UPA 24 h). https://bityli.com/LtiZjhXC

Brazilian Association of Technical Standards (ABNT) NBR 16537. (2018). *Accessibility – Tactile floor signage - Guidelines for design and installation the preparation of projects and installation* [Acessibilidade — Sinalização tátil no piso — Diretrizes para elaboração de projetos e instalação]. Author.

Brazilian Association of Technical Standards (ABNT). NBR 9050. (2020). Accessibility to buildings, equipment and the urban environment [Acessibilidade a edificações, mobiliário, espaços e equipamentos urbanos]. Author.

Brazilian Health System wastes 53% of the cost of care. (2021, October 4). Retrieved May 03, 2022, from Medicina S/A https://medicinasa.com.br/desperdicio-custo-hospital/

Brazilian Institute of Geography and Statistics. (2010). *Discover Brazil - Population: people with disability* [Conheça o Brasil – População: pessoas com deficiência]. https://educa.ibge.gov.br/jovens/conheca-o-brasil/populacao/20551-pessoas-com-deficiencia.html

Brazilian Institute of Geography and Statistics. (2019). *Country has 17.3 million people with some type of disability* [País tem 17,3 milhões de pessoas com algum tipo de deficiência]. https://bityli.com/VLZuSw

Breda, M. E. C, Joaquim, P.N, Testoni, A.K, Schneider, C.F, Mello, V.A & Trindade, L.L. (2018). Teamwork in an emergency care unit. *Revista da Semana Acadêmica do Curso de Medicina da UFFS-Campus Chapecó, 1*(1).

Brito, L. M. P. (2008). *Competence management, knowledge management and learning organizations: instruments of appropriation by capital of the worker's knowledge*. Imprensa Universitária.

Camilo, D. G. G., de Souza, R. P., Frazão, T. D. C., & da Costa, J. F. Junior. (2020). Multi-criteria analysis in the health area: Selection of the most appropriate triage system for the emergency care units in natal. *BMC Medical Informatics and Decision Making*, *20*(1), 1–16. doi:10.118612911-020-1054-y PMID:32085757

Campana, Á. O. (1999). Methodology of scientific research applied to the biomedical area: 2. Investigations in the medical area [Metodologia da investigação científica aplicada à área biomédica: 2. Investigações na área médica]. *Jornal de Pneumologia*, *25*, 84–93. doi:10.1590/S0102-35861999000200005

Cardoso, W. (2020). 1 Introduction Going back to the historical evolution of the productive systems, it is possible to see clear progress in the managerial field of the same, since everything began in an organized way with the scientific administration of Taylor. *He Broug*, *9*, 360–380.

Carvalho, S. A., Tourrand, J. F., & Poccard-Chapuis, R. (2012). Atividade leiteira: Um desafio para a consolidação da agricultura familiar na região da transamazônica, no Pará [Dairy activity: a challenge for the consolidation of family farming in the trans-Amazonian region, in Pará]. *Cadernos de Ciência & Tecnologia*, *29*(1), 269–290.

Castro, A. A. (2001). Systematic review and meta-analysis [Revisão sistemática e meta-análise]. *Compacta: temas de cardiologia*, *3*(1), 5-9.

CEPEA - Centro de Estudos Avançados em Economia Aplicada. *Série de preços* [Price series]. https://www.cepea.esalq.usp.br/br/indicador/leite.aspx

Cereda, A., Jr., Röhm, S., & Lollo, J. A. D. (2009). Mapping using Multicriteria Analysis and Fuzzy Logic as a subsidy to Urban and Regional Planning. 12th Encuentro de geógrafos de america latina, Montevideo, 222-229.

Chabudé, T.G., César, G.C., & Santana, C.J. (2019). Reception and Risk Classification in an Emergency Unit: Experience Report of the Implementation of the Manchester Triage System. *Essays and Science C Agrarian and Health Biologicals*, *23*(2), 121-125.

Charron, R., Harrington, H. J., Voehl, F., & Wiggin, H. (2014). *The lean management systems handbook* (Vol. 4). CRC Press. doi:10.1201/b17201

Chaves. (2021). Fast Track in Emergency departments an Integrative Review. *IFIP Advances in Information and Communication Technology*, *631*, 241–249. doi:10.1007/978-3-030-85902-2_26

Chaves, S. (2022). Fast Track. In *The Upas 24 H - Analysis of Opportunities and Continuous Improvements* [Fast Track Nas Upas 24 H - Análise Das Oportunidades E Das Melhorias Contínuas]. Universidade Federal Fluminense.

Chaves, S. M. D. A., Calado, R. D., Coelho, S. A., Neto, O. B., Santos, A. B., & Bourguignon, S. C. (2021, September). Fast Track in Emergency Services an Integrative Review. In *IFIP International Conference on Advances in Production Management Systems* (pp. 241-249). Springer.

Chay, T., Xu, Y., Tiwari, A., & Chay, F. (2015). Towards lean transformation: The analysis of lean implementation frameworks. *Journal of Manufacturing Technology Management*, *26*(7), 1031–1052. doi:10.1108/JMTM-10-2013-0143

Chiarini, A., & Baccarani, C. (2016). TQM and lean strategy deployment in Italian hospitals: Benefits related to patient satisfaction and encountered pitfalls. *Leadership in Health Services*, *29*(4), 377–391. doi:10.1108/LHS-07-2015-0019 PMID:27707152

Cho, K. W., Kim, S. M., Chae, Y. M., & Song, Y. U. (2017). Application of queueing theory to the analysis of changes in outpatients' waiting times in hospitals introducing EMR. *Healthcare Informatics Research*, *23*(1), 35–42. doi:10.4258/hir.2017.23.1.35 PMID:28261529

Chrusciel, J., Fontaine, X., Devillard, A., Cordonnier, A., Kanagaratnam, L., Laplanche, D., & Sanchez, S. (2019). Impact of the implementation of a fast-Track on emergency department length of stay and quality of care indicators in the Champagne-Ardenne region: A before-After study. *BMJ Open*, *9*(6), 1–8. doi:10.1136/bmjopen-2018-026200 PMID:31221873

Cildoz, M., Ibarra, A., & Mallor, F. (2019). Accumulating priority queues versus pure priority queues for managing patients in emergency departments. *Operations Research for Health Care*, *23*, 100224. doi:10.1016/j.orhc.2019.100224

Coblentz, W. W. (1932). The Copenhagen meeting of the second international congress on light. *Science, 76*(1975), 412-415. 10.1126cience.76.1975.412

Cochran, J. K., & Bharti, A. (2006). A multi-stage stochastic methodology for whole hospital bed planning under peak loading. *International Journal of Industrial and Systems Engineering*, *1*(1-2), 8–36. doi:10.1504/IJISE.2006.009048

Code optimizing C compilers for Microchip PIC® and dspic® dscs. (n.d.). CCS, Inc. Retrieved from http://www.ccsinfo.com/compilers.php

Coelho, S. M., Pinto, C. F., Calado, R. D., & Silva, M. B. (2013). Process improvement in a cancer outpatient chemotherapy unit using lean healthcare. *IFAC Proceedings Volumes, 46*(24), 241-246. 10.3182/20130911-3-BR-3021.00047

Coelho, V. S. P. (2007). The democratization of Health Councils: The paradox of attracting non-allies. *Novos Estudos CEBRAP*, 77–92. doi:10.1590/S0101-33002007000200009

Cong, X., & Pandya, K. V. (2003). Issues of knowledge management in the public sector. *Electronic Journal of Knowledge Management*, *1*(2), 25–33.

Coriat, B. (1994). Thinking Inside Out: The Japanese Model of Work and Organization [Pensar pelo Avesso: o modelo japonês de trabalho e organização]. UFRJ Editora.

Cosenza, C. A. N. (1981). *An Industrial Location Model* [Working Paper]. Martin Centre for Architectural and Urban Sites Studies, Cambridge University.

Cosenza, H. J. S. R. (2020). *5S Organization, Quality and Efficiency of the Health Environment* [5S Organização, Qualidade e Eficiência do Ambiente de Saúde]. doi:10.22409/2675-4924.1

Coughlan, P., & Coghlan, D. (2002). Action research for operations management. *International Journal of Operations & Production Management*, *22*(2), 220–240. doi:10.1108/01443570210417515

Crane, J., & Noon, C. E. (2011). *The Definitive Guide to Emergency Department Operational Improvement - Employing Lean Principles with Current ED Best Practices to Create the "No Wait" Department*. CRC Press.

Crema, M., & Verbano, C. (2021). Simulation modelling and lean management in healthcare: First evidences and research agenda. *Total Quality Management & Business Excellence*, *32*(3-4), 448–466.

Crosby, P. (1989). *Let's Talk Quality*. McGraw-Hill.

Cyrne, C. C. S., Rempel, C., Haetinger, C., & Bortoli, J. (2015). O (não) uso de indicadores de gestão em propriedades leiteiras na Galícia – Espanha [The (non) use of management indicators in dairy farms in Galicia – Spain]. *Holos*, *5*(31), 308–321. doi:10.15628/holos.2015.3249

da Silva, M. H. T., Lima, A. D. C., Teixeria, A. M., Agostinho, R., & Calado, R. D. (2021). *Lean E PNH: a metodologia lean e a política nacionalde humanização* (Vol. 1). Revista Lean Nas Upsa.

da Silva, M. R. B., da Silva Santos, J., de Morais, M. P. D. L., de Armada, H. C. D., de Oliveira, N. S., & Donato, A. G. (2021). Nurses' perception of risk classification in an emergency care unit in the West Zone of Rio de Janeiro [Percepção dos enfermeiros na classificação de risco em uma unidade de pronto atendimento na Zona Oeste do Rio de Janeiro]. *Global Clinical Research Journal*, *1*(1), e2–e2.

Daud, S. (2012). Knowledge management processes in SMES and large firms: A comparative evaluation. *African Journal of Business Management*, *6*(11), 2012.

Davis, B. M. (2010). Applying Lean to the perioperative environment. *AORN Journal*, *92*(S6), S100–S104.

De Amaral, L. C., Nascimento, S.D., Costa, H.G., Viera, L.E.V., Teixeira, A.M., Braga Neto, O.O., & Calado, R.D. (2021). Lean Healthcare – Lean Thinking, Standardized Work and the 8 Health Wastes [Lean Healthcare – Pensamento Lean, Trabalho Padronizado e os 8 Desperdícios na Saúde]. *Universidade Federal Fluminense LabDGE, 2*(1), 16.

de Carvalho, J. C., Ramos, M., & Paixão, C. (2014). A lean case study in an oncological hospital: Implementation of a telephone triage system in the emergency service. *Risk Management and Healthcare Policy*, *7*, 1. PMID:24376365

de Souza Minayo, M. C., Deslandes, S. F., & Gomes, R. (2011). *Social research: theory, method and creativity* [Pesquisa social: teoria, método e criatividade]. Editora Vozes Limitada.

de Souza, A., Guerra, M., Guerra, C. O., Gomide, P. L. R., Pereira, C. M., & Freitas, D. A. (2009). Management control in hospital organizations [Controle de gestão em organizações hospitalares]. *REGE Revista de Gestão*, *16*(3), 15–29.

de Souza, L. B., & Pidd, M. (2011). Exploring the barriers to lean health care implementation. *Public Money & Management*, *31*(1), 59–66.

Deimiling, S. F., & Zanin, A. (2011). Produção enxuta no agronegócio: análise em uma agroindústria do Oeste de Santa Catarina [Lean production in agribusiness: analysis in an agroindustry in the west of Santa Catarina]. Proceedings of Simpósio Engenharia de Produção, 1-15.

Demo, P. (1985). *Introduction of the methodology* [Introdução da metodologia]. Atlas.

Demo, P. (1995). *Scientific methodology in social sciences* [Metodologia científica em ciências sociais]. Atlas.

DeRosier, J., Stalhandske, E., Bagian, J. P., & Nudell, T. (2002). Using health care failure mode and effect analysis™: The VA National Center for Patient Safety's prospective risk analysis system. *The Joint Commission Journal on Quality Improvement*, *28*(5), 248–267. doi:10.1016/S1070-3241(02)28025-6 PMID:12053459

Di Marzo, R. (2017) *The kaizen methodology: Applications and Implementation of the Japanese Model in the West: Lantech Case* [La metodologia kaizen: Applicazioni e Implementazione del Modello Giapponese in Occidente: Caso Lantech]. Division of Scienze Economiche and Aziendali "Marco Fanno", Università Degli Studi di Padova. Retrieved from: http://tesi.cab.unipd.it/61701/

Dorval, M., & Jobin, M. H. (2020). Exploring lean generic and lean healthcare cultural clusters. *International Journal of Productivity and Performance Management*, *69*(4), 723–740. doi:10.1108/IJPPM-01-2019-0057

Dos Santos, A. J., Ribeiro, M. I. L. C., da Silva Melo, C., da Silva, M. M., Silva, A. T., & Alves, A. C. (2021). Demand of patients medicated and referred for hospital admission after risk classification in an Emergency Care Unit. *Brazilian Journal of Health Review*, *4*(5), 18998–19012. doi:10.34119/bjhrv4n5-041

dos Santos, R. F., Sampaio, P. Y. S., Sampaio, R. A. C., Gutierrez, G. L., & de Almeida, M. A. B. (2017). Assistive technology and its relationship to quality of life of people with disabilities [Tecnologia assistiva e suas relações com a qualidade de vida de pessoas com deficiência]. *Revista de Terapia Ocupacional da Universidade de São Paulo*, *28*(1), 54–62.

Drei, S. M. (2020). *Lean healthcare applied in the medical clinic of a medium-sized hospital* [Lean healthcare aplicado na clínica médica de um hospital de médio porte]. Universidade Estadual de Campinas - Faculdade de Ciências Médicas. https://www.slideshare.net/maryamkazemi3/stability-of-colloids%0Ahttps://barnard.edu/sites/default/files/inline/student_user_guide_for_spss.pdf%0Ahttp://www.ibm.com/support%0Ahttp://www.spss.com/sites/dm-book/legacy/ProgDataMgmt_SPSS17.pdf%0Ahttps://www.n

Drucker, P. (1994). *Post-capitalist society* [Sociedade pós-capitalista]. Pioneira.

Drucker, P. (1997). Brave world of knowledge [Admirável mundo do conhecimento]. *HSM Management*, *1*, 63–68.

Duarte, E., Eble, L., & Garcia, L. (2018) 30 years of the Unified Health System. *Journal of Epidemiology and Health Services, 27*(1). Retrieved from: https://scielosp.org/article/ress/2018.v27n1/e00100018/

Erthal, A., Frangeskou, M., & Marques, L. (2021). Cultural tensions in lean healthcare implementation: A paradox theory lens. *International Journal of Production Economics*, *233*(1), 107968. doi:10.1016/j.ijpe.2020.107968

Esain, A. E., Williams, S. J., Gakhal, S., Caley, L., & Cooke, M. W. (2012). Healthcare quality improvement–policy implications and practicalities. *International Journal of Health Care Quality Assurance*.

Escorel, S. (2008). Equity in Health [Equidade em Saúde]. In *Dictionary of Professional Education in Health* (2nd ed.). Rio de Janeiro: EPSJV. Retrieved from: http://www.epsjv.fiocruz.br/publicacao/livro/dicionario-da-educacao-profissional-em-saude-segunda-edicao-revista-e-ampliada

Esper, G. J., Sweeney, R. L., Winchell, E., Duffell, J. M., Kier, S. C., Lukens, H. W., & Krupinski, E. A. (2020). Rapid System Wide Implementation of Outpatient Telehealth in Response to the COVID-19 Pandemic. *Journal of Healthcare Management, 65*(6), 443–452. doi:10.1097/JHM-D-20-00131

Extreme U. V. (n.d.). *Grape Rays And UVB: Difference Between Them* [Raios Uva E UVB: Diferença Entre Eles]. Retrieved from https://www.extremeuv.com.br/raios-uva-e-uvb-diferenca-entre-eles

FAO - Food and Agriculture Organization of the United Nations. (2019). *Gateway to dairy production and products 2019*. https://www.fao.org/dairy-production-products/production/en/

Farias, D. C., & Araujo, F. O. D. (2017). Hospital management in Brazil: Literature review aimed at improving administrative practices in hospitals [Gestão hospitalar no Brasil: revisão da literatura visando ao aprimoramento das práticas administrativas em hospitais]. *Ciencia & Saude Coletiva*, *22*, 1895–1904. doi:10.1590/1413-81232017226.26432016 PMID:28614509

Ferenhof, H. A., Da Cunha, A. H., Bonamigo, A., & Forcellini, F. A. (2018). Toyota Kata as a KM solution to the inhibitors of implementing lean service in service companies. *VINE Journal of Information and Knowledge Management Systems*, *48*(3), 404–426. doi:10.1108/VJIKMS-11-2017-0083

Fernandes, B. (2014). Iramuteq Manual. Academic Press.

Fernandes, H. M. de L. G., Jesus, M. V. N. de, Silva, D. da, & Guirardello, E. de B. (2020). Lean Healthcare in the institutional, professional, and patient perspective: An integrative review. *Revista Gaúcha de Enfermagem*, *41*. Advance online publication. doi:10.1590/1983-1447.2020.20190340

Figueiredo, C. J., & da Silva, M. H. L. (2014). Multicriteria approach and fuzzy logic for product portfolio prioritization in an agroindustrial system. *Operational Research for Development*, *6*(2), 226–242.

Fillingham, D. (2007). Can lean save lives? *Leadership in Health Services*, *20*(4), 231–241. doi:10.1108/17511870710829346 PMID:20698096

Fisher, A. M., Ding, M. Q., Hochheiser, H., & Douglas, G. P. (2016). Measuring time utilization of pharmacists in the Birmingham Free Clinic dispensary. *BMC Health Services Research*, *16*(1), 1–7. doi:10.118612913-016-1787-6 PMID:27687973

Fitzgerald, K., Pelletier, L., & Reznek, M. A. (2017). A Queue-Based Monte Carlo Analysis to Support Decision Making for Implementation of an Emergency Department Fast Track. *Journal of Healthcare Engineering*, *2017*, 1–8. Advance online publication. doi:10.1155/2017/6536523 PMID:29065634

Flach, L., & Antonello, C. S. (2010). Informal Learning theory and its implications for organizations. [A teoria sobre aprendizagem informal e suas implicações nas organizações.] *Gestao. Org*, *8*(2), 193–208.

Fomundam, S., & Herrmann, J. W. (2007). *A survey of queuing theory applications in healthcare*. Academic Press.

Fonseca, A. (2006). *Organizational knowledge assessment methodology*. World Bank Institute.

Forno, A. J., Forcellini, F. A., & Crestani, P. A. (2010). A abordagem enxuta aplicada ao agronegócio: estudo de caso em viveiro de mudas florestais [The lean approach applied to agribusiness: a case study in a forest seedling nursery]. Proceedings of Encontro Nacional de Engenharia de Produção, 2-12.

Franco, L. (2020). *Lean healthcare application for patient flow analysis in Cardiology department* [Doctoral dissertation]. Politecnico di Torino.

Fugate, M., Prussia, G. E., & Kinicki, A. J. (2012). Managing employee withdrawal during organizational change: The role of threat appraisal. *Journal of Management*, *38*(3), 890–914. doi:10.1177/0149206309352881

Gallis, C. (2013). Increasing productivity and controlling of work fatigue in forest operations by using prescribed active pauses: A selective review. *Croatian Journal of Forest Engineering: Journal for Theory and Application of Forestry Engineering*, *34*(1), 103–112.

Gijo, E. V., & Antony, J. (2014). Reducing patient waiting time in outpatient department using lean six sigma methodology. *Quality and Reliability Engineering International*, *30*(8), 1481–1491. doi:10.1002/qre.1552

Gill, S. D., Lane, S. E., Sheridan, M., Ellis, E., Smith, D., & Stella, J. (2018). Why do 'fast track' patients stay more than four hours in the emergency department? An investigation of factors that predict length of stay. *EMA -. Emergency Medicine Australasia*, *30*(5), 641–647. doi:10.1111/1742-6723.12964 PMID:29569844

Gkika, E., Psaroulaki, A., Tselentis, Y., Angelakis, E., & Kouikoglou, V. S. (2019). Can point-of-care testing shorten hospitalization length of stay? An exploratory investigation of infectious agents using regression modelling. *Health Informatics Journal*, *25*(4), 1606–1617. doi:10.1177/1460458218796612 PMID:30179068

Goldwasser, R. S., Lobo, M. S. D. C., Arruda, E. F. D., Angelo, S. A., Ribeiro, E. C. D. O., & Silva, J. R. L. (2018). Planning and understanding the intensive care network in the State of Rio de Janeiro (RJ), Brazil: A complex societal problem. *Revista Brasileira de Terapia Intensiva*, *30*(3), 347–357. doi:10.5935/0103-507X.20180053 PMID:30328988

Gonçalves, J. M. S., Santos, L. C., & Gohr, C. F. (2013). Uma análise das publicações sobre produção enxuta nos principais periódicos nacionais de Engenharia de Produção [An analysis of publications on lean production in the main national journals of Production Engineering]. *Produção em Foco*, *3*(2), 252–277. doi:10.14521/P2237-5163.2013.0004.0003

Gordilho, R. (2018). *Strategic management in hospitals* [Gestão estratégica em hospitais]. Ledriprint.

Graban, M. (2009). *Lean Hospitals: Improving Quality*. Patient Safety and Employee Satisfaction.

Graban, M. (2013). *Lean Hospitals: improving quality, patient safety and employee engagement* [Hospitais Lean: melhorando a qualidade, a segurança dos pacientes e o envolvimento dos funcionários]. Bookmark.

Graban, M. (2016). *Lean Hospitals: Improving Quality, Patient Safety, and Employee satisfaction* (3rd ed.). Taylor & Francis Group.

Green, L. V., & Liu, N. (2015). A study of New York City obstetrics units demonstrates the potential for reducing hospital inpatient capacity. *Medical Care Research and Review: MCRR*, *72*(2), 168–186. doi:10.1177/1077558715572388 PMID:25701578

Grzybovski, D. (2007). *Knowledge Platform and Transgenerational Learning in Family Businesses* [Doctorate in Administration. Lavras Federal University.

Guedes, H. M., Almeida, A. G. P., de Oliveira Ferreira, F., Júnior, G. V., & Chianca, T. C. M. (2014). Risk classification: Portrait of the population assisted in a Brazilian emergency service. *Revista de Enfermagem Referência.*, *4*(1), 37–44. doi:10.12707/RIII13108

Guedes, V. L., & Borschiver, S. (2005). Bibliometry: A statistical tool for the management of information and knowledge, in information systems, communication and scientific and technological evaluation [Bibliometria: uma ferramenta estatística para a gestão da informação e do conhecimento, em sistemas de informação, de comunicação e de avaliação científica e tecnológica]. *Encontro Nacional de Ciência da Informação*, *6*(1), 18.

Hajjarsaraei, H., Shirazi, B., & Rezaeian, J. (2018). Scenario-based analysis of fast track strategy optimization on emergency department using integrated safety simulation. *Safety Science*, *107*(March), 9–21. doi:10.1016/j.ssci.2018.03.025

Hallam, C. R., & Contreras, C. (2018). Lean healthcare: Scale, scope and sustainability. *International Journal of Health Care Quality Assurance*, *31*(7), 684-696.

Henrique, D. B. (2014). *Modelo de mapeamento de fluxo de valor para implantações de lean em ambientes hospitalares: proposta e aplicação* [Doctoral dissertation]. Universidade de São Paulo.

Heymann, E. P., Wicky, A., Carron, P.-N., & Exadaktylos, A. K. (2019). Death in the Emergency Department: A Retrospective Analysis of Mortality in a Swiss University Hospital. *Emergency Medicine International*, *2019*, 1–9. doi:10.1155/2019/5263521 PMID:31565438

Hitti, E. A., El-Eid, G. R., Tamim, H., Saleh, R., Saliba, M., & Naffaa, L. (2017). Improving Emergency Department radiology transportation time: A successful implementation of lean methodology. *BMC Health Services Research*, *17*(1), 1–10. doi:10.118612913-017-2488-5 PMID:28870249

Hoot, N. R., Zhou, C., Jones, I., & Aronsky, D. (2007). Measuring and Forecasting Emergency Department Crowding in Real Time. *Annals of Emergency Medicine*, *49*(6), 747–755. doi:10.1016/j.annemergmed.2007.01.017 PMID:17391809

Hopkins, R. B., Tarride, J. E., Bowen, J., Blackhouse, G., O'Reilly, D., Campbell, K., Lim, M., & Goeree, R. (2008). Cost-effectiveness of reducing wait times for cataract surgery in Ontario. *Canadian Journal of Ophthalmology*, *43*(2), 213–217. doi:10.3129/i08-002 PMID:18347625

Huntzinge, J. (2005). *The Roots of Lean. Lean Enterprise Institute*. Disponível em: https://www.leaninstituut.nl/publications/Roots_of_Lean_TWI.pdf

Hurst, J. (2000). Challenges for health systems in Member Countries of the Organisation for Economic Co-operation and Development. *Bulletin of the World Health Organization*, *78*, 751–760. PMID:10916912

Iasbech, P. A. B., & Lavarda, R. A. B. (2018). Strategy and practices: A qualitative study of a Brazilian public healthcare system of telemedicine. *International Journal of Public Sector Management*, *31*(3), 347–371. doi:10.1108/IJPSM-12-2016-0207

IBGE. (2019). *Macaé*. https://cidades.ibge.gov.br/brasil/rj/macae/panorama

IEA - Instituto de Economia Agricola. (2018). *Valor de produção: Estatística de produção dos principais produtos da agropecuária Paulista 2018* [Production value: Production statistics of the main agricultural products from São Paulo 2018]. http://ciagri.iea.sp.gov.br/nia1/subjetiva.aspx?cod_sis=1&idioma=1

IFCN - International Farm Comparison Group. (2018). *The IFCN Dairy Report 2018: For a better understanding of dairy world*. https://ifcndairy.org/wp-content/uploads/2018/10/Dairy-Report-Article-2018.pdf

Inazawa, F. K. (2009). The role of organizational culture and learning for successful knowledge management. *Perspectives in Information Science, Belo Horizonte*, *14*(3), 2009.

Inman, R. R. (1999). Are you implementing a pull system by putting the cart before the horse? *Production and Inventory Management Journal*, *40*(2), 67.

Instrument for the evaluation of public management. (2010). CICLO.

IPEA. Associação Nacional Dos Servidores da Carreira de Planejamento e Orçamento. (2017). Brazil 2035: scenarios for development [Brasil 2035: cenários para o desenvolvimento]. IPEA.

Ivanov, D. (2020). Viable supply chain model: Integrating agility, resilience and sustainability perspectives—lessons from and thinking beyond the COVID-19 pandemic. *Annals of Operations Research*. Advance online publication. doi:10.100710479-020-03640-6 PMID:32836614

Jessome, R. (2020). Improving patient flow in diagnostic imaging: A case report. *Journal of Medical Imaging and Radiation Sciences*, *51*(4), 678–688. doi:10.1016/j.jmir.2020.08.014 PMID:32950432

John Hopkins University & Medicine. (n.d.). *COVID-19 – Map – Coronavirus Resource Center*. Retrieved from: https://coronavirus.jhu.edu/map.html

Joint Commission on Accreditation of Healthcare Organizations. (2006). *Doing More with Less: Lean Thinking and Patient Safety in Health Care*. Oakbrook Terrace.

Joint Commission Resources. (2013). Lean thinking in healthcare: less waste and queues and more quality and patient safety [O pensamento lean na saúde: menos desperdício e filas e mais qualidade e segurança para o paciente]. *The Bookman*.

Jorma, T., Tiirinki, H., Bloigu, R., & Turkki, L. (2016). LEAN thinking in Finnish healthcare. *Leadership in Health Services*, *29*(1), 9–36. doi:10.1108/LHS-08-2015-0021 PMID:26764958

Jung, H. M., Kim, M. J., Kim, J. H., Park, Y. S., Chung, H. S., Chung, S. P., & Lee, J. H. (2021). The effect of overcrowding in emergency departments on the admission rate according to the emergency triage level. *PLoS ONE, 16*(2), 1–9. doi:10.1371/journal.pone.0247042

Jurberg, C. (2008). Flawed but fair: Brazil's health system reaches out to the poor. *Bulletin of the World Health Organization*, *86*(4), 248–249. doi:10.2471/BLT.08.030408 PMID:18438510

Karam, A. A., Liviu, M., Cristina, V., & Radu, H. (2018). The contribution of lean manufacturing tools to changeover time decrease in the pharmaceutical industry. A SMED project. *Procedia Manufacturing*, *22*, 886–892. doi:10.1016/j.promfg.2018.03.125

Konder, M. T., & O'Dwyer, G. (2016). The integration of the Emergency Care Units (UPA) with healthcare services in the city of Rio de Janeiro. Brazil. Interface-Communication. *Health Education*, *20*(59), 879–892.

Kovalchuk, S. V., Funkner, A. A., Metsker, O. G., & Yakovlev, A. N. (2018). Simulation of patient flow in multiple healthcare units using process and data mining techniques for model identification. *Journal of Biomedical Informatics*, *82*, 128–142. doi:10.1016/j.jbi.2018.05.004 PMID:29753874

Krohling, R. A., & Campanharo, V. C. (2009). Fuzzy-TOPSIS for multicriteria decision making an application to the case of offshore oil spill accidents. In *XLI Simposio Brasileiro de Pesquisa Operacional* (pp. 1731–1742). Academic Press.

Krykhtine, F. L. P., Morim, A. C. D., do Vale, N. G. P., Fortes, L. E. N. S., & Neto, A. G. C. (2013). *Applying fuzzy logic in a multicriteria selection model for multiclients*. X Simpósio de Gestão e Excelência em Tecnologia.

Lacerda, W. A. D., & Santiago, I. M. F. L. (2007). Popular participation in local management of the Family Health Program in Campina Grande, Paraíba. *Journal Katálysis*, *10*, 197–205.

Lack of basic medical supplies hinders pandemic combat in UBS. (2020, August 19). Retrieved May 05, 2022, from University of São Paulo (USP) https://jornal.usp.br/atualidades/falta-de-insumos-medicos-basicos-dificulta-combate-a-pandemia-nas-ubs/

Lakshmi, C., & Iyer, S. A. (2013). Application of queueing theory in health care: A literature review. *Operations Research for Health Care*, *2*(1-2), 25–39. doi:10.1016/j.orhc.2013.03.002

Lantz, B., & Rosén, P. (2016). Measuring effective capacity in an emergency department. *Journal of Health Organization and Management*, *30*(1), 73–84. doi:10.1108/JHOM-05-2014-0074 PMID:26964850

Lanzaro, G. A. (2018). *Using fuzzy logic for speed limit determination on highways*. Academic Press.

Lean Magazine in ECUs (2020). *Initial Diagnostic Report in 50 ECUs*. Author.

Lee, K. H., Austin, J., & Pronovost, P. J. (2016). Developing a measure of value in health care. *Value heal, 19*(4), 323-325.

Leite, H., Bateman, N., & Radnor, Z. (2019). Beyond the ostensible: An exploration of barriers to lean implementation and sustainability in healthcare. *Production Planning and Control*, *31*(1), 1–18. doi:10.1080/09537287.2019.1623426

Levinson, W., & Shojania, K. G. (2011). Bad experiences in the hospital: The stories keep coming. *BMJ Quality & Safety*, *20*(11), 911–913. doi:10.1136/bmjqs-2011-000474 PMID:21964611

Liker, J. K., & Meier, D. (2007). *The Toyota model: Application Manual* [O modelo Toyota: Manual de Aplicação]. Bookman.

Lima, A., Barbosa, C., Sobrinho, A., Calado, R., & Sobral, A. P. (2021, September). Capacity Management as a Tool for Improving Infrastructure in the Lean Healthcare: A Systematic Review. In *IFIP International Conference on Advances in Production Management Systems* (pp. 298-304). Springer. 10.1007/978-3-030-85902-2_32

Lima, F. R. Jr, & Carpinetti, L. C. R. (2015). A comparison between TOPSIS and Fuzzy-TOPSIS methods in supporting multicriteria decision making for supplier selection. *Management & Production*, *22*, 17–34.

Lima, R. T. de S., Fernandes, T. G., Balieiro, A. A. da S., Costa, F. dos S., Schramm, J. M. de A., Schweickardt, J. C., & Ferla, A. A. (2016). Primary Care in Brazil and the Mais Médicos program: An analysis of production indicators [A Atenção Básica no Brasil e o programa Mais Médicos: Uma análise de indicadores de produção]. *Ciencia & Saude Coletiva*, *21*(9), 2685–2696. doi:10.1590/1413-81232015219.15412016 PMID:27653054

Lin, D., Patrick, J., & Labeau, F. (2014). Estimating the waiting time of multi-priority emergency patients with downstream blocking. *Health Care Management Science*, *17*(1), 88–99. doi:10.100710729-013-9241-3 PMID:23690253

Lira, E. G. (2018). *Patient flow management strategies: Multiple case study in radiotherapy clinics in Belo Horizonte* [Estratégias de gestão do fluxo de pacientes: Estudo de casos múltiplos em clínicas de radioterapia de Belo Horizonte]. Academic Press.

Liu, J., Masiello, I., Ponzer, S., & Farrokhnia, N. (2019). Interprofessional teamwork versus fast track streaming in an emergency department—An observational cohort study of two strategies for enhancing the throughput of orthopedic patients presenting limb injuries or back pain. *PLoS One*, *14*(7), 1–16. doi:10.1371/journal.pone.0220011 PMID:31318942

Lobo, C. V. F., Calado, R. D., & da Conceição, R. D. P. (2018). Evaluation of value stream mapping (VSM) applicability to the oil and gas chain processes. *International Journal of Lean Six Sigma*, *11*(2), 309–330. doi:10.1108/IJLSS-05-2018-0049

Loubère, L., & Ratinaud, P. (2014). *Documentation IRaMuTeQ 0.6 alpha 3 version 0.1*. Available at: http://www.iramuteq.org/news

Lourenzani, W. L., Pinto, L. B., Carvalho, E. C. A., & Carmo, S. M. (2008). A qualificação em gestão da agricultura familiar: A experiência da alta paulista [Qualification in family farming management: the experience of high São Paulo]. *Revista de Ciências em Extensão*, *4*, 62.

Lubben, R. (1989). *Just-In-Time: an advanced production strategy. trans* (2nd ed.). McGraw-Hill.

Luciani-McGillivray, I., Cushing, J., Klug, R., Lee, H., & Cahill, J. E. (2020). Nurse-led call back program to improve patient follow-up with providers after discharge from the emergency department. *Journal of Patient Experience*, *7*(6), 1349–1356. doi:10.1177/2374373520947925 PMID:33457586

Machado, G. V. C., Oliveira, F. L. P. D., Barbosa, H. A. L., Giatti, L., & Bonolo, P. D. F. (2015). Factors associated with the use of an emergency service, Ouro Preto, 2012 [Fatores associados à utilização de um serviço de urgência/emergência, Ouro Preto, 2012]. *Cadernos Saúde Coletiva*, *23*, 416–424. doi:10.1590/1414-462X201500040177

Magalhães, R. S. (2007). Habilidades sociais no mercado de leite. *Revista de Administração de Empresas*, *47*, 1–11.

Magnusson, C., Herlitz, J., & Axelsson, C. (2020). Pre-hospital triage performance and emergency medical services nurse's field assessment in an unselected patient population attended to by the emergency medical services: A prospective observational study. *Scandinavian Journal of Trauma, Resuscitation and Emergency Medicine*, *28*(1), 1–19. doi:10.118613049-020-00766-1 PMID:32807224

Maicon Gonzaga. (2022, January 4). *EPI's sterilizer* [Esterilizador de EPI's] [Video]. YouTube. https://www.youtube.com/watch?v=hUFDIk8SWIo

MAPA - Ministério da Agricultura. Pecuária e Abastecimento. (2002). Instrução Normativa N° 51, de 19 de Setembro de 2002 [Normative Instruction No. 51, of September 19, 2002]. Brasília: Mapa.

MAPA - Ministério da Agricultura. Pecuária e Abastecimento. (2018). Instrução Normativa N° 76, de 26 de Novembro de 2018 [Normative Instruction No. 76, of November 26, 2018]. Brasília: Mapa.

Martins, C. C., & Waclawovsky, A. J. (2015). Problems and challenges faced by public managers in the health management process. *Journal of Management in Health Systems, 4*(1), 100-109.

Massuda, A., Hone, T., Leles, F. A. G., De Castro, M. C., & Atun, R. (2018). The Brazilian health system at crossroads: Progress, crisis and resilience. *BMJ Global Health*, *3*(4), e000829. doi:10.1136/bmjgh-2018-000829 PMID:29997906

Matias, D. B. (2021). *Implementation of service strategy in an emergency care unit in Belo Horizonte based on the principles of Lean Thinking and Fast Track* [Implementação de estratégia de atendimento em uma unidade de pronto atendimento de Belo Horizonte baseada nos princípios do Lean Thinking e do Fast Track]. Academic Press.

Mattos, R. (2009, Out 20). The Meanings of Integrality in Attention and Health Care [Os sentidos da integralidade: algumas reflexões acerca de valores que merecem ser defendidos]. In *The meanings of integrality: some reflections on values that deserve to be defended.* Cepesc/IMS/Uerj/Abrasco. Retrieved from: https://lappis.org.br/site/wp-content/uploads/2017/12/Os-Sentidos-da-Integralidade-na-Aten%C3%A7%C3%A3o-e-no-Cuidado-%C3%A0-Sa%C3%BAde.pdf

McGrath, K. M., Bennett, D. M., Ben-Tovim, D. I., Boyages, S. C., Lyons, N. J., & O'Connell, T. J. (2008). Implementing and sustaining transformational change in health care: Lessons learnt about clinical process redesign. *The Medical Journal of Australia*, *188*(6), S32. PMID:18341474

Medeiros. (2021). *Risk communication. CIEVS I CGEMSP I DSASTE I SVS I MS Number 19* [Comunicação de risco. CIEVS I CGEMSP I DSASTE I SVS I MS Número 19]. https://sbim.org.br/images/files/notas-tecnicas/212611-rede-cievs-variante-omicron.pdf

Meirelles, C. S. C., & Oliveir, V. M. S. (2013). Didactics, Teaching and Tutoring in Higher Education. Aracaju. *UnitPós*, *2013*, 15.

Mello, C. H. P., Turrioni, J. B., Xavier, A. F., & Campos, D. F. (2012). Pesquisa-ação na engenharia de produção: Proposta de estruturação para sua condução [Action research in production engineering: a structure proposal for its conduction]. *Production*, *22*(1), 1–13. doi:10.1590/S0103-65132011005000056

Ministry of Health Department of Health Care. (2010). *National Humanization Policy*. Cadernos HumanizaSUS: Training and intervention. Retrieved from: https://bvsms.saude.gov.br/bvs/publicacoes/cadernos_humanizaSUS.pdf

Ministry of Health. (2013). *National Humanization Policy - HumanizaSUS* [Política Nacional de Humanização - HumanizaSUS]. https://www.gov.br/saude/pt-br/acesso-a-informacao/acoes-e-programas/humanizasus

Ministry of Health. (n.d.). *Emergency Care Unit (UPA 24h)*. Available at: https://www.gov.br/saude/pt-br/assuntos/saude-de-a-a-z/u/unidade-de-pronto-atendimento-upa-24h

Ministry of Health. Health Care Department. (2013). *National Humanization Policy*. Retrieved from: https://bvsms.saude.gov.br/bvs/publicacoes/politica_nacional_humanizacao_pnh_folheto.pdf

Min, L. L., Sarantopoulos, A., Spagnol, G. S., & Calado, R. D. (2014). *What is this Lean Healthcare thing?* [O que é esse tal de Lean Healthcare]. Pedro e João.

Min, L. L., Sarantopoulos, A., Spagnol, G. S., & Calado, R. D. (2014). *What's this Lean Healthcare guy?* [O que é esse tal de Lean Healthcare]. Pedro e João.

Mintzberg, H. (1995). Creating effective organizations [Criando organizações eficazes]. São Paulo: Atlas.

Monden, Y. (1998). *Toyota Production System: an integrated approach to just in time. 3*. Engineering and Pressure.

Moraes, R., & Galiazzi, M. D. C. (2006). Discursive textual analysis: Multi-facereconstructive process [Análise textual discursiva: processo reconstrutivo de múltiplas faces]. *Ciência & Educação (Bauru)*, *12*, 117–128. doi:10.1590/S1516-73132006000100009

Moreira, W. (2018). *Systems of knowledge organization: theoretical, conceptual and methodological aspects* [Sistemas de organização do conhecimento: aspectos teóricos, conceituais e metodológicos]. Academic Press.

Morell-Santandreu, O., Santandreu-Mascarell, C., & Garcia-Sabater, J. J. (2021). A Model for the Implementation of Lean Improvements in Healthcare Environments as Applied in a Primary Care Center. *International Journal of Environmental Research and Public Health*, *18*(6), 2876. doi:10.3390/ijerph18062876 PMID:33799752

Moura, E. (2013, July 1). The right to health in the Federal Constitution of 1988 [O direito à saúde na Constituição Federal de 1988]. *Revista Âmbito Jurídico, Cadernos Direitos Constitucionais*. Retrieved from: https://ambitojuridico.com.br/cadernos/direito-constitucional/o-direito-a-saude-na-constituicao-federal-de-1988/

Myszewski, J. M., & Sinha, M. N. (2018). A model for measuring effectiveness of quality management practices in health care. *Leadership in Health Services*, *31*(3), 310–325. doi:10.1108/LHS-03-2018-0020 PMID:30016923

Naidoo, L., & Mahomed, O. H. (2016). Impact of Lean on patient cycle and waiting times at a rural district hospital in KwaZulu-Natal. *African Journal of Primary Health Care & Family Medicine*, *8*(1), e1–e9. doi:10.4102/phcfm.v8i1.1084 PMID:27543283

Neily, J., Ogrinc, G., Mills, P., Williams, R., Stalhandske, E., Bagian, J., & Weeks, W. B. (2003). Using aggregate root cause analysis to improve patient safety. *Joint Commission Journal on Quality and Safety*, *29*(8), 434–439. doi:10.1016/S1549-3741(03)29052-3 PMID:12953608

Nicolaides, A. (2017). *Promoting ethical corporate social responsibility in the events industry*. Academic Press.

Nicolay, C. R., Purkayastha, S., Greenhalgh, A. A. S. N., Benn, J., Chaturvedi, S., Phillips, N., & Darzi, A. (2012). Systematic review of the application of quality improvement methodologies from the manufacturing industry to surgical healthcare. *Journal of British Surgery*, *99*(3), 324–335.

Nino, V., Claudio, D., Valladares, L., & Harris, S. (2020). An enhanced kaizen event in a sterile processing department of a rural hospital: A case study. *International Journal of Environmental Research and Public Health*, *17*(23), 1–20. doi:10.3390/ijerph17238748 PMID:33255618

Nonaka, I., Toyama, R., & Konno, N. (2000). SECI, Ba and leadership: A unified model of dynamic knowledge creation. *Long Range Planning*, *33*(1), 5–34. doi:10.1016/S0024-6301(99)00115-6

Noronha, D. P., & Ferreira, S. M. (2000). Literature reviews. In *Sources of information for researchers and professionals*. UFMG.

Nosek, R. A. Jr, & Wilson, J. P. (2001). Queuing theory and customer satisfaction: A Review of terminology, trends, and applications to pharmacy practice. *Hospital Pharmacy*, *36*(3), 275–279. doi:10.1177/001857870103600307

O'Dwyer, G., Konder, M. T., Reciputti, L. P., Lopes, M. G. M., Agostinho, D. F., & Alves, G. F. (2017). The process of implementing emergency care units in Brazil [O processo de implantação das unidades de pronto atendimento no Brasil]. *Revista de Saude Publica*, *51*, 125. PMID:29236876

OECD. (2003). *Survey of knowledge management practices in ministries/ departments/ agencies of central government*. OECD.

Official Journal of the European Union. Regulation (EU) 2016/425 of the European Parliament and of the Council of 9 March 2016, Art.3 p.7. https://bit.ly/3vgohXj

Ohno, T. (1988). *The Toyota Production System: Beyond Large-Scale Production*. Productivity Press.

Ohno, T. (1997). The Toyota production system beyond production. *The Bookman*.

Ohno, T. (1997). *The Toyota Production System: in addition to large-scale production* [O Sistema Toyota de Produção: além da produção em larga escala]. Bookman.

Oliveira, L. D. S., Costa, D. do N., Oliveira, D. M. de L., Almeida, H. O. C., & Mendonça, I. O. (2018). Quality indicators in hospital emergency services [Indicadores de qualidade nos serviços de urgência hospitalar]. *Cadernos de Graduação:Ciências Biológicas e de Saúde Unit, 4*(3), 173–188. https://periodicos.set.edu.br/index.php/cadernobiologicas/article/view/5177

Oliveira, M. D. D. (2019). *Profile of the demand for services performed by the Emergency Care Unit (UPA) of Tramandaí / RS* [Perfil da demanda de atendimentos realizados pela Unidade de Pronto Atendimento (UPA) de Tramandaí/RS]. Academic Press.

Owen, J. M. (1999). Knowledge management and the information professional. Information Services & Use, 9(1), 7-16. doi:10.3233/ISU-1999-19103

Paim, J., Travassos, C., Almeida, C., Bahia, L., & Macinko, J. (2011). The Brazilian health system: History, advances, and challenges. *Lancet, 377*(9779), 1778–1797. doi:10.1016/S0140-6736(11)60054-8 PMID:21561655

Peimbert-García, R. E., Gutiérrez-Mendoza, L. M., & García-Reyes, H. (2021). Applying Lean Healthcare to Improve the Discharge Process in a Mexican Academic Medical Center. *Sustainability, 13*(19), 10911. doi:10.3390u131910911

Pereira, H., & Barros, R. D. (2008). Humanization [Humanização]. In *Dictionary of Professional Education in Health* (2nd ed.). EPSJV. Retrieved from: http://www.epsjv.fiocruz.br/publicacao/livro/dicionario-da-educacao-profissional-em-saude-segunda-edicao-revista-e-ampliada

Pettersen, J. (2009). Defining lean production: Some conceptual and practical issues. *The TQM Journal.*

Pícoli, R.P., de Oliveira Cazola, L.H., & Maurer, N. M. D. J. S. (2016). Service Users Classified as Risk Level 'Blue'in an Emergency Department. *Cogitare Enferm, 21*(1), 1-7.

Pimentel, V. P., Barbosa, L. M. D. L. H., Machado, L., Adão, L. F., & Reis, C. (2017). *Brazilian health system: management, institutionality and financing* [Sistema de saúde brasileiro: gestão, institucionalidade e financiamento]. Academic Press.

Pimentel, V. P., Gomes, R. D. P., Landim, A. B., Pieroni, J. P., & Palmeira Filho, P. L. (2012). *Health as a development: perspectives for bndes's performance in the health industrial complex* [Saúde como desenvolvimento: perspectivas para atuação do BNDES no complexo industrial da saúde]. Academic Press.

Pinto, R. S., Stocker, T., & de Lima, T. M. (2019). The role of emergency care units: analysis of the performance of the first UPA in the municipality of Pelotas-RS [O papel das unidades de pronto atendimento: análise do desempenho da primeira UPA do município de Pelotas-RS]. *Revista de Gestão em Sistemas de Saúde, 8*(2).

Planning Ministry. Constitution of the Federative Republic of Brazil. (2007). *Constitutional text enacted on October 5, 1988, with the amendments adopted by Constitutional Revision Amendments nº 1 to 6/94.* Federal Senate Undersecretary of Technical Editions. Retrieved from: https://pac.gov.br/infraestrutura-social-e-urbana/upa-unidade-de-pronto-atendimento

Pompeu, A. M., Antônio, J., & Pinheiro, S. (2015). Production models and standardized work: An approach from artisanal production to lean production [Os modelos de produção e o trabalho padronizado : uma abordagem da produção artesanal à produção enxuta]. *Multitemas, 47*, 89–108.

Pozo, J. I. (2008). The learning society and the challenge of converting information into knowledge. *Diretor Udemo, 4*(5), 2008.

Preater, J. (2001). *A bibliography of queues in health and medicine.* Bibliography.

Prometal. (2021, July 20). NR 32 - Safety and health at Work in health services [NR 32 - Segurança e saúde no Trabalho em serviços de saúde]. *Prometal EPIs - Equipamentos de Proteção Individual.* Retrieved from https://www.prometalepis.com.br/blog/50-nr-32-seguranca-e-saude-no-trabalho-em-servicos-de-saude/

Pucci, M., & Cesar, A. M. R. V. C. (2014). The decision-making process of hospital managers. Anais do 14o Congresso USP de Controladoria e Contabilidade.

Pyzdek, T. (2021). The Lean Healthcare Handbook: A Complete Guide to Creating Healthcare Workplaces. Springer. doi:10.1007/978-3-030-69901-7

Quoniam, L., Tarapanoff, K., Araújo Júnior, R. H. D., & Alvares, L. (2001). Intelligence obtained by the application of data mining based on French theses about Brazil [Inteligência obtida pela aplicação de data mining em base de teses francesas sobre o Brasil]. *Ciência da Informação*, *30*, 20–28. doi:10.1590/S0100-19652001000200004

Raimundo, J., & Cadete, M. (2012). Qualified listening and social management among health professionals. *ACTA Paulista Nursing Journal*, 61-17. Retrieved from: https://www.scielo.br/pdf/ape/v25nspe2/pt_10.pdf

Ramos, L. C. F., Spiegel, T., & Assad, D. B. N. (2018). Hospital materials management: A process improvement proposal applied in a university hospital. *Journal of Health Administration*, *18*(70).

Régis, T. K. O., Gohr, C. F., & Santos, L. C. (2018). Lean Healthcare Implementation: Experiences and Lessons Learned in Brazilian Hospitals [Implementação Do Lean Healthcare: Experiências E Lições Aprendidas Em Hospitais Brasileiros]. *Revista de Administração de Empresas / FGV EAESP*, *58*, 30–43. doi:10.1590/S0034-759020180103

Régis, T. K. O., Santos, L. C., & Gohr, C. F. (2019). A case-based methodology for lean implementation in hospital operations. *Journal of Health Organization and Management*, *33*(6), 656–676. PubMed

Ritter, M. D. N., They, N. H., & Konzen, E. (2019). *Introduction to statistical software R* [Introdução ao software estatístico R]. Academic Press.

Rodrigues, R. de C. M., & Carvalho, S. V. de. (2001). A Markovian Decision Model For The Optimization of a Maintenance System With Coxian Repair Times and Unobservable Phases [Um Modelo Markoviano De Decisão Para a Otimização De Um Sistema De Manutenção Com Tempos De Reparo Coxianos E Fases Não Observáveis]. *Pesquisa Operacional*, *21*(2), 159–178. doi:10.1590/S0101-74382001000200003

Rosa, M. S, Costa, M. J. R. P., Sant´Anna, A. C., & Madureira, A. P. (2009). *Manual de Boas Práticas de Manejo-Ordenha* [Manual of Good Milking Management Practices]. Jaboticabal: Funep.

Rosa, C., Silva, F. J. G., Ferreira, L. P., & Campilho, R. D. S. G. (2017). SMED methodology: The reduction of setup times for Steel Wire-Rope assembly lines in the automotive industry. *Procedia Manufacturing*, *13*, 1034–1042. doi:10.1016/j.promfg.2017.09.110

Rother, M., & Harris, R. (2002). *Criando Fluxo Contínuo: um guia de ação para gerentes, engenheiros e associados da produção*. Lean Institute Brasil.

Rother, M., & Shook, J. (2007). *Learning to see: mapping the flow of value to add value and eliminate waste: working manual of a lean tool* [Aprendendo a enxergar: mapeando o fluxo de valor para agregar valor e eliminar o desperdício: manual de trabalho de uma ferramenta enxuta]. Lean Institute Brasil.

Rotter, T., Plishka, C., Lawal, A., Harrison, L., Sari, N., Goodridge, D., Flynn, R., Chan, J., Fiander, M., Poksinska, B., Willoughby, K., & Kinsman, L. (2019). What is lean management in health care? Development of an operational definition for a Cochrane systematic review. *Evaluation & the Health Professions*, *42*(3), 366–390. doi:10.1177/0163278718756992 PMID:29635950

Santos, A. B., Calado, R. D., Chaves, S. M. do A., Nascimento, S. D., Silva, M. B., & Bourguignon, S. C. (2021). MDE-S: A Case Study of the Health Company Diagnostic Method Applied in Three Health Units. *IFIP Advances in Information and Communication Technology*, *631*, 305–313. doi:10.1007/978-3-030-85902-2_33

Santos, A. N. S. (2015). *Patient safety in non-hospital urgent and emergency care units: risk analysis* [Dissertation]. Federal University of Goiás.

Santos, V. M. (2017, July 5). *Lean Healthcare: What is it and how is it changing healthcare?* [Blog post]. Retrieved from https://www.fm2s.com.br/o-que-e-lean-healthcare/

Santos, A. C., Reis, A. C., Souza, C. G., Santos, I. L., & Ferreira, L. A. F. (2020). The first evidence about conceptual vs analytical lean healthcare research studies. *Journal of Health Organization and Management*, *34*(7), 789–806. doi:10.1108/JHOM-01-2020-0021 PMID:32945155

Scalco, A. R., & Souza, R. D. C. (2006). Qualidade na cadeia de produção de leite: Diagnóstico e proposição de melhorias [Quality in the milk production chain: diagnosis and improvement propositio]. *Organizações Rurais & Agroindustriais*, *8*(3), 368–377.

Schafirowitz, G. D. C., & Souza, A. C. D. (2020). Adult users classified as not urgent in the Emergency Care Unit [Usuários adultos classificados como pouco urgentes em Unidade de Pronto Atendimento]. *Interface: Comunicacao, Saude, Educacao*, 24.

Schappo, M. G. (2020, June 16). How does ultraviolet light fight the coronavirus? [Como a luz ultravioleta combate o coronavírus?]. *Questo de Cienceia*. Retrieved from https://bit.ly/3t6k0WK

Schiesari, L. M. C. (2014). External evaluation of hospital organizations in Brazil: Can we do it differently? [Avaliação externa de organizações hospitalares no Brasil: podemos fazer diferente?]. *Ciencia & Saude Coletiva*, *19*, 4229–4234. doi:10.1590/1413-812320141910.21642013 PMID:25272131

Schmidt, E., & Cohen, J. (2014). *The new digital age: Transforming nations, businesses, and our lives*. Vintage.

Scorsolini-Comin, F., Inocente, D.F., & Miura, I.K. (2011). Organizational learning and knowledge management: guidelines for people management. *Rev. Bras. Orientac.*, *12*(2).

Shapoval, A., & Lee, E. K. (2017, November). Optimizing inpatient bed capacity to improve care delivery. In *2017 IEEE International Conference on Bioinformatics and Biomedicine (BIBM)* (pp. 855-860). IEEE. 10.1109/BIBM.2017.8217767

Shingo, S. (1985). *A Revolution in Manufacturing: The SMED System*. Productivity Press.

Shojaei, M., & Saneifar, H. (2021). MFSR: A novel multi-level fuzzy similarity measure for recommender systems. *Expert Systems with Applications*, *177*, 114969. doi:10.1016/j.eswa.2021.114969

Shortell, S. M., Blodgett, J. C., Rundall, T. G., & Kralovec, P. (2018). Use of lean and related transformational performance improvement systems in hospitals in the United States: Results from a national survey. *Joint Commission Journal on Quality and Patient Safety*, *44*(10), 574–582. doi:10.1016/j.jcjq.2018.03.002 PMID:30243359

Silva, J. O. (2009). *Illusory Social Inclusion Processes: a new look at diversity in the educational context* [Processos de Inclusão Social Ilusórios: um novo olhar frente à diversidade no contexto educacional] [Dissertação de Mestrado]. PUCRS, Porto Alegre, RS.

Silva, S.L. (2004). Knowledge management: A critical review guided by the knowledge creation approach. *Ci. Inf.*, *33*(2).

Silva, I. N., Pereira, V. A., & Araujo, L. C. N. (2018). Implementation of the national humanization policy (pnh): Achievements and challenges for health care [Implantação da política nacional de humanização (pnh): conquistas e desafios para a assistência em saúde]. *GEP News*, 2–7. https://www.seer.ufal.br/index.php/gepnews/article/view/4674/3281

Silva, K. S. N., & Santos, S. L. (2014). Units of emergency care (upa) and health promotion: A look from the "system of objects" and "system of actions" [Unidades de pronto atendimento (upa) e promoção de saúde: um olhar a partir do "sistema de objetos" e "sistema de ações"]. *Rev Mov Sociais e Dinâmicas Espac*, *3*(2), 224–246.

Silva, N. F. D. C. D., Vianna, C. M. D. M., Oliveira, F. S. G. D., Mosegui, G. B. G., & Rodrigues, M. P. D. S. (2017). Fuzzy Visa: A fuzzy logic model for Health Surveillance risk assessment for health services waste inspection. *Physis: Journal of Collective Health*, *27*(1), 127–146. doi:10.15900103-73312017000100007

Simões, J., & Bauer, A. (2017). Reproductive and milk production profiles in Serrana Goats. In *Sustainable Goat Production in Adverse Environments* (Vol. 2, pp. 233–243). Springer. doi:10.1007/978-3-319-71294-9_17

Singh, S., Verma, R., & Koul, S. (2021). A collaborative method for simultaneous operations: case of an eye clinic. *OPSEARCH*, 1-21.

Slack, N., Chambers, S., & Johnston, R. (2009). *Production Management* (3rd ed.). Editora Atlas.

Smalley, A. (2005). The Starting Point For Lean Manufacturing: Achieving basic stability. *Management Services*, *49*(4).

Souza, L. E. P. F. D., Paim, J. S., Teixeira, C. F., Bahia, L., Guimarães, R., Almeida-Filho, N. D., ... Azevedo-e-Silva, G. (2019). The current challenges of the struggle for the universal right to health in Brazil [Os desafios atuais da luta pelo direito universal à saúde no Brasil]. *Ciencia & Saude Coletiva*, *24*, 2783–2792.

Tavares, R. S. C. R., Yukita, F., Geraldini, F. L. F., Franco, B. C., & Muniz, J. Jr. (2018). Success Factors For Lean Healthcare Implementation: A Bibliometric Study [Fatores De Sucesso Para Implantação Do Lean Healthcare: Um Estudo Bibliométrico]. *Produto & Produção*, *18*(2). Advance online publication. doi:10.22456/1983-8026.60442

Tekin, M., Arslandere, M., Etlioğlu, M., Koyuncuoğlu, Ö., & Tekin, E. (2018, August). An application of SMED and Jidoka in lean production. In *The International Symposium for Production Research* (pp. 530- 545). Springer.

Terra, J. C. C. (2005). *Knowledge management: The great business challenge*. Terra Forum Library.

The Know Network. (2011). *Eight worldwide criteria in the international certification of auditors in knowledge management processes – Metodologia MAKE – Most Admired Knowledge Enterprises*. The Know Network.

Tlapa, D., Zepeda-Lugo, C. A., Tortorella, G. L., Baez-Lopez, Y. A., Limon-Romero, J., Alvarado-Iniesta, A., & Rodriguez-Borbon, M. I. (2020). Effects of Lean Healthcare on Patient Flow: A Systematic Review. *Value in Health*, *23*(2), 260–273. doi:10.1016/j.jval.2019.11.002 PMID:32113632

Toussaint, J. S. (2008). *Interview of doctor John S. Toussaint on Lean Health Care by R. Hamilton*. https://robinerikhamilton.com/dr-john-toussaint/

Toussaint, J. S., & Berry, L. L. (2013). The Promise of Lean in Health Care. *Mayo Clinic Proceedings*, *88*(1), 74–82. doi:10.1016/j.mayocp.2012.07.025

Tuomi, I. (1999). Data is more than knowledge: Implications of the reversed knowledge hierarchy for knowledge management and organization memory. *Journal of Management Information Systems*, *16*(3), 103–117. doi:10.1080/07421222.1999.11518258

Tupy, O., Manzano, A., Esteves, S. N., Novaes, N. J., Camargo, A. C., Freitas, A. R., & Machado, R. (2002). Planilha para Cálculo do Custo de Produção de Leite na Agricultura Familiar [Spreadsheet for Calculating the Cost of Milk Production in Family Farming]. *Circular Técnica Embrapa*, *32*, 1–11.

Urbizagástegui Alvarado, R. (2002). Lotka's Law in Brazilian bibliometry [A Lei de Lotka na bibliometria brasileira]. *Ciência da Informação*, *31*, 14–20.

Valdiviezo, L.E.V. (2020). *Implementation of a Fast-Track Strategy In Emergency Hospitals* [Implementação De Uma Estratégia Fast-Track Na Emergência De Hospitais]. Academic Press.

Valentim, M. L. P., Lenzi, L. A. F., Cervantes, B. M. N., Carvalho, E. L. D., Garcia, H. D., Catarino, M. E., & Tomael, M. I. (2003). The Competitive Intelligence Process in Organizations. *DataGramaZero, 24*(2).

van de Vrugt, M., & Boucherie, R. J. (2016). Assigning treatment rooms at the emergency department. *Operations Research for Health Care*, *8*, 62–70. doi:10.1016/j.orhc.2015.06.004

Varney, J., Bean, N., & Mackay, M. (2019). The self-regulating nature of occupancy in ICUs: Stochastic homoeostasis. *Health Care Management Science*, *22*(4), 615–634. doi:10.100710729-018-9448-4 PMID:29725895

Vats, A., Goin, K. H., & Fortenberry, J. D. (2011). Lean analysis of a pediatric intensive care unit physician group rounding process to identify inefficiencies and opportunities for improvement. *Pediatric Critical Care Medicine*, *12*(4), 415–421. doi:10.1097/PCC.0b013e3181fe2e3c PMID:20975612

Vieira, T. de O. (2020, January/April). The contribution of document management to knowledge management in organizations: An exploratory approach [O contributo da gestão de documentos na gestão do conhecimento nas organizações: uma abordagem exploratória]. *Questão, Porto Alegre*, *26*(1), 327–350. doi:10.19132/1808-5245261.327-350

Viera, L. V., Reis, M., Chaves, S., Calado, R., Bourguignon, S., & Lordelo, S. (2021, September). Evaluation of Fast-Track Implementation on Emergency Department: A Literature Review. In *IFIP International Conference on Advances in Production Management Systems* (pp. 280-288). Springer. 10.1007/978-3-030-85902-2_30

Viola, D. C., M., Cordioli, E., Pedrotti, C. H. S., Iervolino, M., Bastos Neto, A. da S., Almeida, L. R. N. de, Neves, H. S. de S., & Lottenberg, C. L. (2014). Advanced units: Quality measures in urgent and emergency care [Unidades avançadas: medidas de qualidade no atendimento de urgência e emergência]. *Einstein (Sao Paulo, Brazil)*, *12*(4), 492–498. doi:10.1590/S1679-45082014GS2894

Von Krogh, G., Ichijo, K., & Nonaka, I. (2001). *Enabling Knowledge Creation: Reinventing the Enterprise with the Power of Continuous Innovation* [Facilitando a Criação de Conhecimento: reiventando a empresa com o poder da inovação contínua]. Campus.

Walley, P., & Gowland, B. (2004). Completing the circle: From PD to PDSA. *International Journal of Health Care Quality Assurance*, *17*(6), 349–358.

Wang, H., Kline, J. A., Jackson, B. E., Robinson, R. D., Sullivan, M., Holmes, M., Watson, K. A., Cowden, C. D., Phillips, J. L., Schrader, C. D., Leuck, J., & Zenarosa, N. R. (2017). The role of patient perception of crowding in the determination of real-time patient satisfaction at Emergency Department. *International Journal for Quality in Health Care*, *29*(5), 722–727. doi:10.1093/intqhc/mzx097 PMID:28992161

Weiss, S. J., Ernst, A. A., Derlet, R., King, R., Bair, A., & Nick, T. G. (2005). Relationship between the National ED Overcrowding Scale and the number of patients who leave without being seen in an academic ED. *The American Journal of Emergency Medicine*, *23*(3), 288–294. doi:10.1016/j.ajem.2005.02.034 PMID:15915399

Weiss, S. J., Ernst, A. A., & Nick, T. G. (2006). Comparison of the National Emergency Department Overcrowding Scale and the Emergency Department Work Index for Quantifying Emergency Department Crowding. *Academic Emergency Medicine*, *13*(5), 513–518. doi:10.1197/j.aem.2005.12.009 PMID:16551777

What is EAGLE ? (n.d.). Autodesk. Retrieved from: https://autode.sk/3HztSwm

Where is the waste in healthcare ? (2014, January 23). Retrieved May 03, 2022, from Lean Institute Brasil https://www.lean.org.br/artigos/250/onde-esta-o-desperdicio-na-area-da-saude.aspx

Wijnen, B. F. M., Hemmen, B., Bouman, A. I. E., Van De Meent, H., Ambergen, T., Brink, P. R. G., Seelen, H. A. M., & Evers, S. M. A. A. (2019). Cost-effectiveness of an integrated 'fast track' rehabilitation service for multi-trauma patients: A non-randomized clinical trial in the Netherlands. *PLoS One*, *14*(3), e0213980. Advance online publication. doi:10.1371/journal.pone.0213980 PMID:30901353

Wilson, T. D. (2002). The nonsense of knowledge management. *Information Research*, *8*(1), 8–1.

Womack, J., & Jones, D. T. (2003). *Lean thinking: Banish waste and create wealth in your corporation*. Academic Press.

Womack, J. P., & Jones, D. T. (2003). *Lean Thinking: Banish Waste and Create Wealth in Your Corporation*. Free Press.

Womack, J. P., Jones, D. T., & Roos, D. (2007). *The machine that changed the world: The story of lean production—Toyota's secret weapon in the global car wars that is now revolutionizing world industry*. Simon and Schuster.

Womack, J. T., Jones, D., & Roos, T. (1990). *D. The Machine That Changed the World: The Story of Lean Production*. Rawson Associates.

Xavier, L., Oliveira, M., & Teixeira, E. (2012). Theories used in investigations on knowledge management [Teorias utilizadas nas investigações sobre gestão do conhecimento]. *RISTI*.

Zadeh, L. A. (1965). Information and control. *Fuzzy Sets, 8*(3), 338-353.

Zanon, L. R., Zanin, L., & Flório, F. M. (2016). Evaluation of the use of services provided by emergency care units in a Brazilian municipality. *RGO - Revista Gaúcha de Odontologia, 64*(4), 411–418. doi:10.1590/1981-863720160003000073043

Zibrowski, E., Shepherd, L., Booth, R., Sedig, K., & Gibson, C. (2019). A qualitative study of the theory behind the chairs: Balancing lean-accelerated patient flow with the need for privacy and confidentiality in an emergency medicine setting. *JMIR Human Factors, 6*(1), e11714. Advance online publication. doi:10.2196/11714 PMID:30724743

Zipf, G. K. (1949). *Human behavior and the principle of least effort: An introduction to human ecology*. Academic Press.

About the Contributors

Eduardo Guilherme Satolo is Associate Professor in Faculty of Science and Engineering at São Paulo State University (UNESP), Tupã Campus, lecturing on Business Administration course and Agribussiness and Development Post Graduation Program. Post-Doctorate in Production Engineering from UFF (2018), doctor in Industrial Engineering from the Universidade Metodista de Piracicaba (UNIMEP). Has a master's in Production Engineering from UNIMEP is a graduate in Production Engineering from UNIMEP.

Robisom Damasceno Calado is an Adjunct Professor at the Department of Production Engineering, Universidade Federal Fluminense (UFF), Brazil. He has a postdoctoral degree in Lean Six Sigma and coordinates the LabDGE – Laboratory of Design Thinking, Management and Industrial Engineering at UFF. His current professional activity focuses on teaching and/or research in Industrial Engineering and Management Systems. He currently coordinates the Lean Healthcare Research Project and implementation in 100 Health Emergency Departments, with funding from the Brazilian Ministry of Health. He has over 150 publications and has had over 150 mentors. He has IFIP-APMS publications; IFAC Proceedings, International Journal of Lean Six Sigma and International Journal of Productivity and Performance Management.

* * *

Melissa Felix de Abreu is currently studying Production Engineering at the Fluminense Federal University (UFF), Volta Redonda campus, and attended high school and technical courses in Industrial Automation at the Federal Institute of Education, Science and Technology of Rio de Janeiro, Volta Redonda campus. She is a scholarship student of the Study and Research project for improvement of the Network and Promotion of Access to Health Services, of the Ministry of Health in partnership with UFF through LabDGE - Laboratory of Design Thinking, Management and Industrial Engineering.

Laryssa Amaral is a Researcher at the Design Thinking, Management and Industrial Engineering Research Laboratory (LabDGE) linked to the Fluminense Federal University - UFF (Rio das Ostras). The line of research collaborates in searching for Lean tools and methods applied to health (Lean Healthcare) as shown in published articles. Member of the Project for restructuring and implementing humanization in the patient flow care in UPAs - 24 hours in cooperation between the Ministry of Health and the Universidade Federal Fluminense.

Christiane Barbosa has a Degree in Civil Engineering from the Federal University of Pará (2007), degree in Physical Education from the University of the State of Pará (2006), Master's in Civil Engineering from the Federal University of Pará (2009) and PhD in Civil Engineering from the State University of Campinas (2015). She is currently a professor at the Federal University of Pará. She works on topics related to civil construction, lean production, continuous flow, transport, and logistics.

Alexandre Beraldi Santos is a doctoral student in Science and Biotechnology at Universidade Federal Fluminense - UFF Master in Systems, Programs and Institutions Evaluation at Fundação CESGRANRIO (2019) Bachelor in Business Administration at Faculdade CNEC (2012) Postgraduate in Project Management at Faculdade Unyleya (2018) Postgraduate Graduated in Higher Teaching from Faculdade Unyleya (2018) Master Black Belt Specialist in Lean Six Sigma FM2S - Council for Six Sigma Certification (2021) Quality Manager responsible for the Senior Management of the Municipal Administration Department of Macaé ? SEMAD (2012) General Administrator of the Educational Foundation of Macaé - FUNEMAC (2015) Coordinator of the Planning Sector at the Institute of Administration and Public Policies of Macaé - IAPP (2015) Project Manager of the Faculty Professor Miguel Ângelo da Silva Santos - FEMASS (2017)) Project Manager of the Planning Sector of the Municipal Health Department of Macaé (2021) Currently Value Stream Manager of the Indicators and Goals Management Office - EGIM of the Municipality of Macaé/RJ.

Andrei Bonamigo is an Adjunct Professor at Universidade Federal Fluminense, allocate in the Production Engineering Department of the School of Industrial Metallurgical Engineering of Volta Redonda (EEIMVR). He is a Professor of the professional master's course in production engineering at UFF. He is the coordinator of the Service Engineering Study and Research Group - GEPES. Postdoctoral candidate at the School of Engineering of Lorena (EEL) of the University of São Paulo (USP). Doctor in Production Engineering from the Federal University of Santa Catarina (2017) holds a Master's Degree in Administration from the University of the West of Santa Catarina, Master (Sandwich) at IPS - Polytechnic Institute of Setúbal - Portugal (2014). Specialist in Production Engineering from Instituto Superior Tupy - Joinville/SC (2012). Graduated in Production Engineering - Uninter (2020) and graduated in Mechanical Fabrication by the National Service for Industrial Learning (2010). He is technical in Mechanics - SENAI (2007). He worked as a teacher in undergraduate and graduate courses at the University of the West of Santa Catarina, UCEFF Faculdades and Senai. He served as director/administrator of the company Kata Business Solutions. He has experience in implementing and managing strategies for production management, services, quality management based on Lean thinking, Business ecosystem, ISO 9001 and Industrial service. He is interested in research in the area of ecosystem management of industrial services and co-creation of value in services, Lean Thinking in service management and Knowledge management, entrepreneurship and innovation in industrial services. He is a reviewer of national and international magazines related to the area of Production Engineering and Administration.

Saulo Bourguignon graduated in Biological Sciences (1985) from the UGF, Master's in Biophysics from the Carlos Chagas Filho Institute of Biophysics of UFRJ (1991) and PhD in Cellular and Molecular Biology from the Oswaldo Cruz Foundation (1997). He was Director of the Institute of Biology from April 2007 to January 2015. He was Research Coordinator of the Dean of Postgraduate Research and Innovation at UFF from January 2015 to July 2016. He was chairman of the Research Commission Biosafety (CBio) at UFF from 2016 to July 2019, Director of the Institute of Biology from 2019 to 2023.

Prof. Head of the Department of Cellular and Molecular Biology, professor of the Graduate Program in Science and Biotechnology (PPBI), teaches classes in Cellular and Molecular Biology and Biosafety for undergraduate and graduate courses in the area of Biological and Health Sciences. He works in the areas of Cell Biophysics, Protein Biochemistry and Protozoology of human parasites. The main line of research focuses on the evaluation of the trypanocidal effect, in T. cruzi and Leishmania, of synthetic and natural substances extracted from marine algae and plants, such as compounds derived from naphthoquinones. Currently, he has been working in the area of social inclusion, guiding doctoral students in the development of bilingual teaching material (Libras and Portuguese) such as books, videos and glossaries focused on science, biotechnology and biosafety.Member of the Lean project at UPAS.

Sandra Maria do Chaves graduated in Nursing from the State University of Rio de Janeiro (1982), Graduated in Psychology from the Gama Filho University (1991), Master's in Nursing from the Federal University of Rio de Janeiro (1990), Full Professor at the Gama Filho University (1996)). She was Head of the Nursing Department of Rio das Ostras at Universidade Federal Fluminense for two consecutive terms and the position of Coordinator of the Undergraduate Nursing Course at UFF in Rio das Ostras. PhD in Science and Biotechnology from the Institute of Biology at UFF. https://orcid.org/0000-0002-2985-1410.

Harvey Cosenza holds a postdoctoral degree, doctorate and master's degree in Production Engineering from COPPE/UFRJ and a degree in Industrial Electrical/Electronic Engineering from the Federal Center for Technological Education Celso Suckow da Fonseca (1992). He is currently an Adjunct Professor of the Production Engineering course at UFF. He is part of the group of researchers at LABFUZZY, COPPE / UFRJ and LabDGE, at Universidade Federal Fluminense-UFF. He has experience in academic management, with emphasis on Planning, Design and Control of Production Systems, working mainly on the following topics: Strategic Planning, Business Strategy, Industrial and Business Location, Logistics, Quality, marketing, fuzzy logic, insurance, relationship and sustainable development. He is currently an Adjunct Professor of the Production Engineering course at UFF. He is part of the group of researchers at LABFUZZY, COPPE / UFRJ and LabDGE, at Universidade Federal Fluminense-UFF.

Patrick Da Fonseca is a Master's student in Production Engineering by the Fluminense Federal University (UFF). Conducts research at LabDGE - Laboratory of Design Thinking, Management and Industrial Engineering, in the area of Health Management (Lean Healthcare), with emphasis on simulation and at CESS - Study Center for Sustainable Systems, in the area of sustainability, focusing on the recycling of vessels and offshore structures.

Sérgio Crespo da Silva Pinto is a Professor at Universidade Federal Fluminense UFF. Vice Coordinator of the Doctoral Program in Science, Technology and Inclusion at UFF. Leader of the CNPq research group: Computational Technologies in teaching and learning from the perspective of Diversity, Inclusion and Innovation. Guest professor in the Master's Program in ICTs at the Technological University of Panama. PGCTIN/UFF. LabDGE (Laboratory of Design Thinking, Management and Industrial Engineering). Lattes http://lattes.cnpq.br/./6515044727348778. ORCID: https://orcid.org/0000-0001-6914-2398.

Stephanie D'Amato Nascimento is a Production Engineer, ongoing MBA in Project Management, Black Belt in Lean Six Sigma, Researcher in Production Management at LabDGE (Laboratory of Design Thinking, Management, and Industrial Engineering). Engineer in Lean Healthcare Project Management in Lean in UPA Project, an initiative of the Brazilian Ministry of Health in partnership with Federal Fluminense University.

Milena dos Reis is an Associate Professor in the Production Engineering Department at the Federal University of Rio de Janeiro (UFRJ / Campus Macaé), holds a Pos-doctorate in Fluminense Federal University, a PhD in Production Engineering from the Federal University of Rio de Janeiro, a Msc. in Production Engineering from the Federal University of Minas Gerais (UFMG), Bachelor's degree in Production Engineering from the Federal University of Ouro Preto (UFOP) and a Black Belt Certification - Lean Six Sigma. She teaches Production Management and is a researcher at the Design Thinking, Management and Industrial Engineering Laboratory. She a researcher in the area of Production Management on topics such as Production Planning and Control, Lean healthcare, Lean Six Sigma, Operational Research and Product Engineering, Active learning methodologies in Production Engineering education.

Ilma Fausto is a doctoral student at the Postgraduate Program in Sciences, Technologies and Inclusion (PGCTIn) – Academic Doctorate Dame Comendadora "Cruz do Mérito da Educação" by the distinguished Council of the Brazilian Chamber of Culture. Member of the Research Group TeCEADI. Master in School Education by PPGEEProf - UNIR. Systems Analyst. EBTT Professor in Exclusive Dedication Regime Institute of Education, Science and Technology of Rondônia – IFRO.

Helder Gomes Costa received his PhD in Mechanical Engineering from Pontifícia Universidade Católica do Rio de Janeiro (1994), Brazil. He is currently full professor and the header of the Decision Analysis Group at Universidade Federal Fluminense (UFF), Brazil, acting on the following subjects: decision multicriteria decision making. clustering and performance evaluation. Nowadays, he is the President of the National Association of Post-Graduation and Research in Production Engineering (ANPEPRO), Brazil.

Thaís Lessa Queiroz is a Production Engineer from the Fluminense Federal University. She is currently a researcher at the Laboratory of Design Thinking, Management and Industrial Engineering and participates in the Lean Project at UPAs 24h. Academic performance in the area of Operations Engineering and Production Processes. In the sub-area: Factory and Industrial Installations Project: industrial organization, layout/physical arrangement. Research on lean production management philosophies, focusing on Lean Healthcare.

Fabiana Leta is a Professor of the Postgraduate Course in Science, Technologies, and Inclusion (PGCTIN), Postgraduate Course in Mechanical Engineering (PGMEC) and Mechanical Engineering Department. ORCID: https://orcid.org/0000-0002-6210-3078.

Adalberto Lima holds a degree in Civil Engineering from the Universidade da Amazônia (1990), a degree in Full Degree in Mathematics from the Federal University of Pará (1986), a Master's in Production Engineering from the Federal University of Santa Catarina (1998) and a PhD in Mechanical Engineering from the Universidade Estadual from Campinas (2007). Post-Doctorate at Universidade Federal

Fluminense (2021), Researcher at LabDGE/UFF - Campus Rio das Ostras, Researcher member of the Lean Project at UPAs MS/UFF, Associate Professor at the Faculty of Industrial Engineering at Campus de Abaetetuba/UFPA, Teaches the subjects Planning and Product Development and Introduction to the Lean Production System, Industrial Organization Systems for the Industrial Engineering course. He has experience in the area of Production Engineering, with an emphasis on Planning, Design, Production Management and Lean Production Systems, he was awarded the Professional of the Year 2013 award in Brazil in Management System.

Priscilla Ayleen Bustos Mac-Lean is an Assistant Professor in School of Science and Engineering at Sao Paulo State University (Unesp), Tupã Campus, Brazil, lecturing on Biosystems Engineering course and Agribussiness and Development Post Graduation Program. . Doctor in Animal Quality and Productivity by the Postgraduate Program in Animal Science from the University of São Paulo (2012). Master in Animal Production by the Postgraduate Program in Animal Science (2008) and undergraduated in animal science (2005) from Universidade Estadual de Maringá (UEM). Her research interests include the areas of improvement of the animal production chain evaluating good practices related to product quality and quantity, ambience and animal biometeorology and welfare, working mainly in the productive chains of dairy cattle and sericulture.

Olavo Neto is an Advisor at the Department of Hospital Care and Urgency - DAHU at the Ministry of Health, working in Project Management of Responsible for projects arising from the Institutional Development Support Program - PROADI/SUS carried out in partnership with Hospitals Excellence (Sírio Libanes, Albert Einstein, Oswaldo Cruz, HCor and Moinhos de Vento). Experience in Public Private Partnerships for Development: Implementing Solutions in Brazil. He acted as a focal point for projects carried out in partnership with the Fluminense Federal University on the subject of Lean Healthcare, Infections Related to Health Care and Assessment and Safety of Medical Equipment. Studying Black Belt. Specialist in Health Promotion and Social Development at the Sergio Arouca National School of Public Health, Oswaldo Cruz Foundation - FIOCRUZ. Graduated from FCM - Faculty of Medical Sciences of Paraíba. He is the author of the book "Manual of support to the technical activities of the nutritionist within the scope of the PNAE" launched by the Ministry of Education in 2018.

Aline Oliveira is graduating in Production Engineering at Universidade Federal Fluminense (UFF) - University Campus of Rio das Ostras. Researcher at the Design Thinking, Management and Industrial Engineering Research Laboratory (LabDGE). The research line collaborates with the study of tools applied to health (Lean Healthcare). Member of the Project for restructuring and implementing humanization in the flow of patient care in UPAs - 24 hours, carried out from the partnership between the Ministry of Health / SAES / DAHU and the Universidade Federal Fluminense/RJ, aiming at strengthening the Unified Health System Health - SUS.

José Ricardo Ramos is a Master in Technology and Specialist in Quality and Productivity Management by the Federal Center for Technological Education of Rio de Janeiro (CEFET/RJ - 2000). Mechanic Engineer and Business Administrator from the Catholic University of Petrópolis (UCP - 1978). Adjunct Professor (UCP), in the Engineering, Administration and MBA's courses. It has training in Lean Manufacturing Implementation / Kaizen's & Six Sigma projects by the TBM group. Mastery of production planning and control techniques (PPC, KANBAN, MRP) and Industrial Engineering (Methods, Processes and techniques: GTT, MTM. Team management and development (TTA), back-up training and continuous improvement of products, processes and Maintenance (RCM, TQM, among others). 43 years of experience in the areas of Production, Quality, Engineering, Maintenance, Planning, Management and Direction. Consultant / Specialist in Total Quality, CEP, ISO9000 Standards, Audits and Certification (Lead Auditor by LORIEN / PE-Batalas UK) and Lean Manufacturing. Speaker in the areas of Quality, Administration, Technological Innovations, Strategic Planning, Lean/Lean Production, Six Sigma and 5S, in Brazil and abroad.

Luiz Eduardo Rodrigues is a graduate student of the Department of Nursing, Fluminense Federal University (UFF). Researcher at the Laboratory of Design Thinking, Management and Industrial Engineering (LabDGE - UFF).

Gabriel Santos is a nursing student at the Fluminense Federal University. Anatomy Monitor from 2019 to 2020. Former member of the Pre-University Social and Better Age extension project at the University of UFF on the Rio das Ostras campus. Currently volunteer of Scientific Initiation. Member of the Laboratory of Research, Practice and Simulated Training in Nursing (LAPESE). Scholarship holder in the project: Study and research to improve the network and promote access to health services.

Guilherme Silva is finishing his bachelor's degree in Computer Science at the Fluminense Federal University. Currently researches how the use of technologie might assist and improve the patient lifecycle in Brazilian public medical facilities.

Nilra Silva is a researcher at the Design Thinking, Management and Industrial Engineering Research Laboratory. Line of research on risk prevention in the health sector, HFMEA (Healthcare Failure Mode and Effect Analysis). Currently, the Lean member in the Care Units (UP) with a focus on continuous improvement through Lean Management for Ready and humanization care in the patient flow. Financing cooperated between the Ministry of Health and the Universidade Federal Fluminense, with an interface with DAHU/SAES/MS, with a view to strengthening the Unified Health System - SUS (2020-2022).

Ana Paula Sobral has a degree in Statistical Sciences from the National School of Statistical Sciences (1993), a master's degree in Electrical Engineering from the Pontifical Catholic University of Rio de Janeiro (1999) and a PhD in Electrical Engineering from the Pontifical Catholic University of Rio de Janeiro (2003), with a Sandwich Doctorate at the University of Liége (Belgium). I have experience in the areas of Engineering and Health, with an emphasis on Decision Support Method, working on the following topics: statistical modeling, time series, machine learning, statistical process control and lean healthcare.

Adriana Teixeira is a public health specialist with a Master's degree in Hospital Management. Doctoral student at Fluminense Federal University in the Postgraduate Program in Sciences, Technologies and Inclusion. Graduated in Hospital Administration. Director at the Ministry of Health of the Department of Hospital and Urgency Care - DAHU which is responsible for the General Coordination of Hospital and Home Care, the National Coordination of Urgency and Emergency and the National Force of SUS Coordinated by the ministries of the Labdge/UFF Researcher in the Lean theme Healthcare.

Guilherme Ussuna is a Master in Agribusiness and Development from Universidade Estadual Paulista - UNESP (2020) and Bachelor in Business Administration from Universidade Estadual Paulista - UNESP (2017). He has experience in Innovation (Design Thinking), Continuous Process Improvement - Lean Tools, Process Management linked to Customer Experience (Customer Experience), Customer Relationship Management (CRM - Customer Relationship Management), Communication and Media Relations, Organizations - Methods and Agribusiness. In the Journey through the academy, scientific productions are highlighted in the areas of: Production Management (Lean Production), Innovation, Agribusiness and Agro-environmental Management.

Luis Enrique Viera graduated in Industrial Engineering from the National University of Piura, Master and D.Sc. in Production Engineering from the Federal University of Rio de Janeiro. He is currently an associate professor at the Fluminense Federal University, in the Department of Engineering. He participates in the DGE-Design Thinking Management and Industrial Engineering Laboratory. He has experience in the field of Production Engineering, with emphasis on industrial project evaluation, industrial organization, Lean Six Sigma, Industrial Localization, Design, management and evaluation of Production Systems.

Ana Zeferino is a Chemical Engineer from UNICAMP, MBA from FGV, Master Black Belt from Setec Consulting Group and Lean Practitioner from Lean Institute Brazil. Lactu Senso Maaster Degree Student at Fluminense Federal University. Professor at the Operational Excellence postgraduate course at Hospital Albert Einstein. Improvement consultant for the Social Health Organization Prima Qualitá, promotes the implementation of Lean in the Hospital, in the basic health units (ESF), in the women's clinic and UPA of municipalities in the interior of the state of Rio de Janeiro. Researcher at Lean nas UPAs 24horas in Brazil.

Index

K

L

M

O

P

Q

R

S

T

U

V

W

www.ingramcontent.com/pod-product-compliance
Lightning Source LLC
LaVergne TN
LVHW080647011026
849160LV00014B/1351